DATE DUE

MAY 2 0 2005			

Demco, Inc. 38-293

20 YEARS OF

CENSORED

NEWS

Carl Jensen

AND PROJECT CENSORED

Introduction by Michael Parenti

CARTOONS BY TOM TOMORROW

SEVEN STORIES PRESS / New York

In the U.K.:
Turnaround Publisher Services Ltd., Unit 3, Olympia Trading Estate, Coburg Road, Wood Green, London N22 6TZ U.K.

In Canada:
Hushion House, 36 Northline Road, Toronto, Ontario M4B 3E2, Canada

Library of Congress Cataloging-in-Publication Data

Jensen, Carl.
      20 years of censored news / Carl Jensen and Project Censored
      p. cm.
      ISBN: 1-888363-51-7. — ISBN 1-888363-52-5 (pbk.)
      1. Freedom of the press. 2. Censorship. I. Project Censored (U.S.) II. Title.
PN4736.J46 1997
323.44'5—dc21   97-24373
                                                                         CIP

Book design by Cindy LaBreacht

Seven Stories Press
632 Broadway, 7th Floor
New York, NY 10012

Printed in the U.S.A.

9 8 7 6 5 4 3 2 1

TO DECCA TREUHAFT

aka Jessica Mitford

Author, Censored Judge, and Friend

"Queen of the Muckrakers"

September 11, 1917—July 23, 1996

Table of Contents

Preface

In early 1961, journalist Tad Szulc, of *The New York Times*, wrote an article that revealed the United States was about to launch an invasion of Cuba using CIA-trained Cuban exiles. The story was originally to be published by *The Times* under a four-column headline at the top of page one.

But when word leaked out in Washington that *The Times* planned to run the Szulc story, President Kennedy called James Reston, *The Times*'s Washington bureau chief, asking him to kill it. Reston told Orvil Dryfoos, the publisher of *The Times*, about Kennedy's call and suggested toning down the story and removing the references to the invasion.

As a result, a heavily edited version of the story, with a one column heading, appeared with no mention of the CIA's involvement or that the invasion was imminent.

Kennedy later told *New York Times* Managing Editor Turner Catledge, "If you had printed more about the operation, you could have saved us from a colossal mistake."

It is generally agreed that if the media had widely publicized the coming invasion, Kennedy would have been forced to cancel it.

The New York Times was not the only publication to censor the story. As David Halberstam pointed out in *The Powers That Be*, the media were "remarkably vulnerable to the seductive call of National Security." Television was equally lax in its coverage of the story.

It was not because the media did not know about the proposed invasion. The alternative press, led by *The Nation*, had already published information that was censored by the mainstream media. On November 19, 1960, five months before the invasion, *The Nation* reported the Bay of Pigs invasion plan and urged "all U.S. news media" to check it out. It noted that if the report were true, "then public pressure should be brought to bear upon the Administration to abandon this dangerous and hare-brained project."

But the mainstream media ignored *The Nation*'s plea and the United States suffered one of its worst foreign policy fiascoes.

✖ ✖ ✖ ✖ ✖

More than thirty years have passed since the infamous Bay of Pigs invasion, years in which the issue of censorship, or self-censorship as the case may be, has not receded.

20 Years of Censored News is a report card on the performance of America's news media from 1976 up to 1996. And the media did not pass. In fact, this book is a damning indictment of the national news media for their consistent failure to inform the public of issues critical to its well-being. And it is a disturbing litany of crimes against society by political and corporate leaders during that 20-year period.

20 Years of Censored News is also a resource guide to the first 20 years of the national research project known as Project Censored. Project Censored was founded in 1976 by the author as a seminar in mass media at Sonoma State University in Rohnert Park, California.

The primary objective of Project Censored is to explore and publicize the extent of news censorship in our society by locating stories about significant issues of which the public should be aware, but is not, for a variety of reasons.

Since its inception, the Project has hoped to stimulate journalists to provide more news coverage of under-reported issues and to encourage the general public to demand more coverage of those issues by the media and to seek information from alternative sources.

The essential issue raised by the Project is the failure of the mass media to provide people with all the information they need to make informed decisions concerning their own lives. Only an informed electorate can achieve a fair and just society. The public has a right to know about issues that affect it and the press has a responsibility to keep the public well-informed about those issues.

THE MEDIA MYTH

We have all been brought up to believe in the power and value of the press—the great watchdog of society. It is the nation's ombudsman. It is the muckraking journalist with printer's ink in his blood who is willing to sacrifice all to expose evil. We were taught to believe *The New York Times* prints "All the news that's fit to print." We believed *The Chicago Times* when it said, "It is a newspaper's duty to print the news and raise hell."

I wanted to be a journalist from the time I was eight years old when I saw how important a newspaper, the *New York Daily News*, was to my father. He would bring it home each evening and sit at the kitchen table reading it from cover to cover before dinner. Later I came to believe that a journalist could make a difference and could even help to build a better world. I was in awe of the achievements of the early 20th century muckrakers and seduced by the siren song of Horace Greeley, the 19th century editor of the *New York Tribune*, who rhapsodized:

> "Then hail to the Press!
> chosen guardian of freedom!
> Strong sword-arm of justice!
> bright sunbeam of truth."

Press apologists also like to quote Thomas Jefferson, our third president, who said in 1787, "The basis of our government being the opinion of the people, the very first object should be to keep that right; and were it left to me to decide whether we should have a government without newspapers or newspapers without a government, I should not hesitate a moment to prefer the latter."

Those same apologists conveniently forget to mention what Jefferson had to say about the press in later times: "The man who never looks into a newspaper is better informed than he who reads them, inasmuch as he who knows nothing is nearer to truth than he whose mind is filled with falsehoods and errors." (1799); "Nothing can now be believed which is seen in a newspaper." (1807); "I read but one newspaper and that...more for its advertisements than its news." (1820).

Indeed the media-generated myth of the press as an aggressive, unbiased, honest watchdog of society, is just that—a myth. I fulfilled my childhood dream of becoming a journalist but after witnessing first-hand the kind of reporting it took to be a "successful" journalist, I left that profession for another which, at least, wasn't hypocritical about what it really was—public relations and advertising.

My early disenchantment with journalism only grew through the years as I first witnessed how advertisers could influence the media, and later, as a university professor, when I created a national research project—Project Censored—which explored and exposed the media's failure to cover important issues.

Admittedly, not all media and all journalists are driven by the bottom line but many are, especially the large media corporations and the "brand-name" journalists. The media are more concerned with their next quarterly profit than with the unique opportunity given them by the First Amendment. And most journalists are more concerned with keeping their jobs and increasing their income than with fighting for the public's right to know. This helps explain why millions of Americans turn to the alternative press for reliable information about what is really happening.

America's mainstream mass media basically serve three segments of society today—the wealthy, politicians, and the sports-minded. The news media have done an exceptional job of providing full and, on the whole, reliable information to those who are involved in or follow the stock market and to those who are involved in or follow politics and to those who are involved in or follow sports.

GOLDEN AGE OF MUCKRAKING

At the same time, the media have failed to inform, or protect the interests, of those less fortunate in our society. It was not always this way. For a brief ten year period, at the turn of the century, a period sometimes referred to

as the Golden Age of Muckraking, the media sought out, investigated, and published stories about the plight of all its citizens, including those at the bottom of the economic scale. The works of journalists and authors like Lincoln Steffens, Ida Tarbell, Upton Sinclair, and others, were widely read by many Americans and led to significant social change that benefited the general public.

Lincoln Steffens' *The Shame of the Cities* exposed and cleaned-up municipal political corruption; Ida Tarbell's *The History of the Standard Oil Company* led to the dissolution of that giant monopoly; and Upton Sinclair's *The Jungle*, a powerful exposé of the meat packing industry, led to legislative changes and the first Pure Food and Drugs Act.

Sadly, nearly a century later, problems similar to these still exist. However, the muckrakers and the muckraking publications of yesteryear are not present today. Political bribes in government, earlier exposed by Steffens, are now often given in the acceptable form of PAC money and ignored by the press; the media not only fail to explain the negative impact of monopolies as Tarbell did, but instead act as cheerleaders for giant mergers; and instead of investigating and exposing the hazards and dangers of meat processing and packing as Sinclair did, the media are now content to sensationalize the deaths of children from e-coli rather than expose the conditions that create it.

20 Years of Censored News is a book that reveals, year by year from 1976 to 1995, the stories and issues the major media neglected to tell you about when they were timely and what has happened with them since.

Project Censored had its inception in the summer of 1976. I was then an assistant professor of sociology at Sonoma State University in Northern California and looking for a subject for a seminar in mass media that I taught

each year. For some time I had been curious about how Richard Nixon could have won the 1972 election with a landslide vote nearly five months after the biggest political crime of the century—Watergate.

The break-in at the Democratic National Committee offices in the Watergate complex in Washington, D.C., by the Republican Committee to Reelect the President (CREEP) in June 1972, sparked one of the biggest political cover-ups in modern history. And the press was an unwitting, if not willing, partner in the cover-up. The break-in, by CREEP employees known as the "plumbers," was described as a "two-bit burglary" not worthy of press attention.

The media's lack of interest in the Watergate story even prompted the *Washington Post's* Katharine Graham to wonder, in her 1997 autobiography, *Personal History*, "If this is such a hell of a story, then where is everybody else?" Fortunately, despite the skepticism on the part of their colleagues, Carl Bernstein and Bob Woodward, young reporters at the *Washington Post*, eventually made it a national news story. Bernstein later noted that out of some 2,000 full-time reporters in Washington for major news organizations, just 14 were assigned to the Watergate story on a full-time basis and only six of them on an investigative basis, even six months after the break-in. When Walter Cronkite, the legendary CBS-TV news anchor and America's most trusted man, tried to do a unique two-part series on Watergate on the *CBS-TV Evening News* before the election, a phone call from the Nixon White House to Bill Paley, chair of CBS, resulted in a scaled down version of Cronkite's scheduled program. Thus, it was not surprising that no one was even talking about Watergate on election eve as Woodward told Larry King (6/17/97).

Watergate taught us two important lessons about the press: first, the news media sometimes do fail to cover some important issues, and second, the news media sometimes indulge in self-censorship. It also led to the creation of Project Censored which has now become the longest running internationally recognized news media research project.

NEWS CENSORSHIP IS NOT A CONSPIRACY

It is important to understand that the 200 *Censored* stories you will read about in this book are not examples of some widespread media conspiracy to censor your news. News is too diverse, fast-breaking, and unpredictable to be controlled by some sinister conservative eastern establishment media cabal. However, there is a congruence of attitudes and interests on the part of the owners and managers of mass media organizations. That non-conspiracy conspiracy, when combined with a variety of other factors, leads to the systematic failure of the news media to fully inform the public. While it is not an overt form of censorship, such as the kind we observe in some other societies, it is nonetheless real and often equally as dangerous to the public's well-being.

Other factors accounting for censorship include the following: sometimes a source for a story isn't considered reliable (an official government representative or corporate executive is reliable; a freelance journalist or eyewitness citizen is not); other times the story doesn't have an easily identifiable "beginning, middle, and end" (acid rain just seems to go on for ever and ever); some stories are considered to be "too complex" for the general public (nobody would understand the intricacies of the savings and loan debacle); on occasion stories are ignored because they haven't been "blessed" by *The New York Times* or the *Washington Post* (reporters and editors at most of the more than 1500 daily newspapers in the United States know their news judgment isn't going to be challenged when they write and publish fashionable "follow-the-leader" stories, a practice which leads to the "pack" or "herd" phenomenon in journalism).

Another excuse the media sometimes give is that the story is too old, outdated, or that they've already covered the issue. As we will see, just because a story was covered once doesn't mean the issue has been resolved. Sometimes updating an old story may not only serve the public well but could even result in a Pulitzer for the journalist. One such story focused on the issue of conducting radiation experiments on unsuspecting subjects dating back to the mid-1940s. It was the #8 *Censored* story of 1986. But it wasn't until 1993 that an investigative reporter, Eileen Welsome of the *Albuquerque Tribune*, made it a national issue and won a Pulitzer Prize for her work.

One major factor contributing to media self-censorship is that some stories are considered potentially libelous. Long and costly jury trials, settlements out of court, and occasional multimillion dollar judgments against the media, have produced a massive chilling effect on the press and replaced copy editors with copy attorneys. An equally ominous sign for freedom of the press was revealed in early 1997 when the Food Lion supermarket chain successfully sued ABC-TV after it aired an exposé of its meat packing procedures. Food Lion sued on the basis of a false job application, rather than libel, thereby circumventing libel laws designed to protect the press. Food Lion's argument was that the truth doesn't matter as much as the way the press goes after it.

However, the bottom line explanation for much of the self-censorship that occurs in America's mainstream media is the media's own bottom line. Corporate media executives perceive their primary, and often sole, responsibility to be the need to maximize profits for the next quarterly statement, not, as some would have it, to inform the public. Many of the stories you'll read in this book do not support the financial interests of media publishers, owners, stockholders, or advertisers.

Investigative journalism also is more expensive than the "public stenography" form of journalism practiced at many media outlets. And, of course, there is always the "don't rock the boat" mentality which pervades corporate media boardrooms and then filters down to the newsroom. The latter influence has only been exacerbated by the number of megamedia mergers in recent history. The need to play it safe is becoming pervasive as the stakes are becoming increasingly higher.

CENSORED SUBJECTS

A statistical analysis of the top 200 stories over a 20-year period reveals that while there are some variations from year to year, and from election to election, on the whole, there has been a systematic omission of a select number of issues. The subjects most often censored since 1976 are political, corporate, international, and military issues.

Following are the number and percentage of all 200 *Censored* stories by subject matter from 1976 to 1995:

1—Political	64	32.0%
2—Corporate	37	18.5%
3—International	30	15.0%
4—Military	28	14.0%
5—Environmental	15	7.5%
6—Health	13	6.5%
7—Media	7	3.5%
8—Economic	5	2.5%
9—Education	1	.5%

It was interesting to explore whether there was a difference in the number of *Censored* stories, by subject, and by political administrations. And there was. There were significantly more political, international, and military stories exposed by the alternative media during the Reagan and Bush Administrations than during the Carter and Clinton Administrations. Conversely, there were significantly more corporate and environmental subjects exposed during the Carter and Clinton Administrations.

While there is no fully reliable way to explain these differences, one could speculate that there may have been more reasons or opportunities to expose political, international, and military matters while Reagan and Bush presided over the nation. Or, perhaps Carter and Clinton were more effective in monitoring these sectors during their administrations.

Or it could be that alternative news media, often used as our sources, were more interested in investigating political, international, and military issues during the Republican Administrations and similarly with corporate and environmental issues during the Democrats' incumbency.

However, the most disturbing result of this analysis is the number of issues that have still not been addressed by the major media since Project Censored first raised them.

Of the 200 *Censored* issues, more than three quarters of them can still be classified as overlooked or censored by the mainstream media. Just 46 of the original stories have since received significant attention by the press. Some of the issues from the late 1970s that have been addressed include: acid rain, the fight over who controls the oceans' resources, freezing the elderly to death for non-payment of utility bills, and the commercialization of the Public Broadcasting System (PBS). Examples among the 150 issues that haven't been addressed include problems as near at hand as hazardous over-the-counter drugs and as far from home as the Indonesian repression in East Timor.

By ignoring many critical issues in the past twenty years, the mainstream media have lost the confidence of the American people. Newspapers and network television news programs have lost many thousands—perhaps millions—of readers and viewers as recorded by circulation figures and television ratings. So many so that there is an industry term for the phenomenon: they call it "The Vanished."

However, it is still not too late to attempt to affect some change; we have an abiding faith in the will of the American people to want to know what is really happening in society, and, when so informed, to pressure politicians to do something about it.

The 20-year span of time represented by the 200 stories in this analysis also reminds us of the length of time it takes us, as a society, to recognize and deal with these problems, if, indeed we ever do make the effort. Some examples include acid rain, a problem which we knew about in the early '70s but are only now starting to take seriously; the preventable deaths, injuries, and illness suffered in the workplace, which we knew about in 1976, but have yet to even acknowledge as a major national problem; the threat of male sterility caused by chemical pollution which first came to light in 1977 and yet even in the face of some startling research revelations about the worldwide drop in male sperm counts, it has yet to be put on the national agenda.

The single, most plausible, explanation for our failure to address these and other problems in a timely manner is found in our economic system. Capitalism dictates the need to make a profit—often regardless of the means necessary to achieve that profit. In the future, this era will be seen as one where we truly let significant problems get out of hand, a circumstance which led to the deterioration of much of our health and environment, a time when we permitted the robber barons to strip what was left of our earth's resources, a time when we allowed politicians to sell their souls to the highest bidder, and a time when we were distracted from the real issues of the day by media-hyped events such as the O.J. Simpson trial. It is a time when the few got wealthy at the expense of the many and Mother Earth was left to suffer.

Author Matthew Josephson warned us of the robber barons of the late 19th century, in his aptly titled book, *Robber Barons*, in 1934. Leading the capitalist ruling class of that period, from 1861 to 1901, were Andrew Carnegie, Jay Gould, Pierpont Morgan, John D. Rockefeller, and "Commodore" Cornelius Vanderbilt. And they were the people who provided the fodder for the great exposés by the turn-of-the-century muckrakers. In some cases, most notably with Andrew Carnegie who eventually founded America's public library system, the revelations of the muckrakers had a beneficial influence on the robber barons.

In our time, the one great hope we have for a just and fair society is a "watchdog" press to protect us from the present day robber barons. But, as we have seen in the second half of the 20th century, the media, with rising profit margins, have joined the ruling capitalist class themselves, and are now part of the problem. Today they are little more than lapdogs.

It is impossible to fully measure the impact the failure of the press has had on society. How many thousands, or perhaps millions, of lives would have been saved if the press had done its job instead of ignoring or covering up the problems. The lack of car safety features, the lax regulatory control of the airline industry, the link between tobacco and cancer, and the corporate greed of baby formula manufacturers that led to the deaths of thousands of Third World infants are just a few examples of where the media could have made a difference. How many millions of taxpayer dollars would have been saved if the media had exposed the savings and loan scandal in its infancy? And how much of our nation's resources could have been saved if the media had told the public about the scandalous Mining Act of 1872 that continues to give away valuable minerals and metals from federal lands for a song? Perhaps more than any other single story, the tobacco issue reveals the impact of a flawed press.

CENSORSHIP AND TOBACCO

Some three million people in developed countries worldwide—about one person every ten seconds—will die from smoking cigarettes in 1997. The death toll is expected to reach 10 million deaths annually by 2020. An estimated 60 million people—50 million men and 10 million women—have died or will die from smoking in the last half of this century. These frightening statistics come from a book, titled *Mortality from Smoking in Developed Countries 1950-2000*, published in 1994 by Britain's Imperial Cancer Research Fund, the World Health Organization, and the American Cancer Society. This 553-page report took a critical look at the worldwide death toll of smoking over the long term.

One has to wonder how tobacco came to be such a massive worldwide killer before some measures were taken to try to eliminate it. It wasn't until August 23, 1996, after significant and continuing, albeit belated, media coverage of the hazards of smoking, that the Food and Drug Administration (FDA) issued a regulation restricting the sale of cigarettes and smokeless tobacco to children and teenagers. Finally, in mid-1997, as a result of media exposure, tobacco company whistleblowers, 17 class action suits, and 40 state lawsuits brought by state attorneys general, the tobacco companies capitulated. They agreed to pay more than $368 billion to repay Medicaid and other health costs and to launch anti-smoking educational and advertising programs. More important, the industry agreed to submit to unprecedented new rules that aim to dramatically scale back tobacco's hold over people's lives (*Los Angeles Times*, 6/21/97).

It didn't have to take that long. After all, the link between smoking and cancer was known at least as early as 1938. George Seldes, a muckraking journalist, was the first media watchdog to criticize the press for censoring the connection between tobacco and cancer. In 1938, he tried, without success, to get the press to report the results of a critical five-year study, involving nearly 7,000 persons, by Dr. Raymond Pear of the Department of Biology at Johns Hopkins University. The study revealed that smoking decreased life expectancy. In 1940, when Seldes started his investigative newsletter, *In fact*, he launched a ten-year crusade against tobacco, publishing some one hundred items on the subject in the newsletter. The media continued to ignore the issue and few of his exposés were ever published in the mainstream press.

Project Censored cited the dangers of smoking tobacco as a *Censored* subject in 1979 (tobacco lobby fights self-extinguishing cigarette), 1980 (tobacco companies censor the truth about cigarettes and cancer), 1984 (cigarette advertising and *The New York Times*), 1985 (tobacco industry appeals to children and the Third World; National Institutes of Health seek stronger tobacco plant), and 1995 (ABC spikes new tobacco exposé). But it wasn't until the mid-1990s that the dangers of cigarette smoking were widely publicized in the mainstream media.

How could it be that a massive killer was identified more than half a century ago but was allowed to continue to kill millions of people? One has to ask why our watchdog media, who knew about the problem since 1938, failed to provide an earlier warning about this killer.

JUNK FOOD NEWS

Cynics say that the media give the public what it wants, i.e. "junk food news," because the people are not interested in reading about the issues raised by Project Censored. We contend that the public is not given the opportunity to read or hear those stories in the mainstream media and thus, unfortunately, will absorb only what the mass media offer. As author/poet T.S. Eliot warned presciently in 1923, "Those who say they give the public what it wants underestimate the public taste and end up debauching it."

THIS MODERN WORLD by TOM TOMORROW

The inclusion of personality news, featuring people like Patty Hearst, Elvis Presley, John Lennon, Jim Bakker, Jeffrey Dahmer, O.J. Simpson, and Tonya Harding, among the top ten mainstream news stories in the United States, surely validates T.S. Eliot's warning.

The difference the press can make by doing the right thing is evident in the story of hunger in Africa. Hunger in Africa was consistently nominated as a "censored" subject during the early 1980s. When I would ask journalists why they did not cover the tragedy unfolding there, they would say, "It is not news," or, "Everyone already knows about starving Africans," or, "Nothing can be done about it anyway."

Early in 1984, an ABC-TV News correspondent in Rome came upon information that led him to believe that millions of lives were being threatened by drought and famine in Africa. He asked the ABC home office in New York for permission to take his crew to Africa to get the story. The answer was no.

Later, a BBC television crew, traveling through Ethiopia, captured the horrifying reality of children starving to death. When the world saw the bloated stomachs and bony limbs of the starving children on their television sets, it sparked a worldwide reaction, including an internationally televised rock-fest called Live Aid and the musical anthem, "We Are The World," that reportedly saved the lives of seven million Ethiopians.

Indeed the media can make a difference.

It is the media's responsibility, as true watchdogs of society with the unique protection of the First Amendment, to explore, compile, and present information that people should be aware of in a way that will attract their attention and be relevant to their everyday lives. And, when the media do this, people will read and respond to the issues raised. And journalists need not be embarrassed when they cash their paychecks.

The press does have the power to stimulate people to clean up the environment; to prevent nuclear proliferation; to force corrupt politicians out of office; to reduce poverty; to provide quality health care for all people; to create a truly equitable, fair, and just society. The press had the power to save the lives of millions of smokers more than 50 years ago. Fortunately, it is still not too late for the media to save million of lives in the future. This is why we must all look to, prod, and support a free, open, and aggressive press. We have a free press in the United States guaranteed by the First Amendment and we have the best communications technology in world history. Now let us seek a more responsible and responsive press—a press that earns its First Amendment rights the old fashioned way. Indeed, a press not afraid to do a little muckraking. Then, and only then, will we have the information we need to build a more enlightened and responsive society.

ACKNOWLEDGMENTS

This book would not have been possible if it were not for the investigative efforts of the authors who wrote the top 200 *Censored* stories. Similarly, we recognize the 200 publishers who had the guts to publish those stories. The authors and publications are both cited for each of the 200 stories.

The next acknowledgment must go to all of our *Censored* colleagues across the country who contribute to the success of Project Censored by sending us stories as nominations. We received more than 7,000 nominations during the first 20 years from journalists, educators, librarians, and many others who are concerned with the public's right to know. We are truly grateful to all who have brought those stories to our attention.

Another group critical to the success of the project are the Sonoma State University students who participated as Censored researchers in the annual Project Censored seminars. It was their responsibility to analyze the thousands of nominations received in order to determine whether they qualified as *Censored* stories of the year. Following are those researchers:

CENSORED RESEARCHERS FROM 1976 TO 1995

CENSORED OF 1976—David Cryden, Robert Demers, Leo Dikinis, Robert Elkins, Francine Gersh, John Grauso, Wally Hanley, Larry Hoffman, Dave Houwink, Chanan Kessler, Eric Lehew, Gayle Park, Dave Rigney, Janet Rubin, Matthew Schuss, Susan Skidmore, Jim Szabo, Bruce Walker, Dave Young

CENSORED OF 1977—William Bourland, Linda Endsley, Christine Judge, Melanie Long, Victoria Mann, Nancy Morita, Linnea Mullins, Joyce Quinn, Linda Simone, Ron Sonnenshine, Michael Umble

CENSORED OF 1978—Richard Aliamus, Annelise Jade Bazar, Myrna Blomgren, Winifred Caruana, Emily Center, Dan Cortez, Jim Cyb, Lisa T. Dapprich, Tom Davey, Catherine Drab, Eurie Fogle, Melba Garrett, Linnea Mullins, Terry Rooney, Elis Tipton, Michael Turner

CENSORED OF 1979—Maxine Averbuck, Jeanette Baker, Evelyn Benmergui, Rose Carrara, Chris Carrieri, Robert Cortez, Mark Falcone, John Fengler, Robert Frazee, James Gerlat, George Grosskopf, Marlina Boucher Harrison, Candy Marziano, Roni McKinley, Betty Mekeel, Tim Mosley, Nancy O'Grady, Mary Jane O'Keefe-Caldwell, Claude Plymate, Carolynn Ranch-Apple, Andrew Rangel, Helena Whistler

CENSORED OF 1980—Les Arnold, Tulla Jaffe, Nancy Keller, Drew Longley, Kay McCabe, Nader Mokaram, Gary Sandy, Russ Silbiger, Jim Smith, K.C. Toomire, Bev Brintnall, Maxine Averbuck

CENSORED OF 1981—Robin Beeman, Tom Casler, Ivy Davis, Marilyn Graceffo, Barbara Hayes, Dyan Lea Ellis, Ursula Faasii Liakos, David Ludwig, Will McCracken, Maggie Randle, Jim Rodriguez

CENSORED OF 1982—Lisa Giambastiani, Mindy Lipman, John Sanderbeck, Beverly Saxon, Mary Tinat, Fred Whitted, Charles Zoerner

CENSORED OF 1983—Charles Baker, Jill Butler, Rose Carrara, Susanne Crossman, Meera Damodaran, Lish Hanhart, Johnny Mayorga, Ethan McHenry, Jim Parker, Carol Sales, Maria Saltrese, Karen Scriven, Mary Sullivan, Chase B. Williams

CENSORED OF 1984—Bob Heinritz, Larry McTernan, Ernie Medeiros, Mark Mellander, Pablo Miralles, Laura Sousa

CENSORED OF 1985—Marc Afifi, Sharon Benjamin, Ron Claret, Lisa Coyle, Diane Fennessy, Susan King, Felicia Lipson, Jeff McDonald, Dan Murphy, Charlotte Noda, Nora Norminton, Janet Russell, David Stager, Kathleen Wolff, Jennifer Wood

CENSORED OF 1986—Peggy Sue Alberhasky, Sarah Alcorn, Larry Crowell, Daren Decker, Dave Hoffman, Mike Jasper, Karen Kitchens, Tom Montan, Laura Moore, Nancy Neilson, Bebe O'Brien, Bruce Schwank, Kathy Wolff

CENSORED OF 1987—Frances Caballo, Carolina Clare, Morley Cowan, Nana Nash, Mark Pierson, Lance Plaza, Kevin W. Rose, Roxanne Turnage, Kelly Wendt

CENSORED OF 1988—Karen Baeck, Shawn Connally, Elvia Diaz, Paul Farkas, Stacy Freitas, Robin Imsdahl, Julie Labrincha, Star Lightner, Mark Lowenthal, Andrew Metrogen, Joe Murray, Suellen Ocean, Julie Peterson, Cyrece Puccio, James Sanders, Rick Scott, Claus Sellier, Wendy Silkworth, Robin Watters

CENSORED OF 1989—Michael Accurso, Sally Acevedo, Audrey Auerbach, Alan Barbour, Janie Barrett, Debbie Cohen, Tahd Frentzel, Bill Gibbons, John Gilles, Jim Gregoretti, Tanya Gump, Tim Hilton, Darren LaMarr, Scott McKittrick, Tina Rich, Terril Shorb, Wendy Strand, Heller Waidtlow, Bill Way

CENSORED OF 1990—Andy Alfaro, Dylan Bennett, Todd Borst, Kristine Bush, Devin Carswell, Ed Early, Mandy Fortuna, Rose Ann Fuhrman, Bill Gibbons, Marya Glass, Tally Hastings, Luis Luna, Mike Melfi, Denise Mussetter, Steve Mytinger, Thea Newcombe, Dan Parr, Stephen Scafani, Sherry Sutton, Felicidad Thorpe-Doe, Dirk VanWinkle, Tony Weeks, Greg Wolf

CENSORED OF 1991—Kathy Aanestad, John Aliotti Jr., Danny Bremson, Anne Britton, Maria Brosnan, Erik Cummins, Steve Dunlop, Paula Giebitz, Dena Griffith, Dustin Harp, Craig Haskell, Rachel Kinberg, Robyn O'Connor, Joe Polk, Scott Shawver, Scott Somohano, Ann Steffora, Jackie Stonebraker

CENSORED OF 1992—Diane Albracht, Beverly Alexander, Peter Anderson, Judy Bailey, Jeannie Blake, Serge Chasson, Amy S. Cohen, Amy Doyle, G. John Faiola, Eric Fedel, Kimberly Kaido, Blake Kehler, Kenneth Lang, Therese Lipsey, Jennifer Makowsky, Stephanie Niebel, Nicole Novak, Valerie Quigley, Kimberly S. Anderson, Damon S. Van Hoesen

CENSORED OF 1993—Gerald Austin, Jesse Boggs, Paul Chambers, Tamara Fresca, Tim Gordon, Bill Harding, Courteney Lunt, Katie Maloney, Mark Papadopoulos, Kristen Rutledge, Sunil Sharma, Laurie Turner

CENSORED OF 1994—William Beaubien, Stephen Beckner, Jennifer Burns, Paul Giusto, Lisa Golding, Billy Hawes, Susan Kashack, Kate Kauffman, Dave Lake, Marilyn Leon, Jessica Nystrom, Scott Oehlerking, Lori Stone, Dan Tomerlin

CENSORED OF 1995—Greg Downing, Tina Duccini, Marcie Goyer, Kristi Hogue, Brad Hood, Stephanie Horner, Dylan Humphrey, Doug Huston, Pia C. Jensen, Vanessa Mann, Jon Merwitzer, Amy Niesen, Stephanie Prather, Fritz Rollins, Mary Jo Thayer, Mike Thomas, Justin Twergo, Tami Ward, Nikki Washburn, Lysa Wayne

One of the most difficult challenges of Project Censored is to select the annual "Ten Best Censored" stories from among the top 25 nominations. This responsibility falls on our distinguished national panel of judges who volunteer their efforts and we are grateful for their participation. Following are the judges who selected the top ten censored stories during the first 20 years of Project Censored:

PROJECT CENSORED JUDGES FROM 1976 TO 1995

Shana Alexander, Donna Allen, Jonathan Alter, Edward Asner, Ben Bagdikian, Alfred Balk, Richard Barnet, Steward Brand, Jim Cameron, Hodding Carter, Jeffrey Chester, Shirley Chisholm, Noam Chomsky, Robert Cirino, David Cohen, Ann Crittenden, Everette E. Dennis, Ron Dorfman, Hugh Downs, Joel Dreyfuss, Susan Faludi, John Kenneth Galbraith, George Gerbner, Edward S. Herman, David Horowitz, Charlayne Hunter-Gault, Sut Jhally, Nicholas Johnson, Rhoda H. Karpatkin, James J. Kilpatrick, Charles L. Klotzer, Brad Knickerbocker, Judith Krug, Frances Moore Lappé, William Lutz, Curtis D. MacDougall, Robert MacNeil, Julianne Malveaux, Victor Marchetti, Robert C. Maynard, Mary McGrory, John McLaughlin, Jessica Mitford, Bill Moyers, Jack L. Nelson, Kathleen F. O'Reilly, Michael Parenti, Tom Peters, Herbert I. Schiller, Joseph J. Schwab, George Seldes, Susan Sontag, Alvin Toffler, Jerry terHorst, Mike Wallace, Sheila Rabb Weidenfeld, Mortimer B. Zuckerman

Perhaps one of the greatest tributes to the project is that four of our original judges—Ben Bagdikian, Nicholas Johnson, Jack Nelson, and Sheila Rabb Weidenfeld—participated in Project Censored for 20 years and Noam Chomsky participated for 19 years.

We would not have succeeded if it were not for seven individuals and foundations that have provided critical financial support to the project over the years: The Angelina Fund, Anita Roddick and The Body Shop, The C.S. Fund, Nicholas Johnson, the John D. and Catherine T. MacArthur Foundation, Joshua Mailman, and the Threshold Foundation.

I am especially grateful to Peter Phillips who took over as director of Project Censored when I retired in 1996. There are also three members of the Project's staff who contributed significantly to the success of the Project over the years: former Associate Director Mark Lowenthal and Research Associates Amy Cohen and Marya Glass. Mark and Amy also provided valuable editing suggestions for this book. Brian Wilson, a systems specialist formerly with the Computer and Information Science Department, brought us into the computer age and was the pioneer Webmaster for Project Censored on the Internet (E-mail: project.censored@sonoma.edu; Web site: http:censored.sonoma.edu/ProjectCensored/).

I am indebted to two publishers who had the faith and fortitude to take on a subject that many conglomerate publishers rejected: Joe Woodman, owner of Ventana Press, and publisher of the 1993 Yearbook, and Dan Simon, owner of Seven Stories Press (SSP), publisher of this book and the Censored Yearbooks since 1994. With his advice, support, and friendship over the past six years, Dan Simon has been far more than a publisher. Special thanks are also due to SSP editors Jon Gilbert, Moyra Davey, and Mikola De Roo, and to book designer Cindy LaBreacht. The plaudits for distribution go to Publishers Group West.

I would also like to acknowledge the support of Brian Donoghue and Greg Ruggiero at the Learning Alliance which conducts the annual Censored Awards Ceremony in New York along with Seven Stories Press. Critical research assistance was provided by Judith Rousseau and Joe Cochran of the Sonoma County Public Library and a number of the librarians at the Ruben Salazar Library, at Sonoma State University.

I am grateful to Michael Parenti for his thoughtful and provocative introduction. He reveals six methods of media bias that are systematically used to manipulate the public and explains why we should all be aware of them.

Finally I want to especially thank my wife, Sandra Scott Jensen, for the many hours she spent reviewing early versions of this book and for all the support and encouragement she has given me and Project Censored since its start in 1976.

Carl Jensen
Cotati, California

Introduction

METHODS OF MEDIA MANIPULATION

by Michael Parenti

We are told by people in the media industry that news bias is unavoidable. Whatever distortions and inaccuracies that are found in the news are caused by deadline pressures, human misjudgment, limited print space, scarce air time, budgetary restraints, and the difficulty of reducing a complex story into a concise report. Furthermore, the argument goes, no communication system can hope to report everything. Selectivity is needed, and some members of the public are bound to be dissatisfied.

I agree that those kinds of difficulties exist. Still, I would argue that the media's misrepresentations are not merely the result of innocent error and everyday production problems. True, the press has to be selective— but what principle of selectivity is involved? Media bias does not occur in random fashion; rather it moves in the same overall direction again and again, favoring management over labor, corporations over corporate critics, affluent whites over inner-city poor, officialdom over protesters, the two-party monopoly over leftist third parties, privatization and free market "reforms" over public sector development, U.S. dominance of the Third World over revolutionary or populist social change, nation-security policy over critics of that policy, and conservative commentators and columnists like Rush Limbaugh and George Will over progressive or populist ones like Jim Hightower and Ralph Nader (not to mention more radical ones).

The built-in biases of the corporate mainstream media faithfully reflect the dominant ideology, seldom straying into territory that might cause discomfort to those who hold political and economic power, including those who own the media or advertise in it. What follows is an incomplete sketch of the methods by which those biases are packaged and presented.

OMISSION AND SUPPRESSION

Manipulation often lurks in the things left unmentioned. The most common form of media misrepresentation is omission. Sometimes the omission includes not just vital details of a story but the entire story itself, even ones of major import. As just noted, stories that might reflect poorly upon the powers that be are the least likely to see the light of day. Thus the Tylenol poisoning of several people by a deranged individual was treated as big news but the far more sensational story of the industrial brown-lung poisoning of thousands of factory workers by large manufacturing interests (who themselves own or advertise in the major media) has remained suppressed for decades, despite the best efforts of worker safety groups to bring the issue before the public.

We hear plenty about the political repression perpetrated by left-wing governments such as Cuba (though a recent State Department report actually cited only six political prisoners in Cuba), but almost nothing about the far more brutal oppression and mass killings perpetrated by U.S.-supported right-wing client states such as Turkey, Indonesia, Saudi Arabia, Morocco, El Salvador, Guatemala, and others too numerous to mention.

Often the media mute or downplay truly sensational (as opposed to sensationalistic) stories. Thus, in 1965 the Indonesian military—advised, equipped, trained, and financed by the U.S. military and the CIA—overthrew President Achmed Sukarno and eradicated the Indonesian Communist Party and its allies, killing half a million people (some estimates are as high as a million) in what was the greatest act of political mass murder since the Nazi Holocaust. The generals also destroyed hundreds of clinics, libraries, schools, and community centers that had been opened by the communists. Here was a sensational story if ever there was one, but it took three months before it received passing mention in *Time* magazine and yet another month before it was reported in *The New York Times* (4/5/66), accompanied by an editorial that actually praised the Indonesian military for "rightly playing its part with utmost caution."

LIES, BALD AND REPETITIVE

When omission proves to be an insufficient form of suppression, the media resort to outright lies. At one time or another over the course of forty years, the CIA involved itself with drug traffickers in Italy, France, Corsica, Indochina, Afghanistan, and Central and South America. Much of this activity was the object of extended congressional investigations and is a matter of public record. But the media seem not to have heard about it.

In August 1996, when the *San Jose Mercury News* published an in-depth series about the CIA-contra crack shipments that were flooding East Los Angeles, the major media held true to form and suppressed the story. But after the series was circulated around the world on the Web, the story became too difficult to ignore, and the media began its assault. Articles in the *Washington Post* and *The New York Times* and reports on network television and PBS announced that there was "no evidence" of CIA involvement, that the *Mercury News* series was "bad journalism," and that the public's interest in this subject was the real problem, a matter of gullibility, hysteria, and conspiracy mania. In fact, the *Mercury News* series, drawing from a year-long investigation, cited specific agents and dealers. When placed on the Web, the series was copiously supplemented with pertinent documents and depositions that supported the charge. The mainstream media simply ignored that evidence and repeatedly lied by saying that it did not exist.

LABELING

Like all propagandists, media people seek to prefigure our perception of a subject with a positive or negative label. Some positive ones are: "stability," "the president's firm leadership," "a strong defense," and "a healthy economy." Indeed, who would want instability, weak presidential leadership, a vulnerable defense, and a sick economy? The label defines the subject, and does it without having to deal with actual particulars that might lead us to a different conclusion.

Some common negative labels are: "leftist guerrillas," "Islamic terrorists," "conspiracy theories," "inner-city gangs," and "civil disturbances." These, too, are seldom treated within a larger context of social relations and issues. The press itself is facilely and falsely labeled "the liberal media" by the hundreds of conservative columnists, commentators, and talk-show hosts who crowd the communication universe while claiming to be shut out from it.

FACE-VALUE TRANSMISSION

One way to lie is to accept at face value what are known to be official lies, uncritically passing them on to the public without adequate confirmation. For the better part of four years, in the early 1950s, the press performed this function for Senator Joseph McCarthy, who went largely unchallenged as he brought charge after charge of treason and communist subversion against people whom he could not have victimized without the complicity of the national media.

Face-value transmission has characterized the press's performance in almost every area of domestic and foreign policy, so much so that journalists have been referred to as "stenographers of power." (Perhaps some labels are well deserved.) When challenged on this, reporters respond that they cannot inject their own personal ideology into their reports. Actually, no one is asking them to. My criticism is that they already do. Their conventional ideological perceptions usually coincide with those of their bosses and with officialdom in general, making them faithful purveyors of the prevailing orthodoxy. This confluence of bias is perceived as "objectivity."

FALSE BALANCING

In accordance with the canons of good journalism, the press is supposed to tap competing sources to get both sides of an issue. In fact, both sides are seldom accorded equal prominence. One study found that on NPR, supposedly the most liberal of the mainstream media, right-wing spokespeople are often interviewed alone, while liberals—on the less frequent occasions they appear—are almost always offset by conservatives. Furthermore, both sides of a story are not necessarily *all* sides. Left-progressive and radical views are almost completely shut out.

During the 1980s, television panel discussions on defense policy pitted "experts" who wanted to maintain the existing high levels of military spending against other "experts" who wanted to increase the military budget even more. Seldom if ever heard were those who advocated drastic reductions in the defense budget.

FRAMING

The most effective propaganda is that which relies on framing rather than on falsehood. By bending the truth rather than breaking it, using emphasis and other auxiliary embellishments, communicators can create a desired impression without resorting to explicit advocacy and without departing too far from the appearance of objectivity. Framing is achieved in the way the news is packaged, the amount of exposure, the placement (front page or buried within, lead story or last), the tone of presentation (sympathetic or slighting), the headlines and photographs, and, in the case of broadcast media, the accompanying visual and auditory effects.

Newscasters use themselves as auxiliary embellishments. They cultivate a smooth delivery and try to convey an impression of detachment that places them above the rough and tumble of their subject matter. Television commentators and newspaper editorialists and columnists affect a knowing style and tone designed to foster credibility and an aura of certitude, or what might be called authoritative ignorance, as expressed in remarks like "How will the situation end? Only time will tell." Or, "No one can say for sure." (Better translated as, "I don't know and if *I* don't know then nobody does.") Sometimes the aura of authoritative credibility is preserved by palming off trite truisms as penetrating truths. So newscasters learn to fashion sentences like "Unless the strike is settled soon, the two sides will be in for a long and bitter struggle." And "The space launching will take place as scheduled if no unexpected problems arise." And "Because of heightened voter interest, election-day turnout is expected to be heavy." And "Unless Congress acts soon, this bill is not likely to go anywhere."

We are not likely to go anywhere as a people and a democracy unless we alert ourselves to the methods of media manipulation that are ingrained in the daily production of news and commentary. The news media regularly fail to provide a range of information and commentary that might help citizens in a democracy develop their own critical perceptions. The job of the corporate media is to make the universe of discourse safe for corporate America, telling us what to think about the world before we have a chance to think about it for ourselves. When we understand that news selectivity is likely to favor those who have power, position, and wealth, we move from a liberal complaint about the press's sloppy performance to a radical analysis of how the media serve the ruling circles all too well with much skill and craft.

MICHAEL PARENTI received his Ph.D. in political science from Yale University in 1962, and has taught at a number of colleges and universities. He is the author of thirteen books, including *Democracy for a Few* (6th edition); *Power and the Powerless; Inventing Reality: The Politics of News Media* (2nd edition); *The Sword and the Dollar: Imperialism, Revolution and the Arms Race; Make-Believe Media: The Politics of Entertainment; Land of Idols, Political Mythology in America; Against Empire: Dirty Truths*; and *Blackshirts and Reds: Rational Fascism and the Overthrow of Communism.* Dr. Parenti's articles have appeared in a wide range of scholarly journals and political periodicals. He lives in Berkeley, California, and devotes himself full-time to writing and lecturing around the country.

CHAPTER 1—1976

The Peanut Farmer and the Trilateral Commission

Nineteen-seventy-six was a big year for news with political, international, space, and domestic issues vying for media time and space. According to the Associated Press, the ten biggest news stories of the year were:

1. Jimmy Carter's presidential victory
2. the deaths of China's top political leaders, Chou En-lai and Mao Tse-tung
3. U.S. Bicentennial
4. the economy
5. Legionnaires' disease
6. Viking landing on Mars
7. Washington sex scandals
8. Patty Hearst trial
9. the Israeli Entebbe raid
10. the Chowchilla kidnapping.

The American public was well-informed about these events by their daily newspapers, newsweekly magazines, and network news programs. But there were other stories of major significance that did not receive the same mass media coverage.

THE TOP TEN CENSORED STORIES OF 1976

—And What Has Happened to Them Since

1. Jimmy Carter and the Trilateral Commission (TLC)

1976 SYNOPSIS: In the election year of 1976, Jimmy Carter ran a successful campaign for the presidency which was based on his image as an "outside-of-the-Beltway," peanut-farming, ex-governor of the state of Georgia.

Yet, since the fall of 1973, Carter had been associated with David Rockefeller and other members of an international power elite through his association with the Trilateral Commission (TLC). The TLC, one of Rockefeller's many policy-making organizations, is an alliance of several hundred top political and economic leaders from North America, Japan, and Western Europe. Their aim is to explore common problems facing the three areas and to advise political leaders of possible solutions.

While this side of Carter's background was almost totally ignored by the mass media, the American public was fully informed about his peanut-farming activities, the *Playboy* (lusting in his heart) interview, and Amy's lemonade stand.

According to the Italian publication *Europa*, as cited in *The Review of the News*, Rockefeller and Zbigniew Brzezinski, a founding director of the Trilateral Commission, had agreed on Carter's potential as our next president as far back as 1970.

Supportive of Carter's close relationship with this little-known power elite is the fact that many members of his administration were drawn from the membership rolls of the TLC. Carter's personal choice for vice president, Walter Mondale, was also a member of the TLC.

In 1976, there was a virtual blackout of media information available to the public concerning the relationships between Jimmy Carter, David Rockefeller, and the Trilateral Commission.

SOURCES: *The Crisis of Democracy*, by Michael Crozier, Samuel P. Huntington, and Joji Watanuki, "Report on the Governability of Democracies to the Trilateral Commission," published by New York University Press, 1975; *Seven Days*, 2/14/77, "From the Folks Who Brought Us Light at the End of the Tunnel," by William Minter, and "Trilateral RX for Crisis: Governability Yes, Democracy No," by Noam Chomsky; *The Review of the News*, 8/18/76; *The Berkeley Barb*, 7/30/76, by Gar Smith; *Jimmy Carter/Jimmy*

Carter, by Gary Allen, published by '76 Press, Seal Beach, California, 1976; *American Opinion*, February 1976, "Carter Brings Forth a Cabinet," by Gary Allen; *New York*, 12/13/76, "Carter's Little Kissingers," by Aaron Latham.

UPDATE: Twenty years after ultra conservatives were yelling about one world conspiracies being promulgated by the Trilateral Commission (TLC) and its predecessor, the Council on Foreign Relations, both organizations are still alive and well and headquartered in New York City. And while the *CBS Evening News* did a segment on the TLC on May 2, 1995, discrediting it as an issue fostered only by reactionary right wing groups such as the Liberty Lobby, it still hasn't attracted the attention of most of the other mainstream media.

Instead, the Trilateral Commission has taken on something of a kooky image like that of the Bilderbergers, a very secretive international organization of powerful elites similar to the TLC, but one which also has members from Eastern Europe, Northern Africa, Turkey, and Greece. Not surprisingly, the most strident criticism of the TLC still comes from the ultra-right which sees it as promoting a one world system of government. For example, Glen Donnelson, of North Ogden, Utah, founder and chairman of the conservative Constitutional Forum, accused President Bill Clinton of taking orders from the Trilateral Commission and the Council on Foreign Relations and secretly signing an executive order in 1995 placing all U.S. military forces under the control of the United Nations. This, of course, didn't happen (*The Salt Lake Tribune*, 1/21/96).

For those who want to discover more for themselves, the U.S. headquarters of the Trilateral Commission is located at 345 East 46th Street, Suite 711, New York, NY 10017; phone 212/661-1180; fax 212/949-7268. For additional sources on the Internet, Alta Vista provides sites for information on members of groups "who are gradually taking over the world under their 'New World Order.'" including the Bilderbergers, Council on Foreign Relations, Skull & Bones Society, as well as the Trilateral Commission.

2. Corporate Control of DNA

1976 SYNOPSIS: Since 1973, scientists at university laboratories across the country have been creating new life forms from the gene-carrying DNA of other organisms. The organisms thus created are called DNA Recombinants because they are literally recombined from the DNA of other simple bacteria or viruses. DNA researchers maintain that their work may lead to the creation of new life-saving drugs, new food sources, and cures for cancer and other diseases.

A number of other scientists do not agree. They say that DNA research amounts to dangerous tampering with the evolutionary balance, tampering that could result in the release of hordes of lethal new viruses which could not be detected until it was too late.

Although the National Institutes of Health (NIH) published guidelines for DNA research, opponents of DNA work state the NIH guidelines are hopelessly unenforceable and do not apply to private industry. The federal government appears willing to allow industry a free hand in creating new viruses, bacteria, and enzymes.

SOURCES: *Mother Jones*, Feb/Mar 1977, "DNA: Have the Corporations Already Grabbed Control of New Life Forms?" by Jeremy Rifkin; *Science Magazine*, 10/15/76, "Recombinant DNA: A Critic Asks the Right to Free Inquiry"; *The Progressive*, March 1977, "Life from the Labs: Who Will Control the New Technology?"

UPDATE: Susan Wright, a historian of science at the University of Michigan, charges in a *Nation* article (3/11/96) that genetic engineering is now proceeding rapidly without even the minimal controls established 20 years ago. Following an intense lobbying effort by scientists in the late 1970s, rapid deregulation followed, and regulatory agencies already have allowed more than 2,000 experimental releases of novel plants and microbes.

A host of transgenic creatures is emerging from genetic engineering laboratories including:

✔ *Transgenic plants*—Agrichemical and seed corporations are developing a wide range of transgenic crops and biopesticides, the most visible to date being Calgene's Flavr Savr tomato which made headlines in 1994.

✔ *Animal pharms*—Bio engineers are turning animals into factories to make drugs in their milk or blood, making pigs and chickens with flesh that can be easily microwaved, and producing bovine growth hormone (rBGH) to increase milk production.

✔ *Genetically altered humans*—Corporations are aggressively promoting human gene therapy for life-threatening diseases and talking of treating non-life-threatening conditions like dwarfism even though no genetic cures are yet in sight.

✔ *Military applications*—After maintaining a low profile for military biological sciences in the 1970s, the Defense Department quietly renewed biowarfare research in the 1980s, using the new biotechnology to produce therapeutic agents, detection devices, and vaccines to protect against biological weapons. Susan Wright concludes that it is time for another international conference to examine the genetically reconstructed worlds being designed by corporations and the military before we have a genetic Chernobyl.

The warning raised in the #2 *Censored* story of 1976 suddenly made front page news throughout the world in late February 1997 when a group of Scottish scientists announced they had successfully cloned an adult mammal, a sheep named Dolly, for the first time. The stunning news caused *The New York Times* to belatedly editorialize (2/25/97): "Like most technologies, cloning is bound to have both virtues and vices. But before these advances get too far ahead of us, society will need to sort through what is acceptable and what is the nightmare beyond."

The March/April 1996 issue of *Utne Reader* provides an informative discussion of the "virtues and vices" of genetic engineering, noting that biotechnology profits are expected to rise from the current $2 billion a year to $50 billion by 2000. It also includes an excellent resource guide to organizations and books on this controversial subject.

3. Selling Banned Pesticides and Drugs to Third World Countries

1976 SYNOPSIS: According to a conservative estimate by the World Health Organization, some 500,000 people, the majority of them in Third World countries, are poisoned yearly by banned pesticides and drugs.

Besides poisonings, a rash of miscarriages and birth defects have been attributed to certain banned herbicides. Although these chemicals are banned for use in the United States, domestic drug manufacturing corporations continue to produce and export them to foreign countries.

Drugs never approved by the Food and Drug Administration, and even some never tested, are marketed and sold in some Third World countries. Moreover, they are shipped to countries that have minimal or no drug controls or regulations despite the fact that the products are known to be dangerous.

What the peoples of those countries are being subjected to, and what the U.S. drug and chemical manufacturers are doing there, goes virtually unnoticed and unreported in this country.

SOURCE: *Rolling Stone*, 2/10/77, "Banned Chemicals Shipped Abroad," by David Weir.

UPDATE: By-passing national bans and restrictions, U.S. corporations are still exporting huge quantities of hazardous pesticides to Third World countries according to U.S. Customs records, as reported by Inter Press Service (12/7/95).

The Los Angeles-based Foundation for Advancement in Science and Education, an independent environmental research organization investigating pesticides, obtained the customs records which indicate that the United States exported at least 58 million pounds of the pesticides to more than 12 countries during the 1991-1994 period.

The customs records document up to 30 shipments of hazardous pesticides totaling 11 million pounds to countries where they are officially banned.

Countries importing hazardous pesticides include the Republic of Korea, Singapore, the Netherlands, India, Zimbabwe, Australia, Costa Rica, Israel, Thailand, El Salvador, Brazil, Japan, and France.

Lori Ann Thropp, a senior researcher at the World Resource Institute's Center for International Development and Environment, said that "an increasing number of people are suffering acute poisonings and chronic damage" because government agencies and pesticide firms in developing countries seldom provide sufficient information and precautions.

Please also see update of "The Circle of Poison," #6, 1980.

4. Why Oil Prices Go Up

1976 SYNOPSIS: While most Americans believe the increase in oil prices was due to the Arab oil embargo started in 1973, few are aware that their elected representatives collaborated with the Organization of Petroleum Exporting Countries (OPEC) and Persian oil-producing nations to deliberately inflate the price of oil.

As early as 1971, the U.S. State Department established oil policy priorities during international negotiations, emphasizing the "stability, orderliness, and durability" of supply with no intention of maintaining price limits. Only two years later, the Arab oil embargo disrupted both the cost and continuity of foreign oil.

While gasoline prices were skyrocketing and supplies diminishing at the consumer level, the White House Council on International Economic Policy was reporting economic benefits that the oil price increases were generating in the United States. OPEC surplus revenue started recycling back into the American economy: foreign oil-producers began investing in American enterprises—corporate stocks, real property, and advanced weaponry.

Further, the foreign increases in oil prices meant more money for domestic oil-producers who benefited from increased domestic oil prices and profits. Meanwhile Americans were fighting one another in gasoline lines. While the increases contributed to a worldwide recession, U.S. industries, as the government had speculated, suffered less than their competitors in Europe and Japan.

SOURCE: *Foreign Policy*, Winter Quarter, 1976, "Why Oil Prices Go Up— The Past: We Pushed them," by Vivian H. Oppenheim.

UPDATE: It appears that the harsh lessons of the seventies have been forgotten in the nineties. *New York Times* columnist Thomas L. Friedman wrote (7/4/96) that we responded to the 1973-79 oil crises by raising taxes on gasoline to reduce consumption but we are now lowering them; we were shrinking the size of automobiles but we are now upsizing them; we lowered the speed limits but we are now raising them. Friedman pointed out that before 1979 the United States was importing about 45 percent of its oil and was vulnerable to crises in the Middle East. After 1979, as conservation took hold, oil imports dropped to 32 percent by 1985; since then, oil imports have steadily gone up, topping 50 percent in 1995. Domestic gasoline prices set record highs in the summer of 1996.

The Group of Seven (G-7), an organization of seven major industrial democracies who meet periodically to discuss world economic issues, was founded to deal with the economic fallout and currency disruptions set off by the 1973 oil crisis. The members are Canada, France, Germany, Italy, Japan, United Kingdom, and the United States. The G-7 was renamed the Group of Eight (G-8) in 1997 with the addition of Russia. In his 1996 article, Friedman charged that thanks to the indifference of the G-7 leaders to oil conservation, it is as though the 1973-1979 oil crises never happened. We are now more vulnerable to crises in the Middle East than ever before.

5. The Mobil Oil/Rhodesian Connection

1976 SYNOPSIS: This story reported how "Single-handedly, America's fifth largest corporation is keeping alive a regime that has been not only embargoed but condemned by virtually every nation on earth." The corporation was Mobil Oil; the nation was Rhodesia (known as Zimbabwe since 1980).

The story was released, with supporting documentation, at a press conference held by the People's Bicentennial Commission (PBC) in Washington,

D.C., June 21, 1976. Attending the press conference were more than 40 reporters from America's major newspapers, all three networks and the wire services, as well as radio and freelance people. On the same day, the PBC turned the documentation over to the Treasury Department, the House and Senate Committees on Africa, and Senator Frank Church's subcommittee on multinationals. The only extensive coverage occurred six weeks later when *The New York Times* broke the story, announcing that the Treasury had begun an investigation of the PBC charges. None of the networks, nor *Time* and *Newsweek*, gave coverage to the story.

The story charged that Mobil, by developing a string of dummy companies, post office addresses, and phony order sheets and invoices was able to set up a circuitous "paper chase" thereby disguising the fact that Mobil was selling Rhodesia as much as $20 million a year in oil products, including specialized aviation fuel for Rhodesia's air force.

SOURCE: *Mother Jones*, Sept/Oct 1976, "Let's Make A Deal," by Richard Parker.

UPDATE: Twenty years after the media's failure to pursue the embargo violations by Mobil Oil, the company is still conducting business as usual at the same old stand. While it had to drop an oil exploration project in Zimbabwe's northern Zambezi valley in late 1994 (Reuters, 1/19/95), a Mobil Oil Corp. vice president for new business predicted that "Africa has the long-term growth potential to rival that of anywhere else in the world," noting that Africa has vast reserves of oil and gas (Reuters, 10/13/95). Mobil has not been alone in breaking an international oil embargo. Both the Bush and Clinton Administrations knew that Texaco's Caribbean subsidiary illegally distributed oil in Haiti, breaking that embargo and propping up military dictators (*CounterPunch*, 10/15/94).

6. Some of Our Plutonium is Missing

1976 SYNOPSIS: Inefficiencies of nuclear safeguarding techniques and ambiguities concerning the accountability of nuclear materials pose a real but little known threat to the safety of the American public. An unpublicized General Accounting Office report revealed cases of inadequate security at nuclear plants, including the use of employee honor systems in lieu of posted guards, the lack of effective security screening for new employees, and the strategic "outmanning" of perimeter sentry guards.

Also noted was the lack of a credible inventory system to accurately tabulate amounts of uranium and plutonium being processed. So lax is the current method that the government cannot account for 150,000 pounds of nuclear materials, 11,000 pounds of which is weapon-grade quality. For comparison, 4.4 pounds of plutonium is sufficient to make a bomb large enough to level a city of 100,000 people. Furthermore, any quantity of plutonium is a carcinogen and a lethal poison.

In short, poor government management has allowed the nuclear security situation to degenerate to the point that nuclear supplies can be pilfered by employees, plants can be seized by terrorists, and private organizations involved with atomic energy go virtually unregulated.

SOURCE: *The Nation*, 10/23/76, "Some of Our Plutonium is Missing," by Barbara P. Newman.

UPDATE: Under a new openness policy, Hazel O'Leary, Secretary of Energy, announced the nation's plutonium and uranium stockpile inventories in early February 1996. DOE also acknowledged an accounting discrepancy in which the department couldn't find 2.8 metric tons (MT) of plutonium. Further, it reported it had an excess of 38.3 MT of weapons-grade plutonium that needs to be disposed of and an excess of 174.3 MT of highly enriched uranium. Among other items listed in the DOE report, it was revealed that the U.S. produced or acquired 111.4 MT of plutonium between 1944 and 1994; some 3.4 MT of plutonium were used during wartime or nuclear tests; the U.S. conducted a total of 1,030 nuclear tests between July 1945 through December 1992; and the locations of the nation's plutonium inventory in buried and stored wastes including Pantex, Texas; Rocky Flats, Colorado; Los Alamos National Laboratory, New Mexico; and Hanford, Washington. For a copy of the official explanation of what happened to our plutonium, "Plutonium: The First 50 Years," prepared by the U.S. Department of Energy, call DOE's Center for Environmental Management Information at 800/7-EM-DATA (*Defense Cleanup*, 2/9/96).

7. Workers Die for Corporate Profits

1976 SYNOPSIS: The untold number of injuries, disease, and deaths caused by work hazards in America's industries is a major story which received little, if any, coverage in the mass media. Following are the problems suffered by workers in just one area: America's foundries.

The Occupational Safety and Health Administration (OSHA) estimates that one out of every three foundry workers is injured every year. The mortality rate among furnacemen is 76 percent greater than that of the rest of the working population of their age. The industry averages 70 deaths and 70,000 injuries from accidents every year. No statistics on disease rates, such as those caused by toxic substances (heavy-metal poisoning, crippling lung diseases, like silicosis and talcosis, bronchitis, emphysema, heart disease, etc.) are cited.

OSHA, charged with protecting 50 million workers in four million workplaces, doesn't have the ability to investigate, let alone regulate and implement change in America's workplaces. Senate Armed Services Committee member Dewey Barlett said efforts to make an industry "safer, healthier or more environmentally acceptable...cannot be placed blindly above the higher priorities of a strong economy and adequate military capability."

SOURCE: *Seven Days*, 2/28/77, "America's Foundries: Hell Aboveground," by Charles West.

UPDATE: Nearly two decades later, serious injuries and illnesses from ergonomic workplace hazards are increasing at epidemic rates according to a 121-page report, "Safe Jobs Promises Kept, Promises Broken," prepared by the AFL-CIO for the 25th anniversary of the Occupational Safety and Health Act.

Overexertion and repetitive motion are responsible for a third of all serious workplace injuries; repeated trauma disorders increased by 800 percent in the last decade; and homicide has become the second leading cause of workplace fatalities after transportation (*Work & Family Newsbrief*, 6/1/96). On July 28, 1997, the Associated Press cited a new study that charged job-related injuries are more common than believed—averaging 18 deaths and 36,000 injuries a day.

Please also see update of "Occupational Disease," #5, 1979, and "The Deadly Secrets of the Occupational Safety Agency," the #1 *Censored* story of 1994.

8. Kissinger Uses the CIA to Change Intelligence Estimates

1976 SYNOPSIS: Because the dangers and threats of a nuclear war are the concern of every citizen, the Strategic Arms Limitation Talks (SALT) are of both domestic and international importance. But while the conferences, accords, and summit meetings were given substantial coverage in the media, the public was little aware what really took place.

For example, in 1976, then Secretary of State Henry Kissinger, with the collusion of the Central Intelligence Agency, was accused of manipulating intelligence estimates for use in SALT talk negotiations. According to *Aviation Week*, the integrity of the US-USSR weapons' pacts was left in doubt when Kissinger directed the CIA to alter range estimates for the Soviet Union's Tupolev Backfire bomber. The CIA was ordered to provide McDonnell Douglas, the aerospace firm, with just enough intelligence data to formulate a 3,500 nautical mile range capability.

A similar study by the Pentagon, using all available intelligence information, computed the bomber's range at 6,000 nautical miles. This clearly put the aircraft in the heavy bomber category to be counted in the 2,400 strategic delivery vehicle limit set in the Ford-Breznhev Vladivostok agreement.

Kissinger had already made a separate agreement with the Russians, conceding that the Backfire would not be considered in the heavy bomber category. The directive to the CIA was an attempt to fulfill his commitment.

In response to Kissinger's denial and request for a retraction and apology, *Aviation Week's* editor, Robert B. Hotz, responded that *Aviation Week* was a responsible publication which had verified the facts and offered no apology and no retraction.

SOURCE: *Aviation Week and Space Technology*, 9/13/76 and 9/27/76.

UPDATE: In a lengthy cover-story analysis of the Central Intelligence Agency (CIA) in March 1995, *Commentary* supported *Aviation Week's* 1976 charge of Kissinger's interference. It said that the "worst instances of politicization of the CIA occurred under President Nixon," who shifted much of the intelligence-estimating authority from the CIA to Henry Kissinger so assessments could be reached that justified White House policies. It noted that Nixon and Kissinger disregarded the CIA's skepticism about U.S. ability to verify treaty compliance in an effort to attain an arms-limitation agreement with Moscow.

9. Worthless and Hazardous Non-Prescription Drugs

1976 SYNOPSIS: According to the Food and Drug Administration (FDA), up to 500,000 different non-prescription remedies generate at least $3.51 billion in sales every year, and, according to its investigating experts who amassed 14,000 volumes of evidence on these over-the-counter (OTC) drugs, the people who purchase them are "the victims of a gigantic medical hoax."

The conclusions of intensive independent studies first launched in 1972 by more than 100 leading medical researchers, physicians, and pharmacologists recruited by the FDA are that "at least half the drugs are worthless or of dubious value, and some may be harmful. Most of the products are labeled with misleading claims, and many are advertised with bold lies."

While the industry invests in massive advertising campaigns, it spends comparatively little in developing and testing new drugs: "Major OTC producers spend at least $400 million in network television spots each year...telling consumers, about fifty times a day, that medically ineffective products will really work."

The 1962 Food, Drug, and Cosmetic law requires the FDA to ban any drug if "there is a lack of substantial evidence that the drug will have the effect the manufacturer claims it does." Yet, the FDA leisurely circumvents the law and continues to allow the drug companies to stall taking their unproved products off the market. The FDA attorneys "protect the product in a sort of limbo, tailor-made for the drug companies," allowing the "industry to continue advertising and marketing the products for up to five years or longer while its researchers feverishly try to prove that the drugs really work."

SOURCE: *New Times*, 9/17/76, "Non-Prescription Drugs—The Ultimate Confidence Game," by Daniel Zwerdling.

UPDATE: While the "gigantic medical hoax" of non-prescription remedies still hasn't received major media coverage, the explosion in over-the-counter (OTC) sales since 1976 should sound a strident warning. The 1976 synopsis noted annual sales of non-prescription drugs at $3.51 billion. Recent sales data indicate that OTC drugs generated $5.5 billion in retail sales in 1980; by 1990, sales almost doubled to $10.3 billion; and industry forecasters estimate that OTC sales will leap to $16.7 billion by 1999. Compounding the hazards of self-diagnosis and self-medication promoted by the drug companies, some 600 drug ingredients that were available only by prescription in the 1970s are now routinely sold over-the-counter. Benadryl, Gyne-Lotrimin, Pepcid, Tagamet, Rogaine, and Nicorette are just a few of the widely advertised cure-alls. It also should be noted that when drugs move from a prescription status to non-prescription OTC status, insurance companies no longer cover their cost. One reason that may account for the lack of media coverage on the huge increase in OTC drug sales is the corresponding explosion in advertising dollars spent to promote these products. In the magazine industry alone, drug marketers spent $163 million in 1990; by the end of 1995, that total had ballooned to $502 million, according to the Publishers Information Bureau (*Inside Media*, 2/7/96).

10. The Natural Gas Swindle

1976 SYNOPSIS: This investigative piece reports illegal and unethical activities of gas companies, company connections with government agencies, and motives for creating a natural gas shortage in the 1970s.

Illegalities mentioned include the failure of seven major companies to produce natural gas supply information subpoenaed by the Federal Trade Commission (FTC), the 100 percent increase in prices for new gas from 1972 to 1974, and the ownership of gas stock by 19 key officials of the Federal Power Commission (FPC).

Also noted is the failure of the FPC to issue injunctions against companies "sitting on" federal land leases, to report that gas companies greatly under-estimated gas reserves, and to abide by its own mandate. The companies are charged with using current shortages as "scare tactics" to force deregulation of interstate gas supplies—a legislative act which would produce windfall profits for the natural gas producing companies.

SOURCE: *The Nation*, 1/24/76, "The Natural Gas Swindle," by Robert Sherrill.

UPDATE: The "natural gas swindle" charged by Robert Sherrill in his 1976 article in *The Nation* was ignored by the major media and never turned into a national gas scandal. Instead, the reportedly contrived natural gas shortages led to political in-fighting in Congress on how best to deregulate the industry—which was precisely what the industry was after from the start. Finally, according to a report in *Electricity Journal*, May 1996, when Jimmy Carter became president in 1977, he launched a complex legislative program to phase in deregulation of natural gas prices over the next decade. Much of the complexity of the program was eliminated in the fall of 1992 when Congress passed the Comprehensive Energy Policy Act, which concluded that producers, consumers and the U.S. economy will all benefit from deregulated competition markets" (*Petroleum Independent*, October 1992). It took 16 years but the natural gas industry finally got the deregulation it wanted.

CHAPTER 2—1977

The Lack of Black Progress vs. the Weather

While inclement weather ranked as the top mainstream news story of 1977, the continuing plight of black Americans was cited as the top undercovered news story of the year. According to the Associated Press, the top ten news stories of the year were:

1. The weather
2. The spread of international terrorism
3. Panama Canal treaty
4. Resignation of Bert Lance, Jimmy Carter's director of the Office of Management and Budget
5. Elvis Presley's death
6. Gary Gilmore's execution
7. Collision of two jets at Tenerife in the Canary Islands
8. The Carter Administration's energy policy
9. Capture of the suspected Son of Sam murderer
10. The investigation of Tong-Sun Park's alleged influence peddling in Washington.

THE TOP TEN CENSORED STORIES OF 1977

—And What Has Happened to Them Since

1. The Myth of Black Progress

1977 SYNOPSIS: It took the power blackout and looting of New York City in 1977 for America to rediscover its ghettos. Most of the indices of poverty, illegitimacy, unemployment, and drug abuse that led to the urban riots in the 1960s are now worse.

Half the black population is less than 24 years old and for them the future promises little. Four out of ten minority youths in ghettos will never have a job that provides them with a livelihood or enables them to support a family. This is the human dimension of a black teenage unemployment rate of 40 percent.

Even those blacks who are considered successful, mainly because they have jobs, are losing ground to their white counterparts. The Labor Department reports a growing gap between white and black income, with the wages of white workers increasing twice as fast as those of blacks.

Crime is the greatest urban concern of our time and black youth plays a major role in that problem. In New York City today, the number of black youths under 16 who have been arrested is almost ten times what it was in 1950.

SOURCE: *The Progressive*, November 1977, "Black Progress Myth and Ghetto Reality," by Joel Dreyfuss.

UPDATE: In a speech on race relations to Town Hall Los Angeles (*Los Angeles Times*, 6/4/96), Senator Bill Bradley (D-New Jersey) summarized the current situation for blacks in America: "Economically, black America is in the best and worst of times. Roughly one-third of black America can now be called middle class." However, Bradley continued, "More than 30 percent of blacks live in grinding poverty. Many can't find a job, can't get credit to buy a house or start a business, and increasingly can't make ends meet for necessities, much less save for the future. Indeed, the unemployment rate for blacks is routinely twice that for whites." He also noted that 46 percent of black children live below the poverty line, compared with 17 percent of white children.

2. The War on Cancer

1977 SYNOPSIS: When Richard Nixon began an "all out war" on cancer with the National Cancer Act in 1971, a concerned public expected great strides to be made. Members of the American Cancer Society (ACS) were the major political force behind the Act which resulted in a National Cancer Institute (NCI) budget of over $800 million in 1977, compared to $190 million in 1971.

However, more than six years and $4 billion later, the U.S. still has the highest record for cancer occurrence—fifty percent above the world average—while the chance for an American to survive cancer has not increased more than one percent since the late 1940s. Forty percent of the research funds go to contract research which is barely reviewed and invites abuse and poor quality work.

Probably the most serious problem with cancer research in this country has been the lack of attention given to banning carcinogenic chemicals. Despite government estimates that 60-70 percent of cancer is caused by environmental factors, the ACS has refused to support such bills as the Toxic Substance Control Act and has never pushed a ban on any carcinogenic product.

SOURCES: *New Times*, 11/25/77, "Cancer, Inc.," by Ruth Rosenbaum; *Politiks*, 12/6/77, "Cancer Society Seeks Cure, Neglects Causes," by Jim Rosapepe.

UPDATE: June 1996 marked the 25th anniversary of Nixon's declaration of war on cancer. Yet the incidence of cancer was still rising, 25 years and $30 billion later. A third of Americans get cancer and a fifth die of it. Richard Klausner, director of the National Cancer Institute, admitted, "Promises were made that could not be kept" (*Salt Lake City Tribune*, 6/6/96).

By late 1996, the National Cancer Institute (NCI) reported that the U.S. cancer death rate was going down for the first time since cancer statistics were first kept in the 1930s. Cancer deaths fell 2.6 percent from 1991 to 1995, reversing a 6.4 percent rise from 1971 to 1990. Donna Shalala, Health and Human Services Secretary, announced, "This looks like a turning point in the 25-year war on cancer" (*USA Today*, 11/14/96).

However, critics questioned the reliability of the NCI data. A new analysis by researchers at the University of Chicago, as reported in the *New Eng-*

land Journal of Medicine, revealed that despite 26 years of work, the U.S. government's "War on Cancer" has failed to reduce death rates from the disease substantially. The researchers argue that the battle should shift to another front: prevention (*USA Today*, 5/29/97).

3. Jimmy Carter and the Trilateral Commission: Part II

1977 SYNOPSIS: Although the Trilateral Commission (TLC) was the top *Censored* story of 1976, it was renominated in 1977 since it continued to receive very limited press coverage.

The 1977 nomination reveals that Jimmy Carter's major moves since taking over as president have been in accord with the TLC's recommendations, including 1) a new economic planning agency attached to the White House; 2) some unspecified way of eliminating the pervasive suspicion of the motives and powers of political leaders; 3) reinvigoration of political parties accomplished mainly by making it legal for corporations to support them; 4) a check on press power to include tough libel laws against journalists who insult decision makers; 5) reduced spending for education as it leads to frustration, criticism, and disrespect; 6) government subsidies to major corporations to design unspecified new modes of organization that will head off irresponsible blackmailing techniques; and 7) a new institute for the strengthening of democratic institutions at the public's expense.

SOURCES: *Penthouse*, November 1977, "Cartergate: The Death of Democracy," by Craig S. Karpel; *Esquire*, May 1977, "Where Jimmy Went Wrong," by Taylor Branch.

UPDATE: Please see update of "Jimmy Carter and the TLC," #1, 1976.

4. The Cost of Decommissioning Nuclear Power Plants

1977 SYNOPSIS: The decommissioning of nuclear reactors, which have lifetimes of 30 to 40 years, is a problem that has hardly been considered and has not been resolved. The intensity of radioactivity that will surround shutdown plants—some of it being hazardous for as long as 1.5 million years—will make it necessary for all reactors to eventually be completely decommissioned.

The Nuclear Regulatory Commission seems to assume that income generated by the reactors' use will pay for the enormous costs of decommissioning—but what happens if a reactor fails after only a few years of operation, or if its corporate owners no longer exist, or if the waning industry itself ends? What has not been adequately considered is that nuclear power, which has so far been nourished primarily by government funds, has problems that go beyond the many drawbacks and difficulties cropping up with the reactors themselves—such as low productivity, inadequate safety precautions, dwindling fuel supplies, skyrocketing prices, etc. The issues also extend to what happens when the plants are shut down. The question of waste disposal and how decommissioning costs are going to be paid remains an open one.

SOURCES: *Progressive*, December 1977, "A Landscape of Nuclear Tombs," by Alexis Parks; *Environment*, December 1976, "The Cost of Turning It Off," by Steve Harwood, Kenneth May, Marvin Resnikaff, Barbara Schlenger, and Pam Tames.

UPDATE: An in-depth investigative report on decommissioning nuclear reactors by *The Nation* (9/25/95) reveals that the worst fears cited in the 1977 *Censored* story are being realized and that the public can look forward to another massive taxpayer bailout. By 1988, the Nuclear Regulatory Commission (NRC) belatedly realized that someone would have to pay the cost for decommissioning nuclear reactors. The NRC "mandated that utility companies put money in trust for the day when their nuclear plants end their active lives and are decommissioned." Seven years later those trusts are reported to be in "catastrophic condition."

In just the past three years, "utilities have recalculated decommission costs, almost doubling their initial estimates; thus many trusts are even more underfunded than originally thought." Further, as warned in 1977, due to the high cost of nuclear power, hugely expensive repairs, and a waning nuclear industry, it is expected that "utilities will probably decide to close many facilities prematurely, thus allowing less time for the funds to accumulate."

Nuclear plants were licensed to operate for forty years, but NRC statistics reveal that as of 1993, the average age for a nuclear plant shutdown is 15 years. Further exacerbating the potential economic debacle, the Utility Regulatory Commission, an industry lobbying group, pressured the Federal Energy Regulatory Commission to relax investment guidelines for the trust funds. Now they have begun gambling some of their trust-fund money on volatile stocks rather than the more conservative bonds.

Please also see "The Dangers of Nuclear Power Plants," #1, 1978.

5. The Bottle Baby Scandal in the Third World

1977 SYNOPSIS: With the birthrate in the United States declining, infant formula manufacturers (Nestle and Bristol-Myers in the forefront along with Abbott and American Home Products) began pushing their products on the Third World to ensure their continued profits.

They rely on exploitative and deceptive tactics to sell their products including: 1) giving free samples to mothers so their own milk will dry up, leaving them dependent on expensive formulas; 2) promises of "modernization and heightened status" through use of the formulas, as encouraged by well-financed media campaigns (which include radio and television spots, calendars, billboards, and baby contests); 3) telling new mothers that their own milk is "inappropriate" or may be "unsuccessfully" given to their baby, etc.

The majority of Third World mothers wind up watering down the formulas, using contaminated water, and otherwise malnourishing and infecting their children because they cannot afford to administer formulas in the prescribed way. Parents would have to spend 30-40 percent of their average daily wage to feed their babies on this mother's milk substitute. Malnutrition and denial of natural immunities (which would have been provided had the mother breast-fed) caused by infant formula feeding account for 35,000 deaths and untold brain damage in babies of predominantly Third World countries.

Meanwhile, the profit margins on infant formulas have been documented at up to 72 percent; a billion dollars a year are taken from the Third World countries from the import of these formulas.

SOURCES: *Mother Jones*, December 1977, "The Bottle Baby Scandal," by Barbara Garson; *Seven Days*, 4/19/76, "Into the Mouths of Babes," by Leah Margulies.

UPDATE: As a result of public outrage in the late seventies and through a series of events involving the courts, the U.S. Senate, a group of Catholic nuns, the Securities and Exchange Commission, and concerned citizens, the WHO/UNICEF Code for Marketing Breastmilk Substitutes was drafted, redrafted, and finally adopted by the World Health Assembly in 1981. The final vote was 118 to 1. The United States cast the sole negative vote.

Despite the U.N. Code, a comprehensive exposé published by *Mothering* (12/22/95) revealed that even today, "Billboards and radio jingles encourage women to use formula in order to raise the healthiest baby. Hospital maternity units in developing nations are sometimes sponsored by formula companies...In addition, babies are routinely fed formula and glucose water, and mothers are sent home with unstimulated breasts and free samples of whatever formula paid for the maternity unit."

It is now estimated that "one million infant deaths per year can be prevented by using the world's most economical and effective health protection: breast milk." But Third World mothers are still not being told this and continue to be bombarded with promotions for formula. Anyone interested in this issue would be well advised to look up the original *Mothering* article. It is an exceptionally well-researched history of the problem dating back to 1939 when Nestle was selling sweetened condensed milk as infant food despite research showing it was unsafe for infants. It also contains dozens of names and addresses of organizations and individuals who can be contacted for further information.

Unfortunately, the health issue became increasingly complicated in 1997 as increasing numbers of Third World women, infected with the AIDS virus, were transmitting it to their infants through breast milk. Some observers feel that infant formula may be a powerful weapon to reduce childhood deaths from AIDS. Infant formula critics acknowledge that the data are incomplete but say that the vast majority of Third World infants will be imperiled by renewed promotion of bottle-feeding. Still others say it is imperative to find alternatives to breast-feeding including making safe, affordable formula widely available (*The New York Times*, 6/8/97).

6. The Mass Slaughter by the Khmer Rouge

1977 SYNOPSIS: Execution, starvation, cannibalism, torture, disease, malnutrition were only a few of the violations of human rights made by the Khmer Rouge in Cambodia and Vietnam. A few journalists who conducted interviews with refugees believed that out of a population of seven million, 1.2 million died between 1975 and 1977 alone. In addition, a Catholic missionary reported "15,000 to 20,000 suicides."

Reports also indicated that the Khmer Rouge treated people like slaves and imposed exacting rules. Failure to observe these rules led to immediate execution. Anyone who complained was punished. Rule breaking and complaints applied to such "crimes" as asking for more food, falling in exhaustion, or not meeting Khmer Rouge's own inhumane values.

The so-called "transgressors" were often clubbed to death with objects such as pick handles. When a starving worker was caught cannibalizing, he was tortured to death. Such torture included being buried in the ground up to the shoulders and being beaten to death or impaling their heads on pointed stakes.

In January 1977, the American Security Council invited all three major networks to a conference on the subject, which may have been the most important human rights story of the decade; not one sent a correspondent.

SOURCES: *National Review*, 9/2/77, "The Nation as a Concentration Camp," and 4/29/77, "The New Vietnam"; *The Progressive*, September 1977, "Vietnam: A New Numbers Game," by Robert K. Musih; *TV Guide*, 3/18/78, "Why Do Networks Play Down News From Cambodia?" by Patrick Buchanan; *Newsweek*, 1/16/78, "A New Indochina War," by Kenneth Labich, with Holger Jansen and Lars-Erik Nelson.

UPDATE: When Khmer Rouge executioners killed a million or more fellow Cambodians 20 years ago, it was a major story in the right-wing press but basically ignored by the mainstream media. It wasn't until 1984 when a British-made film, *The Killing Fields*, retold the story that many Americans became aware of the extent of the tragedy.

In 1993, a United Nations-sponsored election brought a measure of calm and renewal to Cambodia. However, the calm did not last long. In early July 1997, a military coup plunged the country back into political chaos and once again Cambodia seemed stuck in the cycle of violence and despair that has stained its history for the last 40 years. According to the Knight-Ridder Newspapers report (7/14/97), "Now, even some longtime [domestic] supporters are giving up and going home."

7. The Cost Benefits of Environmental Quality

1977 SYNOPSIS: American companies are fighting federal environmental and occupational health and safety regulations by warning that government controls would cause massive plant closings.

In fact, few factories would have to shut down, many more jobs would be created than lost, and the price increases would be balanced by the savings in pollution damage and health costs.

The Environmental Protection Agency (EPA), which monitors plant closings that involve 25 or more workers, reported on December 31, 1975, that only 75 plants had closed or curtailed operations because of the cost of complying with the last five years of federal regulations on the environment, with a loss of about 15,700 jobs. Even these dislocations seemed to be concentrated among marginal plants that were already heading for collapse. The number of lost jobs was offset by the increased employment caused by environmental spending—each $1 billion spent creates 66,900 jobs. A Council on Environmental Quality (CEQ) study estimated the total employment related to pollution control at more than a million people.

The CEQ put the combined public and private cost of meeting federal environmental standards in the 1974-1983 decade at $217.7 billion; for 1975, it was $19 billion. For comparative purposes, in 1975, according to the EPA, pollution of the general environment cost $26.6 billion in air and $10 billion in water pollution damage.

SOURCE: *The Nation*, 10/29/77, "Environmental Balance Sheet: Cost Benefits of the Cleanup," by Stephen Solomon and Willard Randall.

UPDATE: In early June 1996, the Environmental Protection Agency released draft results of the most detailed attempt made yet to measure the costs and benefits of cleaning the air (*Washington Post*, 6/17/96). The analysis revealed that "from 1970-90, sulfur dioxide emissions were reduced by 40 percent, carbon monoxide by 50 percent and airborne lead by 99 percent. These and other cuts cost $436 billion, but produced $6.8 trillion in benefits to human health—a staggering return of $16 for every dollar spent." Not included in the analysis were the benefits of limiting air pollution damage to crops, forests, buildings, waterways, and other ecosystems. Nor did it cite the many health effects—including a reduction in cancer from lead and airborne toxic chemicals.

In 1997, as the EPA was preparing to impose a new set of strict air pollution controls, corporate America was once again planning to fight them, but no longer on a cost analysis basis. John M. McManus, manager of environmental strategies for American Electric Power, said, "If we've learned any lesson, it's that you have to engage the debate on a different basis than costs" (*The New York Times*, 6/1/97).

8. Acid Rain Portends an Ecological Disaster

1977 SYNOPSIS: Acid rain, caused predominantly by oil and coal burning, smelting, and car exhaust, has been falling throughout most parts of the East coast of the U.S. The acidity of the rain contaminates the soil, damages crops, stunts the growth of trees by possibly more than ten percent, lowers the pH of even the most remote high altitude lakes, thus wiping out entire native fish species, and causes other potentially disastrous results.

Today, all the fish have died in more than 50 percent of the Adirondack Lakes, about 2,000 feet in elevation—the ones more remote from civilization. Lakes famous for trout for the last century now cannot even support minnows.

Biologists at Cornell University found that rain and snow throughout the eastern U.S. presently falls with 100 times more acidity than it did a generation ago. Further studies indicate that in most areas the soil quickly neutralizes the acid. But in thin, sandy soils, such as those found in high mountainous areas, the acid precipitation runs off, unchanged, into the lakes. The "unbuffered" rain of the 1970s is acidic enough to kill off most freshwater fish east of the Mississippi. In the Adirondacks, most of the water is too acidic to allow fish to reproduce.

The problem is wide-ranging because of the nature of rain. The pollution that causes the acidity (sulfuric and nitric acid) can originate thousands of miles from where the rain finally falls. East coast acid rain could start at the electrical generating plants and industrial sites of Detroit, Chicago, and southern Ontario. Yet the opposition to air cleanup by these plants has been fierce.

SOURCE: *Mother Jones*, December 1977, "Look What They've Done to the Rain," by Alan MacRobert.

UPDATE: Through the years, horror stories about the impact of acid rain continued to appear. It was not until mid-1996 that a light appeared at the end of the tunnel. A U.S. Geological Survey (USGS) report, released June 27, 1996, found that acid rain declined substantially during 1995 throughout the eastern United States, particularly in the mid-Atlantic region and Ohio River Valley (*Washington Post*, 7/1/96). The USGS attributed the decline to federal regulations, specifically the 1995 implementation of Phase I of the Clear Air Act Amendments of 1990. Phase I required certain electric utilities (most of them east of the Mississippi) to cut back on emissions of sulfur dioxide by January 1, 1995. Results revealed that in the year following implementation of the Clear Air Act, 62 eastern sites experienced a 13.8 percent decline in sulfur compounds and an eight percent decline in hydrogen ions, both essential to acid rain formation. However, there is still work to be done; nitrates, which can form nitric acid in water, did not decline during 1995.

9. The Global Battle for the Mineral Wealth of the Oceans

1977 SYNOPSIS: The race to control the ocean floor involves the following conflicting interests: a consortium of three multinational corporations, 20 transnational corporations from six developed nations, and 110 Third World nations represented by the U.N.'s annual Law of the Seas Conference. At stake is 1.5 trillion tons of mineral wealth and who controls production and profits.

The U.N.-supported Law of the Seas Conference has been ongoing since 1958. It discusses fishing rights, territorial waters, and international straits. In 1969, a resolution was passed saying that the ocean floor was a "common heritage of mankind." Third World nations interpret this to mean that all mining would be done under U.N. control. However, the American position would turn the mining control over to private corporations that have the capital and resources to start undersea mining.

Third World nations are arguing for conservation of undersea minerals until land-based minerals are consumed. They also fear that multinational corporations will tend to neglect Third World needs and reap windfall profits from the bountiful ocean floor.

Little is known about the sea bottom or its role in maintaining the planet's environment. Its sediment is rich in microscopic organisms and animal life. Mining companies admit that their hydraulic dredges and continuous line buckets will stir sediment and probably kill any plant or animal life in their path. Nonetheless, they argue that the environmental costs are "insignificant."

The Ocean Mining Associates consortium has filed mining claims extending far over the Pacific where the State Department has no control. American policy has tended to support these claims by multinationals in their conflicts over who controls these regions.

SOURCE: *In These Times*, 12/14/77, "Race to Control the Sea Floor," by David Helvarg.

UPDATE: The United States was globally embarrassed in 1985 when the International Seabed Authority (ISA) and the International Tribunal for the

Law of the Sea rejected as "wholly illegal" the U.S. request to explore parts of the seabed before the Law of the Sea Treaty was finalized. The Ocean Mining Associates, headed by U.S. Steel at the time, had requested exclusive rights to mine manganese nodules in a seabed area of the Pacific Ocean (*UN Chronicle*, September 1985).

Finally, after years of debate over who will control the oceans rich resources, it now appears that the Law of the Sea Treaty proponents have won. The *Financial Times* (4/19/96) reported, "The latest round of negotiations have ended with agreement on the composition of the council to run the International Seabed Authority, the specialized UN agency that will implement the treaty." Satya Nandan, of Fiji, the ISA's secretary general, said, "The objective is to provide the machinery for the administration of the resources of the deep seabed, which are the common heritage of mankind, and the development of those resources so that the international community as a whole may benefit from them." Nandan noted that there is a complex system of representation on the council that ensures that various interest groups are represented and ensures for equitable geographical representation. The way now appears clear for the ISA to begin monitoring the exploitation of minerals from the international seabed (*Financial Times*, 4/19/96).

On October 18, 1996, United Nations Secretary-General Boutros Boutros-Ghali officially inaugurated the International Tribunal on the Law of the Sea in Hamburg, Germany (Federal News Service, 10/21/96).

10. The Untold Side of the Illegal Aliens Story

1977 SYNOPSIS: Up until now, most of the media coverage of illegal aliens has falsely concentrated on their role in draining welfare funds,

creating unemployment, and not paying taxes into a system from which they benefit.

First, to receive welfare, proof of citizenship is required. Further, the illegal aliens are not causing unemployment since the state has tried to get the urban poor to take the jobs in question and failed.

Many employers benefit from illegal workers in that they can demand more work for less pay; they also use threats of calling the border patrol to keep the workers under extreme working conditions.

Ironically, millions of dollars are being spent to apprehend, detain, and repatriate illegal aliens, yet three times as many people continue to get through the security barriers than are returned or detained.

While the mainstream media tell only one side of the story of illegal aliens, it ignores an important question: who, on this side of the border, is profiting from the sweat of the illegal workers?

SOURCES: *New West*, 5/23/77, "California's Illegal Aliens, They Give More Than They Take," and "How Illegal Aliens Pay as They Go," by Jonathan Kirsch and Anthony Cook; *In These Times*, 6/1/77, "Illegal Aliens: The New Scapegoat."

UPDATE: While 20 years have passed since *Censored* asked about the "untold side of the illegal aliens story," the issue remains unresolved and has become an inflammatory one with it being a major political football in the 1996 election year. The nation's attention was focused on the issue on April 1, 1996, when Riverside County, California, policemen were televised beating two Mexicans after their pick-up truck was pulled over. The visual impact of the beatings worsened relations between Mexico and the United

States. *The Economist* (5/18/96) reported that "more than 40 Mexicans have died trying to slip into California this year...the number of illegal aliens caught has jumped 70 percent this year, to around 40,000 a month."

Mexicans complain there is hypocrisy in the assault on illegal aliens. "It is an 'undocumented' Mexican girl, they say, who makes Pat Buchanan's hotel bed, and cheap Mexican labor underwrites the profits of California's garment industry, farms and vineyards. A recent survey for the Centre for U.S.-Mexican Studies found that in Southern California 51 percent of high-tech labor, 95 percent of agricultural labor and 87 percent of hotel staffs are foreign, and overwhelmingly from Mexico."

While the increase in illegal immigration from Mexico to the United States has received some press coverage, the question of how American employers benefit from this labor source remains relatively unexplored by the media. Similarly, relatively little coverage has touched on the relationship between the influx of illegal immigrants from Mexico into America and the passage of NAFTA.

The Continuing Cover-up of the Hazards of Nuclear Power

The tragic mass killings and suicides by members of the Peoples Temple in Guyana easily ranked as the top mainstream news story of 1978. According to the Associated Press, the top ten news stories of the year were:

1. Peoples Temple tragedy
2. The Middle East: Camp David accords, Begin and Sadat win Nobel Peace Prize
3. President Carter announces U.S. recognition of China
4. California passes Proposition 13, tax rebellion spreads across country
5. Death of two Popes, John Paul II assumes papacy
6. U.S. economy
7. Panama Canal treaties approved
8. Collision over San Diego results in worst U.S. air disaster
9. World's first test tube baby born in Britain
10. Mayor George Moscone and Supervisor Harvey Milk shot to death in San Francisco.

THE TOP TEN CENSORED STORIES OF 1978

—And What Has Happened to Them Since

1. The Dangers of Nuclear Power Plants

1978 SYNOPSIS: In 1978, the Union of Concerned Scientists (UCS), a national public interest group, released a report titled "Scientists' Group Judges Federal Nuclear Safety Inspection Effort" that received little news media coverage.

The report criticized the Nuclear Regulatory Commission's (NRC) failure to be a tough inspector of nuclear power plants. UCS spokesman Robert D. Pollard warned, "Nuclear power plants are inherently hazardous. Irrespective of how safe reactors are in theory, federal inspectors cannot be sure they are built and operated safely. This report shows the NRC's inspection efforts are biased against enforcement, undermined by political consideration, weak, and ineffective."

Contrary to the common perception that the nuclear industry is closely regulated, the UCS found: only one to five percent of safety-related nuclear power plant activities are inspected; NRC inspectors spend most of their time inspecting utility records, not the power plants themselves; most regulatory standards are drafted by the nuclear industry itself.

SOURCE: Union of Concerned Scientists, 11/26/78, "Scientists' Group Judges Federal Nuclear Safety Inspection Effort."

UPDATE: Despite the warnings of the Union of Concerned Scientists in 1978, the lessons of Three Mile Island in 1979 and Chernobyl in 1986, and the promises of Bill Clinton to "ensure safety" in the nuclear power industry during his 1992 campaign, the problems and dangers of nuclear power plants are as prevalent today as they were in 1978, if not even more so.

In November 1992, Portland General Electric in Oregon closed its Trojan nuclear power plant because of faulty steam generator tube leaks (*Christian Science Monitor*, 4/4/95). In December 1993, Public Citizen, a private watchdog group, released confidential industry inspection reports revealing that federal inspectors had failed to address hundreds of safety problems that industry teams identified at 56 of the nation's nuclear power plants (*Minneapolis Star Tribune*, 12/16/93). On April 4, 1995, *The Christian Science Monitor* also reported that an inspection of Maine's Yankee nuclear plant discovered steam-generator problems that forced it to close down and led to inspections of steam-generated plants nationwide.

In early May 1996, Northeast Utilities, New England's largest operator of nuclear plants, was accused of unsafe fuel-unloading practices at one of its three Millstone nuclear plants. The safety crisis at Millstone had earlier prompted the NRC to indefinitely close all three reactors there (*Boston Globe*, 5/8/96).

Because of the thousands of safety problems discovered at the Millstone reactor, in October 1996, the Nuclear Regulatory Commission finally ordered every nuclear reactor in the country to begin an exhaustive review of its safety performance (*Boston Globe*, 10/11/96). The day before the NRC announcement, the Critical Mass Energy Project, a consumer advocacy group, urged the NRC to shut down 25 nuclear reactors, almost one-fourth of the nation's nuclear reactors, because they are "disasters waiting to happen" (Associated Press, 10/10/96).

Finally, on January 29, 1997, the NRC sent a message to the industry about its safety problems. It warned, "shape up or there will be drastic consequences." It also added six nuclear reactors to its close watch list, bringing the total number in need of special scrutiny to 14—the highest number since 1988 (Associated Press, 1/30/97).

2. Organic Farming: The Secret Is It Works!

1978 SYNOPSIS: Most Americans have been well propagandized by the U.S. Department of Agriculture and agribusiness corporations. We have been taught to believe that growing organically means growing small, pest-infested fruits and vegetables with brown spots. Or, as Secretary of Agriculture, Earl Butz, said, growing organically is "a primitive method of farming scarcely befitting the needs of a modern nation."

From the Corn Belt to the valleys of California to fertile farmlands in Europe, there is proof which refutes the agribusiness myth. The secret of organic farming is that it works.

In Delano, California, there is a profitable $3 million ranch that has not used a poison on its vineyards in five years. At Washington University's Center for the Biology of Natural System, in St. Louis, researchers have found more than 250 commercial organic farms, ranging up to 800 acres, in the Corn Belt. In the foothills of the Swiss Alps is the $6 million Biolta Ltd. Company which sells picture-perfect organic vegetables to supermarkets all over Switzerland.

Organic farmers like these, ignored by the press, may have the answer to some of the most critical health problems Americans are faced with today. There is mounting evidence that the pesticides used in agriculture are responsible for cancer, mutations, birth defects, and many other health problems.

SOURCE: *The Progressive*, December 1978, "Curbing the Chemical Fix: The Secret Is It Works," by Daniel Zwerdling.

UPDATE: Whether it's an increasing concern for the environment or for one's own health, organic foods and farming have come a long way since our *Censored* story of 1978. The U.S. Department of Agriculture has been steadily increasing its budget for alternative agriculture reaching a record $7 million in 1994; organic sales grew more than 20 percent a year, reaching an estimated $1.5 billion in 1993 (*E Magazine*, October 1994). There's been an increase in organic farms and associations, such as the Northeast Organic Farming Association of New York Inc., and the National Organic Standards Board was formed in 1992 to set national standards and a certification program (*Capital District Business Review*, 6/6/94). And, according to a nation-wide survey conducted by the Organic Farming Research Foundation, the amount of farmland devoted to organic crops has increased ten-fold since 1980 (*BioCycle*, June 1996).

Organic foods received a major boost in the United Kingdom following the "mad cow" disease, a *Censored* story of 1995 (*Financial Times*, 7/6/96). And, Hisataka Suto, a Japanese organic rice grower and true believer, has created his own home page on the Net to promote organic farming to the world. Suto's home page can be accessed at http://www.aizu.com/lab/vr/Farmer/Suto (*The Daily Yomiuri*, 6/16/96).

But perhaps the biggest boost for organic farming in the future occurred on June 19, 1996, when the *Los Angeles Times* reported that an investment group headed by Roy Disney bought a majority interest in organic foods marketer Cascadian Farms. The investment will be used to expand the company's research and development of organic farming and food production.

3. The Government's War on Scientists Who Know Too Much

1978 SYNOPSIS: In 1964, Dr. Thomas Mancuso was commissioned by the Atomic Energy Commission (AEC), predecessor to the Nuclear Regulatory

Commission, to measure how safe nuclear plants are for the people who work in them.

It was the first study of its kind and was therefore invested with special significance. His initial findings were innocuous. However, in 1976, Mancuso and two associates turned up alarming evidence that low levels of radiation, previously thought to be safe, can actually be quite deadly.

Dr. Mancuso's contract with the government was promptly canceled and his funds cut off for the research. He was shoved into premature retirement and the government tried to take possession of his research findings.

Mancuso's predicament, and his study, are particularly disturbing since he was only one of several scientists the government tried to silence for challenging its view of nuclear safety.

In a study of the Hanford facility in Washington, more commonly referred to by residents as "Plutonium City," a Dr. Milham found an unusually high rate of cancer among the workers at the facility. He was unable to conclusively attribute it to the radiation because he did not have access to the records of the employees' radiation exposure. Dissatisfied with the Milham research, the AEC turned to the Battelle Pacific Northwest Laboratories, a Washington research firm the AEC regularly employs. Battelle attributed the unnatural cancer rate to a statistical bias rather than to radiation. The AEC was content with this finding.

The implications of the scientists' research extend far beyond the fate of nuclear workers. If they are right, it means that thousands may die from radiation they are receiving. It means that current government standards on radiation are meaningless, that having x-rays or living next to a nuclear plant can be extremely dangerous, and that our government has sponsored a cruel illusion since the 1940s.

SOURCE: *Rolling Stone*, 3/23/78, "The Government's Quiet War on Scientists Who Know Too Much."

UPDATE: It was not until 1990 that the Department of Energy provided access to the workers' health records at Hanford. One of Mancuso's associates, Dr. Alice Stewart, finally had the opportunity to complete the research after 14 years of stonewalling by the government. By then, the Hanford plant had been closed because of environmental and safety problems. Stewart's new study, the first independent study of the health records of the 35,000 Hanford workers, presents a new, more sinister picture of the risks of small doses of radiation.

It also confirms the original conclusions offered by Mancuso that had been criticized and rejected by the Department of Energy.

Stewart's study concludes: even small doses of radiation are four to eight times more likely to cause cancer than previously believed; older people are far more vulnerable to radiation-induced cancer; and radiation delivered in small doses over time may carry a higher risk of cancer than a higher level of radiation delivered in a single dose *(Houston Chronicle,* 12/8/92).

4. U.S. Exports Death: The Third World Asbestos Industry

1978 SYNOPSIS: Much attention has been focused recently on the health hazards of asbestos, particularly with its use in school classroom ceilings and in hair dryers. That health danger, however, is not as great as the danger posed to persons who work in asbestos plants.

Research indicates that people who work in asbestos plants and inhale the fibers run a significantly higher risk of contracting lung cancer (20 times higher than for people who smoke). Other ailments include the respiratory disease asbestosis and mesothelioma. There also is a 300 to 400 percent increase in gastrointestinal cancer due to the fact that those who inhale the fibers also swallow them.

The situation is all the more tragic in light of the fact that the asbestos industry has been aware of the deadliness of their product since the 1930s and has done nothing about it. Finally, in the late 1960s, the U.S. government began regulating the asbestos industry.

What the American public does not know is that the asbestos manufacturers responded to the new regulations by simply moving their factories to Third World nations such as Mexico, Taiwan, South Korea, India, and Brazil where the regulations were either minimal or nonexistent. Additionally, the corporate profits in these locations were even higher because of the lower wages.

The working conditions in these foreign plants are horrendous. Investigations of asbestos manufacturing plants such as Amatax, which has plants just across the border from El Paso, Texas, and Douglas, Arizona, found the air in the factories thick with asbestos fibers and large clumps of the material clinging to nearby bushes and fences where children play. The penchant young children have for putting things in their mouths makes the situation there all the more frightening.

SOURCE: *Guardian*, 12/20/78, "Asbestos: U.S. Exports Death."

UPDATE: By the 1980s, corporate America finally acknowledged the tragic hazards of asbestos. Major asbestos producers gave up the business either by choice or by bankruptcy; the largest to quit included U.S. Gypsum, Manville Corp., and UNR Industries Inc. of Chicago. The demise of the industry was hastened by a series of EPA orders starting in 1982 and climaxing in 1989 with the Asbestos Ban & Phaseout Rule, which provides for the elimination of 94 percent of all asbestos used in the U.S. by 1997 (*Chicago Tribune*, 4/30/96).

But, as reported by *The National Journal* (6/23/84), seven years after our *Censored* story, multinational corporations were still exporting some of their dirty industries, like asbestos, to Third World countries with weak environmental regulations. Eleven years later, the *Mining Annual Review* (July 1995) updated this continuing trend by reporting a "dramatic upturn in fortunes" for the asbestos industry, now found mostly in developing countries including Mexico, Brazil, South Africa, Zimbabwe, Swaziland, South Korea, Taiwan, China, India, Kazakhstan, Siberia, and Greece.

5. Winter Choice: Heat or Eat

1978 SYNOPSIS: More than 200 Americans died in the winters of 1975, 1976, and 1977, when utility companies shut off their gas and electricity service.

At the same time, thousands of other Americans were forced to make the choice of spending limited funds to pay fuel bills or for medication, food, or rent.

These grim statistics were cited in November 1978, by the Citizen/Labor Energy Coalition, a national group which has started a campaign to have the U.S. Department of Energy and state public utility commissions prevent gas and electric utility companies from stopping service to their customers during extreme weather conditions.

William Hutton, secretary-treasurer of the coalition and executive director of the National Council of Senior Citizens, warned that thousands of people are faced with the choice of "heating or eating." "They face life-and-death economic choices of whether to pay for ever-increasing utility bills, or whether to cut back on food," Hutton said.

Only three states in the United States—Wisconsin, Maryland, and Rhode Island—had legislation to ban utility service shutoffs during winter at that time.

SOURCE: *Solidarity*, 12/1/78.

UPDATE: The deaths of more than 200 Americans who froze to death in the middle-to-late seventies because their utilities shut off service led to a variety of programs, from the local to the national level, to solve the problem. The nation developed the Federal Energy Assistance Program to help needy people pay their utility bills during the winter. In 1985, the program provided $2.1 billion to elderly, handicapped, and poor people. A number of states, primarily in the North, created their own programs for which they spent nearly $200 million in the same year (*The New York Times*, 11/3/85).

In some states, major utilities declared a moratorium on shutting off service to non-paying customers during periods of extreme cold and a growing number of utilities created private fuel funds for the need to which stockholders and customers can donate (*St. Louis Post Dispatch*, 12/22/89). The need for such programs, which have proved successful, was summed up by Michael Mullett, legal counsel for the Citizens Action Coalition in Indianapolis, "In America, we ought not to have people freezing to death because their electricity has been shut off" (*The Courier-Journal*, 11/17/89).

However, in late 1996, President Bill Clinton proposed a 25 percent cut from federal aid to the poor for home heating bills in his fiscal 1998 budget and recommended elimination of the Low Income Home Energy Assistance Program in five years (*USA Today*, 12/11/96).

6. America's Secret Police Network

1978 SYNOPSIS: Compared to the CIA and the FBI, the LEIU (Law Enforcement Intelligence Unit) is a virtually unknown organization. But its power is considerable and its potential threat to our freedom is enormous.

The LEIU links the intelligence squads of almost every major police force in the United States and Canada. Although its members are sworn police officers who work for state and city governments, it is a private club, not answerable to voters, taxpayers, or elected officials. It cuts across the vertical lines of authority of local government, for its members hold certain allegiances to the LEIU that cannot be countermanded by a mayor, county manager, or even a state governor.

Custody of the LEIU's files is the most sacred trust that the organization bestows upon its individual members. The LEIU not only withholds its files from the FBI and other federal authorities but also flatly refuses to show them to anyone who is not an LEIU member.

The LEIU is a private club and therefore not subject to freedom-of-information laws; thus, their files are even more secret than those of the CIA or FBI. Ex-members of the LEIU admit to illegal wiretapping, breaking and entering, and spying on people to gather information for their files. SOURCE: *San Francisco Chronicle*, 11/25/78, "Leaks to the Mob: U.S. Police Network's Big Problem"; *Penthouse*, 1976, "America's Secret Police Network," by George O'Toole.

UPDATE: A year after the LEIU *Censored* nomination in 1978, the American Friends Service Committee released a 3 1/2-year study that revealed that police surveillance of groups and individuals for political purposes is continuing "on a vast scale" in the United States. The study charged that the prime offender was the "old-boy network" in the Law Enforcement Intelligence Unit (*New York Times*, 4/17/79).

In 1991, investigative author Frank Donner's book, *Protectors of Privilege: Red Squads and Police Repression in Urban America*, documented political repression practiced by urban police. Donner described the LEIU as a private organization which served as a conduit for information and technology and may also have helped local departments evade restrictions on their intelligence gathering (*Monthly Review*, November 1991).

On May 10, 1993, the *San Francisco Chronicle* revealed how local police secretly use the LEIU to preserve intelligence files that are supposed to be destroyed. In May of 1995, the LEIU held a criminal-intelligence information training conference in Dallas for police groups throughout the United States (*Orange County Register*, 4/14/95).

While the Law Enforcement Intelligence Unit remains active, it continues to maintain an extremely low profile.

7. The Specter of Sterility

1978 SYNOPSIS: The problem first came to light in 1977 when some production workers at the Occidental Chemical Plant in Lathrop, California, were found to be sterile as a result of exposure to the pesticide dibromochloropropane (DBCP). Various government agencies, including the Environmental Protection Agency and the Food and Drug Administration, swarmed over the case and wound up restricting domestic use of DBCP, which is applied to soil to kill pests that destroy the roots of crops.

Next, the National Institute for Occupational Safety and Health (NIOSH) broadened the investigation to include other industrial compounds to determine their effects on male fertility. What they found was evidence that other agents might cause a reduction in sperm count. Some scientists involved in the project found scientific literature suggesting that sperm counts for the entire male population were lower than they had been 30 years earlier. Mounting evidence revealed that the average sperm count among American men dropped by frightening percentages since a landmark study done in 1951.

The probable causes are chemicals similar to DBCP—herbicides, fungicides, and other elements—which are known to decompose very slowly. Presumably they have worked their way up through the food chain and are finally poisoning man. By this logic, the male reproductive process (and most certainly the female) has been affected by industrial and agricultural poisons associated with modern America for the past 30 to 50 years.

"There is no question in my mind," said Dr. Kenneth Bridbord of the Office of Extramural Coordination and Special Projects at NIOSH in Washington, "but that this is a major problem facing the nation. I would not be surprised, based on the evidence we have looked at so far, to find that the declining sperm count represents a potential sterility threat to the entire male population."

SOURCE: *Esquire*, 4/11/78, "The Spectre of Sterility," by Raymond M. Layne.

UPDATE: In January 1996, *Mother Jones* published an article by investigative writer Michael Castleman in which he documented the continuing decline in sperm counts and pointed out that "the sperm crisis still hasn't cracked prime time...the major media have not given this story the attention it deserves."

But the inattention may be coming to an end. The October 1996 issue of *The Quill* reported that articles on the subject, appearing in *The New Yorker*, *Newsweek*, and *Time* in early 1996, had intensified the "debate over whether chemicals in the environment are wreaking havoc on human reproduction and causing a host of other problems."

In its March 18, 1996, issue, *Time* asked "What's Wrong With Our Sperm?" and suggested one possible cause: chemical pollution. *Time* reported several studies: researchers in Edinburgh, Scotland, reported that men born after 1970 had a sperm count that was 25 percent lower than those born before 1959—an average decline of 2.1 percent a year; a 1995 study of Parisians found a 2.1 annual decline over the past 20 years; New York City's Fertility Research Foundation reported that in the 1960s only about eight percent of the men who came for consultation had a fertility problem, but that number is now up to 40 percent.

Media interest in the subject also was sparked by the publication of *Our Stolen Future* in the spring of 1996. The book concludes that a wide range of reproductive-related ills may be caused by chemical pollutants in the environment. Nonetheless, the subject remains controversial as three new studies, published in May 1996, challenged the thesis suggesting there hasn't been any significant change in the quantity or quality of sperm in the United States (New Orleans *Times-Picayune*, 5/26/96).

On June 17, 1996, *USA Today* reported studies that showed testicular cancer rates are rising sharply in the U.S. and Europe and may be due to environmental chemical pollutants. And on June 30, 1996, the *San Francisco Examiner* reported a new study by the Danish endocrinologist, Dr. Niels Skakkebaek of Copenhagen University, which said that men who consume pesticide-free food produce more sperm than those who do not.

In the final analysis, this story may well represent one of the most crucial early warnings issued by Project Censored. As *Time* magazine concluded its article, "It's conceivable that the average man will be infertile within a century. Even if things are only half that dire, it would be bad news indeed for the human race."

8. The Search for Dangerous Dams

1978 SYNOPSIS: As the United States hastily built nearly 50,000 large dams to curb floods, store drinking water, irrigate crops, generate electricity, create recreational areas, and spur industrial development, it too often neglected questions of the safety of the structures holding back the water.

The result was a vast reservoir of danger. One scientific study concluded that in any year America's dams were 10,000 times more likely to cause a major disaster—one involving 1,000 or more deaths—than were 100 nuclear power plants.

The need to identify America's dangerous dams is urgent. According to Dr. Bruce A. Tschantz, a University of Tennessee civil engineering professor and a White House consultant on dam safety, in any given year, 25 to 30 of the nation's dams may break. Tschantz goes on to say that there are so many large dams and there is such a legacy of neglect that there may be yet more disasters before the backlog of hazards can be erased.

Of the 49,422 large dams (each 25 feet or more in height or capable of impounding more than 16.3 million gallons of water) counted by the Corps of Engineers in a national inventory, about 39,000 have never been inspected by state or federal engineers.

Also, new dams are being built at a phenomenal rate. Dr. Tschantz found that on an average day, five new private dams are completed in America—double the rate of the 1950s. The biggest boom is in dams for recreational lakes, which are sometimes crude earthen structures built by real estate developers without engineering advice.

SOURCE: *Smithsonian*, April 1978, "The Search for Dangerous Dams—A Program to Head Off Disaster," by Gaylord Shaw.

UPDATE: Despite the urgent warnings about dangerous dams issued in 1978, there has been no major national effort to fix them. On May 1, 1989, the Gannett News Service reported that federal investigators say it is "highly probable" that "Coolidge Dam will fail, touching off a flood that could kill as many as 500 people." The 61-year-old central Arizona dam was reported to be one of the five most dangerous dams in the United States.

Although hundreds of dams burst in Georgia during the great flood of 1994—the state's worst natural disaster—officials still haven't strengthened laws requiring regular inspection of Georgia's dams. Nor have they raised standards to protect residents in the state's 100-year flood plains. The *Atlanta Journal* reported (7/2/95) that "the failure of unregulated, man-made dams also contributed to extensive damage to infrastructure and some deaths. More than 230 unregulated dams burst in southwest Georgia."

9. Is Your Diet Driving You Crazy?

1978 SYNOPSIS: Since the turn of the century drastic changes in the American diet have wreaked havoc with our health. Diabetes, hypertension, heart disease, and cancer have all been linked with eating habits. Although it is not exactly known how 126 pounds of sugar and nine pounds of additives consumed annually per capita affect our mental state, there is mounting evidence that 6.4 million Americans now under mental care, as well as 13.6 million in need of it, could be cured through nutrition.

Kaiser Permanente Department of Allergy chief emeritus, Ben F. Feingold, hypothesized in 1973 that one to five million American school children diagnosed as hyperkinetic are actually victims of toxicity due to ingestion of artificially dyed and flavored foods. One hundred "Feingold Associations" claimed great success by applying these findings.

Biochemist and physician Abram Hoffer maintained that 70 percent of prison inmates imprisoned for serious crimes have vitamin deficiencies leading to aggressive behavior. He also found through his research that 90 percent of convicted murderers diagnosed as paranoid schizophrenics suffer from vitamin deficiencies or low blood sugar.

In the 1930s, ten percent of mental patients in the South were suffering from pellagra. It was found to be a B-vitamin, or niacin, deficiency stemming from the high-corn, low-protein diet. Before this discovery, it was not called pellagra; it was called schizophrenia.

Despite such findings, the mental health aspect is the least funded in all nutrition research. The National Institute of Mental Health is funding just one: a $118,000 study of the Feingold hypothesis.

SOURCE: *The Progressive*, May 1978, "Is Our Diet Driving Us Crazy?", by Jeanne Schinto.

UPDATE: In a well-documented, extensive article on foods that benefit brain function, and those that impair it, the May 1996 issue of *Psychology Today* concludes: "You are what you eat."

It notes research over the past 15 years has shown the right foods, or the natural neurochemicals they contain, can enhance mental capabilities: "Nutritional neuroscience, as it's called, is barely in its infancy but it's already turning up some very heady findings. Among them: A diet that draws heavily on fatty foods and only lightly on fruits and vegetables isn't just bad for your heart and linked to certain cancers—it may also be a major cause of depression and aggression in North America. Such a diet is particularly common among men." The article explains the roles played by carbohydrates, sugar, serotonin, vitamins and minerals, antioxidants, and much more.

Garlic aficionados will be particularly pleased to learn about garlic's special healing powers. Garlic's health benefits range from thinning blood and lowering cholesterol to fighting infection and even cancer. A French researcher claims a substance in garlic promotes release of the neurotransmitter serotonin, producing a calming effect. The *Psychology Today* article also reported that Japanese studies on rats and mice suggest the "pungent herb may slow degeneration of brain cells, encourage their regeneration, aid memory in aged animals, and even prolong life."

10. Who Owns America? The Same Old Gang

1978 SYNOPSIS: Alvin Toffler tells us in his best-seller, *Future Shock*, that our society has "managed within a few short decades to throw off the yoke of manual labor." The book, widely quoted by politicians and the wealthy, asserts that "the economic class system is disappearing...redistribution of wealth and income... has ended economic inequality's political significance."

Are we to believe this? The statistics say no. Only four percent of America's population have estates worth $60,000 or more. More than half of all Americans have a "net worth" of $3,000 or less. At the top we find the richest one percent owns one quarter of the net worth of the entire population.

So what is new? Nothing. Economic historians tell us that on the eve of the Civil War (1860), the top one percent owned 24 percent of the whole population's net worth. By 1969, more than a century later, that figure was 24.9 percent. There has been no change since World War II, as studied at roughly five-year intervals. The richest one percent owns a quarter, and the top half of that one percent owns one-fifth of everything in America.

Despite the easily available statistics, by virtue of their silence, the mass media have more often than not perpetuated the myth that class divisions in the U.S. are disappearing. The continuing economic class divisions in our society rarely get any media coverage and ultimately, the media failed to tell Americans who "really owns America."

SOURCE: *The Progressive*, June 1978, "Who Owns America? The Same Old Gang," by Maurice Zeitlin.

UPDATE: In the 1978 *Censored* story, we noted that there has been little change in the distribution of wealth, with the top one percent of society owning about 25 percent of America, dating back to the eve of the Civil War. And we asked, "So what is new?" And answered, "Nothing."

But that is no longer true. There has now been a significant change in

THIS MODERN WORLD by TOM TOMORROW

WHY IS THE AMERICAN PUBLIC SO CRANKY ABOUT THE *ECONOMY* THESE DAYS, ANYWAY? AFTER ALL, A MULTITUDE OF PUNDITS *INSIST* THAT THINGS ARE *GREAT!*

AND WE HAVE *STATISTICS* TO PROVE IT! — NOT TO MENTION COLORFUL CHARTS!

WELL, THIS IS JUST A *CRAZY GUESS* -- BUT *MAYBE* THE PUBLIC HAS BEGUN TO SUSPECT THAT THE *EXPERTS* HAVE A VERY PECULIAR IDEA OF WHAT CONSTITUTES *GOOD ECONOMIC NEWS...*

--AND GIGANTICO STOCK *SOARED* TODAY AFTER 17,000 EMPLOYEES WERE --AH--*DOWNSIZED!* INVESTORS MADE A *BUNDLE!*

HEY, THAT'S *TERRIFIC!*

GRRR...

NOTICE OF TERMINATION

the distribution of wealth, even since 1978; the rich have gotten richer while the poor have gotten poorer. According to Edward Wolff, an economist at New York University, by 1992, the top one percent owned a whopping 42 percent of the nation's wealth, an extraordinary increase in wealth accumulation over an exceptionally short period of time (*The Economist*, 2/24/96). On June 20, 1996, *The New York Times* reported that the gap between the most affluent Americans and everyone else was wider than it had been since the end of World War II. The wealthiest five percent of U.S. households earned more in the early 1990s than the entire 60 percent of households in the middle class. A two-part cover story in *USA Today* (September 20, 23, 1996) charged that the widening income gap threatens to tear America apart. It noted that the gap between rich and poor is greater in the U.S. than any other industrial nation, with the possible exception of Russia with its large underground economy.

The United Nations' "Human Development Report 1996" revealed that the combined wealth of the world's 358 billionaires equals the total income of the poorest 45 percent of the world's population, some 2.3 billion people (*Utne Reader*, November/December 1996). The number of billionaires in the world was raised to nearly 500 in 1997 according to *Forbes* magazine's (7/28/97) annual list of billionaires. According to the *Forbes* report, the world's wealthiest person, Bill Gates, chairman of Microsoft Corp., saw his net worth double to $36.4 billion since 1996.

How could such a significant redistribution of wealth occur in such a short period of time with so little public awareness? Perhaps it is because the mass media today, as a direct result of increased consolidation, have become, in reality, corporate media, and as such they benefit directly from maintaining the status quo.

Media Ignore the Corporate Crime of the Century

While the Iranian revolution and hostage crisis was the top mainstream news story of 1979, the story of what actually led to the revolution and the taking of hostages was one of the top *Censored* news stories of the year. According to the Associated Press, the top ten news stories of the year were:

1. Iranian hostage crisis
2. Accident at Three Mile Island nuclear power plant in Pennsylvania
3. The continuing energy crisis
4. U.S. economy
5. Crash of American Airlines DC-10 in Chicago killing 273 and subsequent grounding of that plane
6. Middle East peace
7. Visit of Pope Paul II to the United States and Ireland
8. Starvation in Cambodia after decade of revolution and counterrevolution
9. The signing of SALT II
10. Challenge to President Carter by Edward M. Kennedy.

THE TOP TEN CENSORED STORIES OF 1979
—And What Has Happened to Them Since

1. The Corporate Crime of the Century

1979 SYNOPSIS: In November 1979, *Mother Jones*, one of America's leading investigative journals, devoted nearly an entire issue to "The Corporate Crime of the Century"—documenting the full scope of American corporate exploitation of Third World countries. *Mother Jones* elaborated on and documented the issues raised in the #3 Censored story of 1976 discussing exporting dangerous products overseas. The crime is called "dumping"—exporting dangerous chemicals, toxic pesticides, and defective medical drugs and devices, which have been restricted or banned in the United States, to less wary Third World countries.

Every pesticide which has been banned or restricted in this country has been exported elsewhere. Some of the pesticides and chemical exports are suspected of causing birth defects, reduced fertility, genetic mutations, cancer, and bone marrow, blood, and respiratory changes. The Food and Drug Administration allows U.S. drug manufacturers to export banned drugs, stale out-dated drugs, and even unapproved new drugs.

When the U.S. nuclear industry encountered difficulties in selling reactors to wary American communities, it turned to countries where dissent can be silenced and political payoffs bring quick results. The U.S. nuclear industry sold its power plants to less-developed countries, and most buyers were nations with strong regional rivalries—Iraq and Iran, Korea and Taiwan, Argentina and Brazil, India and Pakistan.

SOURCE: *Mother Jones*, November 1979, "The Corporate Crime of the Century," by Mark Dowie, Barbara Ehrenreich, Stephen Minken, Mark Shapiro, Terry Jacobs, and David Weir.

UPDATE: To prevent problems caused by our exploitative export policies, President Jimmy Carter signed an executive order on January 15, 1981, creating a uniform notification system for the export of hazardous or domestically restricted products. Just over a month later, on February 17, 1981, newly-elected president, Ronald Reagan revoked the executive order, saying the controls were "unduly burdensome for U.S. industry and would threaten U.S. jobs" (*Journal of Public Policy & Marketing*, Fall 1991).

In April 1994, the Clinton Administration tightened the export policy on pesticides by requiring that foreign governments be notified of the shipments of U.S.-banned or never-registered pesticides, but it didn't stop such exports. On July 11, 1994, the *Boston Globe* ran a well documented story titled "Foul Trade: Using U.S. Exports Can Be Risky," as part of a three-part series on foreign trade. "In the global economy," it reported, "let the buyer beware. Just as some American companies take advantage of weak labor and environmental laws in poor countries, they also manufacture or export products (including powerful drugs and pesticides) that are illegal in the United States, or inappropriate for the Third World consumer being urged to buy them."

Please see also "Selling Banned Pesticides and Drugs to Third World Countries," #3, 1976 and its update.

2. The Embassy Seizure in Iran Should Not Have Been a Surprise

1979 SYNOPSIS: The American people were shocked in 1979 when militant Iranian students seized the American embassy in Iran and held more than 50 Americans hostage. But if the mass media had accurately portrayed what had been happening in Iran and America's involvement there, the events which transpired might not have been so surprising.

While Iranian nationalists were fighting to curb the power of both foreign investors and the despised Iranian monarch, the U.S. media, led by *The New York Times*, were telling Americans in 1978 that the Shah of Iran had a "broad base of popular support" and were portraying him as a modernizing, reform-oriented leader. Meanwhile, Amnesty International described the Shah's regime as the "world's worst violator of human rights."

In that same year, there was an unprecedented general strike and several other protests in which an estimated 10,000 Iranians were gunned down by the Shah's security forces. The response of the U.S. government, an avowed defender of human rights, was to send riot-control equipment, advisers, trainers, and more than $2.5 billion in weapons.

Shah Pahlavi's strong ties to the United States through Henry Kissinger and David Rockefeller served to inflame Iranian nationalists to a fever pitch, climaxing with the seizure of the embassy.

SOURCE: *Mother Jones*, April 1979, "The Iranian Hundred Years' War," by Eqbal Ahmad.

UPDATE: In a commentary on July 15, 1996, *Business Week* reviewed the June 25 explosion in Dhahran that took 19 American lives and injured 547 others. It draws an analogy between Iran in 1976 and Saudi Arabia today. The fear is that the House of Saud may be going the way of the Shah of Iran. During the earlier period, the U.S. establishment and media, led by *The New York Times*, defended the Shah, who had become a desperate and possibly deranged autocrat, fueling the extreme anti-American policies of Iranian rebels. Today, the U.S. establishment supports the 7,000-member House of Saud and the many Al Aud princes. *Business Week* warns that once again America risks being dragged into a tragic, even bloodier, mess than that of Iran. It reports, "Hundreds of thousands of ill-educated young Saudis unable to find work in a stagnant economy fiercely resent America's close ties to the billionaire Al Saud princes who wield near-total power. Such youths are ripe to become supporters of Islamic clerics pursuing a radical anti-American agenda."

3. International Panel Finds U.S. Guilty of Human Rights Violations

1979 SYNOPSIS: When the world's leading proponent of human rights is found guilty of human rights violations, one would expect it to make news. But it didn't in 1979 when the United States was the subject of an international inquiry into human rights violations—and found guilty.

In late 1978, the National Conference of Black Lawyers, the National Alliance Against Racist and Political Repression, and the Commission of Racial Justice of the United Church of Christ filed a petition with the United Nations. It alleged there were consistent patterns of human rights violations with classes of prisoners in the U.S. because of their race, economic status, and political beliefs.

A panel of seven international jurists, experienced in human rights cases, came to the U.S. to investigate violations of the document of the United Nations Universal Declaration of Human Rights and its Standard Minimum Rules on the Treatment of Prisoners.

After a comprehensive national investigation, including interviews with inmates and officials in prisons across the country, the jurists' final report stated there was a "clear prima facia case" of human rights violations in American prisons.

On August 21, 1979, the jurists' findings were announced at a press conference held in the UN's Church Center on UN Plaza. The results were not reported by the mass media. According to a report in *The Village Voice*, when asked why the story wasn't covered, media representatives responded, "The big black story now is Andy Young and the fallout from his resignation." There is only room for one sizable "black story" at a time, media representatives explained.

SOURCES: *The Village Voice*, 9/10/79, "Seven International Jurists Journey to the Heart of Darkness," by Nat Hentoff; *New York Amsterdam News*, 12/9/78, "Human Rights Violations Subject of UN Petition."

UPDATE: Prisoners' rights have been under a new assault since the latest crackdown on crime, led by the "three-strikes, you're out" law. The growing cost of new prisons plagues the already burdened taxpayers. The political solution? "Harness the vast pool of idle inmate labor in the hope that overcrowded prisons can soon pay for themselves. Since 1990, 30 states have legalized the contracting out of prison labor to private companies," according to a report in *The Nation* (1/29/96). While some of the companies pay minimum wage, prisoners receive only about 20 percent of it while the rest goes to state governments or private prison managers. "Inmates working in the California Joint Venture Program receive minimum wage, $4.25, minus the 80 percent that is garnished. In other states, prison wages are even lower. In Colorado, AT&T paid 50 inmate telemarketers $2 an hour."

While cheap labor is what fuels the rise of for-profit prison labor, it also offers employers another benefit: no strikes or union organizing. This charge is echoed by Vincent Schiraldi of the San Francisco-based Center for Juvenile and Criminal Justice: "All over the country states are stripping inmates of their rights. They're losing everything from TV to First Amendment rights. What other labor pool has no access to the media, labor organizers, or other community groups?" One wonders what a UN investigation of our prisons would reveal today.

4. U.S. Electronic Firms Operate Third World Sweatshops

1979 SYNOPSIS: In order to find cheap labor and escape health and safety regulations and the unions, many American corporations are setting up branches or contracting out jobs in Third World countries. American electronics firms are major exporters of jobs abroad. California-based companies alone have 65 Asian branch plants, mainly in Malaysia, Singapore, Hong Kong, Taiwan, and South Korea.

In 1977, the Zenith Radio Corporation's Chicago plant eliminated 5,000 U.S. jobs which paid an average of $5.25 an hour and $1.75 in fringe benefits. According to a company spokesman, workers in Taiwan now produce the same circuit boards for Zenith for an average wage of 36 cents an hour, plus 26 cents in fringes. Because of the mental and physical strains of the job and working conditions, the average working life of these workers is estimated at about ten years.

Conditions in other American firms' branch plants in Asia are similar. Representatives from the American Friends Service Committee investigated conditions at the National Semiconductor plant in the Free Trade Zone, Penang, Malaysia, and found the average wage to be about $2 per day for making integrated circuits for calculators and computers. Similar conditions exist in the textile and apparel industry.

SOURCE: *The Nation*, 8/25/79, "Asia's Silicon Valley," by Diana Roose.

UPDATE: In 1996, similar conditions in the apparel industry became a national scandal when highly paid entertainers and sports figures, such as Kathy Lee Gifford and Michael Jordan, were forced to explain how they could profit from corporations that exploited Third World children (*Time*, 6/17/96).

While the 1979 *Censored* story specifically warned that U.S. electronic firms were operating Third World sweatshops for assembly line production, at the time it was assumed that jobs requiring higher education qualifications would remain in the U.S. Now it appears that is no longer true. There is evidence that the benefits of an education-based economy is not guaranteed for the United States as reported in *The Independent* (12/5/94). A spokesman for the chipmaker Intel warned, "Anybody who still thinks that the only competitive edge of developing countries is cheap, unskilled labour has a lot of catching up to do. Just as Western companies learned in the 1970s and 1980s that manufacturing could be moved virtually anywhere, today it is getting easier to shift knowledge-based work as well." While exporting low-skilled, low-paid assembly line jobs to the Third World is fairly common knowledge now and even encouraged by the government through trade pacts like NAFTA, the fact that these electronic companies are now starting to export their high-skilled, high-paying jobs as well is not widely known.

5. Occupational Disease: Is Your Job Killing You?

1979 SYNOPSIS: Eula Bingham, executive director of the Occupational Safety and Health Administration (OSHA), reports that at least 100,000 workers die each year—and three or four times that number are disabled—as a result of occupational disease.

More important, these are not workplace *accidents* (which occur at the rate of about 2,000 a month) but *illnesses* attributable to the thousands of new chemicals, untested for safety, that are being introduced into industrial products and processes.

Surveys, covering almost a million workers in 5,000 plants, indicate that one worker in four—about 21 million working men and women—currently may be exposed to hazardous substances which can cause disease or death. Twice that number may have had exposure at some point during their working lives, leaving them subject to disablement.

The Department of Health, Education, and Welfare reported that two out of five cancer deaths in the next thirty years will be caused by six industrial chemicals alone—asbestos, nickel oxides, arsenic, benzene, chromium, and petroleum fractions.

One particularly worrisome aspect of occupational disease is in the area of human reproduction, including birth defects, infertility, miscarriages, early menopause in women, and low sperm count in men.

SOURCE: *The Progressive*, November 1979, "Dead on the Job," by Sidney Lens.

UPDATE: The most comprehensive accounting of workplace tragedies ever conducted in the United States, released by the National Institute for Occupational Safety and Health (NIOSH) in 1993, revealed that the workplace death rate is going down—from 7,405 workers killed in 1980 to 5,714 in 1989. Altogether nearly 65,000 workers died from injuries sustained while working in the past decade. However, the study did not examine the number of deaths caused by occupational disease, the subject raised in the 1979 *Censored* story. While OSHA previously estimated as many as 100,000 Americans died each year from illnesses contracted on the job, many safety experts believe that figure may be increasing (*San Francisco Chronicle*, 4/28/93).

Please also see update of "Workers Die for Corporate Profits," #7, 1976, and update of "The Deadly Secrets of the Occupational Safety Agency," #1, 1994.

6. The Worst Nuclear Spill in U.S. History Goes Unnoticed

1979 SYNOPSIS: While the world knew about the disaster at Three Mile Island, few Americans are aware of what was actually the worst nuclear spill in U.S. history, according to officials at the Nuclear Regulatory Commission.

At 5 a.m., on July 16, 1979, 100 million gallons of radioactive water containing uranium tailings breached from a tailing pond into the north arm of the Rio Puerco, near the small town of Church Rock, New Mexico.

Two hours later, workers shored up the hole in the tailing pond dam, but by 8 a.m. the radiation was detectable in Gallup, New Mexico. Radiation was detected up to 50 miles from the site of the spill. Livestock and people were kept away from the river, and children found playing in the water received full-body scans at the Los Alamos nuclear labs in Albuquerque.

Altogether some 1,100 tons of uranium mine tailings (waste) breached from holding ponds, contaminating 250 acres of land and up to 50 miles of the Rio Puerco. On the first day of the accident, state Environmental Improvement Division spokesman Michael Triviso said that samples of the river water indicated radioactivity 6,600 times the maximum standards for drinking water. The Rio Puerco flows into the Little Colorado River which flows into Lake Mead. Lake Mead, in turn, supplies the water for Los Angeles and Southern California.

The Kerr-McGee Company and the United Nuclear Corporation operate the uranium mill and waste storage site.

SOURCE: *Greenpeace Chronicles*, September 1979, "Worst Nuclear Disaster in U.S. History."

UPDATE: Six months after the Church Rock disaster, *The Christian Science Monitor* (1/10/80) reported another major problem resulting from the spill. The Navajo Environmental Protection Committee charged that a percentage of the dam-spill water will percolate into the ground, and when it hits the Mancos Shale it will be redirected northward into the aquifer system where it will remain for a few thousand years. Nonetheless, because of the economic importance of uranium to the area, the *Monitor* noted, "Accidents like the catastrophic Church Rock uranium-tailings spill last summer are almost nonevents—except for the people who live in the Four Corners."

The United Nuclear Corporation closed its mining operation down in 1984 and started a multi-million-dollar cleanup effort (PR Newswire, 1/16/92).

Kerr-McGee, the other company involved in the Church Rock tragedy, was the company cited in the celebrated Karen Silkwood case. Silkwood, an employee at the Kerr-McGee nuclear power plant in Oklahoma, suffered radiation contamination and died after her car was mysteriously forced off the road. At the time she was trying to prove a cover-up by Kerr-McGee.

On August 5, 1995, *The Irish Times*, in an article commemorating the 50th anniversary of the tragedies in Hiroshima and Nagasaki, noted the price we are still paying for nuclear weapons production: "In July 1979, the largest radioactive spill in U.S. history took place at the United Nuclear mill at Church Rock, New Mexico. One hundred million gallons of radioactive water contaminated the drinking water of more than 1,700 Navajo people. In the aftermath of the accident the company refused to supply emergency food and water. Rather than attempting to minimize the damage, the corporation stonewalled for nearly five years before agreeing to pay a paltry $525,000 out-of-court settlement to its victims."

7. The Press Cover-up of the Tragedy in East Timor

1979 SYNOPSIS: Human rights violations rivaling those in Cambodia are occurring in East Timor with the support of the United States but without the American public's knowledge.

In December 1975, Indonesian military forces invaded East Timor following a short-lived civil war there. The little-known war of aggression by Indonesia has continued with the assistance of the United States. The results have been the establishment of Indonesian military rule in East Timor, as well as major violations of the population's human rights and their right to self-determination.

Neutral observers have estimated the number of people slaughtered at 50,000 to 100,000—almost ten percent of the population. Yet the Western press has given little coverage to the massive atrocities committed by the Indonesian forces. The press adheres to the Indonesian-U.S. State Department version of the situation in East Timor, that most of the lives were lost in the civil war prior to the Indonesian intervention. However, other reports cite the number of dead from the civil war at just 2,000 to 3,000.

The U.S. government claims to have suspended military aid to Indonesia from December 1975, when the invasion started, to June 1976. However, military aid during that period was above what the State Department had originally proposed to Congress and it has continued to increase, largely concealed from public knowledge.

SOURCE: *Inquiry,* 2/19/79, "East Timor: The Press Cover-up," by Noam Chomsky.

UPDATE: Today East Timor is sometimes referred to as the site of the world's worst case of genocide, proportionately speaking, since the Holocaust. The Associated Press reported (10/16/96) as many as 260,000 people have died in East Timor. Joseph Szwaja, a Seattle teacher and member of the East Timor Action Network, recounted the horrors on the 20th anniversary of the Indonesian invasion, and asked, "Why has so little been heard in our country about these nauseating abuses?" (*Seattle Times,* 7/18/96) Szwaja attributes the silence to government and corporate interests. The world's leading oil companies were interested in the offshore oil deposits. The United States provided Indonesia with armaments, military training, and political support. Nevertheless, the media were silent.

The U.S. officially suspended its military assistance program to Indonesia in 1992 allegedly because of the East Timor holocaust. In 1996, the U.S. Congress restored grants to Indonesia for military education and training. The U.S. gave Indonesia $600,000 so that it could send its military and civilian personnel to U.S. military educational and training institutes. This reversal of military support for Indonesia was reported in *Jane's Defence Weekly,* on April 17, 1996.

Meanwhile the offshore petroleum industry is reportedly on the brink of a worldwide high growth period, expected to last at least through 1997-1998 and probably to 2002 or beyond. Companies poised to exploit oil reserves off Indonesia and East Timor include Exxon, Conoco, Chevron, Texaco, Maxus Energy, Marathon, Arco, and Unocal (*Offshore,* May 1996).

The New York Times has led the media cheerleaders with an editorial (7/20/96) urging Washington to exert a significant positive influence in Indonesia's future. *The Times* acknowledged that "Washington too often overlooked the Suharto Government's repressive ways along with its forcible annexation and occupation of East Timor. Today a more forthright approach is needed." In defense of Suharto, however, *The Times* pointed out, "The Suharto regime crushed the Communists in a bloody purge, imposed political order and gradually rebuilt the economy." In yet another apologia, Thomas L. Friedman, columnist for *The New York Times,* reported (7/11/97) that "Indonesia has to be the least understood country in the world." Suggesting that Indonesia is misunderstood over the East Timor situation, Friedman didn't mention its oil resources.

For a possible explanation of why the U.S. is still supporting a repressive regime in Indonesia, consider the case of Freeport-McMoRan, a New Orleans-based company that runs the world's biggest gold mine in the Indonesian rainforests. In 1975, Indonesia invaded East Timor with the approval of Henry Kissinger and President Gerald Ford. It then embarked on its genocide of the Timorese. Kissinger is now on the board of directors of Freeport-McMoRan (*The Progressive*, February 1996).

In an ironic twist to the tragic East Timor story, the 1996 Nobel Peace Prize was awarded to Roman Catholic Bishop Carlos Felipe Ximenes Belo and political activist Jose Ramos-Horta for their efforts to bring peace to East Timor—the island that the world knows so little about (*Los Angeles Times*, 10/12/96). In accepting the prize on December 10, 1996, in Oslo, Norway, co-winner Ramos-Horta severely criticized Indonesia and proposed a plan for East Timorese independence (*The New York Times*, 12/11/96).

8. PBS—The Oil Network

1979 SYNOPSIS: As a reaction to the vast wasteland of network television, there arose in the '60s a mighty dream—The Public Broadcasting System (PBS)—an educational and non-commercial television resource. The American people finally were to be exposed to a wide variety of opinion and culture. TV censorship would be relegated to the commercial networks.

The dream never materialized. Instead, public television became the ward of the "establishment"—of corporations, mostly oil companies, that serve as key underwriters. And censorship, while publicly disclaimed by PBS executives, became a way of life in public broadcasting.

Examples given include a controversial documentary called "Plutonium: Element of Risk," which was dropped from the PBS schedule because it failed to conform to PBS's "journalistic standards;" a documentary titled "Blacks Britannica," directed by David Koff, which was termed "unsuitable for Americans" and initially canceled then subsequently aired in a "reorganized or censored" form; and a powerful documentary about the world garment trade called "The Shirt Off Our Backs," which was also "reorganized" before being aired.

The Coalition to Make Public TV Public was formed in New York after WNET (PBS-New York) rejected four films for the station's "Independent Focus" series without a word of explanation to the independent review panel that had recommended them.

In explaining why PBS failed to fulfill its dream, *San Francisco Chronicle* columnist Charles McCabe said, "One of the reasons why this never happened was the takeover of educational television by the petroleum industry. Educational television is now effectively controlled by Mobil, Exxon, Sun, Atlantic Richfield, and suchlike."

SOURCES: *Washington Journalism Review*, April/May 1979, "The Horowitz Affair," by John Friedman; *Jump Cut*, November 1979, "Racism in Public TV," by Joel Dreyfuss; *In These Times*, 2/6/80 and 3/5/80, "Public Television," by Pat Aufderheide; *San Francisco Chronicle*, 6/12/78 and 2/28/80, "The Oil Network," by Charles McCabe.

UPDATE: The dream of an educational and non-commercial public television resource for all Americans ended in 1996 with congressional discussion of the Public Broadcasting Self-Sufficiency Act which would pave the way for the commercialization of PBS. In early 1997, the Clinton Administration eliminated funding for the Public Telecommunications Facilities Program, the network's primary source for equipment funding and infrastructure replacement (Ohio University, "News on Federal Funding for Public Broadcasting," 2/7/97). A one-billion-dollar broadcasting trust fund would assist the public broadcasting industry in making the transition from governmental to private financing. Direct funding for PBS would be phased out by the year 2000 (*Warfield's Business Record*, 3/18/96).

Southern California's flagship public television station, KCET-TV Channel 28, was quick to turn commercial. By early 1997, it was running commercials from American Airlines, Infiniti, Secure Horizons, Chevrolet, Lufthansa, and American Express. Peter Downey, PBS's senior executive responsible for underwriting network guidelines, said the KCET-TV efforts were clearly a trend. "KCET is hardly the first and I doubt that it will be the last station that has gone in this direction. This is a phenomenon that has been in discussion in public television circles for two years now, and most accept it as a natural order of things" (*Los Angeles Times*, 1/14/97).

9. The Most Powerful Secret Lobby in Washington

1979 SYNOPSIS: While many Americans may be aware there are paid lobbyists in Washington attempting to influence their elected representatives, few are probably aware of the most powerful secret lobby in the Capitol.

The Business Roundtable has maintained a deliberately low profile since it was founded in 1972. The chairman, Thomas A. Murphy, is also chairman of General Motors.

Although it doesn't divulge the names of its members, the Roundtable is known to include the chief executives of nearly 200 of the country's richest corporations. Assets of the Roundtable's member companies amount to $1.3 trillion, about half of the nation's total gross national product.

In one way or another, the Business Roundtable, through its extraordinary influence, has affected every American. The Roundtable has successfully bottled up tax reforms, pushed legislation to subject all Federal Trade Commission rulings to a Congressional veto, helped win tax policy rulings favorable to business, supported oil and gas price decontrol, pushed the Energy Mobilization Board to override environmental consideration, blocked the creation of a consumer protection office, and watered down attempts to strengthen antitrust legislation.

Mark Green, director of the Public Citizen's Congress Watch, a Ralph Nader-led group, describes the Business Roundtable as "the most powerful secret lobby in Washington."

SOURCE: *The New York Times Magazine*, 12/9/79, "Big Business on the Offensive," by Philip Shabecoff.

UPDATE: The Business Roundtable is alive, well, still operating in Washington, D.C., and just as secretive as it was in 1979. A *Fortune* article (5/15/95) cited the Business Roundtable as one of the favorites among executives of the *Fortune* 50 top corporations. And they lobby together. Various news sources, including *The National Review, Environmental Action Magazine*, and *Best's Review* reveal that the Business Roundtable has lobbied strongly, and successfully, for NAFTA, for GATT, against health care, against Medicare reform, and for a balanced budget.

10. The 65 Billion Dollar Ghost Bank in Washington, D.C.

1979 SYNOPSIS: When the Chrysler Corporation sought a government loan guarantee to prevent plant closures and massive employee layoffs, it became one of the big stories of 1979. But when Western Union went to the government for a $750 million loan, not a guarantee, it didn't cause a stir among the media.

Western Union needed three quarters of a billion dollars to build a space communications satellite that NASA wanted. But because of its already heavy space shuttle budget, NASA suspected Congress wouldn't appropriate the $750 million for the project.

Instead, Western Union went to a bank that permits the government to do off-the-balance-sheet financial transactions. The bank, called the Federal Financing Bank (FFB) helps the government hide how big the national deficit really is and allows government agencies to go ahead with projects the Congress thought too costly or unneeded.

The FFB is a little known, obscure off-budget government bank that works out of a small office in the Federal Treasury Building in Washington. According to government records, the bank, which only has a handful of staff members, has made up to $65 billion in loans since it started in 1974. For comparison, that sum exceeds the total outstanding loans of the world's largest private bank, the Bank of America.

One of the nation's leading financial publications, *Forbes*, once referred to the FFB as the "Ghost Bank" and said its loan portfolio would "make an examiner wince."

SOURCES: *Chicago Tribune Service*, 12/16/79, "Buck Rogers' High Finance in Costly U.S. Space Venture," by James O'Shea; *Forbes*, 3/15/76, "Ghost Bank."

UPDATE: According to Charles D. Haworth, secretary of the Federal Financing Bank, the bank's holdings on May 31, 1996, totaled $64.9 billion, about the same as reported in the 1979 story. Some recent transactions include a $1.5 billion loan to the U.S. Postal Service (*Wall Street Journal*, 10/2/96); the Fisheries Obligation Guarantee Program for vessel refinancing (Congressional Press Releases, 9/16/96); the General Services Administration and the Pennsylvania Avenue Development Corporation for the construction of the 3.1 million-square-foot, eleven-acre Federal Triangle project, the largest federal building constructed since the Pentagon (*Engineering News-Record*, 9/4/96); and the Madison Guaranty Savings and Loan Association, the S&L of Whitewater fame (*The Washington Times*, 2/6/96). The FFB was also a major player in the Clinton Administration's effort to avoid default in early 1996 by swapping agency securities for Treasuries held by another account (*The Bond Buyer*, 3/20/96).

CHAPTER 5—1980

Biased Coverage of Central America Problems

The national elections, including Ronald Reagan's defeat of Jimmy Carter, dominated the mainstream news media coverage for most of 1980. According to the Associated Press, the top ten news stories of the year were:

1. The presidential election
2. The Iranian hostage crisis
3. The U.S. economy
4. Soviet intervention in Afghanistan
5. Volcanic eruption of Mount St. Helens in Washington State
6. Events in Poland
7. Murder of former Beatle John Lennon in New York City
8. Earthquakes in southern Italy
9. The war between Iran and Iraq
10. (Tie) Boatlift from Cuba and influx of Cuban and Haitian refugees, and the fire that killed 84 persons at the MGM Grand Hotel in Las Vegas.

The root causes of more than a decade of conflict in Central America were overlooked.

THE TOP TEN CENSORED STORIES OF 1980

—And What Has Happened to Them Since

1. Distorted Reports of the El Salvador Crisis

1980 SYNOPSIS: The U.S. media coverage of the outbreak of civil war in El Salvador was dangerously misleading. Either through willful misinformation or ignorance, the major media supported a misguided U.S. foreign policy that threatened to embroil Americans in another Vietnam War.

A popularly promoted media myth was that the current government of the tiny Central American country is a "moderate" junta, struggling to maintain order in the face of left and right-wing extremist minorities. However, Murat Williams, a former U.S. ambassador to El Salvador, and other observers, report that the "left" is more accurately a heterogeneous mix of peasants, students, teachers, priests, nuns, and middle-class businessmen, comprising about 80 percent of the population. What remains is less "center" than "right," comprised chiefly of the military and the oligarchy. The few "moderates" of the civilian-military junta and the Cabinet of 1979 had resigned by January 1980, despairing of any real governmental reforms.

Further, the U.S. press has generally perpetuated the belief that the bulk of El Salvador's estimated 10,000 assassinations in 1980 were the work of "Marxist-inspired guerrillas" or reactionary right-wing forces. But records of the Legal Aid Office of the Catholic Archdiocese of San Salvador show that government military units themselves were responsible for 80 percent of the country's political assassinations.

Another media myth is that Cuban- or Russian-inspired guerrillas were the cause of El Salvador's social upheaval rather than the country's real enemy—a century of economic and social injustice.

There was also much media-generated paranoia regarding Cuban or Russian arms shipments to the "leftist guerrillas," obscuring the reality of an alarming U.S. military buildup in El Salvador. According to the Institute for Policy Studies, U.S. security assistance to El Salvador between 1950 and 1979 totaled $16.72 million; in 1980 alone, more than $5.7 million in U.S. military aid was sent to El Salvador and U.S. military advisers were stationed there.

SOURCES: *America*, 4/26/80, "El Salvador's Agony and U.S. Policies," by James L. Connor; *Christianity and Crisis*, 5/12/80, "El Salvador: Reform as Cover for Repression," by William L. Wipfler; *Inquiry*, 5/5/80, "The Continuing Calamity of El Salvador," and 11/10/80, "Central American Powder Keg," both by Anne Nelson; *The Nation*, 12/13/80, "El Salvador's Christian Democrat Junta," by Penny Lernoux, and 12/20/80, "The Junta's War Against the People," by James Petras.

UPDATE: The Salvadoran civil war continued to 1992 when the United Nations-sponsored peace accords ended the 12-year conflict with the rebels forming a formal political party—the Farabundo Marti National Liberation Front (FMLN). It was also in 1992 that forensic experts unearthed skeletons of children and babies in El Mozote, El Salvador, confirming that hundreds of civilians were killed in the largest massacre in the civil war.

It wasn't until mid-March 1993 that mainstream media in the United States finally reported what the alternative press had been publishing for more than a decade. The government of El Salvador, with the support and funding of the Reagan and Bush Administrations, was responsible for the horrible atrocities during the 12-year conflict. The atrocities, which took the lives of an estimated 75,000 people—Salvadoran civilians, including many women and children—were supported with more than $6 billion in economic and military aid, including $1 billion in covert aid, furnished by the Reagan and Bush Administrations.

For a well-documented comprehensive analysis of the tragedy in El Salvador, please see "The Truth of El Mozote," the 74-page *New Yorker* cover story (12/6/93) by Mark Danner.

2. NSA: Big Brother is Listening to You

1980 SYNOPSIS: Compared to many other nations governed by less democratic regimes, most U.S. citizens take both the right to privacy and free speech as a given in their daily lives. Harrison E. Salisbury, respected Pulitzer Prize-winning editor and foreign and domestic correspondent for *The New York Times*, described the difference between a free democracy and a totalitarian state: "We had no censorship; we had freedom of communication; no one listened in when we talked on the telephone; our mails were secure; no government spy read our telegrams or cables."

But then Salisbury added, "That was before I heard of the NSA. Those initials are not exactly your household acronym. If I ask my neighbor what is the country's biggest security agency, he will name the CIA or FBI. He will be wrong. The National Security Agency (NSA) is the biggest, and not one American in 10,000 has even heard its name."

The NSA is the behemoth of U.S. security outfits with an annual appropriation of more than $2 billion and a staff of more than 22,000. Everything it does is classified.

The NSA monitors all message traffic in the world—cable, wireless, satellite, telephone, coded, uncoded, scrambled, private, business, diplomatic, military. Every telephone call, wireless and cable message to and from the U.S. is automatically recorded. In 1973, the NSA reportedly retrieved more than 24 million individual communications including private, personal, supposedly inviolable messages of ordinary Americans. The latter are reputedly screened out and fed into a 20-ton-a-day destruct furnace—but no one knows for sure.

Harrison notes that all this is 100 percent against the law and violates every provision of the Bill of Rights.

SOURCES: *Penthouse*, November 1980, "Big Brother is Listening to You," by Harrison Salisbury; *The Progressive*, November 1980, "Somebody is Listening," by Loring Wirbell.

UPDATE: While the NSA spy tactics are illegal and a violation of our Bill of Rights, Harrison Salisbury's 1980 charges have not caused the agency to rethink its tactics nor the mass media to focus on the issue. The NSA is still virtually invisible to the American public, and according to an *Austin American-Statesman* report (1/7/96), still runs the nation's most ambitious spying operation, eclipsing the CIA in budget and personnel. Its operations cost nearly $1 million an hour, $8 billion a year, and it oversees tens of thousands of eavesdroppers in listening posts from Alaska to Thailand. And now, instead of cutting back with the end of the Cold War, the NSA apparently is expanding its activities in at least three new directions—international economic spying, a domestic war on computer hackers, and an ongoing battle with terrorists.

During the tense auto trade negotiations in Tokyo in early 1995, the NSA eavesdropped on telephone conversations between Japanese automakers and Japanese government officials, passed it back to CIA headquarters at Langley for processing, and bounced minute-by-minute information back to the U.S. delegation in Tokyo (*World Trade*, June 1996). On June 30, 1996, the British *Mail On Sunday* reported that world leaders meeting at the G-7 (renamed the Group of Eight (G-8) in 1997 with the addition of Russia) economic summit in France the previous week were furious that every classified message they sent home was being intercepted by the NSA and sent back to the U.S. to be deciphered. However, while Japan, France, and Germany all complained about U.S. eavesdropping, the trade ties are too valuable to permit the issue to become a major diplomatic incident.

On June 25, 1996, John M. Deutch, CIA director, announced plans to create a "cyberwar" center at the National Security Agency to focus the government's effort to understand and combat the threat from hacking attacks by governments, terrorists, and "mischievous 16-year-olds" (*International Herald Tribune*, 6/26/96).

However, not all NSA spying is sinister. Following the mid-July tragic accident of TWA Flight 800 off Long Island, NSA started sifting through several weeks of messages gathered through its international eavesdropping tactics seeking any bits of relevant information (*The Christian Science Monitor*, 7/22/96). In the wake of the TWA 800 tragedy and the Olympic bombing in Atlanta, there was renewed pressure in Washington to expand federal authority for wiretapping.

3. The Continuing Censorship of the Nuclear Issue

1980 SYNOPSIS: Three Mile Island (TMI), the worst accident in the history of the commercial nuclear energy program in the United States, proved to be a blessing for pro-nuclear propagandists. Using the catch phrase "no one died at TMI," the nuclear power industry embarked on a slick nationwide campaign to resell nuclear power to the American public. America's Electric Energy Companies directed its campaign at the media with an advertisement in *Columbia Journalism Review* (March/April 1981) using the headline "Three Mile Island has made nuclear power even safer."

Meanwhile, more than a half-dozen nuclear-oriented stories were nominated for "best censored" of 1980, including the following:

NO ONE DIED AT TMI—The Pennsylvania Health Department released a report entitled "No Infant Deaths Caused by TMI" that was widely publicized by the media. However, a devastating study by Dr. Ernest J. Sternglass, a protégé of Albert Einstein and a professor of radiation physics at the University of Pittsburgh, which refutes that report went unpublicized. Using the government's own data, Dr. Sternglass laid the blame for a minimum of 430 infant deaths in the U.S. on TMI.

SOURCE: *Harrowsmith*, June 1980, "The Silent Toll," by Thomas Pawlick.

URANIUM MINING IN REMOTE NEW JERSEY—While the Nuclear Regulatory Commission (NRC) recommends that facilities for mining and milling uranium be confined to "remote areas," Exxon and Standard Oil of New Jersey started exploratory drilling for uranium in an area of northern New Jersey where four cities and six towns, with a combined population of close to one million, now derive their water supplies.

SOURCE: *In These Times*, 11/19-25/80, "Uranium Rush Threatens New Jersey," by Ann Spanel.

THE HIDDEN U.S. NUCLEAR WAR—Some 235 nuclear bombs have been detonated in the hidden 17-year nuclear war the U.S. has fought against itself. An atomic weapon is detonated underground nearly every three and one-half weeks at the U.S. nuclear test site in Nevada. New evidence supplied by a former high-ranking Air Force official and other sources indicates that radiation from these tests may be seeping into the atmosphere.

SOURCE: *Pacific News Service*, 7/2/80, "Underground Tests Every Three Weeks," by Norman Solomon.

2,300 NUCLEAR PLANT "INCIDENTS"—Critical Mass, an antinuclear group affiliated with Ralph Nader, announced that more than 2,300 incidents, including operational errors and mechanical failures, were reported at the nation's nuclear power plants in 1979.

SOURCE: *The New York Times*, 7/14/80, "2,300 Incidents Reported At Nuclear Plants in 1979," Associated Press.

UPDATE: Uranium mining in New Jersey, once a major industry there, came to an official end on August 9, 1989, when New Jersey Governor Thomas Kean signed a bill declaring a formal moratorium on uranium mining in the state (UPI, 8/9/89).

Left in limbo by the 1992 moratorium on underground nuclear testing, the Nevada Test Site's future is uncertain, according to a *Salt Lake Tribune* report (2/20/96). Four possible scenarios for the site include continuing current operations to maintain readiness in case testing is resumed; discontinue all operations except monitoring and security; expand uses for military training and defense-related research; return uncontaminated sections to the public for recreational and educational use. Incredibly, in July 1996, Nevada's U.S. Senator Harry Reid volunteered his state as a nuclear test site again to give Nevada's economy a boost (*Washington Times*, 7/23/96). The offer was rejected by the Senate.

April 26, 1996, marked the 10th anniversary of the world's worst nuclear power plant accident—Chernobyl. It is now known that some 4,300 people died as a direct result of the accident and that many of the 350,000 cleanup workers are now ill (*Los Angeles Times*, 4/27/96). And the lives of millions of others were affected, mostly in Ukraine, Russia, and Belarus. Despite the tragic warning of Chernobyl, safety problems continue to beset America's nuclear industry. For a frightening compilation of nuclear accidents and events compiled in a daily calendar over a year's span, see the Greenpeace Internet site, http://www.greenpeace.org/~comms/nukes/chernob/rep02.html.

4. The Bendectin Cover-up

1980 SYNOPSIS: Richardson-Merrell Inc., the company that brought us thalidomide, has now produced another drug charged with causing birth defects: Bendectin.

Described as a "low-level" teratogen (defined as an agent causing development malformations), Bendectin is suspected of causing heart disorders, limbs reduced in size or missing, cleft lips and palates, and a disease in which the brain is formed outside the skull, in about one percent of the children whose respective mothers took the drug.

What is most alarming about this statistic is that Bendectin has been prescribed to about 30 million women since it was introduced in 1956. With an estimated 1.5 million women taking the drug in 31 countries around the world every year, if the incidence of deformity is as low as 2-5 in 1,000, as suggested by one study, Bendectin could still be creating between 3,000 and 7,500 deformed children each year.

While evidence shows that Richardson-Merrell and the Food and Drug Administration each have on file numerous reports of birth defects suspected to be the results of Bendectin, the reports have been largely ignored and unreported.

SOURCES: *Mother Jones*, November 1980, "The Bendectin Cover-up," by Mark Dowie and Carolyn Marshall; *Science*, 10/31/80, "How Safe is Bendectin?" by Gina Bari Kolata.

UPDATE: In the 1980s, an increasing number of parents began suing Bendectin's maker, Merrell, claiming their youngsters' handicaps resulted from the use of Bendectin. According to a *Minneapolis Star Tribune* report (4/3/96), the cost of insurance and litigation became so onerous that the maker of Bendectin was losing money and was finally forced to stop production of the drug. Nonetheless, the controversy continues with lawsuits slowly moving through the judicial system.

5. Something is Rotten in the Global Supermarket

1980 SYNOPSIS: While modern technology has increased worldwide food production and raised per capita income, millions of landless peasants in Third World countries face starvation and malnutrition.

Prime agricultural lands in Third World countries have increasingly been converted to the production of cash export crops by vast transnational agribusiness firms. While this succeeded in increasing exports and ameliorated balance of payments problems for underdeveloped countries, the benefits did not accrue to everyone.

Multinational corporations increased their profits, taking advantage of cheap labor resources abroad. Foreign governments and the few landed gentry also benefited from the arrangements. But peasant farmers were driven from their subsistence lands when the multinationals arrived. New technology production did not offer enough employment opportunities to compensate for the massive displacements. Those who managed to find seasonal work in agribusiness were not paid enough to cover their subsistence food needs.

Vast migrations of hungry peasants fled to the cities where employment opportunities were not much better. The specter of urban poverty, filth, and slums proliferated throughout the Third World.

SOURCE: *The Nation*, 2/9/80, "The Profits of Hunger," Richard J. Barnet.

UPDATE: Despite the dire 1980 warnings about the problems in worldwide food production, funding for agricultural research targeted to Third World countries declined drastically during the 1980s and continues to decline, according to the International Food Policy Research Institute (IFPRI), a Washington-based institute that monitors trends affecting the world's food supply. The IFPRI reported that while scientific advances in agriculture have boosted worldwide food production in recent decades, a record explosion in the world's population will outstrip food production in coming years if research on new farming technologies and food policies is neglected (*Chicago Tribune*, 4/4/94).

One hopeful sign is the formation of the Tufts International Famine Centre at University College, Cork, Ireland, according to Dr. J. Larry Brown, of Tufts University in Boston. He said for the first time, widespread famine and disaster related deaths could be prevented. The Centre would seek to establish better early warning systems, research, and analysis, as well as training, technical support and early mobilization of international agencies and the media when necessary (*The Irish Times*, 11/20/95).

6. The Circle of Poison

1980 SYNOPSIS: The export of banned pesticides from the industrial countries to the Third World is a scandal of global proportions still little covered by the major news media. To compound the problem, investigative reporters David Weir and Mark Shapiro have discovered that from 50-70 percent of the chemicals are not used to grow food for the hungry but are actually used on luxury crops like coffee and bananas destined for the U.S. and Europe—creating a "circle of poison."

Dangerous pesticides create the circle of poison by endangering the workers in American chemical plants, injuring Third World workers in the fields where they are used, and, finally returned to us in the food we import.

The U.S. is one of the world's top importers of food and at least ten percent of our imported food is officially estimated to be contaminated. Moreover, the Food and Drug Administration's (FDA) most commonly used test fails to measure 70 percent of the almost 900 food tolerances for cancer-causing chemicals.

At least 25 percent of the U.S. pesticide exports are products that are banned, heavily restricted, or have never been registered for use in the U.S. Many have not been independently evaluated; others, like DDT, are familiar poisons, widely known to cause cancer, birth defects, and genetic mutations. Yet the Federal Insecticide, Fungicide and Rodenticide Act explicitly states that banned or unregistered pesticides are legal for export.

SOURCE: *The Nation*, 11/15/80, "The Circle of Poison," by David Weir and Mark Shapiro.

UPDATE: According to *Total Health* (February 1995) Americans are consuming more fruits and vegetables, which is good for us, but in the process are ingesting more insecticidal toxic substances. Equally disturbing, according to *Business and Society Review* (January 1995), the U.S. depends on Latin American produce for about 20 percent of its annual produce sales. In turn, Latin America depends on U.S.-banned pesticides. Roughly ten percent of the annual $22 billion in global pesticide sales is of such pesticides. Latin American farmers often use these pesticides on export crops such as bananas, cocoa, coffee, corn, rice, sugar cane, soybeans, and tomatoes.

As a result, tests by the U.S. Food and Drug Administration show that residues of U.S.-banned pesticides still contaminate some five percent of imported produce. While this shows a substantial improvement since 1980, it also confirms that the circle of poison is still spinning. Meanwhile, the National Cancer Institute has launched a major, three-year agricultural health study to examine cancer risks among workers who have direct exposure to pesticides. The study, launched in 1996, will involve about 75,000 adult subjects (*Environmental Health Perspective*, April 1996).

Unforeseen in earlier studies was the impact of NAFTA on the "circle of poison" as noted in a 1997 study by a number of watchdog groups including the Economic Policy Institute and the Institute for Policy Studies. The report, titled "The Failed Experiment: NAFTA at Three Years," revealed that NAFTA had weakened food safety inspections. While imports of fresh and frozen fruits from Mexico grew by more than one-third since NAFTA was enacted, some shipments of strawberries, lettuce and carrots have had illegally high levels of pesticide residue of 18.4 percent, 15.6 percent, and 12.3 percent, respectively (*San Francisco Examiner*, 6/29/97).

7. Space Wars

1980 SYNOPSIS: While Americans thrilled to the new adventures of Luke Skywalker and Darth Vader, they were unaware that real-life counterparts in Washington and Moscow have been busily developing a set of weapons just as spectacular as anything George Lucas ever put on the screen.

But these real-life killer satellites and laser weapons will prove a lot deadlier than *Star Wars* toys if they're ever put to use. Russia and the United States are locked into a race of time and technology to place super-sophisticated anti-satellite (ASAT) weapons in orbit above the earth.

Nuclear powered satellites, armed with high energy lasers and particle beams, designed to destroy any target including those on Earth with pinpoint accuracy up to 4,500 miles away, will lead to the development of ABM space stations capable of destroying a thousand enemy missiles in a matter of minutes. The technology would make a pre-emptive first strike feasible and make technological parity between the superpowers absolutely imperative. In effect, it locks the two into an arms race for outer space which neither can afford to lose.

SOURCES: *New West*, 4/21/80, "Space Wars," by Jacques Gauchey; *Mother Jones*, August 1980, "No Need for Star Wars"; *Inquiry*, 9/1/80, "Laser-Rattling in Outer Space," by David Ritchie; *Space For All People*, Newsletter for Citizens for Space Demilitarization, 1980 issues.

UPDATE: The early concerns about space war weapons became a reality on March 23, 1983, when President Ronald Reagan, in a surprise segment during a televised speech about Grenada, announced the Strategic Defense Initiative (SDI) which he described as a "peace shield" in space (*Los Angeles Times*, 7/8/96). However, with the passage of time, and billions of dollars, SDI, or Star Wars, came to be seen as technically unfeasible, immensely expensive, and just plain stupid. This despite strong support from Newt Gingrich who said, "Young people like space." Finally, President Bill Clinton and Congress canceled Star Wars and shifted the focus of the program to ground-based missile defense in 1993 (*Defense News*, 7/15/96).

But Star Wars didn't die. First, it made a stealthy return in the Republicans' Contract with America as part of the National Security Restoration Act (*The New Republic*, 12/5/94). It raised its head again at a 1995 meeting of the Western European Union meeting at Lisbon with Europeans considering their own space-based defence shield (*The Guardian*, 5/4/95). In 1996, presidential candidate Bob Dole took up the cudgel for Star Wars (*Los Angeles Times*, 7/8/96). While still a Senator, Dole had introduced the Defend America Act of 1996 which would have implemented strategic defenses. The price tag, estimated at $31 billion to $60 billion, made it easy for Congress to table it in June. Nonetheless, Dole continued to make stump speeches for a ballistic missile defense.

Star Wars, like its Hollywood namesake, just won't go away.

8. Tobacco Companies Censor the Truth About Cigarettes and Cancer

1980 SYNOPSIS: The American tobacco industry uses its substantial advertising revenue to discourage magazines from publishing stories on a major health hazard—cigarette smoking. That was the conclusion of an article published by the American Council on Science and Health (ACSH) and also announced in a press conference in San Francisco. Despite the serious charges, it received little press coverage.

ACSH's examination of the reporting record of major national magazines showed that most that accepted cigarette advertising had not published a single major story on the health dangers of smoking during the previous five years.

The ACSH article also cited an earlier *Columbia Journalism Review* survey of coverage of the cigarette-cancer link in leading national magazines over a seven-year period. *CJR* Managing Editor R.C. Smith reported a "striking and disturbing" pattern that revealed that "advertising revenues can indeed silence the editors of American magazines."

SOURCES: *ACSH News & Views*, February 1980, "Conspiracy of Silence?" by Beverly Mosher and Margaret J. Sheridan; ACSH press release, San Francisco, 1/29/80, "New Report Says Tobacco Industry Uses Ad Revenue to Discourage Anti-smoking Magazine Stories."

UPDATE: After years of censorship and limited coverage, a combination of new research on the hazards of smoking, effective whistleblowers from the tobacco industry, and well-publicized congressional hearings, the tobacco/cancer issue was finally put on the front burner by the media in 1994. However, the tobacco industry did not roll over easily. While it was a censor itself in 1980, it attempted to reverse roles in the 1990s and claimed it was now the victim of censorship. The tobacco companies went on the offensive after the Clinton Administration's proposal in August 1995 to ban some advertising, such as the Marlboro Man and Joe Camel from certain media, and to eliminate tobacco brand names from sporting events.

Then, on August 23, 1996, President Clinton declared nicotine an addictive drug and gave the Food and Drug Administration broad jurisdiction to regulate cigarettes and smokeless tobacco (*Los Angeles Times*, 8/24/96). Two years of relentless, albeit belated, media coverage helped reverse more than two centuries of the government's hands-off policy toward the nation's tobacco industry.

9. The Oil Companies' Monopoly on the Sun

1980 SYNOPSIS: In the early seventies, it was said that we wouldn't have solar power until the oil companies got a monopoly on the sun. Now it appears that this is happening.

Within the last five years, a powerful elite of multinational oil companies, aerospace firms, utilities, and other large corporations has been quietly buying into the solar industry. The group's aim appears to be to squeeze out smaller competitors and control development so that alternative energy sources will never threaten its massive investments in fossil fuels and nuclear power.

Most of these are the same corporations that for years have been viewed by alternative energy activists as solar's worst enemies. In countless advertisements, political campaigns and conferences, they have branded solar technology as impractical and expensive, a source of power that at best will someday provide one percent of our national energy needs.

Now, however, solar technology appears interesting to companies like Shell Oil, Atlantic-Richfield, Northrop, Amoco, Exxon, and Mobil—all corporate giants that have taken control of solar power firms in the last several years.

Further, the federal government is even helping them in their efforts toward monopolization. More than 90 percent of the federal solar energy budget for research and development has ended up in the coffers of the largest corporations in the United States.

SOURCES: *New West*, 8/11/80; *Mother Jones*, September-October 1980.

UPDATE: Following the energy crisis in the early 1970s, entrepreneurs rushed to develop solar power projects to free America of its oil dependency. Many of them went broke or were bought out by large corporations, including the big oil companies, as revealed in the 1980 story. By 1994, *Time* magazine was ready to announce a "sunny forecast" for solar energy and Shell International Petroleum in London predicted renewable power, particularly solar, would dominate world energy production by 2050. By 1996, the first large, commercially competitive solar power projects were underway. In India, the Rajasthan State Electricity Board signed a 25-year power purchase agreement with Amoco/Enron Solar for power. In China, Amoco/Enron signed an agreement with the State Science and Technology Commission which could lead to a solar cell manufacturing centre and 150MW generating facility. Bob Kelly, co-chairman of Amoco/Enron Solar, a joint venture between Amoco, the U.S. oil company, and Enron, North America's largest natural gas company, announced, "We think there is a great big market out there and we are going for it" (*Financial Times*, 7/3/96). It took some time, but the big oil companies finally got their monopoly on the sun. A stirring account of the battle for the sun is contained in *Who Owns the Sun? People, Politics and the Struggle for a Solar Economy* by Daniel M. Berman and John T. O'Connor, published by Chelsea Green, 1997.

10. Poisoned Water, Poisoned Land

1980 SYNOPSIS: Each year some 78 billion pounds of poisonous chemicals are dumped into 51,000 sites throughout this country where they enter the underground water supply. Many of these mixtures are lethal on contact, many are carcinogenic, and many can last in the environment for up to 100 years. Despite the enormity of this problem, the Environmental Protection Agency (EPA) has failed to monitor where the toxic wastes go.

Aside from direct contact, the greatest threat from careless toxic waste disposal is through the water supply. Ground wells often are located near chemical waste deposits. And, by the government's own estimate, 90 percent of our waste materials are improperly disposed of.

While a federal consultant has estimated it would cost up to $50 billion just to clean up existing dumps, the EPA is nearly two years behind in implementing regulations covering current toxic waste disposal.

SOURCES: *Penthouse*, May 1980, "Poisoned Water," by Michael H. Browne; *The Progressive*, July 1980, "Poisoned Land," by Barry Jacobs.

UPDATE: The most comprehensive recent update on our water supply is found in a lengthy, well-documented article in the May 1996 issue of *Consumers Digest*, entitled "How Safe is Your Water?" Everyone concerned with their water supply is advised to read this special report. It reported that the Safe Drinking Water Act (SDWA), originally passed in 1974 to ensure safe drinking water, was updated in 1986 to monitor for 83 specific contaminants and 25 additional contaminants every three years. Nonetheless, in 1994, some 30 million Americans were served by water systems that violated one or more public health standards.

Consumers Digest pointed out, "Although most water systems do a responsible job of reporting hazards, a lack of agency reporting and poor awareness make public drinking-water safety one of the most powerful issues of our time." The potential severity of the problem became apparent in 1993 when Milwaukee-area residents succumbed to a little known protozoan nicknamed "Crypto." It took 104 lives and sickened some 400,000 others. "Crypto" is naturally present in up to 87 percent of surface water supplies. In July 1996, the EPA announced a five-year $50 million effort to learn more about microbial hazards such as "Crypto" (Associated Press, 7/11/96).

While our water supplies may still be contaminated, for the first time the public will now be aware of it. In early August 1996, Congress passed and President Clinton signed a bill authorizing $7.6 billion for loans to improve deteriorating water systems and requiring customers to be notified of chemicals and bacteria in the water they drink (Associated Press, 8/7/96).

Consumers Digest concluded, "On the whole, Americans enjoy drinking-water supplies that are among the best in the industrial world."

That may be. But in 1995, Americans drank 2.7 billion gallons of bottled water, almost 60 percent more than a decade earlier. Bottled water was the fastest-growing beverage category in the 1990s, comprising 11.1 percent of the total refreshment beverage market (*The Tampa Tribune*, 10/28/96). The home water filtration system industry also profited from Americans' skepticism about the quality of their water. The sale of home water filters increased by 26 percent since 1990 and reached $1.4 billion in 1996; more than 25 percent of adults use one or more types of home water treatment devices (*The Houston Chronicle*, 10/8/96).

Please also see update of "Our Water is Running Out," #5, 1981.

CHAPTER 6—1981

The True Causes of American Economic Problems

While the status of the U.S. economy often ranks among the top ten mainstream news stories of the year, the causes underlying our frequent economic crises don't make the news. This untold story was the top *Censored* story of 1981. According to the Associated Press, the top ten news stories of the year were:

1. The assassination attempt on President Reagan
2. Return of the hostages from Iran
3. The Anwar Sadat assassination
4. The attempt on Pope John Paul II
5. The new conservative administration in Washington
6. The American economy
7. The flights of the Space Shuttle Columbia
8. The air traffic controllers strike
9. Appointment of Sandra Day O'Connor,
    the first woman Supreme Court justice
10. Political developments in Poland.

THE TOP TEN CENSORED STORIES OF 1981

—And What Has Happened to Them Since

1. The Real Story Behind Our Economic Crisis

1981 SYNOPSIS: In the past, we have been told that factors such as the over-regulation of business and the "declining moral fiber of the American worker" caused the worst economic crisis since the depression.

However, testifying before the California Senate Committee on Industrial Relations, a UCLA professor, Maurice Zeitlin, outlined one basic cause that was not widely publicized.

In brief, Zeitlin said we no longer have a competitive economy, and that monopoly, militarism, and multinationalization are at the root of our economic crisis. Following are just a few of the points he made to support his thesis:

1. The 200 largest non-financial corporations control at least 60 percent of the net capital assets of all American companies;
2. the 20 largest manufacturing corporations alone control about a third of the total net capital assets and get some 40 cents of every dollar of profit made by all the manufacturing companies in the country;
3. the 100 largest commercial banks control about half of the deposits of the nearly 14,000 banks in the country;
4. the 400 largest U.S. companies played the foreign-exchange markets and gambled against the American dollar, fueling inflation and diverting capital from productive and job-creating investments in the U.S.

SOURCE: *Voice*, January 1981, testimony by UCLA Professor Maurice Zeitlin, California Senate Committee on Industrial Relations, 12/9/80.

UPDATE: Since Maurice Zeitlin's 1981 warning about the impact of monopolization and multinationalization, corporate America has indulged itself in an unparalleled merger mania and spread out on a global basis. In its annual listing of *Fortune*'s Global 500: The World's Largest Corporations, *Fortune* magazine reported (8/5/96) that mergers and restructuring have touched nearly every company in every industry and vaulted a number of them onto the Global 500 list. It noted, "Nowhere is the trend toward globalization more apparent than in the U.S., home of the largest number of global 500 companies. The 153 U.S. companies on the list had an 11 percent increase in profits." *Fortune* also said that while the companies broadened their horizons, they also continued to downsize their existing operations with massive layoffs.

The *Fortune* prognosis was confirmed by a 1997 international study revealing that the rich now control more of the world's wealth. The authors found that the amount of world wealth controlled by millionaires rose an average of eight percent a year in the last decade and accelerated to ten percent in 1996 (*Financial Times*, 4/28/97).

Mergers in the banking industry were equally impressive. The *Institutional Investor* reported (July 1996), "The value of U.S. bank deals completed in just the first four months of this year—$42.3 billion—is nearly twice the previous all-time annual record of $23 billion set in 1995. The record for the largest-ever deal in U.S. banking was broken three times in the past 12 months, most recently by the $10.9 billion acquisition of First Interstate Bancorp by Wells Fargo & Co."

For a confirmation of Zeitlin's thesis on the dangers of monopolization and multinationalization, please see update of "Who Owns America," #10, 1978.

2. Injustice at Greensboro after KKK and Nazi Attack

1981 SYNOPSIS: One of the most flagrant miscarriages of justice in American civil rights history almost went unnoticed.

It started on November 3, 1979, when five Communist Workers Party (CWP) demonstrators were murdered on the streets of Greensboro, North Carolina, by members of the Ku Klux Klan and the American Nazi Party. The murders were recorded live on cameras from four television stations. One year later, the men charged with the brutal killings were acquitted. The story might have ended there if it had not been for the Institute for Southern Studies, a private, nonprofit organization that monitors reports of civil liberties violations.

After its own six-month investigation, the Institute produced evidence that revealed the following: Greensboro officials maintained an "intimate alliance" with the accused; Greensboro police were aware of Klan/Nazi intentions to disrupt the CWP "Death to the Klan" rally two weeks before it occurred; the District Attorney acted to "systematically" weaken the government charge against the Klansmen and Nazis; local government officials, the Justice Department's Community Relations Service, and other agencies used "harassment, intimidation, and red-baiting" to thwart legal, non-violent demonstrations and rallies protesting the killings.

Despite the overwhelming evidence of a miscarriage of justice at Greensboro and the protests of civil rights groups, it was not until March 8, 1982, that the Justice Department impaneled a federal grand jury to hear evidence about the deaths of the five demonstrators.

SOURCES: *The Institute for Southern Studies*, 1981, "The Third of November"; *Organizing Notes*, November/December 1981, "Greensboro, North Carolina: Two Years and No Closer to Justice."

UPDATE: In the years following the Greensboro massacre, criminal charges were brought against the KKK gunmen in both state and federal courts. Despite the overwhelming evidence, the prosecution lost both times. The state jury found the defendants not guilty of murder and the federal jury acquitted them on charges of conspiring to violate the demonstrators' civil rights (*Newsweek*, 4/8/85).

Finally, in 1985, a federal civil suit seeking $48 million in damages was brought by civil rights attorney Danny Sheehan on behalf of relatives of the slain demonstrators and several people wounded by the gunfire. In June, the jury found eight of 45 defendants guilty and ordered them to pay a penalty of $405,000 to the families of the deceased. The eight included members of the Ku Klux Klan, American Nazi Party, and the Greensboro police (*Regardies The Business of Washington*, June 1988).

While this ended the judicial process, the Greensboro massacre will not soon be forgotten. On February 9, 1996, the world premiere of "Greensboro" opened in Princeton, New Jersey. Emily Mann, a Broadway playwright/director, referred to her play as a "theatre of testimony"—a memory play (*Back Stage*, 2/9/96).

3. Burying America in Radioactive Waste

1981 SYNOPSIS: Radioactive waste is accumulating daily throughout the United States and the government doesn't seem to know what to do with it. Following are brief highlights of some of the radioactive waste stories of 1981 along with their sources:

RADIOACTIVE WASTE IN THE SEA—From 1946 to 1970, barges and planes dropped radioactive trash into 50 ocean dumps up and down the east and west coasts of the United States including prime fishing areas that serve the top 20 cities in the country. To this day we don't know how dangerous they are.

SOURCE: *Mother Jones*, July 1981, "You Are What They Eat," by Douglas Foster.

THE MILITARY'S UNKNOWN A-WASTE—While public interest generally focuses on commercial nuclear power plants, wastes from atomic weapons production accounts for half the radioactivity and more than 90 percent of the volume of nuclear waste in the U.S., including some 77 million gallons of high level liquid waste. Most of the weapons-related liquid waste is stored in 169 temporary underground tanks at the Hanford nuclear reservation in Washington.

SOURCE: *Christian Science Monitor*, 12/28/81, "Military's A-Waste— A Growing Problem," by Brad Knickerbocker.

THE $120 MILLION BURIAL CHAMBER THAT DIDN'T WORK—The Department of Energy's (DOE) Waste Isolation Pilot Project in New Mexico, focal point of industry and government hopes for early disposal of nuclear waste, sprung a fatal leak in December 1980. After the DOE spent $120 million carving out a burial chamber in "permanently stable" salt, a drill struck a large body of hot salt water making the site unsuitable for nuclear-waste storage.

SOURCE: *This World, San Francisco Chronicle*, 2/7/82, "Bury the Nuclear Dream," by Daniel Deudney.

WHAT DO YOU DO WITH A DEAD REACTOR?—On July 23, 1976, Pacific Gas & Electric's Humboldt Bay nuclear reactor in Northern California shut down for refueling—and has not reopened since. The plant is located in an earthquake zone and regulators shut it down due to fear of possible ground movement. Now the facility is a leading candidate to become the largest light-water commercial reactor in the nation ever to be decommissioned. The problem is that PG&E apparently does not know how to decommission the nuclear plant.

SOURCE: *Mother Jones*, January 1981, "Taking Apart Your Neighborhood Nuke," by John Ross.

UPDATE: More than 15 years later, radioactive waste is building at an even greater level—nuclear sludge and other highly radioactive by-products of nuclear energy generation are nearly overflowing their storage pools at more than 100 power plants across the country—and the government still doesn't seem to know where to bury it for up to 10,000 years.

Nonetheless, under a 1982 law, the government was committed to start disposing of the radioactive waste by January 31, 1998. That date has now slipped to 2010 and more than $4 billion already has been spent on the project according to a report in the *Los Angeles Daily News* (6/3/97). While Nevada's Yucca Mountain, a site near Death Valley, appears to be the most likely candidate for a permanent repository, politicians were trying to buy time in 1996 by building a temporary storage site on Nevada nuclear test grounds about 100 miles north of Las Vegas and within 50 miles of the Yucca Mountain site (*Los Angeles Times*, 7/17/96; *Minneapolis Star Tribune*, 8/1/96).

Government scientists at a conference on Natural Phenomena Hazards in July 1996 warned that many U.S. nuclear weapons production and storage centers are vulnerable to earthquakes, tornadoes, floods, and other natural disasters. It noted that magma from volcanic activity at the Yucca Mountain site "could ascend directly through the repository...compromising the integrity of the waste isolation system" (Associated Press, 7/15/96).

In late 1996, the Energy Department announced a two-track plan to get rid of 50 tons of highly radioactive surplus plutonium from the nuclear weapons stockpile. Some of the material will be "immobilized"—encased in glass or ceramic blocks and consigned to a permanent underground repository. The rest will be combined with conventional nuclear power plant fuel and burned in commercial electric-generating plants. In selecting the two methods, the Energy Department rejected options such as launching the plutonium into space or dumping it into the ocean (*Washington Post*, 12/9/96).

Meanwhile, the Humboldt Bay nuclear reactor that was shut down 20 years ago was mothballed in 1983 and still has not been decommissioned.

4. A Hungry Child Died Every Two Seconds in 1981

1981 SYNOPSIS: While world leaders debate the nuclear arms race and others warn of untold casualties from a nuclear holocaust, an estimated 50 million people quietly starve to death each year. In addition, according to a United Nation's (UN) report released in 1980, more than a half billion people—one out of every nine human beings—are severely malnourished.

In 1981, the price of a child's life was $100 but much of the world found it too high a price to pay. Thus, every two seconds of 1981, a child paid that price with its life. According to figures projected at this time, 17 million of the children born in 1982 would also die before their fifth birthday. "This [1981] has been, therefore, another year of 'silent emergency'; of 40,000 children quietly dying each day; of 100 million children quietly becoming disabled in mind or body; of 200 million six- to eleven-year-olds quietly watching other children go to school; of one-fifth of the world's people quietly struggling for life itself," the UN report said.

SOURCE: *Senior Scholastic*, 10/16/81, "Earth's Hungry Millions," by Peter M. Jones.

UPDATE: In the 22 years since the first World Food Conference was held in 1974 to deal with imminent famine, the number of undernourished people in the world declined despite an overall growth in population of 1.5 billion. Science came to the rescue with the "green revolution" in agriculture—the use of hybrid varieties of grains in combination with massive doses of chemical fertilizers and pesticides—to greatly increase crop yields.

Faced with 2.5 billion more mouths to feed in the first quarter of the next century, delegates to the second World Food Summit that concluded in Rome on November 17, 1996, once again appealed to science—this time in biotechnology and food-preservation techniques—to save the planet. The problem of hunger is still urgent. An estimated 800 million people are said to be undernourished and some 200 million children go to bed hungry every day (*Los Angeles Times*, 11/18/96).

The Rome summit pledged to cut the number of hungry people from more than 800 million to 400 million by 2010, to enhance the role of women in traditional societies, and to lower the rate of population growth (*Sacramento Bee*, 12/1/96).

5. Our Water is Running Out and What's Left is Being Poisoned

1981 SYNOPSIS: From coast to coast, the water supply, once thought to be unlimited, is disappearing. In early 1981, New York's reservoirs, usually at 80 percent of capacity at that time, were only 34 percent full. In mid-April, 1981, the rural Illinois town of Eldorado had 12 days of water left. The water level in Tucson's 250 wells are declining by two feet a year. The water table at Grant County, Kansas, has dropped more than 100 feet since 1940. Similarly, water levels are falling drastically in the Ogalla aquifer, perhaps the largest underground reserve of fresh water in the world which runs from Texas to South Dakota.

Meanwhile, the nation's remaining water supply is increasingly threatened by chemical contamination. The major villains are dangerous solvents and other compounds, many of them poisonous, discharged by industry.

SOURCES: *The Progressive*, July 1981, "Wringing America Dry," by John Opie, and "Making Deserts Bloom," by Robert L. Reid; National Wildlife Federation, April 1981, "How Safe is the Water We Drink?" by Marvin A. Zeldin.

UPDATE: While the water shortages noted in the 1981 story did not materialize, the contamination of our water continued to be a problem.

On August 6, 1996, President Clinton signed into law the 1996 Safe Drinking Water Act. Termed "significant public health legislation," the Act authorizes $6 billion over the next six years to improve the nation's drinking water and targets federal resources as real health risks (Congressional Press Releases, 8/6/96). The legislation means for the first time, most Americans will receive detailed annual reports on the safety of their tap water. They'll learn the source of their drinking water, whether it contains chemicals or contaminants and what the health consequences might be. The bill also contains a "right to know" provision that guarantees better public access to information and more of it. It requires most public utilities to provide these "plainly worded" reports to customers. Mailings are expected to begin within two to three years (*The Houston Chronicle*, 10/8/96).

Please also see update of "Poisoned Water, Poisoned Land" #10, 1980.

6. Training Terrorists in Florida

1981 SYNOPSIS: While the Reagan Administration publicly opposes international terrorism, terrorists are being trained in the United States with its knowledge, if not assistance.

Guerrilla training camps are openly operating in Florida with the knowledge of the federal government and in apparent violation of federal law. While an investigation by the Pacifica National News Service found no proof of active U.S. involvement in the camps, the Justice Department, by passive acceptance, condones their existence.

Camp Libertad, located only five miles outside Miami, is one of the camps where exiled Cubans and Nicaraguans prepare for attacks on their homelands. The 600-acre camp is surrounded by barbed wire and guarded by men with AR-15s, the basic combat weapon of the American Army. The camp's paramilitary activities, once limited to small groups who trained in the Everglades, has expanded into a large, well-organized structure of camps. Americans, mostly ex-Green Berets, participate in the training.

The activities appear to violate a number of federal laws that prohibit any organized attempt by private citizens to overthrow or undermine another government. One of these laws, the U.S. Neutrality Act, states, in part, that it is unlawful to "provide or prepare a means for, or furnish the money for or take part in, any military or naval expedition or enterprise" against any government with which the United States is at peace.

SOURCE: *Pacifica National News Service*, Los Angeles, California, 9/9/81, "The Miami Connection," by Ronnie Loveller.

UPDATE: Terrorist or guerrilla training has changed in at least two ways since the 1981 story. While Camp Libertad once trained Cubans and Nicaraguans for attacks on their homelands, unofficial militia camps now train U.S. citizens for attacks on their own government. The existence of the militia camps, such as the 80-acre Michigan Militia camp at Wolverine, Michigan, started to receive media attention in the aftermath of the tragic Oklahoma City bombing (*The Boston Herald*, 4/24/95).

There also is the official U.S. terrorist training of Latin American officers at the School of the Americas at Fort Benning, Georgia. Critics charge that the foreign officers receive training in executions and torture. On September 20, 1996, the Pentagon released training manuals that contained references to executing guerrillas, beatings, drunkenness, and coercion as methods of obtaining information (Associated Press, 9/21/96). Alumni of the school have been implicated in the murders of priests, nuns, and others in Latin America, including the 1989 murders of six Jesuits and two women in El Salvador. The School of Americas Watch, an activist group opposed to training terrorists, holds protests at the school and advocates closing it down (*Newsday*, 8/15/96).

7. The Insanity of Nuclear Weapons

1981 SYNOPSIS: The more Americans learn about the true hazards of nuclear weapons, the more concerned they are with the possibility of a nuclear holocaust. Following are a few of the nuclear-related stories, and their sources, that should have received more media coverage in 1981:

NUCLEAR ACCIDENTS WILL HAPPEN—On November 2, 1981, we almost nuked Scotland but few Americans ever heard about it. A fully-armed Poseidon missile was dropped 17 feet from a crane during a transfer operation from the submarine, USS Holland, to the USS Los Alamos, a mother ship. Fortunately for Scotland, the Poseidon did not detonate, although it could have.

SOURCE: *New Statesman*, 11/27/81, "Accidents Will Happen," by Norman Solomon and Duncan Campbell.

THE REAL "BIAS" IN OUR NUCLEAR STRATEGY—Recent reports indicate that our super-sophisticated intercontinental ballistic missiles (ICBMs) may not be as accurate as originally thought. The "bias factor," resulting from unpredictable variations in gravity, atmospheric conditions, and wind velocity, could throw a missile off target by as much as a quarter of a mile, failing to destroy a hardened missile silo target.

SOURCE: *Inquiry*, 10/5/81, "Bombs Awry," by Fred Kaplan.

UNCLE SAM AND NUCLEAR PROLIFERATION—Since 1959, the State Department, the Export-Import Bank, and U.S. producers of nuclear reactors have worked together to supply 49 reactors to 12 nations throughout the world, including Libya, Iraq, and South Africa. We don't really know how those reactors are being used.

SOURCE: *San Francisco Chronicle*, 9/6/81, "How U.S. Spread Nuclear Power Around the World," by Howard Jaffe.

WHAT CALIFORNIANS DON'T KNOW—Many Californians are living in an enormous nuclear bunker and they aren't aware of it. The large-scale, secretive, and virtually self-regulated use of radioactive materials by military bases in California include an estimated 1200 nuclear weapons on at least 12 bases (more than half of which are located in or near major urban areas and some are sitting on active earthquake faults) and as many as 19 Navy vessels powered by 29 nuclear reactors with home ports in California harbors.

SOURCE: *New West*, April 1981, "Where the Bombs Are," by David E. Kaplan.

NO "SAFE" LEVEL OF RADIATION—New research being conducted at the Lawrence Livermore weapons laboratory in California and the Oak Ridge National Laboratory in Tennessee suggests that 15 years of radiation research may be invalid with the amount of radiation toxicity understated.

SOURCE: *Science*, 5/22/81, "New A-bomb Studies Alter Radiation Estimates," by Eliot Marshal.

RADIATION FROM UNDERGROUND—While not as dangerous as the open-air nuclear tests of the 1950s, the underground nuclear tests in Nevada exposed Americans to dangerous levels of radiation through the '60s, '70s, and since. On September 25, 1980, an underground test broke through the earth scattering its radiation to the winds in a process known as venting. Ventings have been covered up and kept from public disclosure because of their classified status. However, in 1980, General Mahlon Gates, operation manager for the Nevada test site, admitted that at least 40 ventings had occurred.

SOURCE: *The Washington Monthly*, January 1981, "Another A-bomb Cover-up," by Raymond E. Brim and Patricia Condon.

UPDATE: The end of the Cold War in 1989 led to a dismantling of nuclear weapons in the United States as well as abroad. As a result, according to Secretary of State Warren Christopher, "Every American is more secure." Christopher noted, "Thousands of nuclear warheads, built to destroy America, have themselves been destroyed. Those that remain in Russia no longer target our homes. Three of the four nuclear states that succeeded the Soviet Union have abandoned nuclear weapons" (*Time*, 5/27/96).

Even Helen Caldicott, one of the world's leading anti-nuclear activists, is somewhat optimistic. In a lengthy cover story in *The Nation* (4/29/96), Caldicott suggests, "The window of opportunity to eliminate nuclear weapons is once and for all wide open: Never before in the fifty-year history of the nuclear age has it been possible to envision global nuclear disarmament, and an end to plutonium production as well."

However, Caldicott also warns of continuing problems: the threat of nuclear war, impending nuclear meltdown, nuclear waste contamination, nuclear space explosions, and nuclear terrorism. She concludes, "I wrote in *Nuclear Madness* in 1979, 'As a physician, I contend that nuclear technology threatens life on our planet with extinction. If present trends continue, the air we breathe, the food we eat, and the water we drink will soon be contaminated with enough radioactive pollutants to pose a potential health hazard far greater than any plague humanity has ever experienced.' I still stand by those words."

On July 29, 1996, China conducted a nuclear test despite worldwide protests, and shortly before international negotiators started discussing a global testing ban. China, the only nuclear power still conducting nuclear tests, promised it would be the last one (Associated Press, 7/29/96).

Please also see update of "The U.S. Against the World on Nuclear Issues," #7, 1982.

8. Union Busting With Briefcases Not Blackjacks

1981 SYNOPSIS: A new breed of union busters, known as labor relations consultants, stalks the land. Modern Management, Inc., the largest of the new consulting firms, employs 100 consultants, most of them with advanced degrees in psychology, business, or industrial relations.

Union leaders charge that the sole intent of these consultants is to prevent union organizing and to eliminate existing unions.

An unpublicized investigation by the U.S. House Subcommittee on Labor-Management Relations concluded that firms such as Modern Management "come dangerously close to justifying whatever means are necessary" to defeat unions. Some techniques show how to: legally weed out potential union sympathizers before they are hired; turn supervisors into an anti-union organizing force while restricting campaigning by union supporters; make employees fear reprisals for unionization or expect rewards for voting against the union; and delay elections or contract negotiations so long that union sympathizers lose faith in the union.

SOURCES: *National Catholic Reporter*, 4/17/81, "Congress, Labor Board Reports Blast 'Anti-Union' Consulting Firms"; *The Nation*, 6/13/81, "Secrets of a Union Buster"; both by Kinsey Wilson and Steve Askin.

UPDATE: The labor movement has been in retreat ever since former President Ronald Reagan fired 11,400 striking government air-traffic controllers en masse on August 5, 1981. The trend toward union-busting firms, portrayed in the 1981 *Censored* story, continued to increase and, according to a *Los Angeles Times* story (9/5/93), has been variously estimated to be a $100-million to $1-billion annual enterprise. Law firms devoted to management-side labor law tend to lead the assault. The "Report and Recommendations by the Dunlop Commission on the Future of Worker-Management Relations" led a reviewer to conclude that organized labor has been beaten "nearly to death." But the report also concluded that a reaction to union-busting has started and that a revival of unions can be expected (*Challenge*, March 1996).

One hopeful sign for unions was the Senate defeat of a national right-to-work law, which would have further weakened the labor movement, on July 10, 1996 (*Arkansas Democrat-Gazette*, 7/11/96).

For the record, Modern Management Inc., the union-busting firm cited in the 1981 synopsis, is no longer in business (*Philadelphia Business Journal*, 11/11/94).

9. Defense Vulnerability and the High Cost of Whistle-Blowing

1981 SYNOPSIS: The central nervous system of America's military machine is a data processing network called Wimex. Unfortunately, this mighty communications system does not work. The 35 Honeywell computers the Department of Defense bought in 1971 were obsolete before they were installed; an agency report in 1976 indicated the "network crashes approximately every 35 minutes"; a 1977 exercise at six of the sites revealed that the network functions only 38 percent of the time at four of them; and the giant early warning NORAD site in Colorado was plagued by false warnings of nuclear attacks.

One person, John Bradley, an engineer originally charged with testing the Wimex prototype, discovered the problem in 1973. Since then he has been trying to convince people that the computers controlling the defense of the nation are dangerous, incompetent, and may, in fact, trigger a holocaust.

For his efforts, Bradley was first criticized, then transferred, and later charged with "inefficiency, resisting competent authority and making false and misleading statements about (the system's) reliability." He was then fired.

On March 8, 1982, the House Government Operations Committee reported the warning system is plagued by "severe and potentially catastrophic deficiencies" because of failings in the Pentagon's procurement of computer equipment.

SOURCES: *Inquiry*, September 1981, "The High-Cost of Whistle-Blowing," by Rhonda Brown and Paul Matteucci; *San Francisco Examiner*, 3/9/82, "Our Feeble Missile Attack Warning System."

UPDATE: After considerable attention and billions of dollars, Wimex finally started to operate correctly, and, in fact, played a key communications role for President George Bush during the Gulf War. However, Canada Newswire reported (3/7/96) that with more than 100 million computers now linking telecommunications used by both civilians and the military, society could face an electronic Pearl Harbor of epic proportions. It noted the "Pentagon has revealed that Wimex computers are broken into twice daily and that one hacker was recently caught downloading 'tasking orders' for Air Force jets."

While the Major Fraud Act, passed in 1988, was supposed to protect whistleblowers who are fired as a result of furnishing information, the reality is that the practice of firing whistleblowers in corporate America continues today. Nor is this injustice limited to corporate America. For example, on December 24, 1996, *The New York Times* reported that a respected chemical weapons researcher investigating the illnesses of Gulf War veterans for the Arms Control and Disarmament Agency and the State Department was abruptly dismissed for talking to the veterans and government whistleblowers.

10. Cultured Killers—Biological Weapons and Third World Targets

1981 SYNOPSIS: Following World War II, biological warfare (BW) was advanced through funding by the CIA, the Department of Defense (DOD), and the Navy with hundreds of BW projects at corporations and universities throughout the country.

The research was banned in 1969 due to public pressure. Existing BW stocks were to be destroyed and further research confined to "defensive purposes." Yet, in 1975, it was learned that a CIA project still maintained BW stocks at Fort Detrick, Maryland, with covert connections to "specific assassination plans."

Race-specific weapons such as cocci (Valley Fever) and tuberculosis have been researched only by the DOD as biological warfare agents. Third World countries are considered to be particularly vulnerable targets for a BW attack due to dispersed rural populations with poor health and nutritional status and barely sufficient agriculture for sustenance.

There is a lack of distinction between offensive research, which is banned, and defensive research, which is still permitted. The DOD says it is funding cocci research to develop a vaccine.

SOURCE: *Science for the People*, July 1981, by A. Conadera.

UPDATE: The #6 *Censored* story of 1987 revealed that despite the international agreement which banned development of germ-warfare agents, the Pentagon's research budget for infectious diseases and toxins has increased ten-fold since fiscal 1981. Further, most of the 1986 budget of $42 million went to 24 U.S. university campuses where the world's most deadly organisms are being cultured in campus labs. Similarly, the #6 *Censored* story of 1993 revealed that the U.S. Army has resumed biological agent testing at its Dugway, Utah, test site which had been declared unsafe a decade earlier.

By the mid-1990s, a new acronym, NBC, was being used to describe nuclear, biological, and chemical warfare. The use of biological weapons, at one time unimaginable, had become a reality. On March 20, 1995, a Japanese doomsday cult, Aum Shinri Kyo (Supreme Truth), unleashed a nerve gas attack in Tokyo's subway that killed 12 and sickened more than 5,500 commuters (*The Independent*, 7/17/96). In mid-June 1996, the U.S. Defense Department admitted that American troops in the 1991 Gulf War may have been exposed to Sarin, the same nerve agent used in Tokyo (*Newsday*, 6/29/96).

In late August 1996, the U.S. Army's long-delayed, $12 billion program to destroy the nation's chemical weapons through incineration was started in a new $650 million Tooele Chemical Agent Disposal Facility southwest of Salt Lake City. Shortly after it started, it was shut down. A small amount of Sarin nerve gas was found in the end-of-the-line filters that clean factory air before releasing it into the desert skies. After being closed five days, the plant started up again and plant officials assured its 600 workers and the public the gas leak had posed no health risk (*The New York Times*, 9/1/96). Nonetheless, low levels of Sarin were again detected at the plant in late January 1997. Once again, officials assured critics none of the Sarin was released outside (*USA Today*, 1/27/97).

.

CHAPTER 7—1982

Fraudulent Safety Tests Deceive the American People

While the top mainstream news story of 1982 dealt with the U.S. economy, it still ignored the basic causes for the crisis, cited as the top *Censored* story of 1981. According to the Associated Press, the top ten news stories of the year were:

1. The U.S. economy
2. Seven die from cyanide-laced extra-strength Tylenol
3. War in the Falklands
4. The death of Leonid Brezhnev
5. Israel invades Lebanon
6. John Hinckley, Jr. found innocent of Reagan assassination attempt by reason of insanity
7. Massacre in Palestinian camps in Lebanon
8. First artificial heart transplant
9. Air Florida crash in Washington, D.C.
10. Football strike.

THE TOP TEN CENSORED STORIES OF 1982

—And What Has Happened to Them Since

1. Fraudulent Testing Provides an Illusion of Safety

1982 SYNOPSIS: Industrial Bio-Test (IBT) was the largest testing lab in the country. It conducted about one-third of the toxicity and cancer testing of chemicals in America—as many as 22,500 safety tests over the last decade.

In 1981, the former president of IBT and three ex-subordinates were indicted for allegedly fraudulent tests on four specific chemicals. The four suspect chemicals were TCC, an antibacterial agent used in deodorant soaps; naprosyn, an arthritis medication; and seconor and nemacur, both pesticides. During the experiments, IBT substituted live rats for those which died and did not keep proper identification of the test animals; it also provided the Food and Drug Administration (FDA) with false information and made a practice of shredding documents.

IBT had conducted tests for nearly 30 years and its corporate clients included Proctor and Gamble, Armour, Upjohn, Dow, 3M, and Shell; government clients included the Army, Department of Defense, Environmental Protection Agency, the FDA; and the World Health Organization.

Meanwhile, a major investigation by *Mother Jones* and the Center for Investigative Reporting into testing laboratories, standard-setting boards, and regulatory agencies that oversee the science of testing for safety, revealed that much of the research aimed at ensuring a safer world is either fraudulent or useless.

SOURCES: *FOCUS/MIDWEST*, September 1982, "Testing Fraud," by Judith and Mark Miller; *Mother Jones* and the Center for Investigative Reporting, 1982, "The Illusion of Safety," by Mark Dowie, Douglas Foster, Carolyn Marshall, David Weir, and Jonathan King.

UPDATE: Three top executives of Industrial Bio-Test Laboratories were indicted and convicted in 1983 for claims that they had conducted safety tests on pesticides when, in fact, they had not (*New York Times*, 3/2/91). Edwin Johnson, director of the EPA pesticide office, assured the public the IBT affair was not the "hidden public-health disaster that some had feared." However an analysis of the IBT case by MIT's *Technology Review* (February 1984) warned that despite the EPA assurances, the motive for laboratories to cheat was still there and that EPA had little commitment to enforcing quality standards.

The MIT warning was prescient. In March 1991, the EPA launched another investigation into laboratory testing fraud. Craven Laboratories of Austin, Texas, was accused of understating the residues of pesticides widely used on fruits and vegetables (*Washington Post*, 3/13/91). In February 1994, Dr. Don Allen Craven was sentenced to five years in prison for faking dozens of tests meant to detect pesticides in food, and he and his company were ordered to pay $3.7 million in restitution. Fourteen ex-employees also pleaded guilty. The Craven Labs case triggered a $15 million nationwide review of pesticides used on food crops. Nonetheless, skeptics charged that the testing system still didn't work and questioned EPA's ability to police private labs (*The Dallas Morning News*, 2/26/94).

Corporate clients of the test labs were not always unwitting participants in fraud. In October 1991, Monsanto Company was charged with using falsified lab data on animal studies that were used to judge the health and environmental effects of polychlorinated biphenyls (PCBs), once used as lubricants for electrical transformers. The fraudulent tests were conducted by IBT during the 1969-1971 period (*St. Louis Post Dispatch*, 10/29/91). In September 1994, Thermal Science Inc., maker of a fire retardant, was indicted for conspiring with a St. Louis testing lab, Industrial Testing Laboratories, to fabricate tests and falsify test results. The retardant, Thermo-Lag, which the Nuclear Regulatory Commission admits is deficient, is used in 70 nuclear power plants (*Chicago Sun-Times*, 9/30/94).

2. Americans "Bugged" by Super-Secret Spy Court

1982 SYNOPSIS: Unbeknownst to most Americans, there is a super-secret spy court in Washington, D.C. It passes judgment on intelligence agency requests to spy on Americans in this country.

The U.S. Foreign Intelligence Surveillance Court was created in 1978 following the Watergate era when "national security" was often invoked to justify excessive domestic surveillance of U.S. citizens. The court was charged with the task of preventing such constitutional abuses.

The court, located in a lead-enclosed vault (to prevent it from being bugged) on the sixth floor of the Justice Department, is unlike any other court in this country. It isn't listed as an official government operation; it doesn't appear in the Government Organization Manual; it is not mentioned in the United States Court Directory.

The court's decisions are never published; at the end of each year, it issues a two-sentence annual report. The first lists the number of applications for surveillance; the second shows the number approved.

The court's record is remarkable. Through 1981, it heard a total of 962 requests. It has issued 962 orders allowing electronic surveillance. Not one request has been denied.

The secrecy surrounding the court is exceptional. One spokesman for the Justice Department acknowledged that the court exists but refused to say where.

SOURCES: *San Francisco Examiner*, 10/24/82, "America's Super-Secret Spy Court," by Laurence McQuillan.

UPDATE: The Foreign Intelligence Surveillance Act (FISA), a 1978 law that permits secret bugging and wiretaps of individuals suspected of being agents of a hostile foreign government or international terrorist organization, even when the target is not suspected of committing any crime, has come a long way since the 1982 *Censored* story.

In an extensive investigative article, the *Washington Post* (6/23/96) reviews the background and current activities of the FISA, and its super-secret court in the Justice Department. It reveals that unannounced search and surveillance efforts for reasons of "national security," without specific evidence of any crime, is increasingly common. In 1994, federal courts authorized more wiretaps for intelligence-gathering and national security purposes than they did to investigate ordinary federal crimes—576 over 554. In 1995, the court authorized a record 697 national security wiretaps on American soil, outside normal constitutional procedures. While thousands of applications for wiretaps had been made by mid-1996, the court never rejected even one. Its approval record remains at 100 percent.

Further, the *Post* reported that in early 1996 the Justice Department asked for a change in its FISA charter to include criminal prosecutions as a secondary purpose of counterintelligence investigations. While civil libertarians objected, strongly opposing the proposal to expand the purpose of such "black-bag jobs," Congress dismissed such arguments and passed the law.

The *Post* article said, "For the first time in modern U.S. history, Congress had institutionalized a process for physical searches outside of Fourth Amendment standards."

3. Is This the End of Equal Opportunity in America?

1982 SYNOPSIS: Without real public input, without vociferous public debate, and without significant media coverage, the Reagan Administration has attacked the federal equal opportunity program in America.

In January 1982, Max Benavidez, editor of *Equal Opportunity Forum*, warned that the federal machinery for the protection of equal opportunity was almost totally destroyed: "From federal contract compliance (Department of Labor) to Title IX (Department of Education) to employment (Equal Employment Opportunity) to government advocacy of the law (Department of Justice), the Reagan Administration has stripped away the traditional role of government in protecting the rights of disenfranchised citizens."

In December 1982, his ominous warning was given credibility by a study released by Women Employed, a Chicago-based working women's organization. It found that "dramatic reduction in enforcement activity, combined with agency policy changes and budget cuts, threaten to dismantle the entire federal enforcement apparatus. The damage currently being done to the federal equal opportunity enforcement mechanisms will set back efforts toward that goal for years to come."

SOURCES: *Equal Opportunity Forum*, January 1982, by Max Benavidez; *Labor Notes*, 12/21/82, "Reagan Administration Dismantles Equal Opportunity Enforcement."

UPDATE: Affirmative action became a major issue in the 1996 presidential election year. Both of the top candidates agreed some change was necessary. While Bill Clinton said, "Mend it, don't end it," Bob Dole said, "I think now we've reached a point where we need to move on." Then the nation looked to California where a controversial referendum, Proposition 209, designed to end state government-sponsored affirmative action programs, had been put on the California ballot. On November 5, 1996, California voters overwhelmingly voted to end affirmative action. The vote in favor of 209 was heavily Republican, white, and male (*Los Angeles Times*, 11/7/96).

The passage of 209 ended the political campaign, but the bitter debate about fairness and opportunity had just started. The ballots were hardly counted before student protests erupted on California campuses and a federal judge issued an order temporarily blocking Proposition 209. The proposition began its lengthy and costly course to the U.S. Supreme Court. And the 1982 warning about the end of equal opportunity in America suddenly became terrifyingly real.

4. Agent White: The Super Agent Orange

1982 SYNOPSIS: When Agent Orange, the well-known chemical killer, wasn't strong enough to do the job in Vietnam, the U.S. Army brought in a defoliant known as Agent White.

A powerful pesticide manufactured and sold by Dow Chemical under the trade name of Tordon, Agent White is used as an agricultural chemical. Its generic name is picloram. Tordon products are so poisonous that the Environmental Protection Agency (EPA), which registers more than 2,000 pesticides, classifies Tordon as one of 37 "restricted use" pesticides. Only trained applicators with a special permit are allowed to use it.

Tordon has been used most heavily in forested rural areas like Cherokee County, North Carolina. Now, Cherokee County residents believe that picloram, liberally applied to forest and farmland from one end of Cherokee to the other for as long as anyone can remember, is washing off the land and poisoning groundwater supplies from which most county residents draw their water. And, they believe it is killing more than vegetation.

In 1976, less than one in seven people died in Cherokee from cancer, a figure below the national average. By 1979, nearly one in four died of cancer countywide—60 percent above the nation's average and nearly double the state average. Since 1979, Cherokee physicians say cancer-related deaths appear to be even more numerous.

Dow Chemical claims that Tordon is no more lethal than table salt. Dow bases its evidence on two studies done by Industrial Bio-Test Labs of Illinois and a third done by GulfSouth Research Institute.

SOURCE: *Inquiry*, 3/15/82, "Agent White: It Kills Weeds, Bushes, Trees— and Maybe People," by Keith Schneider.

UPDATE: Three months after the *Inquiry* article about Tordon, *The New York Times* (6/7/82) confirmed Tordon was suspected of causing an increase in cancer deaths in western North Carolina. After a significant increase in the number of deaths due to cancer, a leading pathologist said, "There's no doubt in my mind that picloram (Tordon) is a carcinogen."

In early 1983, the *Washington Post* (1/30/83) reported the controversy raging over allegations of a cancer epidemic caused or abetted by Tordon, and said there were "lawsuits pending in at least seven states alleging Tordon has caused cancer and other illness."

Despite the fact that the Army stopped using Tordon in the Vietnam War because of potential ecological damage, despite the controversy over the carcinogenic effect of Tordon, despite the lawsuits across the country, and despite the fact that the discredited Industrial Biotest Labs had tested the chemical for toxicity for Dow (see the 1982 #1 *Censored* story about fraudulent testing labs), Tordon is still in use today. For example, *The Denver Post* reported July 6, 1996, that despite the public protests, helicopters sprayed 880 acres of Colorado's Boulder County with the herbicide Tordon.

5. What is Really Happening in Central America?

1982 SYNOPSIS: The 1982 media coverage of the deadly and widespread battles taking place in Central America was limited and confusing. The paradoxical media reports on El Salvador and the Nicaragua/Honduras situation has made it virtually impossible to ascertain what is really going on.

But while the media reports from El Salvador, Nicaragua, and Honduras might be limited and often incomprehensible, we hear even less from Guatemala, where the situation may be even worse.

When General Efraim Rios Montt took power in a military coup in Guatemala on March 23, 1982, he was lauded by some as a savior. For example, commenting on the situation in Guatemala at the time, *The New York Times* said, "Left-wing terrorism is quiet after a decade and a half of turmoil."

Montt, a born-again Christian, once was forced to leave the country because of public outcry over his repression and bloody campaign against Indian campesinos. When he returned to power, the Vietnamization of Guatemala was stepped up with pacification programs, fortified hamlets, and search-and-destroy missions in what Montt referred to as a "beans and rifles" program.

SOURCES: *Four Arrows: The Horror and the Hope* and various news sources.

UPDATE: Guatemala, a key indicator as to what happens in Central America, became the subject of two additional *Censored* stories: the #15 story of 1988 which asked, "What's Happening in Guatemala?" and the #5 story of 1989, which charged there was "Guatemalan Blood on U.S. Hands."

Nevertheless, it was not until March of 1995 that Guatemala was finally put on top of the media's news agenda with revelations that a Guatemalan military officer on the CIA payroll had been involved in the murders of an American citizen and a guerrilla commander. Questions raised by Project Censored since 1982 were finally answered with sordid disclosures of the complex web of relations between various agencies of the U.S. government and the Guatemalan military over the last 40 years.

Guatemala's civil war was the longest and deadliest in Central America, having taken the lives of up to 200,000 unarmed civilians, primarily highland Indians. It started in 1960, six years after the 1954 U.S. intervention ousted the popularly elected government of Jacobo Arbenz, and ended in 1995. The war officially ended with an accord signed December 29, 1996.

Today, Guatemala has a new president, Alvaro Arzu, who has plans to advance peace negotiations and to establish civilian control over the army. Additionally, the Clinton Administration does not seem ideologically committed to the Guatemalan army, as was the case with Reagan and Bush (*Foreign Policy*, 6/22/96).

Please also see update of "Guatemalan Blood," #5, 1989.

6. Ronald Reagan: America's Chief Censor

1982 SYNOPSIS: Late in 1982, *New York Times* journalist David Burnham sounded a warning that deserved far more coverage than it received. Burnham charged:

"In its first 21 months in office, the Reagan Administration has taken several actions that reduce the information available to the public about the operation of the government, the economy, the environment, and public health. The actions have included increasing the authority of govern-

THIS MODERN WORLD by TOM TOMORROW

THE DEBATE OVER A T.V. RATINGS SYSTEM INITIALLY STRUCK *US* AS A LUDICROUS WASTE OF *TIME*...

MR. PRESIDENT-- SLOBODAN MILOSEVIC ON LINE 2!

WELL, TELL HIM TO CALL BACK! I'M WORKING ON THE V-CHIP RIGHT NOW!

...BUT THEN WE STARTED THINKING ABOUT OTHER THINGS THE PRESIDENT AND CONGRESS *COULD* BE SPENDING THEIR TIME ON-- LIKE, SAY, DISMANTLING WHAT'S LEFT OF THE SOCIAL SAFETY NET--

--AND IT OCCURRED TO US THAT WASTING AS MUCH OF THEIR TIME AS *POSSIBLE* PROBABLY ISN'T A BAD IDEA...

...WHICH IS WHY WE'D LIKE TO PROPOSE A FEW *OTHER* POSSIBLE PUBLIC CRUSADES FOR 1997...

ment officials to classify data, cutting back on the collection of statistics, eliminating hundreds of government publications, and reducing the staff of the National Archives."

Columbia Journalism Review editors noted while presidents traditionally have regarded the Freedom of Information (FOI) Act with discomfort, President Reagan "has tried everything from amputation to lobotomy" to weaken it.

An article in *Organizing Notes* reported how journalists, scholars, consumer advocates, environmentalists, labor unions, civil rights activists, and countless other citizens regularly used the FOI act to produce disclosures that benefit the lives of nearly all Americans.

SOURCES: *The New York Times*, 11/14/82, "Government Restricting Flow of Information to the Public," by David Burnham; *Columbia Journalism Review*, March/April 1983, "Keeping Government Honest"; *Organizing Notes*, May 1982, "Government Secrecy," by Maureen Weaver.

UPDATE: If Reagan paved the way for increased governmental censorship, as noted above, and Bush continued the assault on the First Amendment, one might expect Bill Clinton to reverse the trend. However, while the assault on the First Amendment is not as formidable as it was during the Reagan/Bush era, Clinton has also raised some free speech questions. These include his push for three hours a week of children's educational programming, his call for "family programming," his anti-tobacco crusade, and his signature on the Telecommunications Bill which requires new TVs to have the v-chip to lock out violent shows and bans "indecent" material from the Internet.

The specter of governmental censorship is increasingly real because the news media who are supposed to keep such measures in check fail to function as watchdogs on the government and our society. As *Foreign Policy* (3/22/96) points out, "Correspondents, editors, pundits, and publishers who work for major media outlets tend to see themselves as members of an opinion-making elite. They consider themselves on an intellectual and social par with high-level policymakers, an attitude that increases the prospect of their being co-opted by ambitious and determined policymakers." This is an attitude that leads to self-censorship.

7. The United States Against the World on Nuclear Issues

1982 SYNOPSIS: On December 9, 1982, the United Nations General Assembly voted on three resolutions concerning the nuclear issue and world peace.

Two of the resolutions, both opposed by the United States, would ban testing nuclear weapons but not nuclear explosions for peaceful purposes. The votes were 124 votes for and 2 against with 19 abstentions on the first resolution; 114 for and 4 against with 26 abstentions on the second.

The third resolution called for a treaty outlawing all nuclear blasts.

It was overwhelmingly adopted by a vote of 111 to 1 with 35 abstentions. The United States alone voted against the rest of the world.

Kenneth L. Adelman—accused of lying to the Senate Foreign Relations Committee when it was considering his nomination by President Reagan to head the nation's Arms Control and Disarmament Agency—defended the U.S. vote, saying the resolution would not reduce the nuclear threat.

SOURCE: *The New York Times*, 12/10/82, "U.N., in 3 Votes, Asks Ban on Nuclear Arms Tests," by Eric Pace.

UPDATE: In 1996, ironically on the 51st anniversary of the nuclear bombing of Hiroshima and Nagasaki, delegates from 61 nations of the Conference on Disarmament met in Geneva, Switzerland, to complete negotiations on a Comprehensive Nuclear Test Ban Treaty. Negotiations reached an impasse when India vetoed the treaty, but a group of nations agreed to informally present the U.N. General Assembly with a report on the conference's work. On September 10, 1996, the General Assembly overwhelmingly endorsed a global treaty to ban all nuclear test blasts (Associated Press,

9/11/96). The vote was 158 for the treaty, with three against (India, Libya, and Bhutan) and five abstentions.

Fourteen years after the United States was the lone dissenter in the world for banning nuclear tests, it finally joined the rest of the world community and voted for the Comprehensive Nuclear Test Ban Treaty. On September 24, 1996, using the same black pen that John F. Kennedy used 33 years earlier to sign the world's first nuclear pact, President Clinton put the opening signature on the global treaty (*USA Today*, 9/25/96). However the treaty still requires passage by a two-thirds majority of the U.S. Senate, where some Republicans have reservations about the pact (Associated Press, 9/25/96).

8. American Industrialists Traded with the Nazis

1982 SYNOPSIS: In a shocking exposé of American corporate greed, investigative author Charles Higham revealed a disgraceful if not criminal collaboration of some of America's largest corporations with Nazi Germany not only before but *during World War II.*

Higham documents his claims with information gathered through the National Archives and the Freedom of Information Act. His book, *Trading with the Enemy,* gives evidence that such industrial and financial giants as DuPont, Rockefeller, Ford, Chase Manhattan Bank, ITT, General Motors, and Standard Oil collaborated with the Nazis either for monetary gain or because they were Nazi sympathizers hoping for a German victory.

Higham claims that Standard Oil, among other examples, supplied fuel for German U-boats through neutral Spain. It continued providing fuel until 1944 and in the process contributed to the deaths of numerous American merchant seamen.

ITT was the supplier of communications and other equipment for the buzz bombs that devastated London.

Ford maintained a motor plant in Vichy France that turned out tanks and troop carriers for the Third Reich.

Chase Manhattan Bank trafficked in the gold market through the Nazi-controlled Bank for International Settlement in Basel. The source for some of the gold it bought and sold: dentures and wedding rings from death camps.

Most of the corporations were interlocked with the German industrial giant I.G. Farben, the company that produced the poison gas for the death camps and ran the largest camp, Auschwitz, for its slave labor.

SOURCE: *Trading with the Enemy: An Exposé of the Nazi-Money 1933-1949*, by Charles Higham, Delacorte Publishing, NY, 1982; *San Francisco Chronicle*, 2/9/83, review by Carl Vogel.

UPDATE: Charles Higham, author of the 1982 source, *Trading with the Enemy*, wrote a follow-up book, *American Swastika*, published by Doubleday in 1985. In this well-researched book about spies, Nazi sympathizers, and anti-Semitic public officials, Higham concluded that "forces of camouflage, protection, and support for the anti-Semitic cause still exist in the United States" (*The New York Times*, 6/23/85).

In 1953, the assets of I.G. Farben, which American companies worked with during World War II, were divided; the company today remains basically a trust to settle claims and lawsuits from the Nazi era (*Des Moines Register*, 8/27/95). While I.G. Farben rejected claims from survivors in the past, on July 3, 1996, the German Constitutional Court ruled that slave laborers from the Nazi era can at last press their claims in court (*The London Times*, 7/4/96). On August 21, 1996, about 70 surviving slave workers sold by the Nazis to I.G. Farben more than 50 years ago protested outside a shareholders' meeting in Frankfurt to press for compensation (*USA Today*, 8/22/96).

Additionally, while the story of looted Nazi gold in Swiss banks made headlines in late 1996, there was no mention of Chase Manhattan Bank's alleged trafficking in the gold market through a Nazi-controlled bank.

Ironically, the 1917 Trading With the Enemy Act, which was ignored by the U.S. government during World War II when American corporations traded with the Nazis, is now being used to sanction Cuba (*Washington Post*, 6/24/95).

9. Politicians and Fertilizers Threaten Nation's Food Supply

1982 SYNOPSIS: In February 1982, the Congressional General Accounting Office reported that the American food production system, which feeds the United States and ten percent of the rest of the world, "is threatened by growing scarcity of basic resources." It forecast a food crisis that may dramatically overshadow the energy crisis over the next decade.

President Reagan responded to this pessimistic forecast by encouraging America's farmers to take a record 82.3 million acres out of production. In fact, more than one out of every three acres of land normally planted with major crops will be idle under this new federal program.

Meanwhile, *The New Farm*, an agricultural trade journal, ran a six-part series revealing how America's farmers could save billions of dollars while being more productive. The series pointed out how soil testing labs routinely over-prescribe fertilizers. Test plots harvested at the *New Farm's* Rodale Research Center revealed the amount of fertilizer recommended by the 70 test labs studied in the series was totally useless.

The senior researcher in the study estimated that unreliable test lab practices exposed by the magazine's series are causing farmers to literally waste about $2 billion a year on unnecessary fertilizer. The study revealed how America's farmers could save billions of dollars and still maintain, if not increase, their yield.

SOURCES: *The New Farm,* January-September 1982, "Testing...Testing" by George DeVault; *San Francisco Chronicle*, 3/23/83, "One-third of Farmland to Lie Idle."

UPDATE: Since *The New Farm* warning in 1982, there has been increasing concern with the toxic effects of fertilizers and the financial loss from over-fertilizing. Meanwhile, the trend toward organic farming has been growing. Richard Taylor, a commercial grower in Fallbrook, California, did a complete turnaround when he noticed his plants were turning brown because of over-fertilizing. He switched to organic growing methods, his plants thrived, and he went on to become president of the local chapter of the California Certified Organic Farmers (*Los Angeles Times*, 11/5/92). Disney World, which employs 500 people in horticulture and agriculture, uses satellite precision farming methods to tell how much fertilizer to apply, which saves money by not over-fertilizing and improves production (*Chicago Tribune*, 11/27/94). The nation's wine business is also curtailing reliance on pesticides, herbicides, and artificial fertilizers and moving toward organic farming of grapes for wine (*Minneapolis Star Tribune*, 7/31/96).

Please also see update of "Organic Farming," #2, 1978.

10. Toxic Waste Firms Target Indian Reservations

1982 SYNOPSIS: Once again, American Indians are being threatened. This time corporate America wants their land. The threat comes in the form of representatives of firms like Browning-Ferris Industries (BFI) who want the land, not for its natural resources, but for "chemical residual management facilities"—a trade term for toxic waste dumps.

In its efforts to obtain dump sites on Indian land, BFI acquired a listing of tribes through a system of "introductions" provided by the U.S. Bureau of Indian Affairs (BIA). Then BFI approached many tribes including the Chemehuevi and Haulapai in Arizona, the Duckwater Shoshone in Nevada, the Muscogee in Oklahoma, and the Cherokee in North Carolina.

There are several reasons why Indian lands seem so attractive to BFI. First, they appear easily attainable to corporate boards because tribes are now suffering from the effects of severe cutbacks in federal funding. BFI offered one tribe "a million or more a year, which is pretty attractive to a small tribe like ours," said Conkie Hoover, Secretary-Treasurer of the Chemehuevi.

Second, BFI could use the issue of tribal sovereignty to its advantage. Although federal environmental regulations would apply, the expectation is that monitoring and enforcement of these laws would be a great deal more difficult than on non-Indian land because of the remoteness of most proposed sites and the fact that only Indian votes are of any consequence on Indian land.

Further, the Bureau of Indian Affairs, a federal agency, appears to play a supportive role in this type of exploitation. The BIA provides "introductions"—these occur when a company (such as BFI) submits a list of requirements to the BIA, which then provides the company with a list of tribes that fill the requirements. The BIA does no research into the company (they would have found that BFI had a very questionable environmental track record), nor the project it proposes.

SOURCES: *Native Self-Sufficiency*, May 1982, published by the Tribal Sovereignty Program, edited by Paula Hammett.

UPDATE: The plans of the BIA, BFI, and other waste disposal companies to "persuade" Native Americans to turn their reservations into nuclear waste dumps did not consider the power of Grace Thorpe, daughter of legendary Olympic athlete Jim Thorpe, a low-key retiree doing what she called "typical grandmother stuff."

When she discovered that 17 American Indian tribes, including her own, Oklahoma's Sac and Fox Nation, had applied for $100,000 grants from the Department of Energy to consider their reservations as sites for nuclear-waste storage, she took action. Calling radioactive waste "the most lethal poison known in the history of man," she rallied her tribal members to bring the issue to a vote. Members defeated the plan, even though it could have brought millions of dollars a year to any reservation chosen as a "monitored retrievable storage" (MRS) site.

Grace Thorpe quickly became a national activist against MRS facilities on Indian lands, and, as president of the National Environmental Coalition of Native Americans, she led successful efforts to get other tribes to withdraw as well. As *The Christian Science Monitor* pointed out in a story about Grace Thorpe (11/10/94), "People like Grace Thorpe illustrate the ability of a single individual to effect change."

CHAPTER 8—1983

Two Ways to Look at International Events

Nineteen-eighty-three was a big year for mainstream news coverage of international and military issues. According to the Associated Press, the top ten stories of the year were:

1. Marines massacred in Beirut terrorist bombing
2. Soviets down South Korean airliner KAL 707
3. U.S. invades Grenada
4. American economy: inflation down, unemployment drops, and deficit rises
5. Soviets break off arms talks, missiles deployed in Europe
6. Nuclear freeze drive in U.S., anti-nuclear movement in Europe
7. Lech Walesa wins Nobel Peace prize
8. Menachem Begin resigns in Israel
9. Weather: winter storms, spring floods, drought, and hurricanes
10. James Watt resigns as Secretary of Interior.

International and military issues also dominated the top overlooked stories of the year, but with a different focus.

THE TOP TEN CENSORED STORIES OF 1983

—And What Has Happened to Them Since

1. Israel: Merchant of Death in Central America

1983 SYNOPSIS: President Reagan's policy objectives in Central America circumvent Congressional objections with quiet help from Israel.

Israel, now the fifth biggest exporter of arms in the world, is the largest supplier of weapons to Latin America. It is also a major source of training in intelligence and counterinsurgency techniques.

Israel sustains Reagan's Latin America policies by supporting the "contras" fighting the Sandinista government in Nicaragua; aids El Salvador's leaders despite continuing human rights violations and right-wing death squads; turns Honduras into the chief gendarme of Central America; builds up Costa Rica's security forces; and supplies Guatemala's repressive military forces with weapons to fight increasing internal opposition.

Israel's support for repressive regimes in Central America is not new. After Somoza's National Guard killed journalists in 1978, President Carter cut off all U.S. aid to Nicaragua. However, Israel, bolstered by U.S. aid, picked up the slack and provided 98 percent of Somoza's arms until July 2, 1979, just two weeks before the Sandinistas won the final battle.

Israel is the largest recipient of U.S. foreign aid, receiving about one-third of all U.S. foreign aid in the last ten years.

SOURCES: *CovertAction Information Bulletin*, Winter 1984, "Israeli Arms in Central America," by Clarence Lusane; *The New York Times*, 12/17/82, "Israel Stepping Up Arms Sales to Central America," by Leslie H. Gelb.

UPDATE: Israel's reputation as a "merchant of death" has not diminished since 1983. *Agence France Presse* (7/15/94) reported that between 1975 and 1992, Israeli arms exports leapt 75 percent in a world market that had contracted by 45 percent. Israel was the sole country to increase arms exports during the world arms market recession.

During the 1970s, Latin America was Israel's largest market for arms, accounting for 50 to 60 percent of its total military exports. An estimated one-third of its total arms exports of $1.2 billion went to Argentina and El Salvador alone. In a report on "the Israel/Latin American connection," the *Journal of Electronic Defense* (March 1994) described Israel as "a faithful if pricey arms supplier during the years when Chile faced an embargo because of the armed forces' human-rights abuses."

From 1979 through 1994, after the Latin American market dried up, China became the biggest customer for Israel's arms export industry, according to a *Los Angeles Times* report (12/28/94).

Meanwhile, Israel remains the largest recipient of U.S. foreign aid, receiving $3 billion out of the estimated $12.2 billion fiscal 1997 U.S. foreign aid budget (Reuters, 7/25/96).

2. The U.S. Never Dropped Out of the Arms Race

1983 SYNOPSIS: President Reagan contended that the U.S. needed to launch a massive military build-up to counter decades of stagnation and inactivity in the area of weapons development. Yet the following actions taken since the late 1960s make it clear that the U.S. never fell behind the USSR in the arms race and in fact, led the race in most sectors:

1. Deployed 496 Poseidon submarine-launched ballistic missiles;

2. Replaced 192 of these missiles with the still more advanced, more powerful and longer-range Trident I missiles;

3. Deployed 72 additional Trident I missiles on new Ohio class submarines;

4. Improved the accuracy of the Trident I missiles;

5. Constantly upgraded and modernized our B-52 bomber force;

6. Completed deployment of the FB-111A strategic bomber;

7. Completed deployment of the Short Range Attack Missile carried by both B-52s and FB-111As;

8. Deployed over 200 radar-elusive long-range strategic Air Launched Cruise Missiles;

9. Developed 550 Minuteman III ICBMs, the world's first MIRV missiles;

10. Replaced the warheads on 300 of these ICBMs with twice the explosive power;

11. Improved the accuracy of all Minuteman IIIs;

12. Tripled the hardness of our Minuteman silos and installed a system for rapid retargeting to improve response time.

President Reagan also deployed 572 Pershing II and Cruise missiles in Europe, restarted construction of the MX ICBM and the B-1 bomber, and increased development of chemical and biological weapons and space-based laser weapons.

SOURCE: *Washington Post National Weekly Edition*, 12/12/83, "We Never Dropped Out of the Arms Race," by Thomas J. Downey.

UPDATE: In the four decades following the explosion of the world's first hydrogen bomb on a small Pacific island on November 1, 1952, the United States and the Soviet Union engaged in an expensive nuclear arms race that finally drove the Soviets to bankruptcy and almost did the same to the United States. Richard Rhodes, Pulitzer Prize-winning author and scholar on the development of atomic and hydrogen bombs, estimates the arms race cost the U.S. $4 trillion—which equaled the entire national debt in 1994 (*Minneapolis Star Tribune*, 10/1/95). For information on how the Reagan Administration duped the American public into supporting the arms race, please see *Censored* story #1, 1984, "Soviet Military Build-up."

3. Detailed USSR Nuclear Freeze Proposal Ignored by the U.S.

1983 SYNOPSIS: Following arms control talks, President Reagan consistently vilified USSR representatives and the U.S. press provided front page coverage of their militant posture. But when the USSR made a detailed proposal to remove the threat of nuclear war, most Americans never heard about it.

Such a proposal was made on October 5, 1983, by Andrei Gromyko, USSR Minister of Foreign Affairs, in two letters to Javier Perez de Cuellar, Secretary-General of the United Nations. Along with the letters were draft resolutions for freezing nuclear weapons and condemning nuclear war.

The draft resolution for a nuclear freeze included the following points: 1) to cease the build-up of all components of nuclear arsenals, delivery systems, and all kinds of nuclear weapons; 2) not to deploy nuclear arms of new kinds and types; 3) to establish a moratorium on all tests of nuclear weapons; and 4) to stop production of fissionable materials for the purpose of creating nuclear weapons.

It also called for the "USSR and the USA, which possess the largest nuclear arsenals, to freeze, in the first place and simultaneously, their nuclear arms on a bilateral basis by way of example to the other nuclear states."

The draft resolution condemning nuclear war echoed the sentiments of millions of Americans increasingly concerned about nuclear war who supported a nuclear freeze.

SOURCE: *Soviet Life Magazine*, December 1983.

UPDATE: Please also see update of "The U.S. Against the World on Nuclear Issues," #7, 1982.

4. America's Agricultural Disaster of 1983— A PIK in a Poke

1983 SYNOPSIS: In early 1983, President Ronald Reagan introduced a new federal program called Payment In Kind, or PIK. It was designed to reduce surpluses by giving farmers government-owned surplus crops which they can then sell, in return for leaving their own crop lands idle.

The PIK program created a major national agricultural disaster that received virtually no coverage in the press:

1. One third of all eligible crop land in the U.S. was left unplanted, more than three times the acreage originally expected to be in the program;

2. About 250,000 jobs were lost among suppliers, farm laborers, and in farm-related industries;

3. Hundreds of fertilizer, farm-equipment, and seed dealers were forced out of business;

4. Feed prices increased significantly, hurting poultry, pork, and cattle growers;

5. Billions of dollars in farm-export sales were lost;

6. Federal laws which prohibit the USDA from giving more than $50,000 to any single farm were knowingly broken;

7. Giant farm corporations and major grain companies profited by millions of dollars while smaller farmers went bankrupt;

8. An extra $11 billion for farm aid will be charged to the taxpayers;

9. Total farm subsidies were increased to about $28 billion—more than we spend on welfare for the entire poverty population in the country;

10. Now we can expect more than $20 billion to be added to consumer food bills in 1984.

Despite all this, John Block, Secretary of Agriculture, said PIK "has proved to be one of the most successful farm programs in agriculture's history" and it appears it will be repeated in 1984.

SOURCES: *The New Farm*, November 1983, "A PIK in a Poke," by Rodney Leonard; *Washington Post National Weekly Edition*, 11/21/83, "Grain Trades and Conglomerates Benefit from PIK," by Ward Sinclair.

UPDATE: Despite John Block's optimism about the Payment In Kind program, it did turn out to be a PIK in a poke. In the final analysis it cost the taxpayers more than $50 billion, accomplished little, and hastened the end of farm subsidies in the United States (*Wisconsin State Journal*, 12/23/94). In early April 1996, President Bill Clinton signed the 1996 Freedom to Farm Act which reformed farm subsidies for the first time in 60 years. The reform starts with the conversion of subsidies per unit of production to lump-sum payments which are reduced to zero over seven years, and eliminates federal planting directives, leaving farmers free to plant as much or as little of a crop as they choose (*The Montgomery Advertiser*, 4/5/96). On August 20, 1996, wire services reported the new program a success with nearly 99 percent of eligible farmers signed up for the seven-year production flexibility contracts.

5. KAL 007 and 269 Innocent Pawns in US-USSR Spy War

1983 SYNOPSIS: On September 1, 1983, a Soviet jet shot down Korean Air Lines flight 007, killing 269 men, women, and children, including 61 Americans.

The two super-powers reacted as expected. The Soviet Union first issued denials and then grudgingly admitted it had shot the airliner down. President Reagan responded with righteous indignation saying the brutal event was "an act of barbarism, born of a society that wantonly disregards individual rights and the value of human life."

While the U.S. press provided massive coverage to Russia's foolish denials, the U.S. outrage, and the unsuccessful search for survivors, it suddenly dropped the story when the search for the "black box" was abandoned. This was also when serious questions concerning U.S. responsibility in the disaster were being raised.

It is now known that U.S. intelligence had an overriding interest in Soviet military activities in the area overflown by the Korean airliner. Ernest Volkman, national security editor for *Defense Science Magazine*, reported that Korean Air Lines planes regularly overfly Soviet airspace to gather military intelligence. A U.S. official, with close ties to military intelligence, said some foreign government-owned airliners are fitted in this country with cameras and other devices for intelligence collection. Two former Air Force communications intelligence specialists charged the U.S. government could have interceded in the attack on the Korean jet.

SOURCES: *San Francisco Examiner*, 9/4/83, "Aviation Experts Don't Rule Out Possibility KAL jet was Spying," by Knut Royce; *Denver Post*, 9/13/83, "U.S. Spy Plane Capable of Interceding in Attack on Korean Jet," by Tom Bernard and T. Edward Eskelson; *The Progressive*, October 1983, "Collision Course"; *The Guardian*, (London), 12/17/83, "KAL 007: Unanswered Questions," by R.W. Johnson (reprinted in *World Press Review*, March 1984).

UPDATE: Thirteen years after the tragic downing of KAL 007, the case is still going through courts and the facts are still disputed. On April 6, 1996, *The New York Times* reported that 147 of the 269 passengers on the flight had had their cases settled for $75,000 and that other cases were still pending in Japan or the Philippines. In March 1996, the *ABA Journal*, trade journal of the legal profession, noted the Supreme Court limited damages that can be won by survivors of people killed in international air crashes over water to financial losses, excluding compensation for loss of companionship or punitive damages. The onerous $75,000 limitation was finally dropped in November 1996 (*USA Today*, 11/13/96).

6. Journalist Challenges Press Coverage of Central America

1983 SYNOPSIS: We are still not getting the full story of what is happening in Central America. There are a variety of explanations for this, not the least of which is the intimidation and assassination of journalists. In addition, there is the misinformation disseminated by our own State Department and the confusing and complex political situation in that region.

The range of obstacles to reliable press coverage in the area is well documented by Michael Massing's *Columbia Journalism Review* article which suggested that the recall of a *New York Times* reporter seemed to send a signal to the rest of the press to go soft on El Salvador.

However, not all journalists were confused by the political situation, intimidated by the terrorists, manipulated by the Reagan Administration, nor transferred home by their newspapers.

One such journalist is Peter D. Fox, city editor of the *Billings Gazette* in Montana. After a 12-day study mission to Central America, he wrote a series of articles with revelations which were cited by one observer to be "as important to Central America as Harrison Salisbury's 1966 *New York Times* revelations were to Vietnam." In his lead article, Fox reported "what we saw and learned during our time in Managua and the countryside was alarming because it did not correspond with what we had been reading in U.S. newspapers, seeing on U.S. television, and hearing from our U.S. government."

Fox cannot be easily accused of being a "bleeding heart liberal journalist taken in by Communist propaganda." Rather, he is a conservative, former U.S. intelligence officer, who supported President Reagan's Central American policy until he went there himself. Then Fox was so outraged over what he saw his country doing that he publicly resigned his commission in the U.S. Army National Guard.

SOURCES: *Billings Gazette*, 8/31, 9/4, 9/18, and 9/25, 1983, "Another Side of the Fight," by Peter D. Fox; *Columbia Journalism Review*, November 1983, "About-face on El Salvador," by Michael Massing; *The Ithaca Times*, 12/1/83, "A Conversion Story," by John E. Milich.

UPDATE: Peter D. Fox subsequently left the *Billings Gazette* and is now the Director of Public Information for the University of Wisconsin System. While his 1983 transformation created some problems, he never regretted his decision to tell it the way it was, and would do it again. He particularly recalls the support he received from his colleagues at the *Gazette* and in the National Guard. In 1995, he was invited to rejoin the Guard and is now a Lieutenant Colonel in the Wisconsin National Guard. While the mainstream press ignored his story in 1983, Fox was gratified that some ten small-town, middle-America newspapers in the Lee Enterprises News Corporation, which owned the *Gazette*, reprinted his series on El Salvador.

Please also see update of "El Salvador Crisis," #1, 1980.

7. U.S. Media Neglect South Africa Politics

1983 SYNOPSIS: In 1983, most Americans had heard of Lech Walesa and Poland's Solidarity movement, but few Americans knew about Nelson Mandela and South Africa's African National Congress.

The U.S. media provided substantial coverage to Walesa's heroic fight against a communist government; however, they provided little coverage of Mandela's equally heroic fight against the apartheid regime in South Africa—a symbol of racist oppression for many Americans and other people throughout the world.

Despite international ostracism of South Africa's racist policies, some 600 North American companies continue to do business with South Africa and at the time, U.S. investments were estimated at about $10 billion. Disregarding a 1982 U.N. resolution outlawing export of dangerous products to other countries, the Upjohn Company reportedly still provided the South Africa regime with Depo Provera—a drug outlawed in the U.S. Ignoring the potential for nuclear confrontation and holocaust, West Germany, Israel, and the U.S. provided South Africa with nuclear technology. In September 1983, the State Department approved an application by Westinghouse to bid on a $50 million ten-year contract to maintain and supply South Africa's two nuclear stations. Western intelligence sources believed that South Africa was capable of producing nuclear weapons and that it may have tested a nuclear device in the South Atlantic in 1979.

One reason few Americans may have heard about Nelson Mandela, the widely respected political leader in South Africa, may be because of the official and unofficial relationship between South Africa and Washington, D.C. South Africa spent considerable sums of money on Capitol Hill and the Reagan White House to maintain those relationships.

SOURCES: *i.d.a.f. News Notes,* U.S. Committee of the International Defense and Aid Fund for South Africa, October 1983; *Daily World,* 9/15/83, "South Africa, Poland, and the U.S. Press," by Tafataona P. Mahoso; *Washington Post National Weekly Edition,* 3/26/84, "South Africa's Capitol Connections," by Rick Atkinson.

UPDATE: Lech Walesa, the darling of the U.S. press in the early eighties, turned out to be a Cinderella story that went full circle: from electrician at the Gdansk shipyard, to leader of the Solidarity Movement which ultimately brought down Poland's communist government, to Nobel Peace Prize winner in 1983, to Poland's first democratically-elected president, to a failed attempt at re-election, and finally back to Gdansk as an electrician. Ironically, on August 8, 1996, the Gdansk shipyard went bankrupt, rendering the birthplace of Solidarity a victim of the free-market economy it helped create (Memphis *Commercial Appeal,* 8/9/96).

After spending 27 years in prison, Nelson Mandela, who was ignored by the press in the early eighties, went on to become the leader of South Africa's African National Congress (ANC). On May 10, 1994, following the ANC victory in the country's first universal-suffrage election, Mandela was inaugurated as South Africa's first black president. He subsequently became one of the world's best known and most respected political leaders. Few men have been so widely admired in their own lifetime. In 1993, he was awarded the Nobel Peace Prize along with Frederik W. de Klerk, who had helped engineer the transition from apartheid to democracy.

Meanwhile, in 1995, under the leadership of Nelson Mandela, South Africa helped to broker an agreement making the Nuclear Non-proliferation Treaty permanent and, with other African nations, established a nuclear-weapon-free zone on the African continent. South Africa dismantled its unacknowledged nuclear weapons in 1991 (*Bulletin of the Atomic Scientists*, July 1996).

Finally, on May 8, 1996, South Africa adopted a new constitution that guarantees equal rights for all and completes the country's official transformation to democracy (*USA Today*, 5/9/96).

8. The Censored Safety Record of the U.S. Nuclear Navy

1983 SYNOPSIS: Since the 1950s, the U.S. Navy has annually testified before Congress that there has never been an accident involving a naval reactor, or any release of radioactivity which has had a significant effect on individuals or the environment.

That statement stands in sharp contrast to a published list that documents 126 accidents involving nuclear powered vessels, including accounts of fires, floods, collisions, and sinkings. Among the accidents cited were 37 involving the reactors on these ships, including 13 discharges of radioactive material into U.S. coastal waters.

The U.S. Navy recorded these events as "incidents" and "discrepancies" and not as accidents. Therefore, through naval nuke-speak, the Navy can claim there were no "accidents." And for the past 15 years, there hasn't been a radiological survey of nuclear ports in the U.S. by independent agencies.

SOURCE: *Oceans Magazine*, July 1983, "When Incidents are Accidents: The Silent Saga of the Nuclear Navy," by David Kaplan.

UPDATE: The nuclear safety record of the U.S. Navy continues to be an unknown and unreported story in the United States. So-called "incidents" continue to occur with minimal press notice. On May 17, 1996, the nuclear-powered submarine Jacksonville and a Saudi Arabian-flagged container ship collided in a dense fog off the Virginia Beach coast. No injuries were reported to either crew but the merchant ship took on water through a 21-foot gash in its hull. There was no report of nuclear weapons aboard the

U.S. submarine. This was the third collision for the 15-year-old Jacksonville in the same vicinity in the past 14 years (*The Norfolk Virginian-Pilot*, 5/18/96).

However, the safety problems of Russia's nuclear navy are better known and reveal a frightening story. According to *The Scotsman* (4/22/96), a secret document by the International Atomic Energy Agency (IAEA) in 1991, entitled, "Accidents and Losses at Sea Involving Radioactive Material," lists seven Soviet nuclear subs lost at sea between 1963 and 1989. The sinkings involved a total of eight nuclear reactors and more than 24 nuclear weapons in the Pacific, Atlantic, and Norwegian and Mediterranean seas. London-based nuclear consultant Dr. John Large, who has been helping the Russian government solve the environmental and technical problems of its dumped and retired submarines, said, "Two U.S. nuclear submarines have been lost in similar circumstances." He also speculated that the British HMS Sheffield sank with two or three nuclear depth charges during the Falklands War.

It was not until November 1996 that the full implications of Soviet nuclear submarine accidents became known. Keay Davidson, a *San Francisco Examiner* science writer, reported (11/24/96) that when a Soviet submarine sank 600 miles east of Bermuda in the Atlantic Ocean in late 1986, its nuclear warheads, containing perhaps 200 pounds of radioactive plutonium-239, broke open and spilled unknown amounts of the deadly element into the sea. Traces of plutonium were later discovered on floating submarine debris. Davidson said that while the plutonium might settle and stay put because of slow water circulation and sticky seafloor mud, some plutonium might have been absorbed into the rich food chain in the ocean's upper layers as the sub sank. If so, some particles of plutonium, which remain dangerously radioactive for tens of thousands of years, may have been ingested by some of the fish which migrate thousands of miles in a single season, as far as the Atlantic coastal fisheries.

9. DNA: U.S. Key to Biological Warfare?

1983 SYNOPSIS: In 1969, President Richard Nixon pledged we would never develop or use biological weapons (BW); in 1972, he signed the Convention on the Prohibition of the Development, Production, and Stockpiling of Bacteriological and Toxin Weapons, which bans even the possession of such agents.

Yet, over the years, under the guise of "defensive" research, the Department of Defense (DOD) has sponsored a broad program of studies involving the latest techniques of genetic engineering. The Pentagon's BW researchers are using recombinant DNA (gene splicing) technology. The alleged thrust of the current research reportedly is to develop vaccines that will protect the U.S. or allied troops and populations against biological agents that might be used by the enemy.

According to the National Science Foundation, expenditures on biological research by DOD have increased 54 percent since 1980, reaching $100 million in 1983. The Army is studying the effectiveness of aerosol immunization in which the vaccine would be inhaled rather than swallowed or taken by injection. While aerosol immunization is more dangerous and less effective than standard methods, it could be done clandestinely.

For example, in the 1950s, the Army sprayed "simulants"—supposedly innocuous germs—over San Francisco Bay and in New York City subways to test this process. Unknown numbers of unwitting civilians were exposed to the germs. Details of the experiment were not revealed until the late 1970s.

SOURCE: *The Nation*, 12/10/83, "DNA—Key to Biological Warfare," by Charles Piller.

UPDATE: Please see update of "Biological Weapons," #10, 1981, and update of "Biowarfare Testing," #6, 1993.

10. The DOD's Cost-plus Contracting System Taxpayer Swindle

1983 SYNOPSIS: The United States has a federal contracting system that encourages overruns, inefficiency, and fraud but the mass media are not concerned.

Rockwell International, one of the nation's largest space and defense contractors, fired at least two employees for reporting contract fraud to NASA's Inspector General. These two, along with other former and current Rockwell employees, all alleged that Rockwell illegally transferred cost overruns to get the government to pay.

Like other defense suppliers, Rockwell has two types of contracts with the government. The first, fixed price contracts, are negotiated in advance with a set price, and any cost overruns must be absorbed by Rockwell. The second, cost-plus contracts, are like open-ended price tags, with the government covering all expenses no matter how high they go. The B-1 bomber is a fixed price contract, for example, while the Space Shuttle is a cost-plus contract.

The employees revealed that Rockwell was shifting the billing for extra time and money spent on a fixed contract to the cost-plus contracts. Employees were told to bill work done on the B-1 (fixed) to the Space Shuttle (cost-plus).

The U.S. Justice Department began to investigate and suddenly the case was dropped for several years. When it finally was re-opened, Rockwell lawyers agreed to an out-of-court settlement. A month later, the cases were settled with no admission of guilt on Rockwell's part. Rockwell agreed to pay the government $500,000 and to invest $1 million in a computerized time-keeping system that supposedly would ward off abuses. Government watchers were incensed the Justice Department settled for so little and left the door open for future abuses.

SOURCE: *Common Cause,* March 1983, "Whistleblower!," by John Hanrahan.

UPDATE: The Defense Department's cost-plus contracting system, an incredible license to steal which the 1983 story warned about, is alive and well and even more profitable today. Journalist Robert Scheer points out (*Los Angeles Times,* 1/23/96) the military-industrial complex enjoyed the Reagan/Bush years when they had a Cold War field day, but still weren't disturbed when peace broke out: "Instead, they have enjoyed five years of unprecedented profits by laying off workers while continuing to sign up government cost-plus contracts, which guarantees top executive bonuses."

The massive taxpayer rip-off is so outrageous that even some segments of the defense industry are embarrassed by it. In a treatise on technical integrity, the American Institute of Aeronautics and Astronautics (AIAA) Technical Committee on Space Transportation, published in *Aerospace America* (July 1996), acknowledged: "As long as the government awards cost-plus contracts and allows contractors costly overruns to correct mistakes and fix poor-quality work, contractors are likely to over-promise." The AIAA committee said that work to recover from poor technical performance should not produce a profit as it now does.

A recent beneficiary of the cost-plus contract scam is none other than former Defense Secretary Dick Cheney. *The Patriot Ledger* reported (3/23/96) that the expanding needs of U.S. troops in Bosnia mean rising profits for the construction subsidiary of Houston-based Brown & Root, a subsidiary of Halliburton Co., which is headed by Cheney. It has a cost-plus contract that guarantees rising profits for Brown & Root's Bosnia operation. Cheney's company is expected to collect $500 million for contracting services in Bosnia by the time the troops come home. That's $308 million more than the Pentagon's original cost-estimate to build barracks, latrines, and other necessities.

Please also see *Censored* story #4, 1993, "The Real Welfare Cheats: America's Corporations," and *Censored* story #3, 1994, "The Secret Pentagon Plan."

CHAPTER 9—1984

Orwell's 1984 Ignored by the Media

In 1984, the year of George Orwell's prophecy, the mainstream media concentrated on the presidential election. And it ignored Orwell's warnings for the future of our society as reported in alternative press articles about governmental disinformation and threats to our civil liberties. According to the Associated Press, the top ten news stories of the year were:

1. The Reagan landslide
2. The gas leak in Bhopal
3. Geraldine Ferraro nomination
4. Indira Gandhi assassination
5. Bombing of U.S. Embassy annex in Beirut
6. Ethiopian famine and African drought
7. Summer Olympics in Los Angeles
8. Heart transplants in "Baby Fae" and William Schroeder
9. U.S. economy: low inflation, high deficits, recovery
10. San Ysidro McDonald's massacre of 21 people.

THE TOP TEN CENSORED STORIES OF 1984

—And What Has Happened to Them Since

1. The Well-Publicized Soviet Military Build-Up Scare Was a Lie

1984 SYNOPSIS: Information, available to the national press but not publicized by it, revealed U.S. leaders and militarists lied about the Soviet arms build-up and knowingly used false information to inflate Soviet military expenditures. The time honored technique of referring to the Soviet Union's massive build-up of military weapons was used to promote higher military budgets by instilling fear in the American public—a technique that proved highly effective during the 1976-1981 period.

The Myth of the Massive Soviet Build-up: In 1983, testimony before the Joint Economic Committee, the Central Intelligence Agency (CIA) made a significant *downward* revision of its estimate of Soviet military spending for the period 1976-1981 which went almost unreported in the press. The new estimate showed an increase of only two percent per year overall and no increase in the buying of weapons.

Inflating Soviet Military Expenditures: The CIA was responsible for estimating Soviet military spending. The agency's methodology was to compute what the Soviet military would cost *if built and operated in the U.S. using U.S. prices and wages!* For example, to compute personnel costs, the CIA assumed a Soviet conscript's salary to be $575 a month, which was what the U.S. Army paid a private. Actually, the Soviet conscript got four or five rubles, about eight dollars a month.

Despite the evidence to the contrary, President Ronald Reagan, his Secretary of Defense Casper Weinberger, and others continued to cite the "unrelenting" Soviet build-up as justification for increasing U.S. military expenditures at the expense of sorely needed social programs.

SOURCES: *Defense Monitor*, Vol. XIII, #4, 1984, "Taking Stock: The U.S. Military Build-up"; *Aviation Week & Space Technology*, 2/13/84, "Soviet Defense Spending," by William H. Gregory.

UPDATE: Eight years after the 1984 *Censored* exposé, additional analyses confirmed the CIA presented the U.S. government, and the rest of the world, with a false picture of Soviet military spending. The major impact was to exaggerate Soviet military spending and to encourage the U.S. to divert more of its resources to military purposes. The end result led to foreign and domestic economic policies and decisions that cost the United States hundreds of billions of dollars in wasted resources (*Challenge*, May 1992). On May 20, 1992, CIA Director Robert Gates admitted the CIA intelligence data had been cooked to portray the Soviet economy as stronger than it was. Finally, on November 2, 1995, the Associated Press reported the Pentagon was reviewing billions of dollars in arms purchases that may have been based on bogus estimates of Soviet strength during the Cold War.

2. Reagan's Attacks on Civil Liberties

1984 SYNOPSIS: Under the rubric of fighting terrorism, President Ronald Reagan proposed serious threats to our civil liberties in 1984 which were ignored by the media.

The little-known threats were contained in four anti-terrorist bills sponsored by the President under the guise of fighting sabotage and assassination; the bills would criminalize domestic opposition to U.S. intervention in the Third World and authorize FBI investigations of legal political activity.

The most threatening of the bills is called the Prohibition Against the Training or Support of Terrorist Organizations Act of 1984 (HR5613 and S2626), a loosely worded, vague document that makes American citizens liable to criminal penalties for exercising their constitutional rights under the First Amendment.

The most damaging portions of the proposed act were offensive to a few senators and representatives who sent the legislation back to the administration demanding that certain portions be clarified. They included:

✔ The Secretary of State would have unilateral power to determine that a group or government is "terrorist," based on their "acts or likely acts"; similarly, anyone charged under it would be forbidden from arguing that any organization or government on the list was wrongly included;

✔ It would be a crime to act in concert with, train, or serve in any organization designated by the Secretary of State to be an intelligence agency or armed force of any foreign government, faction, or international terrorist group;

✔ Any logistical, mechanical, maintenance or similar support services to the armed forces, or any intelligence agency, or their agents, of any government, faction, or international terrorist group designated as such by the Secretary of State would be prohibited.

While the legislation did not pass last year, it is expected to be reintroduced in 1985. If successful, Reagan's efforts to curtail the people's right to dissent could easily pave the way for our intervention in Central America or elsewhere.

SOURCES: *Guardian*, 7/25/84, "If These Laws Pass, Watch Out," and 8/22/84, "FBI 'terrorizes' the Solidarity Movement," by Eleanor Stein and Michael Ratner; *Wall Street Journal*, 4/27/84, "White House Seeks to Broaden Authority to Thwart Growing Terrorism Threat."

UPDATE: The onerous terrorism Act of 1984 was not passed in 1985. However, in the wake of terrorist attacks at Dhahran, Oklahoma City, and the New York Trade Center, President Clinton signed an anti-terrorist bill on April 24, 1996. It substantially broadened the government's authority to investigate and deport foreign terrorists, provided the right to use secret evidence against suspects, and added restrictions on habeas corpus (*The Economist*, 4/20/96). It reminded civil liberties supporters of the anti-terrorist proposals by Ronald Reagan in 1984. In August 1996, in the wake of the Centennial Olympic Park bombing and the TWA Flight 800 explosion off New York, efforts were made to further strengthen the bill by adding provisions, supported by Clinton, to add taggants to gun powder and to significantly increase the FBI's wiretapping authority. Both provisions were killed by the House Republican leadership as Congress was rushing to adjourn (New York Times Service, 8/12/96).

3. Nicaragua: Fair Elections Versus an Unfair Press

1984 SYNOPSIS: Contrary to U.S. media predictions, the November 4, 1984, Nicaraguan national elections were not rigged by the ruling Sandinistas nor were they the rubber-stamp of Soviet Communism.

News stories circulated before the elections suggested that the Sandinistas were staging the elections to promote the impression of democracy, while holding on to complete political control. Further, there were reports of intimidation and military coercion at the voting booths.

In fact, as events were to prove, the election was the very model of fairness itself. More than 70 percent of eligible voters cast ballots, with a third of the votes going to opposition parties on both the political left and right. Further, had the Sandinistas wanted to "rig the election," they would have chosen the United States' version of representative democracy by using a "winner-takes-all" format that would have given the Sandinistas virtually all the seats in the assembly.

Instead, the proportional representation form of democracy was chosen, based on Western European models, in which the percentage of votes garnered translates directly into percentage of seats won in the National Assembly. This method actually favors the opposition by allowing them fair representation, and supports the means to form political power bases at a national level—something the American political system thwarts.

The election also revealed the fallacy of official U.S. claims of Soviet domination of Nicaraguan politics: total Communist Party votes accounted for only 3.9 percent of votes cast.

Finally, accounts of election day activities revealed no evidence of election fraud and no violence—except by the CIA-backed contras.

SOURCE: *Christianity and Crisis*, 12/24/84, "What Really Happened on November 4?" by Andrew Reding.

UPDATE: Despite the doomsayers in the wake of the Sandinista revolution, Nicaragua could boast of a strong constitutional base of a free and fair democratic process as it approached the 1996 election year, according to John R. Hamilton, Acting Deputy Assistant Secretary of State for Inter-American Affairs. He noted that following the free and fair regional election of 1994, the National Assembly approved an electoral law for the 1996 national elections. The Nicaraguan electoral law provides for a formal voter registration process with greater safeguards than before.

Thus, it was not surprising the election on October 20, 1996, went smoothly with Arnoldo Aleman, former mayor of Managua, handily defeating Daniel Ortega, former president and Sandinista leader (*Los Angeles Times*, 10/27/96).

Ironically, as *The New York Times* pointed out (10/27/96), "all three of the Central American countries [Nicaragua, El Salvador, and Guatemala] wracked by leftist insurrection throughout the 1970s and 1980s will be governed by right-wing presidents."

4. CIA and the Death Squads—Immoral and Illegal

1984 SYNOPSIS: Even while President Ronald Reagan publicly condemned the Salvadoran Death Squads, a paramilitary apparatus responsible for the deaths of thousands of Salvadoran leftists and peasants, the U.S. Central

Intelligence Agency (CIA) continued to train, support, and provide intelligence to forces directly involved in Death Squad activities.

We now know this involvement began as far back as 1964 and possibly earlier. Since the Kennedy Administration, U.S. officials from the CIA, the Armed Forces, and the State Department have been responsible for the following activities in El Salvador:

1) The formation of ORDEN, a paramilitary and intelligence network that grew into the Death Squads; 2) The formation of ANSESAL, the elite presidential intelligence service that relied on Death Squads as "the operative arm of intelligence gathering"; 3) Enlisting Jose Alberto Medrano, founder of both ORDEN and ANSESAL, into the CIA; 4) Supplying detailed surveillance information on Salvadoran individuals later murdered by Death Squads; 5) Training ORDEN leaders in the use of automatic weapons and surveillance techniques, and carrying some of those leaders on the CIA payroll.

Due to public outcry, President Reagan publicly denounced the Death Squads, yet CIA support, in the form of personnel training and intelligence gathering, continued.

All this is in violation of the Foreign Assistance Act of 1974, which prohibits spending U.S. funds "to provide training or...financial support for...law enforcement forces of any foreign government, or any program of internal intelligence or surveillance on behalf of any foreign government." Not only were the CIA's ties with Salvadoran Death Squads immoral, they actually violated the letter of the law.

SOURCE: *The Progressive*, May 1984, "An Exclusive Report on the U.S. Role in El Salvador's Official Terror: Behind the Death Squads," by Allan Nairn.

UPDATE: Human rights groups say right-wing death squads murdered about 40,000 of the 70,000 people killed during the 1980-1992 civil war in El Salvador. Today, death squads are still reported to be roaming El Salvador. On October 13, 1996, the *Washington Post* reported that paramilitary groups have become more visible with political kidnappings, extortion, two car bombings, and threatening communiqués like those of the death squads in the 1980s.

As to U.S. involvement with death squads, on July 16, 1996, the *Atlanta Constitution* belatedly editorialized: "Congress should prohibit CIA collusion with death squads." On January 27, 1997, the *Baltimore Sun* reported a newly declassified CIA training manual, entitled "Human Resource

Exploitation Training Manual—1983," that describes torture methods used on dissidents in Central America.

5. Worst Radiation Spill in North America is Ignored

1984 SYNOPSIS: In 1976, a group of doctors at the Centro Medico, in Juarez, Mexico, bought a radiation therapy unit, the Picker 3000, from an x-ray equipment company in Fort Worth, Texas. The unit was left in an empty warehouse for seven years until late December 1983, when a local worker removed a tungsten wheel from the unit to sell as scrap. The wheel contained the unit's radioactive source: 6010 tiny pellets each containing 70 microcuries of cobalt-60. The worker sold the unit to a nearby junk dealer for ten dollars.

At the junkyard, the wheel was picked up with an electromagnet and accidentally scattered the pellets throughout the yard. Unknowingly, the yard's 60 employees and every piece of metal in the junyard was dusted with lethal doses of radiation. Later, when a pick-up truck from the junkyard was parked in a city driveway, some 200 citizens in Juarez also were contaminated with a lethal dose of cobalt-60.

Most of the contaminated scrap metal and pellets were trucked 220 miles south of Juarez to a smelting plant. The metal was melted down, contaminating more than 5,000 tons of steel. An estimated 700 tons were contracted for use in kitchen table legs and reinforcement beams, some of which were sent to the U.S. Much of the remaining 4,300 tons of contaminated steel was used for foundation supports in homes throughout Mexico. All of it may never be retrieved, according to officials who proposed to recycle the metal for use in dams and bridges, where human exposure is considered minimal.

The entire tragedy might never have been discovered if it hadn't been for an accidental event. A truck delivering some of the contaminated steel bars to a construction site in the Los Alamos National Lab, in New Mexico, made a wrong turn and headed past a radioactive materials control station, tripping the alarm.

The 60 junkyard employees are expected to die of cancer or leukemia and an estimated 200 other citizens in Juarez are expected to die or display signs of cancer or leukemia within the next few years.

SOURCES: *Science*, 3/16/84, "Juarez: An Unprecedented Radiation Accident," by Eliot Marshall; *Guardian*, 6/20/84, "'Worst Radiation Spill in North America' Still Spreading," by Robby Newton and Ellen Kahaner.

UPDATE: While the worst radiation spill in North America received some additional coverage in 1984, it appears there has been no follow-up coverage to the accident or the victims. UPI reported (5/2/84) that the cobalt-60 tainted metal would be buried in a low-level nuclear waste dump to be established about 20 miles south of Juarez. The story noted there would be no U.S. effort to verify the site is safe, "even though both Juarez and El Paso, Texas, draw their water from the same underground aquifer which crosses the border and underlies both cities." On May 4, 1984, the *San Diego Union-Tribune* reported that "geiger counters have been installed at all California-Mexico border crossings to prevent radioactive steel from entering the United States." The June 1984 issue of *Nuclear News* acknowledged the accident may turn out to be the largest radioactive spill in North America and confirmed the earlier reports on the new dump site and the radiation monitors at every border crossing.

6. The Red-Herring of "Left-wing" Terrorism

1984 SYNOPSIS: Since the closing days of World War II, the United States has attacked "left-wing" terrorism while supporting "right-wing" terrorism around the world as a means of fighting communism.

The Reagan Administration in particular consistently proved itself to be a political body that reviled the horrific specter of "leftist" terrorism and singled out the political left as the international source of brutal, fanatic terrorism. This is not quite the whole story as indicated by the following:

1) In Guatemala, a nation ruled by a right-wing military, one hundred people are killed or disappear every month; 2) El Salvador's right-wing death squads still operate with impunity; 3) The contras in Nicaragua routinely rape, torture, and murder women, children, the aged, and other "enemies of democracy;" 4) The nation of Chile, whose military dictator Augusto Pinochet Ugarte is frequently compared to Hitler, lives in a nightmare of political torture, murder, and mutilation; 5) Right-wing European organizations like "Rose of the Winds" and its successor, "P-2," account for more murders and terrorist acts than leftist groups like the PLO and the Red Brigades; 6) Right-wing terrorists include Stefano Delle Chiaie, one of the principals in the terrorist bombing at the Bologna railway station in 1980.

Terrorism, whether from the left or the right, should be a target of all nations concerned with democracy and human rights; the press should reflect this rather than support the administration's red-baiting rhetoric.

SOURCE: *CovertAction Information Bulletin*, Fall 1984, "The Fascist Network," by Edward S. Herman.

UPDATE: The need to support "right-wing" terrorists as a means of fighting communism seemed to disappear or go underground with the end of the Cold War. At the same time, "left-wing" terrorism became less of a threat as the media spotlight focused on the actions of "right-wing" terrorists. *Jane's Intelligence Review—Year Book* reported (12/31/94), "The threat of ideological terrorism of the extreme left is no longer significant in France, Italy, Germany, and the Benelux countries...However, the threat of extreme right-wing terrorism in Europe is far more serious." In America, the threat of "right-wing" terrorism became a reality as the public was belatedly informed of the cruel activities of "right-wing" death squads in Central America and Haiti. In 1987, a *"Los Angeles Times* investigative series first documented right-wing terrorism in Vietnamese communities in the United States" (*The Quill*, April 1996). Finally, the growth and activities of the U.S. militia movement, as well as the 1995 Oklahoma City bombing, also contributed to the national awareness of "right-wing" terrorism.

7. Death of a Nation: The Tragedy of Transkei

1984 SYNOPSIS: While the tragedy of apartheid in South Africa gets increasing media attention, the American press ignores its most devastating effects.

The white-minority government in Pretoria created the "independent" black state of Transkei, in 1976, on the east coast of South Africa, as part of its apartheid policy of separate political and economic development for blacks.

Transkei, also known as the Homelands, is a virtual wasteland, incapable of sustaining its burgeoning population. The land is desert-like, harsh, and arid, and the African drought, considered the worst in Africa in 50 years, affects the Homelands more than the rest of the nation. The impact of the drought, particularly in Ethiopia, has been well-publicized, but Transkei's tragedy has been kept secret by the South African government.

Transkei is ignored by black African nations; unrecognized as a state by the United Nations; and overlooked by the United States. Nonetheless, blacks are being deported there by the tens of thousands yearly as the Pretoria government attempts to further strip them of South African citizenship. As a result, the Homelands face a bleak future, for its people have to rely on Pretoria for most of their economic assistance, support that diminishes as the drought continues.

Unless immediate action is taken, blacks forced into the Homelands surely will die. Starvation and malnutrition will claim the young and old first, and then work on the survivors. Finally, Pretoria won't have to worry about world opinion anymore, for it will have achieved the ultimate goal of its separatist movement—genocide.

SOURCES: *Christian Science Monitor*, 4/3/84, "South African Blacks Struggle for Survival in Winter Recession," and, 4/30/84, "South African Relief Groups Find Better Ways to Combat Hunger," both by Paul Van Slambrouck; *New Statesman*, 8/19/84, "South Africa: Drying Out," by Philip Willan; *U.S. News & World Report*, 7/28/80, "Transkei: A Nation Only On the Map," 8/22/83, "Another Deadly Famine Stalks Black Africa," both by Robin Knight.

UPDATE: While Transkei was reincorporated into South Africa after the 1994 general elections, many of the problems continued. One of the challenges was the integration of Transkei and other vastly different forces of the old South African Defence Force into one national defense force, a process that threatened national security (*Jane's International Defence Review*, 3/1/96). The effects of years of apartheid also continued. On a trip through his own home province of Transkei, Nelson Mandela blamed racial oppression for the blatant misery on every hand (*Swiss Review of World Affairs*, 5/2/96).

8. Orwell's 1984 Arrived While the Press Slept

1984 SYNOPSIS: On March 9, 1984, *New York Times* columnist William Safire reported that Reagan's sweeping new censorship law, National Security Directive-84 (NSDD-84), had been withdrawn due to congressional opposition to the use of lie detectors and lifelong censorship requirements.

Throughout the remainder of 1984, *The New York Times* and the *Washington Post* printed articles that alternately praised Congress for resisting an extraordinary attempt to gag American citizens with prior restraint and chiding the Reagan Administration for its ill-advised attempt to deprive federal employees of their constitutional rights.

As late as December 28, 1984, the *Times* reported, "Under pressure, the Reagan Administration has withdrawn National Security Directive 84...".

Incredibly, the information was inaccurate and the celebration was premature.

When the 98th Congress adjourned in October 1984, the Reagan Administration had successfully implemented the largest censoring apparatus ever known in the United States through the continued implementation of NSDD-84.

Now, for the first time in history, more than three and a half million federal employees in the 12 largest federal agencies are required to submit their speeches, articles, and books for pre-publication review by their superiors—for the rest of their lives.

While columnists debated the "relative" accuracy of George Orwell's dark predictions for 1984, Ronald Reagan seized the initiative, tore up the Bill of Rights, and flushed it down the toilet with an audacity that would have flabbergasted even Orwell.

SOURCES: *Bill of Rights Journal*, December 1984, "They've Got a Secret," by Angus Mackenzie; *The New York Times*, 12/28/84, "Censorship of Its Employees Would Harm Government," by Thomas Ehrlich.

UPDATE: The media's disinformation about NSDD-84 essentially went unchallenged until outgoing U.N. ambassador Jeane Kirkpatrick created a stir by refusing to undergo federal review before publishing any article or book for the rest of her life (*MIT Technology Review*, November 1990). Nonetheless, while two of the thirteen provisions in NSDD-84 finally were rescinded, its basic assault on the First Amendment remained. According to *Columbia Journalism Review* (November 1991), "Steven Garfinkel, director of the federal Information Security Oversight Office, says his campaign to have government employees sign secrecy contracts is now nearly 100 percent complete." Some 143,531 federal employees in 48 agencies signed obligations to secrecy and censorship in just the six-month period between October 1, 1989, and March 31, 1990.

9. Three Stories That Might Have Changed the 1984 Election

1984 SYNOPSIS: Like the censored Watergate story of 1972, there were three potentially explosive political stories available to America's press that might have changed the results of the 1984 election.

But not one of them was put on the national agenda. The stories:

PAUL LAXALT. Considered to be President Reagan's closest friend, Nevada Senator Paul Laxalt was high on Reagan's list of potential nominees to fill the next U.S. Supreme Court position. *60 Minutes* produced an extraordinary documentary about Laxalt's political contributions from supporters linked to organized crime, some highly questionable loans, his efforts to limit FBI investigations into Nevada gaming operations, and his own Carson City casino which engaged in illegal skimming operations. Mike Wallace said it was a story that could change the course of the 1984 election. It was never shown by *60 Minutes*.

SOURCES: *Mother Jones*, August 1984, "Senator Paul Laxalt, The Man Who Runs the Reagan Campaign," by Robert I. Friedman; *The Nation*, 7/24/82, "The Senator and the Gamblers," by Bob Gottlieb and Peter Wiley; *Village Voice*, 3/12/85, "Networks Knuckle Under to Laxalt: The Story That Never Was Aired," by Robert I. Friedman and Dan E. Moldea.

EDWIN MEESE. Edwin Meese, a close personal friend of President Reagan, was named the top law enforcement officer in the United States. However, what few people know is that in the late '60s and early '70s, as a California state official, Edwin Meese directed a secret operation involving a wide variety of illegal and unconstitutional activities aimed at subverting the antiwar movement in California. As U.S. Attorney General, Meese continued his unconstitutional counterinsurgency program by restructuring the Federal Emergency Management Agency (FEMA) to combat domestic terrorism.

SOURCES: *Village Voice*, 2/26/85, "From the Man Who Brought You SWAT: Return of the Night of the Animals," by James Ridgeway; *San Francisco Bay Guardian*, 2/20/85, "Meese Acknowledges Counter-Insurgency Role," by Paul Rauber.

CHARLES WICK. Nancy and Ronald Reagan traditionally spent Christmas Eve with their good friends Mary Jane and Charles Wick. Wick, President Reagan's biggest single private fund-raiser in 1980, was later rewarded with the directorship of the U.S. Information Agency (USIA). In early 1984, *ABC-TV News* bought a well-documented story that revealed that Wick owned a nursing home in Visalia, California, that had what a state inspector called the worst nursing home conditions he had ever seen in California. During an unannounced inspection, one patient was found lying face down on the floor in a pool of blood and died soon after. ABC spent several months investigating and filming the story in California and Washington. Then, just as the story was ready for final edit, it was suddenly killed. There was a report from a reliable source that a call directly from the White House to ABC killed the story.

SOURCE: *Mother Jones*, November 1984, "What the Senate Didn't Know About Charles Z. Wick," by Seth Rosenfeld and Mark Shapiro.

UPDATE: PAUL LAXALT. Despite the allegations never aired by the *60 Minutes* exposé, Paul Laxalt has done very well since 1984. As a lobbyist, he has lobbied Congress on the behalf of the Generic Pharmaceutical Industry Association and the Competitive Long Distance Coalition on the telecommunications bill (*Roll Call*, 8/15/96). The *Washington Post* (7/26/96) reported Laxalt was a senior advisor to presidential candidate Bob Dole. And *The New York Times* (7/9/96) identified Laxalt as an influential advisor to Dole on behalf of Las Vegas.

EDWIN MEESE. The man who once tried to convert the nation's emergency assistance agency (FEMA) into a right-wing operation to combat domestic terrorism was brought down and shoved out of office by serious corruption allegations (*Charleston Post and Courier*, 7/14/96). Nonetheless, he now shares his conservative views at George Mason University where he serves on the board (*The Virginian-Pilot*, 6/29/96). He recently joined the Board of Visitors of Pat Robertson's Regent University School of Law (*The Washington Times*, 7/7/96). He also is a fellow at the Heritage Foundation, a conservative think-tank, where he serves along with fellow Jack Kemp, Bob Dole's 1996 pick for vice presidential candidate (*The Washington Post*, 7/16/96).

CHARLES WICK. Wick, who was Tommy Dorsey's musical arranger before he went into the nursing home business, returned to his celebrity social life after leaving the USIA. While there was continuing media coverage about Wick's social life, in which he was linked with various political figures including Ronald Reagan, Margaret Thatcher, and Walter Annenburg, Richard Nixon's ambassador to the Court of St. James (*Newsday*, 2/7/95; *Daily Variety*, 5/8/95; and *Equity-Vancouver*, November 1995), there never was another mention of his nursing home scandal until 1993 when columnists Jeff Cohen and Norman Solomon mentioned it in a piece they wrote about news media self-censorship (*Arizona Republic*, 8/17/93).

10. Myth of the Peaceful Atom— U.S. and U.K. Break Nuclear Treaty

1984 SYNOPSIS: The Nuclear Non-Proliferation Treaty, of which the United States and the United Kingdom are signatories, calls for a clear distinction between civil and military nuclear technologies. Specifically, Article VI of the treaty forbids the use of civil nuclear byproducts, such as reactor wastes, in the manufacture of nuclear weapons. Israelis used this provision of the treaty as an excuse for the bombing of a nuclear reactor in Iraq.

In 1958, the U.S. and U.K. signed a Mutual Defence Agreement. As part of this agreement, six to seven tons of plutonium from civilian reactors in Great Britain have been shipped to the United States for use in the manufacture of nuclear weapons—an open violation of the Non-Proliferation Treaty. U.S. Energy Secretary Donald Hodel has admitted that two to three tons of this plutonium have been made into nuclear warheads, some of which are currently deployed on Cruise missiles in England.

Dr. Ross Hesketh, a research physicist who began working with the Central Electricity Generating Board (CEGB) in England in 1959, became concerned about the use of civil plutonium for military purposes and began to protest publicly in 1981. After a campaign of systematic harassment, Hesketh was fired in June of 1983; a subsequent storm of public protest resulted in his rehiring by the CEGB, tantamount to an admission of guilt by CEGB. Hesketh later resigned from the CEGB and later became director of the European Proliferation Information Center.

While the story of how the United States and the United Kingdom broke the Nuclear Non-Proliferation Treaty was well covered in England, it was not put on the national news agenda in the United States.

SOURCES: *Sanity,* November 1984, "Plutonium Lies"; and press releases, correspondence, and articles which appeared in British publications during 1984 (including *The Daily Telegraph, New Scientist, The Guardian, Financial Times, New Statesman, New Society,* and *Nuclear Engineering International*) from Mr. David Lowry, Researcher, Energy Research Group, The Open University, Milton Keynes, England.

UPDATE: Despite the violations of the Nuclear Non-Proliferation Treaty (NPT) by key members United States and the United Kingdom, the NPT conference continued to exist. On May 11, 1995, the NPT was made permanent when conferees voted for an indefinite extension by acclamation. The next NPT review conference was scheduled for 1997 (*Nuclear News,* June 1995).

However, in apparent defiance of the international treaty, in late 1996, scientists at U.S. nuclear weapons labs were considering whether to conduct underground bomb tests that would stop just short of chain reaction explosions according to a report in the *San Francisco Examiner* (12/1/96). Some Third World leaders and anti-nuclear activists have warned that such tests would violate the spirit of the treaty, though clearly that has been done before.

CHAPTER 10—1985

International Terrorism vs. U.S. Terrorism

Nineteen-eighty-five was the year Coca Cola changed its formula and while the media covered every possible angle of that Junk Food News story, it completely failed to report the heaviest aerial bombardment that ever took place in the Western Hemisphere. According to the Associated Press, the top ten news stories of the year were:

1. Mideast terrorism
2. Reagan-Gorbachev summit
3. Volcano eruption in Colombia
4. Mexico City earthquake
5. AIDS and the death of Rock Hudson
6. Air crashes, particularly Japan Airlines Flight 747
7. African famine
8. U.S. farm crisis
9. South Africa
10. Spies and defectors.

THE TOP TEN CENSORED STORIES OF 1985

—And What Has Happened to Them Since

1. Fiercest Aerial War in America is Unreported in U.S. Press

1985 SYNOPSIS: While the President of El Salvador, José Napoleon Duarte, boasted about the decline in death squad killings, the people of El Salvador were victims of the most intense saturation bombing ever conducted in the Americas.

From June 1984, when the U.S. provided Duarte with the largest air force in Central America, the Salvadoran Air Force dropped over 3,000 tons of U.S.—made bombs on civilian populations, causing more than 2,000 deaths. Between January and mid-March of 1985, there were more than 105 attacks on civilian populations. These missions were often directed by U.S. military leaders.

Investigative journalist Alexander Cockburn asked, "How is it that over the past two years the United States has been organizing, supplying, overseeing and in many cases actually executing the heaviest bombing and most ferocious aerial war ever seen in the Americas and not one coherent report of the extent, viciousness, or consequences of this campaign has ever appeared in any major U.S. newspaper or magazine?"

Cockburn reported the aerial war was responsible for most of El Salvador's 500,000 internal refugees and for many of the 750,000 refugees outside the country's borders. More than one-fifth of the Salvadoran population of five million became refugees—a higher percentage than the corresponding figure in South Vietnam at the height of that war.

Patrick M. Hughes, director of Refugee Legal Services, in Laredo, Texas, wrote Project Censored to say, "The most outrageous omission in the press is the refusal to report the bombing campaigns in El Salvador."

SOURCES: *The Nation*, 6/1/85, "Remember El Salvador?", by Alexander Cockburn; *Refugee Legal Services*, Laredo, Texas, 1/24/86, letter from Patrick M. Hughes, Director.

UPDATE: Two weeks after Alexander Cockburn wrote the 1985 source article about the El Salvador aerial war, he reported that he watched for news of the bombing in *The New York Times*, *The Washington Post*, and the *Miami*

Herald, and found none. Instead the press continued to herald Duarte's Administration despite the fact that "the death squads were at their worst in his first term and the aerial war had risen to a climax in his second" (*The Nation*, 6/15/85). While the media ignored the largest aerial war ever conducted in America, protesters attempted to get the message to the public. In October 1985, students at Brown University and the University of Michigan jointly protested the media's cover-up of the bombing in El Salvador (*The Nation*, 11/30/85). Protesters urging the United States to stop the bombing rallied in August 1986 at the Illinois State Fair, where President Ronald Reagan was making a major speech on farm policy (*Chicago Tribune*, 8/13/86). And protesters interrupted Macy's 63rd annual Thanksgiving Day parade in 1989 when they were arrested for marching with an unauthorized 30-foot-long bomb-shaped balloon that read "Stop the bombing in El Salvador" (*UPI*, 11/23/89).

The American media were loathe to report the U.S.-supported aerial war in El Salvador, but the Russian news agency, TASS, eagerly reported the U.S. complicity in the brutal bombing of civilians in El Salvador (*TASS*, 1/25/87).

Please also see update of "El Salvador Crisis," #1, 1980.

2. Military Toxic Waste: More Dangerous and Not Regulated

1985 SYNOPSIS: Since before World War II, the U.S. military has been on a chemical and technological binge. While we are now becoming aware of the legacy of thousands of poisonous industrial waste sites, we haven't been told about the hundreds, perhaps thousands, of potentially more dangerous military toxic waste sites.

There are two major differences between military and industrial waste. First, the military problem includes exposure to many different forms of radiation, weapon tests, and dangerous, obsolete weapons whose disposal poses a nearly insolvable problem. Second, and equally important, the military is not subject to Environmental Protection Agency (EPA) regulations which govern industrial waste procedures. Further, the military annually generates more than 500,000 tons of hazardous waste, more than the five largest chemical companies combined.

Military toxic hazards range from chemical solvents that destroyed the well water supply of Hipps Road residents in Jacksonville, Florida, and poisoned a ranch in Eureka, Nevada, to radioactive waste in half a dozen sites in the Midwest and South.

Among the most acute hazards at the 392 military installations the EPA says need cleanup are 500,000 rockets, leaking nerve gas, stored in several sites; old Agent Orange manufacturing and storage areas; and exotic chemicals, such as RDX and other World War II explosives, that have contaminated wells in towns like Grand Island, Nebraska.

SOURCE: *Recon*, Winter 1986, "Pentagon Dumps Toxics On All of Us," by Will Collette.

UPDATE: Military toxic waste was an ongoing, unresolved problem long before Project Censored's first 1985 citation and in 1990 was the subject of yet another *Censored* story, titled "Military's Toxic Legacy to America." Meanwhile the military has been less than forthright in dealing with the problem. In early 1991, the military was caught selling toxic and explosive chemicals to unsuspecting civilian buyers at Defense Department surplus material auctions (*MIT Technology Review*, July 1991). In 1994, another *Censored* story revealed how the Air Force was illegally burning toxic materials at the super-secret Groom Lake Air Force Base (Project on Government Oversight, September 1994). Only now are the true costs of military toxic pollution becoming known. The McClatchy News Service reported on May 29, 1995, that the McClellan Air Force Base in California is the most polluted base in America, and taxpayers will have to pay the bill, expected to be at least $700 million. And in early 1996, two environmental groups charged the U.S. Navy with polluting Treasure Island—which will have to be cleaned up before being turned over to San Francisco in 1997 (*San Francisco Examiner*, 3/6/96).

3. Still Unreported: Ten Years of Genocide in East Timor

1985 SYNOPSIS: One of the top ten *Censored* stories of 1979 was "The Tragedy in East Timor." It revealed that since 1975, neutral observers estimated the number of Timorese people slaughtered with U.S.-supplied arms at 50,000 to 100,000—about ten percent of the population.

Ten years later, in 1985, Amnesty International (AI) reported that up to 200,000 East Timorese, a third of the population, died as a result of Indonesian aggression in the region, a tragedy still unreported by the American press.

Amnesty International released a report on human rights violations in June 1985, which indicated that, despite Indonesian claims of peace in the province and "normality," the Indonesian troops continued with waves of killings, "disappearances," and political arrests.

An Indonesian military manual obtained by AI clearly acknowledges the use of torture and interrogation procedures that contravene international law. The manual states, "If the use of physical violence is unavoidable, make sure that there are not Common People...around to witness it, so as not to arouse the antipathy of the Common People."

SOURCE: *Amnesty Action*, Summer 1985, "East Timor: A Decade of Killing, Torture, and Indonesian Claims of 'Normality.'"

UPDATE: Please see update of "The Tragedy in East Timor," #7, 1979.

4. The Reagan Autocracy

1985 SYNOPSIS: In November 1981, the American Civil Liberties Union warned, "What we are witnessing is a systematic assault on the concept of government accountability and deterrence of illegal government conduct." Since Reagan's election in 1980, the Reagan Administration conducted a successful campaign to exalt the power of the presidency and to undermine the power of the law, the courts, Congress, and the people.

On February 17, 1981, the President signed Executive Order (EO) 12291 which set up a framework for (presidential) management of the rule-making process. Under this order, the White House can nullify acts of Congress that the President considers too costly.

The order threatened to make "cost-benefit principles," imposed and manipulated by the White House, supreme over the statutory mission given by Congress to the executive agencies of the government, in violation of the doctrine of separation of powers.

By 1983, the "Reagan Autocracy" had begun to affect millions of people living near nuclear power plants. Under the director of the budget office, the Nuclear Regulatory Commission and the Environmental Protection Agency suspended some of their most important safety regulations because cost factors were not built into health regulations.

A change adopted in 1984 to "Circular A-122—Cost Principles for Nonprofit Organizations" and a Presidential executive order banned "any organization that seeks to influence...the determination of public policy" from participating in the federal government's lucrative on-the-job charity drives.

On January 24, 1985, again without public notice, Executive Order 12498 gave the White House power to not only impose cost-benefit analysis but to review, control, approve, or suppress any agency activity "that may influence, anticipate, or could lead to the commencement of rule-making proceedings at a later date."

SOURCE: *Harper's*, November 1985, "Liberty Under Siege," by Walter Karp.

UPDATE: The potentially dangerous impact of Reagan's two unpublicized executive orders cited in the 1985 story, #12291 of 1981 and #12498 of 1985, can clearly be seen in two recent events.

On May 11, 1996, a Valujet DC-9 crashed in the Florida Everglades west of Miami killing all 110 people aboard. The accident was caused by a fire in the cargo-hold. Nearly three years earlier, on August 10, 1993, Joseph M. Del Balzo, acting administrator of the Federal Aviation Administration, wrote Carl W. Vogt, then chairman of the National Transportation Safety Board (NTSB), saying the FAA would not implement the NTSB's recommended safety rules to combat the threat from cargo-hold fires on some commercial airliners. The reason given was that the cost of compliance would exceed $350 million, making the proposal a "major rule" as defined in Reagan's 1981 Executive Order 12291 (*USA Today*, 5/21/96).

In November 1996, six months after the tragic crash, the FAA suddenly reversed its long-held position that it was too expensive to put fire detection and suppression systems in all airline cargo-holds. It now wants to require them. On December 13, 1996, the *Los Angeles Times* reported the airline industry would voluntarily retrofit its jetliners with cargo-hold fire detection systems. However, more than a year after the tragic accident, hazardous cargo still was carried on both passenger and cargo planes, and fire-detection systems weren't installed (*USA Today*, 5/9/97).

The other Reagan Executive Order, #12498, paved the way for onerous censorship. When James Hansen, director of the Goddard Institute for Space Studies, presented his findings to the U.S. government that the increase in droughts and storms are "clearly" consequences of the greenhouse effect, his use of the word "clearly" to describe the relationship was suddenly changed to "probably." This revision to a scientific report was made under Reagan's EO #12498, which allows scientific research to be skewed "for conformity with administration policy." It also stops federal agencies from admitting they have been forbidden to collect data on a range of sensitive topics (*The Observer*, 4/24/94).

5. Media Merger Mania Threatens Free Flow of Information

1985 SYNOPSIS: The drive for profits, coupled with the collapse of the Federal Communications Commission (FCC) in 1985, paved the way for the specter of an international information cartel. Not surprisingly, the information cartel did not report on the previous year's media merger mania.

Herbert Schiller, internationally renown media critic, pointed out that the FCC, historically a weak defender of the quality of the nation's interest, abandoned all consideration of the public interest. Now the number of TV and radio stations that a license holder may acquire has been nearly doubled; the traditional obligations of station owners to serve the public's information needs have either been eliminated or weakened severely; standards limiting the number of commercials that may be aired each hour have been relaxed; the requirement that programming logs be kept has been eliminated; children's programming guidelines have been ignored; and license renewals for stations have become virtually automatic.

Media firms bought, sold, bartered, or merged include American Broadcasting Companies, Capital Cities Communications, Metromedia, Prentice-Hall, *The New Yorker*, KTLA-TV Los Angeles, and The Tribune Company. The year ended with the awesome $6.3 billion RCA/NBC takeover by General Electric.

The GE-RCA merger especially worried consumer advocate Ralph Nader, who said, "The big now get bigger by buying each other, rather than by making and selling better products. This is the worst takeover yet, because it's one conglomerate taking over another conglomerate." Nader added, "The level of self-censorship due to conglomerate owners and bottomline mentality in the broadcast media is increasing greatly."

SOURCES: *The Nation*, 6/8/85, "Behind the Media Merger Movement," by Herbert Schiller; *San Francisco Chronicle*, 12/23/85, "For Big Brother, It Was a Very Good Year," by Tom Shales, Washington Post Writers Group.

UPDATE: The media mergers of 1985 pale in contrast to the major media merger mania witnessed a decade later in 1995. University of Maryland media professor Douglas Gomery, author of nine books on the economics and history of the media, said of 1995, "It's been a crazy year, with media mergers seeming to happen on a daily basis" (*American Journalism Review*, December 1995). And while concerned groups such as Consumers Union, the Consumer Federation of America, and the Media Access Project make efforts in Washington to slow media merger mania, they win an occasional concession, but lose the war.

In February 1996, President Clinton signed the sweeping telecommunications reform bill (the #1 *Censored* story of 1995), which paved the way for even bigger mergers now and in the future (*USA Today*, 7/22/96). Criticism of the bill came from an unexpected source. Molly Ivins noted in her column (*Minneapolis Star Tribune*, 1/11/96) that even Bob Dole had several problems with the bill, and reportedly had referred to it as a "big, big corporate welfare project." Unfortunately, the media merger mania has probably not run its course yet. Noting that some $97 billion in media deals were signed in just the first half of 1996 versus $46.6 billion in the first half of 1995, a media stock analyst said this "may be the tip of the iceberg."

Please also see other media merger stories, #1, 1987; #1, 1989; #1, 1992; and #1, 1995.

6. The Birth Defect Crisis and the Environment

1985 SYNOPSIS: Conservative statistics reveal that 12 out of every 100 babies born in the United States this year will have a serious, often incurable mental or physical health disorder. While statisticians disagree as to whether we are experiencing an epidemic of birth defects, they all acknowledge the number of disabled newborns has doubled since the late 1950s and that some of the worst abnormalities are increasing at alarming rates. Of the 16 major (sentinel) defects under surveillance at the Centers for Disease Control (CDC)—defects from missing limbs to missing brains—seven have increased at rates ranging from 20 to 300 percent.

Recent studies have directly linked specific environmental and chemical agents to some of the defects that are increasing. Critics charge there has been a rise of birth defect clusters around environmental catastrophes:

1) Love Canal, where studies show that 56 percent of the children born near the notorious toxic dump were mentally or physically disabled; 2) Shiprock, New Mexico, near a uranium mining site, where there are so many deformed children that the community now hosts its own Special Olympics; 3) Woburn, Massachusetts, where the childhood cancer rate is two and a half times the national average and a cluster of children was discovered

with severe birth deformities. The community pinpointed birth defects in an area of town where burned toxic wastes had contaminated local drinking wells.

Love Canal, Shiprock, and Woburn are but three of hundreds of birth defect clusters currently known to the birth defects branch of the CDC in Atlanta, where 50 new "potentially important" clusters are reported every year.

SOURCE: *Mother Jones*, January 1985, "Terata," by Christopher Norwood, and "Manhattan Project for the Unborn," by Mark Dowie.

UPDATE: One of the most frightening outbreaks of babies born with birth defects occurred in the spring of 1991, when three anencephalic babies were born in a 36-hour period in the Rio Grande Valley. Since this was an extremely unusual incidence of this rare and fatal birth defect in which a baby is born without a brain, numerous scientists and health researchers flocked to the area. While they learned that Brownsville, Texas, had the highest rate of anencephaly in the country, ongoing research by the Centers for Disease Control and Prevention and the Texas Department of Health have not yet determined the cause. Possible causes include environmental, genetic, and nutritional factors (*The Houston Chronicle*, 6/6/95).

A lawsuit by 28 families in the Brownsville area against 40 maquiladoras, including General Motors, was settled for $17 million before the case went to trial in 1995. Supporting documents showed some of the plants used toxic chemicals at levels that were not allowed in the United States and that some even violated less stringent Mexican environmental laws. The environmental situation in the area has improved since 1991 with some factories switching to less-toxic materials and updating their emission equipment. Birth defect rates along the border have dropped since the original outbreak although they remain higher than the national average (Associated Press, 7/4/97).

A statewide survey by the California Department of Health Services released in June 1997 revealed that living near hazardous waste sites appears to raise the risk of birth defects in infants. Communities were warned about potential problems in building housing near waste sites (*San Francisco Examiner*, 6/16/97).

Environmentally caused birth defects are not limited to the United States. Life expectancy in the Soviet Union has dropped to 58 years and is as low as 45 in some regions. The extent to which environmental problems are blamed is shown by the increase in birth defects. Statistics for the past few years show that congenital defect rates have been growing faster than the rates of other diseases. One Russian health and environmental specialist said, "Contamination of chemical and radioactive substances in the environment is a serious cause of pathologies" (Inter Press Service, 4/21/95).

Despite the depressing statistics, there may be some progress being made. The *Morbidity and Mortality Weekly Report* (3/15/96) by the U.S. Department of Health and Human Services reported the 1993 final infant mortality (death before age one year) rate for the United States was 8.4 deaths per 1000 live-born infants—the lowest rate ever recorded.

7. Administration Releases Phony "Star Wars" Test Results

1985 SYNOPSIS: Officials of the Reagan Administration reportedly covered up scientific failures with the "Star Wars" project in an effort to sell the program to a skeptical American public. According to a *New York Times* report, while scientists working on the project were not allowed to talk to the press about test failures, administration officials did talk about successful test results.

Frustrated by the government's disinformation campaign, two top scientists, one at Livermore and another at Los Alamos, resigned from the program.

Ray Kidder, another physicist at Livermore, was quoted as saying, "The public is getting swindled by one side that has access to classified information and can say whatever it wants and not go to jail, whereas we (the skeptics) can't say whatever we want. We would go to jail, that's the difference."

The X-ray laser, pet project of physicist Edward Teller, who sold "Star Wars" to President Reagan, produced completely unreliable results when tested. The test inspired one scientist to conclude, "instead of a weapon we have a toy." Nonetheless, it was Teller, also known as "father of the H-bomb," who leaked that the test took place on March 23, 1985, and his cronies then put out word that it was highly successful.

Further, while the administration said its anti-missile program is non-nuclear, the X-ray laser depends on a nuclear explosion for its energy. And it was the insistence on continuing the "Star War" tests that was a major reason Reagan wouldn't even listen to the Soviet proposal for a comprehensive test ban, despite public sentiment for one.

SOURCES: *The New York Times*, 12/4/85, "A 'Star Wars' Cover-up?", by Flora Lewis; *In These Times*, 11/6/85, "Scientists say no to Star Wars," by David Moberg.

UPDATE: On July 23, 1994, *The New York Times* confirmed that Star Wars officials conducted a deception program in the 1980s to make it appear that the ballistic missile-defense system worked when it didn't. While some senior military officials thought it might be necessary to inform selected members of Congress of the deception, Congress was not informed. When members of the Senate Armed Services Committee learned of the deception in a briefing in September 1993, they said they wished they had known about it back in 1984. Senator David Pryor of Arkansas said, "It is an outrage that Congress did not find out about it until ten years had passed and $35 billion was spent" on the Star Wars program.

8. The Doomsday Communications System

1985 SYNOPSIS: The Ground Wave Emergency Network (GWEN) is a supersecret communications system designed to function after a nuclear war begins, which will enable political and military leaders to establish and maintain communications during an extended nuclear war.

Studies have shown that an electromagnetic pulse (EMP), resulting from a nuclear explosion, will cripple entire continental power and communication lines, as well as radio stations, command posts, radar system, and aircraft and missile electronics.

Utilizing low frequency radio waves, GWEN will link "sensor sites, command posts, and land-based nuclear forces." Under a contract with the RCA Corporation, the Air Force proposes to construct hundreds of relay nodes in communities across the nation. Each GWEN node consists of a tower 300 feet high, an underground copper screen 600 feet in diameter, and buildings to house other equipment.

The first phase of GWEN, with nine relay nodes, was built in the Midwest during 1984 without media exposure or widespread public knowledge.

SOURCES: *Recon*, Winter 1986, "National No-GWEN Alliance," by Lois Barber; *Physics and Society*, July 1985, "Estimating Vulnerability to Electromagnetic Pulse Effects," by John M. Richardson.

UPDATE: In 1993, Congress declared GWEN obsolete and suspended funding (*Minneapolis Star Tribune*, 1/26/94; *The Salt Lake Tribune*, 2/19/94). In 1994, protesters of proposed "doomsday towers," in six states, including communities like Lastrup, Minnesota, and Kanab, Utah, received letters from Assistant Secretary of Defense Emmett Paige, Jr., saying the department will terminate construction contracts for 29 towers to be built at sites across the United States. Since the GWEN project started ten years ago, 58 towers were built, two were under construction, and 23 others were planned.

In 1995, GWEN, which cost taxpayers $500 million, was declared one of the top "bombs" on the list of the Atomic Age—projects canceled after the United States had already spent the money (*The Denver Post*, 7/13/95).

9. Federal Government Rips Off the Homeless

1985 SYNOPSIS: The primary federal assistance agency created solely to aid the homeless in the United States is the Homeless Task Force, in the Department of Health and Human Services. The task force, formed in 1983, was to provide federal resources to the homeless by making "sharing agreements" with other federal agencies. A subcommittee of the House Committee on Government Operations released a study on homelessness in 1985 which revealed how "sharing agreements" have worked:

1) The major sharing agreement of 1984 was made with the Department of Defense (DOD), which received $8 million to renovate vacant military facilities for use as emergency shelters; although DOD found 600 potential sites, only two were renovated at a cost of less than $1 million; the remainder of the money was spent on routine maintenance of army reserve facilities;

THIS MODERN WORLD   by TOM TOMORROW

2) Under another agreement, the DOD was to provide surplus food to food banks that supply homeless shelters and soup kitchens; only 39 of 195 commissaries actually provided food, and then in such limited amounts that it was described in federal records as "minimal";

3) The Department of Housing and Urban Development (HUD) was to provide vacant single-family homes; at the end of 1984, HUD held 9,225 unsold homes in its enormous inventory, but only 10 of these were provided under the agreement;

4) The General Service Administration promised to provide surplus federal buildings for use as emergency shelters; out of 3,874 available buildings, the agency only managed to find three to use as emergency shelters.

SOURCE: Pacific News Service, 12/20/85, "Washington's Foot-Dragging Role in Dealing With the Homeless," by Polly Leider.

UPDATE: The Homeless Task Force and its "sharing agreements" program failed in its fight against homelessness as foreseen by the 1985 *Censored* story. It was succeeded by the McKinney Act, passed by Congress in 1987, which was designed to bring federal, state, local and non-profit sectors together to work on ending homelessness.

The concept of using vacant military facilities to house the homeless continued under the McKinney Act. Some military facilities already being put to such use include the former Mather Air Force Base, near Sacramento (*Sacramento Bee*, 2/25/96); U.S. Army Corps of Engineers property near North Nashville (*The Tennessean*, 4/8/96); and the old Charleston Naval Base in South Carolina (*Charleston Post and Courier*, 8/14/96).

However, federal solutions to the homeless problem remain inadequate as a result of budget cuts, the Not In My Back Yard (NIMBY) attitude, and

a decreased public concern with the problem (*Journal of Housing & Community Development*, March/April 1996; *America*, 4/13/96).

Not surprisingly, a national survey, released by the U.S. Conference of Mayors on December 16, 1996, revealed that hunger and homelessness in the nation's cities increased in 1996 for the 12th straight year. The mayors predict that cuts in welfare benefits in 1997 will make the problem even worse (*USA Today*, 12/16/96).

10. High-tech Health Hazards: A New American Nightmare?

1985 SYNOPSIS: According to California labor statistics, "Poisonings are twice as common among semiconductor workers as they are among employees in other industries...and work-related illnesses occur three-and-one-half times more frequently in the semiconductor industry than in manufacturing as a whole."

High-tech health problems include:

✔ Respiratory Disease: occupational asthma, shortness of breath, and other respiratory problems were traced to liquid solder flux, used to clean boards during soldering;

✔ Chemical Sensitization: exposure to toxic chemicals may damage the body's immune system by destroying "T-cells" which suppress reactions to chemicals;

✔ Hypertension: electronics workers suffered extreme hypertension possibly caused by demanding assembly quotas, incessant monitoring, and production "speed-ups";

✔ Radiation Hazards: high-tech etching equipment can produce above-standard exposure to radio frequency radiation;

✔ Reproductive Problems: solder fumes and many of the solvents used in high-tech plants can cause damage to the reproductive system including spontaneous abortion;

✔ Cancer: cyanide and arsenic compounds and other carcinogenic substances used in the electronic industry can cause cancer.

Since 1980, cutbacks in Occupational Safety and Health Administration funding and reductions in inspections already have made health matters worse in the high-tech industry. Now the Reagan Administration has called for a "voluntary compliance" program that could exempt thousands of plants from surprise inspections.

SOURCES: *The Progressive*, October 1985, "Dead End in Silicon Valley," by Diana Hembree; *Ms. Magazine*, March 1986, "A New American Nightmare?", by Amanda Spake.

UPDATE: In 1987, Diana Hembree (author of the 1985 *Censored* story) and Sarah Henry provided a follow-up to the earlier story, reporting that "more than 100 Silicon Valley employees have sued their companies for workers compensation, blaming their illnesses on exposure to toxic chemicals on the job." They noted the Silicon Valley problem has implications for more than one million employees, mostly women, who work in electronic production in the U.S. (*The San Diego Union-Tribune*, 1/5/87). On May 2, 1989, *MacWeek*, a computer trade journal, reported a California workers' compensation judge ruled for the first time that an electronic industry worker's exposure to solvents on the job caused a disabling disease. More recently, the *Oregonian* (12/10/95) published an investigative piece on the rapidly growing computer chip industry in Oregon. It noted in California's Silicon Valley, the industry failed to recognize the risks it posed to workers and the environment, and as those early mistakes proved costly, the industry began to master its toxic tools. It concluded the "industry's recent safety record is good."

U.S. Spies on its Own Citizens

While the mainstream media covered some aspects of the Iran arms/contra scandal, it failed to report what happened to outspoken U.S. citizens who disagreed with the Reagan Administration's Central American policies. According to the Associated Press, the top ten news stories of the year were:

1. Challenger space shuttle disaster
2. Iran arms/contra funding scandal
3. Chernobyl nuclear power plant accident
4. U.S. bombing of Libya
5. Philippine's ouster of Ferdinand Marcos
6. Income tax reform
7. Reagan/Gorbachev Iceland summit
8. Mideast terror
9. War against drugs
10. U.S. economy.

THE TOP TEN CENSORED STORIES OF 1986

—And What Has Happened to Them Since

1. Criticizing the President's Policies Can Be Dangerous

1986 SYNOPSIS: Political opponents of the Reagan Administration's Central American policies became the targets of mysterious break-ins, IRS audits, FBI questioning, and physical surveillance. Congressman Don Edwards (D-California), a former FBI agent, charged, "The administration is using the various independent agencies of the United States Government for their political purposes."

A three-part television report by San Francisco's KRON-TV "Target 4" investigative group revealed the following:

The IRS sent a letter to *Sojourners*, a non-profit ecumenical Christian magazine based in Washington, D.C., that opposes aid to the contras and other Reagan policies, threatening the group's tax-exempt status; the offices of former U.S. Ambassador to El Salvador Robert E. White, who opposes the administration's Central American policies, were mysteriously broken into; former FBI informant Frank Varelli admitted spying on the Committee in Solidarity with the People of El Salvador (CISPES) and said FBI agents broke into a CISPES office in Dallas; FBI agents were ordered to follow, photograph, and conduct extensive background checks on members of the All People's Congress to determine if the group had a propensity for violence.

In another report, UPI revealed that dozens of American citizens and groups critical of Reagan's policy on Central America say they have been harassed by the Internal Revenue Service, the FBI, or the Customs Service after visits to Nicaragua.

Finally, the Women's Building in San Francisco was broken into and the files containing the names and home addresses of women involved in Central American peace issues and radical feminist politics had been examined.

SOURCES: *KRON-TV "TARGET 4,"* 2/18/87-2/20/87, "Heat on the Left" series, by anchor-reporter Sylvia Chase, producer Jonathan Dann, and Angus Mackenzie of the Center for Investigative Reporting; *San Francisco Examiner, UPI*, 2/19/87, "Nicaragua Visitors: U.S. Harasses Us," by Neil

Roland; *San Francisco Examiner*, 3/13/87, "Info-thieves Hit the Women's Building," by Warren Hinckle.

UPDATE: On January 2, 1989, *The Boston Globe* reported it had received documents that revealed FBI director William Sessions misled Congress about the scope and duration of the FBI's five-year nationwide probe of groups critical of President Reagan's policies in Central America.

The Senate Intelligence Committee report on the FBI's activities released in July 1989 revealed the CISPES investigation involved the efforts of 52 FBI offices and spawned 178 spinoff investigations covering 2,375 individuals and 1,330 groups.

The Senate Committee concluded the CISPES investigation should never have been opened, was improperly expanded, and continued even though it was based on unreliable information. Sessions delivered an unprecedented apology for the bureau's behavior, disciplined six agents, agreed to purge the FBI files of the CISPES data, and the FBI adopted 33 procedural reforms to reduce chances of a repeat performance (*The Nation*, 10/30/89; *The National Journal*, 12/30/89).

Please also see the update of "Salvador Crisis," #1, 1980, for confirmation of what CISPES and other groups had to say about U.S. policies in Central America; and the update of "Foreign Intelligence Surveillance Court," #2, 1982, to learn how the federal government continues to spy on American citizens to this day.

2. Official U.S. Censorship: Less Access to Less Information

1986 SYNOPSIS: Under President Reagan's direction, the government has significantly reduced public information with little if any media attention. Since 1980, the American Library Association has documented administration efforts to eliminate, restrict, and privatize government documents.

In 1985, the Office of Management and Budget required annual reviews of agency publications and detailed justification for proposed periodicals; required cost-benefit analyses of government information activities; encouraged maximum reliance on the private sector for dissemination of government information; and required cost recovery through user charges.

During 1986, the government launched a new "disinformation" program that allows deliberately false, incomplete and misleading information, including altered technical information, to be released in order to impede the transfer of accurate technological information to the Soviet Union. The government also developed a new category of "sensitive information" to further restrict public access to a broad range of unclassified data.

SOURCE: *American Library Association*, Washington Office, "Less Access to Less Information By and About the U.S. Government: II," December 1986.

UPDATE: Evidence of the success of Reagan's efforts to reduce public access to information was revealed in an analysis of the government's secrecy system by Tom Blanton, executive director of the National Security Archive, a Washington, D.C.-based research institute. Blanton concluded an obsession with secrecy still chokes the information arteries of the U.S. government. Some of the problems cited by Blanton included: The Freedom of Information Act has become practically unusable because of bureaucratic processing delays; the National Archive is overwhelmed with old secrets; the official history of our country is replete with censored facts that foreigners are aware of but U.S. citizens aren't; the federal culture of secrecy is so seductive that security clearances are status symbols. Nonetheless, on an optimistic note, Blanton noted President Clinton ordered the first post-Cold War review of the government's enormous secrecy system, a move which could result in the release of millions of secret documents and a wholesale rewrite of our recent history (*American Libraries*, September 1993).

Since 1986, the ALA has continued to document efforts to restrict and privatize government information in their ongoing chronology "Less Access to Less Information By and About the U.S. Government." This chronology is released as a supplement to the ALA Washington Office Newsletter and electronically at http://www.ala.org/washoff/lessaccess.html. A reprint of ALA's 1996 chronology is available in book form in *Censored 1997* (New York: Seven Stories Press, 1997) by Peter Phillips & Project Censored.

3. Personal Privacy Assaulted Without Public Debate

1986 SYNOPSIS: In 1986, the FBI was quietly given extraordinary powers to look into the most private files of Americans "suspected of being in the employ of a foreign power."

This latest invasion of privacy was provided for in the Intelligence Authorization Bill for 1987, which was passed by Congress with little debate or press coverage, in the heat of the end-of-session scramble in late 1986 when senators and representatives were anxious to return home.

In the aftermath of the U.S.-Russian "spy" incident, when *U.S. News & World Report* correspondent Nicholas Daniloff was arrested as a spy in Russia and later exchanged for Russian spies in the U.S., FBI counterintelligence officials persuaded a gullible Congress the bill was needed because they lacked the resources and information to catch Americans selling secrets to the enemy.

Specifically, the bill gives the FBI access to financial records and telephone toll logs of individuals suspected of espionage. Those files include data from banking institutions and telephone companies which reveal some of the most intimate and private details of a person's daily activities. Historically, this type of information was considered off-limits to government.

SOURCE: *The National Reporter,* Fall/Winter 1986, "News Not In The News: Reach Out and Crush Someone," by Don Goldberg.

UPDATE: The invasion of personal privacy has increased rapidly in the last decade with the growth and power of computer systems and telecommunications. The new technologies have given business, as well as government, the ability to gather immense amounts of personal information on everyone. At the same time, the American public has become more concerned with this issue. A public opinion poll by Louis Harris & Associates in 1993 found 83 percent of Americans are concerned about threats to their personal privacy. This is a five point increase from the year before and a 49 percentage point increase since 1970.

A report titled "Privacy and the National Information Infrastructure: Safeguarding Telecommunications-Related Information," issued by the U.S. Department of Commerce in October 1995 warned, "The real danger is the gradual erosion of individual liberties through the automation, integration and interconnection of many small, separate record-keeping systems, each of which alone may seem innocuous, even benevolent and wholly justifiable." The report concluded, "Information privacy can never be absolute in a sociological setting; no individual who lives in a society can have total control over each bit of personal information" (*Chicago Daily Law Bulletin*, 4/27/96).

The San Diego-based Privacy Rights Clearinghouse, administered by the University of San Diego's Center for Public Interest Law, provides the first privacy help-line of its kind in the country. Its phone number is

619/298-3396 and its E-mail address is prc@privacyrights.org and its Web page is www.privacyrights.org (*The San Diego Union-Tribune*, 7/2/95).

4. Pro Contra Media Coverage—Paid for by the CIA

1986 SYNOPSIS: According to Edgar Chamorro, former head of the contra communications office, "approximately 15 Honduran journalists and broadcasters were on the CIA payroll and our influence was thereby extended to every major Honduran newspaper and television station." In his affidavit submitted to the World Court in September 1985, Chamorro also said that the same tactic was employed by the CIA in Costa Rica in an effort to turn the newspapers and television stations of that country against the Nicaraguan government.

Carlos Morales, a Costa Rican professor of journalism and editor of the University of Costa Rica's liberal weekly *La Universidad*, said at least eight Costa Rican journalists, including three "top editors," received monthly payments from the CIA, either directly or through contra groups with offices in Costa Rica.

In 1977, after a Senate Select Committee on Intelligence report disclosed the CIA had maintained working relationships with 50 American reporters over a period of years, the agency announced new rules that barred it from entering into "any paid or contractual relationship" with U.S. journalists, including freelancers and stringers.

However, the regulations said nothing about entering into such relationships with foreign journalists, or about allowing agency operatives to pose as foreign journalists. It now appears the agency does both, thereby jeopardizing press credibility.

In his affidavit, Chamorro said he had been paymaster for the Nicaraguan Democratic Force (FDN) and had received money from the CIA to bribe Honduran journalists and broadcasters to write and speak favorably about the FDN and to attack the government of Nicaragua and call for its overthrow.

SOURCES: *CovertAction Quarterly*, Summer 1986; *Columbia Journalism Review*, March/April 1987, "Contra Coverage—Paid For By the CIA," by Martha Honey.

UPDATE: Given that the CIA once had 50 American journalists on its payroll—a policy banned in 1977—and subsequently paid Central American journalists, as noted in this *Censored* story, it should not be surprising that the CIA is now seeking official permission to hire journalists (*Washington Post*, 7/31/96). Nor should it be surprising that the Council on Foreign Relations, the predecessor to the Trilateral Commission (cited in the #1 *Censored* story of 1976), would prepare a report, entitled "Making Intelligence Smarter," in early 1996, which recommended that the CIA resume the practice of using clergy or news correspondents. The report generated immediate concern from various human rights groups including the Maryknoll Sisters, who questioned whether there was even a need for "an agency such as the CIA" (*National Catholic Reporter*, 4/26/96).

5. President Reagan and the Fascist "World Anti-Communist League"

1986 SYNOPSIS: Members of the World Anti-Communist League (WACL)—an extremist right-wing international cartel of sorts—include such luminaries as Ferdinand Marcos, Rev. Sun Myung Moon, and Adolfo Calero, commander in chief of the armed forces of the FDN contras.

One of the most important people in the WACL is retired U.S. Major General John Singlaub. Singlaub began his military and intelligence career as an OSS member during World War II. In 1976, he became Chief of Staff of both the United Nations and U.S. Army Forces in South Korea. He was removed in 1977 after he publicly criticized President Jimmy Carter's withdrawal of troops from Korea.

Singlaub joined WACL in 1980 and formed an American Chapter called the United States Council for World Freedom. Singlaub subsequently was elected its president.

According to one exposé, the WACL is so extreme that the ultra-conservative John Birch Society shunned it and advised its members to do likewise. The WACL was described by Scott and Jon Lee Anderson, authors of *Inside the League*, an exposé of the WACL, as "largely a collection of Nazis, fascists, anti-Semites, sellers of forgeries, vicious racialists, and corrupt self-seekers."

At the 17th Annual WACL Conference held in San Diego, California, Singlaub read a letter from President Ronald Reagan which said in part, "The World Anti-Communist League has long played a leadership role in drawing attention to the gallant struggle now being waged by the true freedom fighters of our day. Nancy and I send our best wishes for future success."

SOURCES: *UTNE Reader*, August/September 1986, "Moonies, Loonies, and Ronnie," by Eric Selbin; *Briarpatch*, November 1986, "In League with the Devil: The World Anti-Communist League," by George Martin Manz; *St. Louis Journalism Review*, March 1987, "Inside the League," by Scott and Jon Lee Anderson.

UPDATE: John Singlaub and the World Anti-Communist League (WACL), now with a new name, are both still alive and spreading their venom around the world. On September 17, 1994, *The Irish Times* reported that the WACL was now known as The World League for Freedom and Democracy (WLFD). It may be assumed that the end of the Cold War in 1989 and the demise of worldwide communism initiated the name change. A delegate to a recent WLFD convention held, in of all places, Moscow, noted the WLFD is sponsored by Taiwan and South Korea, and now that communism is defeated, it would be turning its attention to "global affairs, the need for peace initiatives and co-operating with developing countries."

Since the 1986 *Censored* story cited above, the WACL/WLFD and Singlaub have been noted for producing "troops of killers" while ostensibly organized to provide support for Corazon Aquino from the right-wing in the Philippines (*Village Voice*, 2/27/96) and for supporting the vicious RENAMO movement in Mozambique (*Guardian*, 8/6/94).

Please see *Censored* story #3 of 1989 for more information about the Mozambique holocaust.

6. Lethal Nerve Gas Production in Residential Areas

1986 SYNOPSIS: Although the military has been under orders from Congress since 1984 to dispose of nerve gases by 1994, they are currently being manufactured and tested in 46 U.S. communities, in 26 states across the country—usually without the knowledge of the residents.

For example, Geomet Technologies does nerve gas research only 100 yards from an elementary school in Gaithersburg, Maryland. Representative Michael Barnes (D-Maryland), whose district includes the Geomet lab, said, "The Army has indicated that, in effect, it has no policy with regard to the location of the testing facility."

Despite the 1984 Congressional order, there has been a boom in nerve gas research in recent years. In fact, chemical warfare funding increased five times to $400 million in 1985.

Twenty-seven major universities, including four medical schools, have chemical warfare contracts. Fifteen of the sites are licensed for full-strength chemical warfare materials (the others work with diluted substances). Since 1981, accidents have been reported at two facilities—both licensed for full-strength work.

At least 40 of the nerve gas sites are located in large metropolitan areas (such as Los Angeles, Baltimore, Chicago, and New Orleans), where an accidental release could imperil thousands of people.

SOURCES: *Recon*, Winter 1987, "Nerve Gas in Residential Areas"; *The New York Times*, 2/28/85, "Research on Nerve Gas Suspended in Cambridge"; *USA Today*, 3/11/87, "Risks Near Chemical Warfare Dumps Cited," by Wayne Beissert.

UPDATE: The 1994 deadline for the disposal of nerve gas passed unheralded by the media. However, on August 22, 1996, the U.S. Army finally began destroying the U.S. stockpile of rapidly deteriorating chemical nerve weapons in a $650 million incinerator at Tooele, Utah. It was an inauspicious start. On August 25, 1996, it shut down for five days after a nerve gas leak was discovered (*USA Today*, 8/26/96). This marked the beginning of a $12 billion effort to eliminate 31,000 tons of mustard and nerve gas packed into three million rockets, land mines, bombs, mortars, missiles, and canisters stored in eight states. The incineration process, which will not be complete until 2004, was protested by environmental groups that charged it was dangerous (Associated Press, 8/23/96).

The New York Times reported (8/23/96), without explanation, that "The Pentagon will still maintain a site for production and testing of new weapons." On April 24, 1997, despite long-standing opposition by Senator Jesse Helms, and with a last-minute nudge from President Clinton, the U.S. Senate overwhelmingly ratified the Chemical Weapons Convention which would ban such weapons (Knight-Ridder Newspapers, 4/25/97). The worldwide treaty banning chemical weapons went into effect, without ratification from Russia, Iraq, and North Korea, at midnight, April 28, 1997.

7. Contragate: The Costa Rica Connection

1986 SYNOPSIS: As 1986 ended, each day seemed to bring new evidence of the Reagan Administration's involvement in the Iran-contra arms scandal. But even now, one major chapter in the sordid story remains to be told.

It involves Lt. Col. Oliver North and those to whom he reported; it involves two American journalists and their $22 million lawsuit against a group of U.S.-backed mercenaries operating in Miami and Central America; it involves a conspiracy to murder dissident contra leader Eden Pastora and the U.S. ambassador to Costa Rica, Lewis Tambs—and blame both acts on the Sandinistas; it involves a drug trafficking ring operating out of contra bases and airstrips on the property of a shadowy U.S. rancher in Costa Rica; it involves a cover-up that included the torture and murder of a key journalistic source; and it involves the continued threats against the lives of the two journalists who sought to expose the whole incredible plot.

The lawsuit was filed by the Christic Institute, a public interest law firm with a long track record of taking on, and winning, important political cases, like the successful Karen Silkwood suit against Kerr-McGee.

The two plaintiffs, Tony Avirgan and Martha Honey, are veteran journalists who had worked for news organizations such as ABC, *The New York Times*, *The London Times*, and the BBC. They started investigating the contra-Costa Rica connection after Avirgan was injured in the assassination attempt against Pastora on May 30, 1984, known as the La Penca bombing. It left three journalists dead and more than a dozen injured.

Michael Emery, author of the articles used as a source for this nomination, is the co-author of *The Press and America*, an authoritative book on press history. He also is a former UPI reporter, U.S. Army public information officer, and chair of the Journalism Department at California State University, Northridge.

SOURCE: *San Francisco Bay Guardian*, 12/3/86, "Contragate: The Costa Rica Connection," and 2/4/87, "Christic Institute Officials Detained in Costa Rica," both by Michael Emery.

UPDATE: The aftermath of the La Penca bombing produced a mystery story with a surprise ending and is well-documented by Martha Honey in the book, *Hostile Acts: U.S. Policy in Costa Rica in the 1980s* (University Press of Florida, 1994). After years of investigations and trials, the Christic Institute suit was lost. Nonetheless, Honey, who was frustrated with the way Daniel Sheehan, head of the Christic Institute, handled the case, kept searching for the truth about La Penca. In the surprising conclusion of her search, she discovered definitively that the bomber was a Sandinista agent. However, there were still "too many questions left, too many cover-ups and lies by the U.S. government about La Penca, to rule out the possibility that the CIA may have been involved in some way" (*The Progressive*, January 1995). Please refer to Martha Honey's book for the full story. Please also see update of "U.S. Contra Drug Connection," #2, 1987.

8. U.S. Agencies Conducted Radiation Tests on Humans for 30 Years

1986 SYNOPSIS: Human experimentation crimes comparable to those we censured the Nazis and Japanese for committing during World War II were committed in the United States by official federal agencies during peace time. And yet, when the government confessed to these crimes in October of 1986, the story wasn't picked up by the press.

From the mid-1940s until the 1970s, federal agencies conducted heinous radiation exposure experiments on hundreds of human beings around the country. Some were reportedly volunteers, but for others there is no record of informed consent. The extraordinary report was released by the House Energy and Commerce Subcommittee on October 24, 1986. It documented how the Atomic Energy Commission (AEC) and its successor, the Energy Research and Development Authority, financed studies involving researchers from government laboratories and such institutions as the Sloan-Kettering Institute for Cancer Research in New York and the University of California at Berkeley.

The purpose of the experiments was to expose humans to radiation to determine its effect on fertility and other biological functions, and to study how the human body absorbed and retained radioactive contaminants.

In one major experiment involving inmates at the Washington State Prison and the Oregon State prison, the testicles of 131 inmates were exposed to large doses of radiation. In Richland, Washington, 14 human subjects were immersed in tritium, a radioactive form of water, or given the material to drink or inhale, to measure retention and excretion. In another study, progesterone, a hormone found in women, was "labeled" with small amounts of radiation and injected into three patients, one of whom was ten weeks pregnant.

SOURCE: *The New York Times*, 10/24/86, "Volunteers Around U.S. Submitted to Radiation."

UPDATE: Following major media coverage in 1994 of the horrifying human radiation experiments, the *Los Angeles Times* reported (10/4/95) that President Bill Clinton apologized to the survivors and families of those who were subjects of the government-sponsored radiation experiments. He also ordered his cabinet to devise a system of relief, including financial compensation. On December 25, 1995, the *Cincinnati Enquirer* reported the Department of Energy had spent more than $22 million researching the human radiation experiments, a sum which could have settled all the claims brought by class action suits. It was not until late 1996 that the first substantial settlements were made. The federal government agreed to pay $4.8 million to settle the claims for 12 of the victims (*Los Angeles Times*, 11/20/96). Please see *Censored* story #6 of 1994 for information about the 1947 AEC memo that revealed why the experiments were censored.

9. Irradiated Veterans: VA Caught Destroying Claims Evidence

1986 SYNOPSIS: In August 1986, the Veterans' Administration (VA) was caught red-handed, shredding thousands of case records of contested radiation injury claims. The shredding took place in spite of a federal court order placing all such records at the disposal of attorneys representing the injured veterans in a class-action suit.

Since the 1940s, hundreds of thousands of military personnel were exposed to nuclear radiation. Throughout more than 40 years of nuclear weapons tests, production, storage, and handling, human subjects reportedly have received dangerous radiation doses. Most claims for VA benefits related to these incidents have been stalled or improperly denied. It is not uncommon for a radiation claim to languish in the VA's labyrinthine bureaucracy for five years or longer. Significant information, such as dosage records, was discarded or destroyed. These and other irregularities finally led the National Association of Radiation Survivors (NARS) to file a class action lawsuit against the VA. Another veterans' group, Swords to Plowshares, also joined the suit.

Initially, ranking VA officials denied accurate records of radiation exposures even existed. Then NARS received two anonymous letters that described a widespread pattern of abuse inside the department. Specific reports and documents were listed, containing data the VA previously claimed did not exist. NARS demanded this new information under federal court order.

Instead of producing the disputed evidence, VA officials apparently ordered a general purging and shredding of VA case files. The VA's own attorney admitted in court that millions of pages of relevant documents had been and were still being destroyed.

SOURCE: *VVA Veteran*, November 1986, "Scandal Hints Plague VA"; January 1987, "The Scandal Deepens."

UPDATE: More than a decade after the 1986 exposé about the Veterans' Administration document shredding, America's "atomic veterans" are still seeking access to treatment and compensation.

Pat Broudy, legislative director of the National Association of Atomic Veterans, testified before the House Committee on Veterans' Affairs Subcommittee on Compensation, Pension, Insurance and Memorial Affairs, on April 30, 1996 (Federal News Service, 4/30/96). He charged that, "In order to prove a claim before the Department of Veterans Affairs (VA), we must have medical and service records, which we felt had been classified and/or destroyed by the VA, Defense Nuclear Agency, Department of Defense, and the Department of Energy." He then told about years of stonewalling the veterans had received from the various government agencies.

The *Bulletin of the Atomic Scientists* (January 1995) reported the VA had relied on three studies to reject veterans' claims and noted that all three have subsequently been criticized by independent reviews for faulty databases. It adds, "A new study is under way, but won't be completed for a couple of years."

In contrast, when it came to the Gulf War and veterans' complaints of Gulf War Syndrome symptoms, the Veterans' Administration changed its attitude. It acknowledged the problems as early as 1992 and established a nationwide program to provide free medical examinations.

10. The Lethal Plutonium Shuttle

1986 SYNOPSIS: As tragic as it was, the explosion of the space shuttle Challenger in January 1986 could have been even worse.

The next shuttle, scheduled for launch in May 1986, would have carried an unmanned spacecraft fueled with 46.7 pounds of toxic plutonium-238.

John Gofman, co-discoverer of uranium-233 and a former associate director of the government's Lawrence Livermore Laboratory, said, "If the plutonium (from the scheduled shuttle flight) gets dispersed in fine pieces, the amount of radioactivity released would be more than the combined plutonium radioactivity returned to earth in the fallout from all the nuclear weapons tests of the United States, the Soviet Union, and the United Kingdom—which I have calculated has caused 950,000 lung cancer fatalities...It is a crazy idea—unless shuttle launches are 100 percent perfect."

Dr. Helen Caldicott, founder of Physicians for Social Responsibility, said that one pound of plutonium, "if uniformly distributed, could hypothetically induce lung cancer in every person on earth."

Despite the Challenger explosion, NASA, although now thoroughly aware of the global risks involved, plans to go ahead with plutonium-fueled space probes when shuttle missions begin again.

SOURCE: *The Nation*, 2/22/86, "The Lethal Shuttle," and 3/15/86, "Plutonium Cover-up?"; *Common Cause*, July/August 1986, "Red Tape and Radioactivity"; all by Karl Grossman.

UPDATE: Ten years later, Karl Grossman, source of the 1986 story, was still warning, "Despite enormous danger and expense, the U.S. government is pushing ahead with development of nuclear technology in space" (Progressive Media Network, 5/22/96). He noted NASA is scheduled to launch the Cassini space probe to Saturn in October 1997 with 72.3 pounds of plutonium-238 fuel aboard—the largest amount of plutonium ever used in a space probe.

The Cassini probe will be launched on top of a Lockheed Martin-built Titan IV rocket—a number of which have exploded in the atmosphere. If the Cassini comes in too close to the Earth during its "slingshot maneuver," expected in 1999, and there is an "inadvertent re-entry," the space probe could break up in the Earth's atmosphere, raining plutonium back down on the Earth's surface. "If that happens," Grossman warned, "NASA's *Final Environmental Impact Statement for the Cassini Mission* acknowledges, 'Approximately five billion of the estimated seven billion to eight billion population...could receive 99 percent or more of the radiation exposure.'"

Sadly, there is no reason to gamble with the Earth's population. A 1994 European scientific breakthrough led to the development of new high performance silicon solar cells for deep-space missions. Please also see other *Censored* plutonium shuttle stories, #10, 1987, and #3, 1988.

Grossman's fears were realized in part on November 17, 1996, when a Russian Mars 96 space probe, traveling at 17,000 mph, re-entered the atmosphere and burned. It was carrying 200 grams of plutonium. Early, widespread media coverage reported the Russian spacecraft had fallen harmlessly into the Pacific Ocean some 1,800 miles off the coast of Chile (*Washington Post*, 11/18/96). Subsequently it was reported that the spacecraft had re-entered the atmosphere and actually burned up over the desert between Chile and Bolivia.

John Pike, head of space policy at the Federation of American Scientists, warned, "If you liked Mars 96, you'll love Cassini." Noting that a Titan IV rocket, which will launch Cassini in late 1997, blew up in 1993, Pike predicted the chance of a similar failure at between one in ten and one in twenty (*Christian Science Monitor (CSM)*, 12/17/96). *CSM* also revealed that there already have been eight space mishaps, including Russia's Mars 96, that have deposited radioactive materials on earth with little if any media coverage. These events amounted to more than twelve pounds of plutonium-238 and 135 pounds of uranium-235.

The spectacular explosion of a Delta rocket 13 seconds after it was launched from Cape Canaveral on January 17, 1997, did little to allay Grossman's fears (Associated Press, 1/18/97).

Another Grossman story about the Cassini was named the top *Censored* story of 1996.

CHAPTER 12—1987

Information Monopoly Limits Public Access

In 1987, the mainstream news media focused on the Iran/contra scandal but again missed an important part of the story. While the #2 *Censored* story of 1987, cited below, told the rest of the story, it wasn't widely covered by mainstream media until 1996. According to the Associated Press, the top ten news stories of the year were:

1. The Iran arms/contra affair
2. Stock market meltdown
3. Reagan/Gorbachev summit in Washington, D.C.
4. Persian Gulf conflict and U.S. involvement
5. Battles over Reagan nominees to the U.S. Supreme Court
6. Jim Bakker/Jessica Hahn story and the PTL scandal
7. Presidential campaign including Gary Hart's withdrawal and re-entry
8. The spread of AIDS
9. U.S. air disasters, particularly the crash of Northwest Flight 255 that killed 156 people but saw a four-year-old survive
10. The rescue of Jessica McClure from a well in Texas.

THE TOP TEN CENSORED STORIES OF 1987

—And What Has Happened to Them Since

1. The Information Monopoly

1987 SYNOPSIS: The rapidly increasing centralization of media ownership raises critical questions about the public's access to a diversity of opinion. Unsurprisingly, the impact of this media monopolization of information on a free society continues to be ignored by the mass media itself.

In 1982, when media expert Ben Bagdikian completed research for his book, *The Media Monopoly*, he found that 50 corporations controlled half or more of the media business. By December 1986, when he finished a revision for a second edition, the 50 had shrunk to 29. About a half year later, when he wrote an article for *EXTRA!*, the number was down to 26.

Bagdikian also warned that a number of serious Wall Street analysts of the media are predicting that by the 1990s, a half dozen giant firms will control most of our media.

Bagdikian notes that of 1700 daily papers, 98 percent are local monopolies and fewer than 15 corporations control most of the country's circulation. A handful of firms have most of the magazine business, with Time, Inc. alone accounting for about 40 percent of that industry's revenues. The three networks, Capital Cities/ABC, CBS, and NBC, still have majority access to the television audience, and most of the book publishing business is controlled by fewer than a dozen companies, with major categories like paperback and trade books dominated by still fewer firms.

Even worse, this situation is exacerbated by the conflict of interest inherent in interlocking boards of directors with major newspaper chains, influential newspapers and magazines, and the electronic media solidly interlocked with corporate America. The prevailing corporate concern with the bottom line, coupled with traditional publishers' tendency to avoid controversy, fosters wide-spread self-censorship among writers, journalists, editors, and news directors.

SOURCES: *EXTRA!*, June 1987, "The 26 Corporations That Own Our Media"; *Multinational Monitor*, September 1987, "The Media Brokers," both by Ben Bagdikian; *UTNE Reader*, January/February 1988, "Censorship in Publishing," by Lynette Lamb; *The Media Monopoly*, by Ben Bagdikian, Beacon Press, 1983.

UPDATE: *The Baltimore Sun* reported (4/3/96) that "the speed with which the media landscape has changed is remarkable. In 1983, media critic Ben Bagdikian's book *The Media Monopoly* was touted as a 'startling report on the 50 corporations that control what America sees, hears and reads.'" Today, *The Sun* adds, his "startling report" seems quaint. As indeed it is.

Bagdikian's fifth edition of *The Media Monopoly*, published in 1997, reveals, "In the last five years, a small number of the country's largest industrial corporations has acquired more public communications power—including ownership of the news—than any private businesses have ever before possessed in world history." In effect, Bagdikian charges, these new monopolies have created a new communications cartel within the United States.

By 1996, the 26 corporations controlling the media in 1987 had shrunk to just ten. The dominant ten are Time Warner, Disney, Viacom, News Corporation Limited (Murdoch), Sony, TeleCommunications, Inc., Seagram (TV, movies, cable, books, and music), Westinghouse, Gannett, and General Electric.

Bagdikian concludes that the warning expressed in the first edition of his book, "Media power is political power," has come to pass to a degree once considered unthinkable.

2. The United States and its Contra-Drug Connection

1987 SYNOPSIS: Though mounting evidence, with substantive and alarming implications in terms of U.S. foreign policy and the Reagan Administration's propriety, pointed to a large-scale contra/CIA drug smuggling network, most of the major U.S. media under-reported it in 1987.

Testimony by convicted drug smugglers as well as private citizens for CBS's *West 58th Street* program, along with the Christic Institute's federal lawsuit under the RICO statute and before congressional committees, provided a startling picture of large-scale drug trafficking under the auspices of the U.S. government/contra supply network.

According to the Christic Institute (a Washington, D.C., based interfaith legal foundation), "Contra narcotics smuggling stretches from cocaine plantations in Colombia, to dirt airstrips in Costa Rica, to pseudo-seafood companies in Miami, and finally, to the drug-ridden streets of our society." The Christic Institute's investigation, sanctioned by the U.S. Attorney's Office in Miami, provided evidence supporting allegations that 1) a major "guns-for-drugs" operation existed between North, Central, and South America that helped finance the contra war; 2) the contra leadership received direct funding and other support from major narcotics traffickers; 3) some contra leaders were directly involved in drug trafficking; 4) U.S. government funds for the contras went to known narcotics dealers; and 5) the CIA helped Miami-based drug traffickers smuggle their illicit cargo into the U.S. in exchange for their help in arming the contras.

SOURCES: *The Christic Institute Special Report*, November 1987, "The Contra-Drug Connection," by The Christic Institute; *Newsday*, 6/28/87, "Witness: Contras Got Drug Cash," by Knut Royce; *The Nation*, 9/5/87, "How the Drug Czar Got Away," by Martin A. Lee; *In These Times*, 4/15/87, "CIA, Contras Hooked on Drug Money," by Vince Bielski and Dennis Bernstein.

UPDATE: Despite nearly a decade of charges about the CIA and its contra drug smuggling connection, mainstream media failed to put the issue on the national agenda. Finally, starting on August 18, 1996, the *San Jose Mercury News* published an extraordinary three-part series that confirmed the #2 *Censored* story of 1987.

Using the Freedom of Information Act, newly declassified federal reports, court testimony, and interviews, investigative journalist Gary Webb of the *Mercury News,* revealed the contra drug smuggling network, exposed the CIA's role, and made an important connection between the flawed foreign policy of Reagan and Bush in the 1980s and America's drug-devastated streets of today.

Anyone who wants to understand how crack cocaine became the scourge of America's urban centers during the greatest crackdown on drugs in history, is urged to read the *Mercury News* series, available in libraries and on the Internet at www.sjmercury.com/drugs/. The *Mercury News* series

THIS MODERN WORLD   by TOM TOMORROW

CIA TIES TO OPIUM AND HEROIN SMUGGLERS DURING VIETNAM ARE A MATTER OF HISTORICAL *RECORD*... LONGSTANDING ALLEGATIONS OF AGENCY COMPLICITY IN CONTRA-COCAINE TRAFFICKING ARE SUPPORTED BY A *MOUNTAIN* OF EVIDENCE...

...MAYBE YOU SHOULD HAVE FOCUSED ON HELPING THE *CIA* "JUST SAY NO," NANCE...

AH, RONNIE, DEAR... DID YOU LEAVE THE *DOOR* OPEN AGAIN?

THE LATTER HAVE RECENTLY RESURFACED, DUE TO A SERIES IN THE SAN JOSE MERCURY NEWS--

--WHICH THE NEW YORK TIMES FINALLY DEIGNED TO ACKNOWLEDGE-- IN AN APPALLINGLY PATRONIZING ARTICLE ABOUT AFRICAN AMERICAN *OUTRAGE* THAT THE GOVERNMENT MAY HAVE HELPED BRING DRUGS INTO THEIR COMMUNITIES...

SO-- JUST BECAUSE THE U.S. GOVERNMENT HAS A LONG HISTORY OF LIES AND DECEIT-- AND CIA CONNECTIONS TO DRUG RUNNERS OVER SEVERAL DECADES ARE THOROUGHLY DOCUMENTED--

--THEY ACTUALLY THINK THIS MIGHT BE *TRUE?*

THOSE NEGROES WILL BELIEVE *ANYTHING!*

The New York Times

prompted long overdue investigations by the CIA, Justice Department, Congress and the mass media. Not surprisingly, three of the nation's largest newspapers—*The New York Times* (10/21/96), the *Washington Post* (10/4/96), and the *Los Angeles Times* (10/20/96)—which hadn't investigated and reported the original charges by the Christic Institute, were quick to investigate and report the *Mercury News* charges in a transparent effort to discredit them. The old "not exposed here" process is embarrassingly evident in these belated efforts.

Ironically, on May 11, 1997, Jerry Ceppos, executive editor of the *Mercury News*, published a column saying the paper made mistakes in its "Dark Alliance" series and that he did "not believe that top CIA officials knew of the relationship." Series author Webb disagreed and said he stood by his stories (*San Francisco Examiner*, 5/12/97). The Internet series is now prefaced by a statement directing readers to the May 11 column for "an understanding of this document or story." In July 1997, Webb told Project Censored he was taken off investigative reporting and exiled to Cupertino, a small community west of San Jose.

3. Secret Documents Reveal Danger of Worldwide Nuclear Accidents

1987 SYNOPSIS: On March 11, 1987, NBC broadcast a documentary, "Nuclear Power: In France It Works." It could have passed for a lengthy pro-nuclear-power commercial. Missing from anchorman Tom Brokaw's introduction was the fact that NBC's owner, General Electric, is America's second largest nuclear power salesman and the third largest producer of nuclear weapons systems.

One month after the NBC documentary, there were accidents at two French nuclear installations, injuring seven workers. *The Christian Science Monitor* reported a "potentially explosive debate" in France, with new polls showing a third of the French public opposing nuclear power. That story was not reported on *NBC News*. NBC's policy is typical of the media silence about reactor incidents, which helps explain the industry's undeserved reputation for safety.

The lid on Pandora's nuclear safety box was partially opened last year when the West German weekly *Der Spiegel* published 48 of more than 250 secret nuclear reactor accident reports compiled by the International Atomic Energy Agency (IAEA). The report of previously secret IAEA documents was translated into English for the first time and published in David Brower's *Earth Island Journal* in 1987.

Some of the nuclear "incidents" you never heard about occurred in Bulgaria, Argentina, West Germany, Czechoslovakia, Pakistan, East Germany, Belgium, Canada, and on the French-Belgian border.

Der Spiegel said in several of the previously unreported slip-ups "a meltdown was a real possibility." Worse yet, *Der Spiegel* found that human error "is most advanced in North America...sometimes with hair-raising results." A survey of official records since the Three Mile Island reactor meltdown in 1979 shows there have been more than 23,000 mishaps at U.S. reactors—and the number is increasing.

SOURCES: *Earth Island Journal*, Summer 1987, "Secret Documents Reveal Nuclear Accidents Worldwide," by Gar Smith with Hans Hollitscher; *EXTRA!*, June 1987, "Nuclear Broadcasting Company."

UPDATE: The real danger of worldwide nuclear accidents, cited above, was most evident in the accidents at Chernobyl in Russia and at Three Mile Island in the United States. And together they apparently sounded the death knell for the nuclear power industry. At the time of the Chernobyl disaster on April 26, 1986, there were 394 reactors, with a capacity of 266,000 megawatts, in operation worldwide. Another 160 reactors were under construction. By contrast, today there are just 434 operating reactors. The combined capacity of all plants operating and those under construction is 15 percent lower than it was a decade ago. In 1995, for the first time since the beginning of civilian nuclear power, ground was not broken for a single new reactor. The list of countries no longer building nuclear plants is headed by the United States. The last U.S. plant was finished in February 1996; the last Canadian plant was finished in 1993. Since the late 1970s, 120 of the proposed North American nuclear plants have been canceled. Reasons for the demise of the nuclear power industry include safety hazards and accidents, the inability to solve the problem of nuclear waste disposal, and the continuing proliferation of fissile materials (*Bulletin of the Atomic Scientists*, May 1996).

4. Reagan's Mania for Secrecy: Decisions Without Democracy

1987 SYNOPSIS: On December 3, 1986, President Ronald Reagan signed Public Law 99-494 proclaiming 1987 "The Year of the Reader." The blatant hypocrisy of that act was clear throughout 1987 as the Reagan Administration outdid itself in its efforts to control, interpret, manipulate, disinform, and censor all forms of information the public might read.

Typical of the Reagan Administration's efforts to control its own destiny and the nation's history was the Justice Department memorandum filed in a lawsuit that would have enabled Reagan to control the history of his involvement in the Iran/contra scandal. The administration was seeking to overturn a 1986 federal court ruling that limited Richard Nixon's right to block the release of his White House papers. The Justice Department memorandum would have allowed Nixon to withdraw any documentation he thought should be suppressed. In effect, Nixon would have been in control of U.S. history between 1968 and 1974. If Nixon had won, with Reagan's support, it would have paved the way for Reagan to control U.S. history from 1980 to 1988.

While alarming, this was just the tip of the iceberg when it came to Reagan's mania for secrecy. Following are just three groups that tried to warn the public about what was happening but were met with mainstream media indifference:

✔ People For the American Way: A report titled "Government Secrecy: Decisions Without Democracy," published in December 1987, provides more than 100 pages of well-documented charges about the growing secrecy system and its danger to American democracy.

✔ The Reporters' Committee for Freedom of the Press: In March 1987, the Reporters' Committee issued a "FYI Media Alert" about how the Reagan Administration and its supporters restrict public and media access to government information and intrude on editorial freedom.

✔ The American Library Association: The ALA released its 1987 updated "Less Access to Less Information By and About the U.S. Government: IX," covering 1987. The chronology provides a damning indictment of Reagan Administration efforts to "restrict and privatize government information."

SOURCES: *The Nation*, 5/23/87, "History Deleted"; *Government Decisions Without Democracy*, December 1987, by People For the American Way; *FYI Media Alert 1987*, March 1987, "The Reagan Administration & The News Media," by the Reporters' Committee for Freedom of the Press; *The American Library Association*, Washington Office, "Less Access to Less Information By and About the U.S. Government: IX," December 1987, by Anne A. Heanue.

UPDATE: Fearing that he would destroy historic Watergate papers, former President Richard Nixon was denied ownership of his White House Papers on the grounds that he served only as a trustee for the American people. On April 12, 1996, after more than two decades of often bitter litigation over the release of Nixon's documents and tapes, the National Archives and attorneys for the Nixon estate agreed that virtually all of his secretly recorded White House tapes may be heard by the public starting in the fall of 1996 (*Los Angeles Times*, 4/13/96).

Ironically, the Clinton Administration, which had pledged to do away with excessive secrecy within government, made it more difficult for future public access to official documents when it provided National Security Council documents the same broad protection from public scrutiny normally reserved for White House papers. This means that security council records will no longer be subject to the Freedom of Information Act (*The New York Times*, 3/26/94).

Please also see earlier *Censored* stories on Reagan and censorship: #6 of 1982, #8 of 1984, #4 of 1985, and #2 of 1986.

5. Bush's Personal Agenda in the Iran Arms Deal

1987 SYNOPSIS: Initially, Vice President George Bush's acknowledged support for the ill-fated secret arms shipments to Iran was interpreted as evidence of his loyalty to the policies of President Reagan.

Now however, other evidence suggests that Bush, far more than President Reagan, promoted the Iran initiative, took part in key negotiations, and conferred upon Oliver North the secret powers necessary to carry it out. It also has been charged that Bush actively promoted the Iran arms sales because of an economic motive the President did not share—the desire to stabilize plunging oil prices in 1986.

Peter Dale Scott, co-author of *The Iran Contra Connection* and former senior fellow at the International Center for Development Policy in Washington, suggests Bush's primary concern in early 1986 was to stabilize falling crude oil prices by promoting a common price policy between the United States and the oil producers of the Persian Gulf, including, above all, Iran and Saudi Arabia.

Further, Scott says, the interest in higher oil prices was an explicit goal in some of Oliver North's secret arms negotiations with the Iranians. The price of oil reflected the concerns of Bush, a former Texas oilman, rather than that of Reagan, a free market advocate.

Bush's mission to Saudi Arabia was to persuade its leaders to help stabilize oil prices that were rapidly falling to under $10 a barrel. His trip was successful. Saudi Arabia's King Fahd received the Iranian petroleum minister in the autumn of 1986 and the two countries agreed to OPEC arrangements for boosting oil prices to $18 a barrel. The $18 price brought economic relief to oil-producing states like Texas, which were the key to Bush's political base.

SOURCES: *Pacific News Service*, 12/21/87, "Bush Had Oil Policy Interest in Promoting Iran Arms Deals," by Peter Dale Scott.

UPDATE: By the time the 1988 election between George Bush and Michael Dukakis came along, there was ample information available about the Iran/contra issue and Bush's involvement, but the mainstream press failed to press the subject. By 1990, the question "Where was George?" was being asked so often the media could hardly ignore it, but they let him off the hook with his disingenuous "out of the loop" explanation.

Finally, by 1992, the press could no longer ignore the issue. Bush's own colleagues were giving him away: John Poindexter revealed how Bush endorsed Reagan's scheme to conceal the plan's specifics; General Richard Secord charged that Bush "was not out of the loop"; former National Security Council aide Howard Teicher claimed that Bush "knew from day one" about the arms-for-hostages deal; additional evidence of Bush's involvement was found in Caspar Weinberger's incriminating memo, which was supported by entries in Bush's own personal diary; and all of it was confirmed by the memoirs of former Secretary of State George Schultz.

Nonetheless, George Bush was never held accountable for his actions. The official explanation of the Iran/contra conspiracy was offered on January 18, 1994, when Lawrence Walsh, the special Iran/contra prosecutor, ended his seven-year, $37 million investigation, clearing both Ronald Reagan and George Bush of criminal responsibility. However, he did blame them for fostering a climate that emboldened subordinates to break the law. He reported that White House aides "skirted the law, some of them broke the law, and almost all of them tried to cover up the president's willful activities" (*Denver Post*, 1/19/94). In a final shameful act, George Bush pardoned the key players in the Iran/contra scandal in the closing days of the investigation.

6. Pentagon Biowarfare Research in University Laboratories

1987 SYNOPSIS: Overshadowed by Star Wars and overlooked by the media, the push toward biowarfare was one of the Reagan Administration's best kept secrets. The research budget for infectious diseases and toxins increased tenfold since fiscal 1981 and most of the 1986 budget of $42 million went to 24 U.S. university campuses, where the world's most deadly organisms were being cultured in campus labs.

The amount of military money available for biotechnology research is a powerful attraction for scientists whose civilian funding resources dried up. Scientists formerly working on widespread killers like cancer began using their talents to develop strains of such rare pathogens as anthrax, dengue, Rift Valley fever, Japanese encephalitis, tularemia, shigella, botulin, Q fever, and mycotoxins.

Many members of the academic community find the trend alarming, but when MIT's biology department voted to refuse Pentagon funds for biotech research, the Reagan Administration forced it to reverse its decision.

Since the U.S. is a signatory to the 1972 Biological and Toxic Weapons Convention which bans "development, production, stockpiling, and use of microbes or their poisonous products except in amounts necessary for protective and peaceful research," the university-based work is being pursued under the guise of defensive projects aimed at developing vaccines and protective gear.

SOURCES: *Isthmus*, 10/9/87, "Biowarfare and the UW," by Richard Jannaccio; *The Progressive*, 11/16/87, "Poisons from the Pentagon," by Seth Shulman; *Wall Street Journal*, 9/17/86, "Military Science," by Bill Richards and Tim Carrington.

UPDATE: The #6 *Censored* story of 1993 revealed that the Army quietly resumed its biowarfare testing at a new laboratory built 70 miles southwest of Salt Lake City at the Dugway Proving Ground. In September of that year, safety concerns were raised when the Dugway Proving Ground was cited for 22 violations of state hazardous-waste regulations, ranging from inadequate record-keeping to improper dumping of poisonous chemicals. Testing subsequently resumed.

On the flip side of the coin, the public will be pleased to learn that in 1988, the U.S. Post Office stopped delivering microorganisms used by the Army in its biowarfare research, including anthrax, Q fever, and plague. The Postal Service was apprehensive about the Army's growing research program on the ingredients of biological war (*Science*, 7/1/88).

Please also see update of "Biological Weapons," #10, 1981.

7. Biased Coverage of the Arias Peace Plan by America's Press

1987 SYNOPSIS: On August 7, 1987, five Central American nations—Costa Rica, El Salvador, Guatemala, Honduras, and Nicaragua—made international history when they signed a regional peace proposal that was authored by Costa Rican president, Oscar Arias.

The proposal, known as the Arias Peace Plan, set specific guidelines and target dates for each nation to comply with in order to stabilize Central America and bring peace to the region.

Two separate studies monitoring U.S. press coverage of the Arias plan revealed a startling bias in how America's leading newspapers covered the region following the historic August 7 pact.

The Media Alliance, a San Francisco-based nonprofit organization of media professionals, monitored stories about the peace plan that appeared in seven major dailies—*The New York Times, Los Angeles Times, Christian Science Monitor, San Jose Mercury News, San Francisco Chronicle, San Francisco Examiner*, and the *Oakland Tribune*. More than 80 percent of the articles published during the first six months after the pact focused almost entirely on Nicaragua—the Reagan Administration's demands on Nicaragua's Sandinista government, the prospects for renewed contra aid, or the extent to which Nicaragua was abiding by the Arias plan. Meanwhile serious human rights problems and violations of the plan by the governments of El Salvador, Honduras, and Guatemala went largely unreported.

The other study by the New York-based Fairness and Accuracy In Reporting (FAIR), a national media watchdog group, concluded the peace accord set off a U.S. media reaction that "showed once again the extent to which White House assumptions are shared by the national press corps" and how "Reagan's obsession with Nicaragua has turned into a media obsession." FAIR's 90-day analysis of *The New York Times* found that *The Times* devoted three times as many column inches of news space to events in Nicaragua than it did to Honduras, Guatemala, and El Salvador combined.

SOURCES: *San Francisco Bay Guardian*, 1/6/88, "On Central America, U.S. Dailies Parrot Reagan Line," by Jeff Gillenkirk; *EXTRA!*, August/September 1987, "Media Put Reagan Spin on Arias Plan," by Jeff Cohen and Martin A. Lee.

UPDATE: The mainstream American news media did not provide adequate coverage of Oscar Arias and his peace plan for Central America. Nevertheless, Arias, who served as president of Costa Rica from 1986 until 1990, gained international prominence for his efforts at conflict resolution in Central America. The Arias Peace Plan set in motion the process by which cease-fire talks were started and rebels laid down their arms in exchange for amnesty in El Salvador and Nicaragua.

The Arias plan was criticized by the Reagan Administration, which called it "fatally flawed." The Nobel prize committee didn't think so and awarded Arias the Nobel Peace Prize in 1987 (*The Cleveland Plain Dealer*, 4/19/94). Since leaving office, Arias has worked as president of the Fundacion Arias which is dedicated to promoting world peace.

8. Dumping Our Toxic Wastes on the Third World

1987 SYNOPSIS: Exporting our hazardous and toxic wastes to Third World countries is a growth industry. The exported material includes heavy metal residues and chemical-contaminated wastes, pharmaceutical refuse, and municipal sewage sludge and incinerator ash. The risks involved for countries that accept our wastes range from contamination of groundwater and crops to birth defects and cancer.

Traditionally, the majority of U.S. toxic waste exports have gone to Canada, where regulations are less stringent than in the U.S. But now the most abrupt increase is in shipments to the Third World where the regulations are either nonexistent or loosely enforced.

Creating the search for new overseas markets is an explosion in the volume of recorded hazardous wastes being produced in the U.S. According to the General Accounting Office, the amount rose from about nine million metric tons in 1970 to at least 247 million in 1984; other experts place the current figure closer to 400 million metric tons.

U.S. officials, aware of the sensitive legal and foreign policy questions involved, are reluctant to crack down on illegal dumpers and, in fact, the government itself is responsible for generating a significant portion of the hazardous waste exports. One large illegal operation broken up last year received more than half its toxic wastes from various branches of the federal government, mainly the military.

The key U.S. government officials responsible for monitoring waste traffic claim they are powerless, saying that once the waste leaves the country they can't do anything about it.

SOURCES: *The Nation*, 10/3/87, "The Export of U.S. Toxic Wastes," by Andrew Porterfield and David Weir.

UPDATE: When the United States stopped shipping toxic wastes to Canada, it looked to Africa and Central America as new dump sites for its waste. However, as the *Singapore Straits Times* reported (6/21/95), these Third World countries became aware of the potential hazards of importing toxic wastes and started fighting back. In 1986, only three countries had banned waste imports; by 1989, the number had risen to 103. As a result, Asia became the final frontier for the West to dispose of its waste. Between 1990 and 1993, the U.S., Australia, Canada, Germany, and Britain shipped more than 5.4 million tons of toxic wastes to countries in Asia.

On May 31, 1996, the *Xinhua News Agency* reported that China accused the United States of illegally dumping trash near Beijing and filed a protest to the secretariat of the Basel Convention, the body that monitors the international agreement on the transfer of hazardous wastes. Xing Demao, director of the Bureau for Inspection for Shandong province, asked, "Why do some countries strictly control export of their advanced technology and equipment but openly permit the export of harmful waste they produced?" (*San Francisco Chronicle*, 6/1/96)

In 1995, the United Nations approved amendments to the 1989 Basel Convention that will bar export of hazardous waste from industrial to developing countries by the end of 1997. The ban was enacted despite protests from the U.S. and some other industrialized countries (*Journal of Commerce*, 9/25/95).

9. Torture in El Salvador: A Censored Report from Mariona Prison

1987 SYNOPSIS: In late 1986, a 165-page report was smuggled out of the Mariona men's prison in El Salvador. The report was compiled by five imprisoned members of the Human Rights Commission of El Salvador (CDHES). The report documented the "routine" and "systematic" use of at least 40 kinds of torture on political prisoners in El Salvador.

The report made three main points: first, torture is systematic, not random; second, the methods of torture are becoming more clever; and finally, it is part of the U.S. counterinsurgency program there—with U.S. servicemen often acting as supervisors.

The Marin Interfaith Task Force of Mill Valley, California, assembled the smuggled report from Mariona prison into a document titled "Torture in El Salvador" and distributed it to major newspapers and other mainstream media nationally.

Only one newspaper gave the actual report substantial coverage. The *San Francisco Examiner* ran two articles by freelance journalist Ron Ridenhour, who quoted State Department spokesman James Callahan as saying the CDHES, the only Salvadoran human rights group recognized by the United Nations, is a communist "front organization."

SOURCES: *The Nation*, 2/21/87, "After the Press Bus Left"; 11/14/87, "The Press and the Plan," both by Alexander Cockburn; *San Francisco Examiner*, 11/14/86, "In Prison, Salvador Rights Panel Works On," by Ron Ridenhour.

UPDATE: Herbert Anaya, the head of El Salvador's nongovernmental Human Rights Commission (HRC) and one of the five prisoners who compiled the Mariona Prison report, was assassinated on October 26, 1987. He was the fourth member of the HRC to be killed since it was founded in 1978; at least three others have disappeared and are presumed dead (*Washington Post*, 10/28/87). During the civil war there were a number of efforts by the guerrillas to storm Mariona Prison in an effort to release political prisoners. One of the most successful occurred June 17, 1991, when rebels blasted a huge hole in the side of the prison allowing 132 prisoners to escape (*Chicago Tribune*, 6/19/91). Unfortunately, the end of El Salvador's civil war on January 16, 1992, did not end the horrors of Mariona Prison. A recent report by Human Rights Watch cites "horrendous overcrowding, rampant violence, insufficient food, and primitive sanitary conditions." Mariano Prison, built to house 800 prisoners, now holds 2,381 and has taken on the look of a crowded slum (*The Washington Post*, 6/25/96).

10. Project Galileo Shuttle To Carry Lethal Plutonium

1987 SYNOPSIS: Despite scientific warnings of a possible disaster, NASA is pursuing plans to launch the Project Galileo shuttle space probe which will carry enough plutonium to kill every person on earth. Theoretically, one pound of plutonium, uniformly distributed, has the potential to give everyone on the planet a fatal case of lung cancer, according to Helen Caldicott. Galileo will have 49.25 pounds of plutonium on board, most of it plutonium-238, a radioisotope 300 times more radioactive than the one used as fuel for atomic bombs.

Critics of the plan, such as Dr. John Gofman, professor of medical physics at the University of California, and Michio Kaku, professor of nuclear physics at the City University of New York, claim that putting Galileo's plutonium payload into space is both risky and unnecessary.

NASA downplays the possibility of the release of plutonium in an accident, stressing the substance will be encapsulated in "clads" made from iridium alloy in a graphite shell. The Department of Energy (DOE) contends that clads can withstand explosive pressures up to 2,200 pounds per square inch. However, a DOE safety analysis report on the Galileo mission obtained under the Freedom of Information Act states that from the viewpoint of potential nuclear fuel release, the most critical accidents would occur on the launch pad. Launch pad accident scenarios, such as "tipovers" and "pushovers" are estimated to generate explosive pressures as high as 19,600 psi.

SOURCE: *The Nation*, 1/23/88, "The Space Probe's Lethal Cargo," by Karl Grossman.

UPDATE: Please see update of "Lethal Shuttle," #10, 1986.

CHAPTER 13—1988

Another Censored Presidential Election

While the top mainstream news story of 1988 was about the election of George Bush, the top under-reported news story of the year revealed why Bush should not have been elected. According to the Associated Press, the top ten news stories of the year were:

1. The election of George Bush
2. Earthquake in Armenia
3. drought in the Midwest
4. USS Vincennes' downing of Iranian passenger jet
5. America's re-entry into space with the shuttle Discovery flight
6. Reagan's decision to open talks with the Palestinian Liberation Organization
7. End of eight-year Iran/Iraq war
8. Threats to the nation's environment
9. Gorbachev's announcement of Soviet troop reductions
10. Forest fires in Yellowstone and other national parks.

THE TOP TEN CENSORED STORIES OF 1988

—And What Has Happened to Them Since

1. George Bush's Dirty Big Secrets

1988 SYNOPSIS: Richard H. Meeker, president of the Association of Alternative Newsweeklies and publisher of *Willamette Week*, in Portland, Oregon, charges that if the average American voter had been reading the alternative press' coverage of Election '88, George Bush would not have been elected president. Here are just ten stories that might have made a difference if the establishment press had bothered to investigate and report them with the same intensity as the alternative press:

✔ George Bush and his relationship with a network of anti-Semites with Nazi and fascist affiliations

✔ Bush's connection with the 1980 "October Surprise Working Group," which reportedly sabotaged Jimmy Carter's efforts to have the hostages in Iran released

✔ Bush's role in delaying the Watergate investigation after Richard Nixon put him in charge of the Republican National Committee

✔ Bush's role as a CIA "asset" in 1963 when he ran the Zapata offshore oil drilling company

✔ Bush's role in encouraging the CIA to go back to "business as usual" when he took over the CIA in 1976

✔ Bush's relationship with Manuel Noriega while he was CIA chief and Noriega was Panama's chief of military intelligence and a paid CIA informant

✔ Bush's support for the secret 1986 arms shipments to Iran

✔ Bush's failure as Drug Czar for the Reagan Administration

✔ Bush's questionable judgment in buying real estate with restrictive racist covenants after he was sworn in as Vice President

✔ Bush's anti-environmental efforts as head of the Presidential Task Force on Regulatory Relief 1981-1983.

SOURCES: *San Francisco Bay Guardian*, 11/2/88, "George Bush's Dirty Secrets," by Richard Meeker; *EXTRA!*, September/October 1988, "The GOP-Nazi Connection."

UPDATE: One of Bush's unpublicized secrets of 1988 focused on his reported relationship with anti-Semites. In 1988, Frederic Malek, a Bush campaign adviser, resigned after it became known that he had compiled a list of Jews while in the Bureau of Labor Statistics during the Nixon Administration. In 1992, Frederic Malek was George Bush's campaign manager (*The Nation*, 3/16/92). Another 1988 secret was Bush's Zapata/CIA connection. In 1991, Bush's oldest son, George W. Bush, was the third largest stockholder in a small Texas oil company that surprisingly won extremely lucrative offshore drilling rights in the Persian Gulf. Once the Gulf War ended, among those reaping benefits from this extraordinary deal were the President's son, George W. Bush, and New York attorney Alan G. Quasha and his father, William H. Quasha. According to *Common Cause Magazine* (Spring 1991), "The elder Quasha is a prominent Manila attorney who represented the Philippine branch of the Nugan Hand Bank, which collapsed in early 1980 amid charges that it was laundering money and had been involved with the CIA."

The issue of buying real estate with restrictive racist covenants was recalled in 1992. Bush sent a letter to the Chicago Bar Association (CBA) commending it on its nomination for an award created by the CBA to honor the late Earl Burrus Dickerson. As the *Chicago Daily Law Bulletin* noted (3/15/95), Dickerson successfully argued before the U.S. Supreme Court that "restrictive real estate covenants barring sales to minorities could not be enforced."

In 1992, Bush reprised his earlier anti-environment stand. According to *Newsweek* (6/22/92), Bush embarrassed himself by looking like the anti-environment president at the ecology summit held in Rio de Janeiro. By posing the debate as the United States versus the world, Bush alienated not only the green vote but a good many moderates.

2. How the EPA Pollutes the News and the Dioxin Cover-up

1988 SYNOPSIS: Reports of improvement in environmental pollution levels in 1988 were a deliberate attempt by the Environmental Protection Agency (EPA) to mislead and pacify the public, according to Jim Sibbison, a former EPA press officer. Equally disturbing, the news media have contributed to this disinformation campaign by treating EPA press releases as reliable news reports. For example, on July 28, 1988, in the midst of a summer during which medical waste washed up on East Coast beaches, *The New York Times* published a reassuring front page story about successful sewer-system pollution control by Philip Shabecoff, its environmental reporter.

The Reagan Administration, in an effort to reduce EPA appropriations from Congress, encouraged EPA officials to soft-pedal pollution stories. Further, since Reagan first took office, executives from industry met secretly over the years with officials of the White House's Office of Management and Budget (OMB) to discuss pending EPA regulations affecting their companies. The OMB allowed the executives to suggest revisions in these regulations to reduce costs to their industry. The EPA then made the necessary changes and the "acceptable" regulations went into effect.

Another example of EPA malfeasance began in February 1987 when the American Paper Industry (API) discovered dioxin, a highly hazardous substance, in the bleaching process of its paper mills. As a result, the industry had to conclude the inevitability of dioxin being present in some of its products, including disposable diapers, office stationery, coffee filters, tampons, milk cartons, butter cartons, cereal boxes, tissues, and paper plates. A month later, a confidential API plan described the public health threat posed by dioxin as a public relations problem and set a primary goal to "keep all allegations of health risks out of the public arena."

Subsequently, internal documents from API, leaked to Greenpeace, substantiated how EPA and industry officials were working together to limit public knowledge about the hazards of dioxin.

SOURCES: *Columbia Journalism Review*, November/December 1988, "Dead Fish and Red Herrings: How the EPA Pollutes the News," by Jim Sibbison; *Greenpeace*, March/April 1989, "Whitewash: The Dioxin Cover-up," by Peter Von Stackelberg.

UPDATE: In 1990, the Clean Air Act Amendment required the EPA to establish limits for emissions of dioxins from incinerators. While the EPA was ordered to put the rules in place by April 1995, the process was delayed to mid-1997 (*The Sunday Gazette Mail*, 7/7/95).

Meanwhile, the residents of a small neighborhood in Pensacola, Florida, live in the deadly shadow of a hill they call "Mount Dioxin." The dioxin-contaminated hill was built by the EPA in 1991. As a result, the EPA then planned the largest evacuation from a dioxin waste site since it emptied the Missouri town of Times Beach in 1983; it was to become the third-largest permanent relocation ever from a hazardous waste site, after Times Beach and the infamous Love Canal neighborhood in Niagara Falls, New York (*St. Petersburg Times*, 6/23/96). After five years of stonewalling residents, on October 3, 1996, the EPA, agreed to relocate all 358 families living around "Mount Dioxin." The relocation will cost taxpayers a minimum of $18 million (Associated Press, 10/4/96).

3. Project Galileo: The Risk of a Nuclear Disaster in Space

1988 SYNOPSIS: Prior to the Challenger disaster on January 28, 1986, the National Aeronautics and Space Administration (NASA) set the odds of a shuttle crash at one in 100,000. It turned out that one in 25 launches could end in tragedy.

Yet, despite the Challenger disaster, NASA plans to launch a shuttle on October 12, 1989, that will carry enough radioactive plutonium to kill every person on earth. Nearly 50 pounds of plutonium is to be used in the space probe which will explore the atmosphere of Jupiter in the proposed Galileo mission. NASA insists the risks of carrying the plutonium payload is minimal and that the possible scientific gains are substantial.

But many scientists who are experts in the field of radioactivity are apprehensive. They see three possible disaster scenarios—a launchpad explosion, in which the shuttle's liquid fuel would be ignited and the plutonium released, would contaminate Cape Canaveral and environs; a Challenger-like explosion in the upper atmosphere would disperse the poisonous plutonium over a broader area; and any serious space mishap within the Earth's 22,000-mile gravitational pull could spread the uranium derivative even more widely over the Earth.

SOURCES: *The Long Island Monthly*, October 1988, "The Fire Next Time," by Karl Grossman; *EXTRA!*, September/October 1988, "*Newsday* Spikes Article on C*****ship," by Dennis Bernstein.

UPDATE: Fortunately for the world's population, the Galileo space probe mission was successful. However, space missions posing similarly disastrous consequences if anything goes wrong continue to be scheduled. For example, the Cassini probe, which is to carry more than 70 pounds of plutonium on board, is currently slotted for a launch in October of 1997.

Please see update of "Lethal Shuttle," #10, 1986, for further information on the Cassini.

4. Radioactive Waste and the Dangers of Food Irradiation

1988 SYNOPSIS: Despite serious questions concerning effectiveness and consumer safety, the U.S. Department of Energy (DOE) plans to set up 1,000 food irradiation facilities around the country within the next ten years. Food irradiation is a process in which food is put on a conveyor belt and exposed to radiation from a radioactive source such as cobalt-60 or cesium-137.

As a process that can utilize radioactive waste, food irradiation is particularly attractive to DOE since it "completes the nuclear fuel cycle," reducing wastes that require disposal to a minimum.

The DOE's planned facilities are of the same type as Radiation Sterilizers in Decatur, Georgia. An accident occurred there on June 6, 1988, in which a capsule containing deadly radioactive cesium broke open, contaminating the irradiation chamber, adjacent offices, and 25,000 gallons of water. Ten workers were exposed to the cesium and 70,000 medical supply containers and milk cartons had to be recalled after several milk cartons, waiting to be shipped to Florida, revealed radioactivity. DOE had previously declared the cesium capsules to be fool-proof.

Safety concerns are not limited to irradiation facilities. Research indicates the evidence of somatic and genetic hazard from consuming irradiated foods is far greater than either the Food and Drug Administration or the proponents of irradiated foods are willing to admit.

SOURCES: *The Workbook*, April/June 1988, "Food Irradiation: Its Environmental Threat, Its Toxic Connection," by Judith H. Johnsrud, Ph.D.; *Northern Sun News*, December 1988, "Update on Food Irradiation," by JoAnne Korkid.

UPDATE: The Department of Energy's plan to set up 1,000 food irradiation facilities around the country in the next ten years, as noted in the 1988 *Censored* story, has not come about yet and, according to Martin Teitel, author of *Rain Forest in Your Kitchen*, probably never will. Teitel points out, in the March 1996 issue of *Sierra*, "Proponents (of irradiation) fondly pictured miniature nuclear facilities scattered about the countryside that would briefly nuke meat and produce to reduce shrinkage, extend shelf life, and kill mold, fungi, bacteria, and insects. Its other big appeal, of course, was that irradiation facilities would function as repositories for the nuclear industry's radioactive waste.

"Critics pointed out the contamination risks to workers and surrounding communities, and that consumers would ingest increased numbers of carcinogenic 'free radicals' in irradiated foods. Cities passed ordinances mandating the labeling of irradiated foods, activists threatened boycotts, and the public said no thanks. Irradiation is still commonly used on spices, but that's about it. A Florida experiment in irradiating strawberries bombed, and there are no known plans for more such ventures."

5. Acid Rain—One of America's Biggest Killers

1988 SYNOPSIS: When acid rain was selected as one of the top ten *Censored* stories of 1977, its toll was cited in terms of contaminated soil, damaged crops, dying trees, and dead fish. Acid rain became a household word, but few people were aware of its devastating toll in human terms. By 1988 there was strong circumstantial evidence that suggested acid rain was a significant threat to human health and lives—one of the "best kept secrets about airborne pollution."

In 1986, the Brookhaven National Laboratory of New York estimated that acid rain annually kills 50,000 Americans as well as 5,000 to 11,000 Canadians. The Office of Technology Assessment (OTA), an advisory body to Congress, rated acid rain much more dangerous in 1988 than it had been in the previous three years.

A study by Dr. Cedric Garland, Director of Cancer Epidemiology at the University of California at Berkeley, revealed a pattern of increased cancers occurring throughout the "acid rain belt" cutting across northeastern U.S. and eastern Canada. Statistics from the area appear to support Dr. Garland. During the five-year period of 1982-1986, deaths from lung cancer in Vermont rose 28 percent; breast cancer deaths increased from 77 in 1980 to 103 in 1986, a 34 percent increase.

While an early warning of the human dangers of acid rain was first sounded in the 1940s, statistical studies are just beginning to document the harm wreaked by toxic metals released by acid rain. In addition to lethal metals, such as lead, aluminum, mercury, and cadmium, acid raindrops often contain man-made chemicals such as DDT and PCBs.

SOURCE: *Vanguard Press*, 1/28/88, "Acid Rain Is Killing Five to 20 Times as Many Americans as AIDS," by Merritt Clifton.

UPDATE: Evidence of the deadly nature of acid rain and the microscopic particles that create it continues to mount. The Council of Economic Priorities, a corporate watchdog group, reported that high levels of sulfur dioxide, a major cause of acid rain and respiratory problems, have been linked to disease and death in more than ten countries (*PR Services*, February 1996). *The Richmond Times-Dispatch* reported (8/1/96) that the sulfur compounds from factories can be transformed in the atmosphere to sulfuric acid, and fall to Earth as acid rain. The particles may cause increased respiratory disease, lung damage, and even premature death. One study, by the Natural Resources Defense Council, a non-profit environmental group, cited in the *Asbury Park Press* (6/24/96), "determined that 64,000 people in major American cities may be dying annually from lung or heart problems aggravated by breathing microscopic particles of soot (which create acid rain)."

On January 17, 1997, the EPA released tougher clean-air standards that would tighten limits on emissions of chemicals and tiny particles that form smog and soot. Five months later President Clinton approved the EPA regulations. The new standards toughen emission limits for ozone and particulate matter. Particulate matter is often carried long distances by wind and brought back to land by precipitation called acid rain. The EPA said the new regulations will prevent about 15,000 premature deaths each year (*Sacramento Bee*, 6/26/97).

Ironically, there are still some who discount the impact of acid rain. *Oilweek*, an oil industry trade magazine, asked (4/1/96), "How many people realize that acid rain turned out to be a false alarm in North America?"

6. America's Secret Police Network—LEIU Part II

1988 SYNOPSIS: The Law Enforcement Intelligence Unit (LEIU) was one of the top ten *Censored* stories of 1978. Ten years later, we find that this secretive unofficial police intelligence organization is alive and well and more powerful than ever. It also is still virtually unknown.

In June 1988, the *Los Angeles Times* reported the LEIU was considering suspension or even termination of the Los Angeles Police Department's membership because two of its police detectives from an organized crime unit allegedly leaked confidential information from LEIU files.

A variety of police agencies have been barred from the powerful, super-secretive organization in past years for suspected security breaches, including the Las Vegas Police Department and the Houston Police Department.

Knowing that the FBI, CIA, and virtually every other agency with the authority to spy, has "gone off the reservation" at one time or another and used their power to threaten our liberties, it is alarming to know there is a national, private intelligence agency which is not answerable to any public authority.

SOURCES: *Los Angeles Times*, 6/24/88, "Intelligence Units Across U.S. Probe Alleged LAPD Leak," by William K. Knoedelseder Jr., Kim Murphy, and Ronald L. Soble; *Penthouse*, December 1976, "America's Secret Police Network," by George O'Toole.

UPDATE: Please see the update of "Law Enforcement Intelligence Unit," #6, 1978.

7. Children are Paying the Third World Debt With Their Lives

1988 SYNOPSIS: A key finding in the UNICEF report, "The State of the World's Children," issued late in 1988 revealed that nine hundred million people, mostly women and children, suffered because their nations used essential resources to repay debts to bankers in industrialized nations.

UNICEF Executive Director James Grant called for a world summit to save an estimated three million children who he said die each year from easily preventable diseases. More than half a million of those children died in 16 developing nations in 1987 because their debt-burdened governments had to cut back on social spending.

Previously, deaths among the young had been falling. A decade of immunization against basic diseases was saving 1.5 million lives a year. However, due to economic hardship, the 40 poorest countries in the developing world halved health spending over the course of several years and cut education budgets by a quarter.

UNICEF cited the two major causes of the worsening conditions: rising debt repayments and falling commodity prices. In 1988 Third World debt stood at more than $1 trillion, while debt repayment took almost a quarter of the developing world's export revenues.

Lawrence E. Bruce, Jr., president of the UN Children's Fund, charged the "mounting debt payments of so many of these developing countries to Western institutions are quite literally snatching food and medicine out of the mouths of millions of children."

SOURCES: *San Francisco Examiner*, 12/21/88, "Children Hardest Hit By Resurgence of Global Poverty," by John Madeley, of the *London Observer; USA Today*, 12/21/88, "World's Children Pay Debt With Their Lives," by Marilyn Greene.

UPDATE: On September 28, 1996, the world's seven wealthiest industrial nations, the so-called Group of Seven (G-7), renamed the Group of Eight

(G-8) in 1997, approved a plan to relieve up to $7.7 billion in debts of about 20 of the world's most heavily indebted countries, many of them in Africa. The plan will cover up to 80 percent of the debt the debtor nations hold individually (Associated Press, 9/29/96). Apparently the plan didn't include Haiti, where violent anti-government strikes broke out on January 16, 1997. The strikers were protesting the government's austerity program inaugurated in response to pressure from international lending institutions (Associated Press, 1/17/97).

However, the continuing problem of worldwide hunger among children was reflected in data released by the U.N. Food and Agriculture Organization (*Knight-Ridder Tribune*, 10/27/96): 200 million children are malnourished; 11 million children under age five die as a result of hunger and malnutrition; and millions more have diseases related to vitamin and mineral deficiencies, bad food, and water.

The 1996 UNICEF report, "The State of the World's Children," changed the focus from the impact of poverty to that of war. In the past ten years, the report says, wars have left two million children dead, four million to five million disabled, and 12 million homeless. Further, as reported in *World Press Review* (January 1996), "The 1990s have brought a vicious new breed of warfare" as guerrilla and government armies have resorted to the use of children to fill the role of combatants. A report by Save the Children in late 1996 revealed that an estimated 250,000 soldiers under 18—both boys and girls and some as young as five years old—are serving in some 33 armed conflicts around the world (Associated Press, 11/1/96).

8. A Constitutional Convention is Just Two Votes Away

1988 SYNOPSIS: There is a little-known, but potentially explosive, dedicated effort underway to call a constitutional convention to amend the U.S. Constitution. The Constitution requires two-thirds (34) of the states to call for such a convention before the nation may hold one to consider amending the Constitution.

As of now, 32 states have called for such a convention—we are now just two states away from holding a constitutional convention.

Some of those seeking the convention want to add "urgently needed...popular" constitutional changes, like balancing the federal budget, requiring voluntary prayer in public schools, and restricting abortions. Others want to add women's rights to the Constitution, make Senate and House terms longer, abolish the electoral college in selecting a president, limit terms for Supreme Court justices, and restrict the rights of the criminally accused.

While some changes may be worthy, we already have proven ways to get them into the Constitution. Further, opponents to the convention are concerned since there are no legal bounds as to what such a convention could do. Indeed, many have been opposed to an open-ended call for such a convention because it could become a runaway event in which every crackpot suggestion for constitutional change would be permitted.

The National Taxpayers Union, the conservative lobby behind the current push for a constitutional convention, acknowledges the drive is essentially part of a strategy to force Congress to draft its own balanced budget amendment.

SOURCES: *The Economist*, 5/21/88, "The Constitution: Lid On to Keep the Worms Out"; *USA Today*, 3/3/89, "Debate: We Shouldn't Tinker with Constitution."

UPDATE: On September 13, 1993, New Jersey Senate Majority Leader John Dorsey withdrew his support for a resolution to add New Jersey to the list of states calling for a convention to amend the U.S. Constitution (*Bergen Record*, 9/14/93). If it had passed, New Jersey would have been the 33rd state to call for a constitutional convention, just one short of the needed 34 states. The effort then stalled. Finally, on March 1, 1995, *The Atlanta Constitution* reported that while up to 32 states had voted for the convention since 1976, "Those votes have no legal weight now, but demonstrated support for the idea." Like the Equal Rights Amendment, time ran out on the call for a constitutional convention (*ABA Journal*, February 1996).

9. U.S. Refuses to Abide by International Court of Justice

1988 SYNOPSIS: The World Court of the United Nations, otherwise known as the International Court of Justice, passed down a ruling finding the United States in violation of international law as a result of the Reagan Administration's support of the contra war effort.

As a result, the U.S. may have to pay billions of dollars in reparations for damages caused in Nicaragua. At the same time, it is suffering the loss of international credibility because of its non-compliance with third party adjudication by the World Court.

New York Congressman Ted Weiss, speaking in the House of Representatives on October 21, 1988, tried to warn the nation of the danger of ignoring the court's ruling when he said, "Mr. Speaker, the Reagan Administration's decision to withdraw from the World Court's compulsory jurisdiction violated a solid policy of support over the past four decades."

In full view of the world, the U.S. is facing charges of hypocrisy for its failure to uphold its own most cherished values of adherence to the rule of law. The stubborn refusal of Washington to deal constructively with the World Court can only lead our foreign allies and enemies alike to conclude that America submits itself to decisions of the World Court only when the decisions are in favor of its own national interest.

SOURCES: *Los Angeles Times*, 9/25/88, "U.S. Snub of World Court Won't Avert Day of Reckoning," op-ed article by Howard N. Meyer; *Congressional Record*, 10/21/88, "The World Court," by Hon. Ted Weiss; *Our Right To Know*, Summer 1988, "The World Court and Nicaragua," by Howard N. Meyer.

UPDATE: Shortly after Violeta de Chamorro was elected president of Nicaragua in 1990, with generous campaign funding from the Bush Administration, she withdrew Nicaragua's World Court claim against the United States (*Newsday* "Viewpoints," 11/8/93). But while the United States was not forced to pay reparations for the damages caused in Nicaragua, it did suffer the loss of international credibility because of its non-compliance with the ruling.

In November 1994, in a discussion of the role of the UN's International Court of Justice in cases such as Yugoslavia and Rwanda, international law expert Benjamin B. Ferencz was asked, "Does the United States support the idea of international law?" He responded, "The United States plays games with the idea. It's a hypocritical, deceitful game that's being played. We say we are not against it in principle, but we'll find enough problems to make sure it never moves." Ferencz pointed out that in the 1980s, the Court found the U.S. mining of harbors in Nicaragua to be an unlawful act but the United States ignored the finding (*National Catholic Reporter*, 11/11/94).

In 1996, in a close decision by the World Court concerning the use of nuclear weapons, critics pointed out that the Court didn't have any power to enforce its decisions. They noted how the U.S. ignored the court's ruling in the Nicaragua case (*Washington Post*, 7/9/96).

10. The Abuse of America's Incarcerated Children

1988 SYNOPSIS: The mental, physical, and sexual abuse children suffer inside America's juvenile-justice system is a tragic story shared by thousands of young people.

On any given day, there are an average of 2.5 million children of both sexes between the ages of five and 19 years incarcerated in America's juvenile detention facilities. Of that number, more than 1.2 million are sexually abused by their peers. Nearly 150,000 more are being abused by their state-employed counselors and staff members.

The physical abuses these children suffer range from rape to spankings to beatings with fists, whips, ropes, and chains. The mental abuses they suffer range from emotional and physical neglect to a sense of being unwanted by parents to indefinite periods of isolation inside filthy solitary-confinement cells.

The issue of abuse of incarcerated children has received little media exposure because they have an even less influential voice than their adult counterparts in the nation's political process.

SOURCES: *Arete*, "I Cried, You Didn't Listen," by Dwight Boyd Roberts with Jack Carter; personal letter, 2/21/89, from Jack Carter.

UPDATE: While there has been a significant increase in juvenile crime since this *Censored* story of 1988, there has been little discussion of how juveniles are treated when incarcerated. National statistics from the U.S. Department of Justice, the General Accounting Office, and the FBI, reported that juvenile court cases involving violent crimes such as murder and rape increased 68 percent between 1988 and 1992; 61 percent of juveniles in jail for violent crimes in 1993 thought it was "okay to shoot someone who hurts or insults you"; 61,000 juveniles were arrested on weapons offenses in 1991, a 103 percent increase over 1985; and 2,200 juveniles committed murder in 1991, a 127 percent increase over 1984 (*Sunday Advocate*, 4/7/96).

Worsening the problem is the fact that as juvenile jail facilities became overcrowded, more juveniles had to be jailed with adult criminals. The *Kentucky Courier-Journal* (7/31/96) characterized the situation of many juvenile facilities when it said, "Anyone who believes that state-sanctioned abuse of juveniles went out with the 19th century should read U.S. District Judge William O. Bertelsman's account of how young people are treated at the Kenton County Jail. It sounds like it came from a Charles Dickens novel." In California, the nation's most populous state, demands are being made for an overhaul of the juvenile justice system now based on the Juvenile Court Law enacted in the 1940s (*The Fresno Bee*, 7/9/96).

Global Media Lords Control World Media

In 1989, the mainstream news media heralded the fall of communist regimes in Eastern Europe, but failed to report the U.S. support for a repressive regime in Guatemala. According to the Associated Press, the top ten news stories of the year were:

1. Communism crumbles in Eastern Europe and Gorbachev works to reform Soviet Union
2. Chinese crackdown on student-led-pro-democracy movement in Tiananmen Square
3. Exxon Valdez oil spill
4. California's Loma Prieta earthquake
5. Abortion debate
6. International drug war
7. Hurricane Hugo batters the Caribbean and South and North Carolina
8. Scandals, trials, and resignations in the federal government
9. Federal government moves to rescue savings and loan industry
10. Oliver North is convicted and the Iran-contra investigation continues.

—And What Has Happened to Them Since

1. Global Media Lords Threaten Open Marketplace of Ideas

1989 SYNOPSIS: A handful of mammoth private organizations, driven by bottom line profit considerations, have begun to dominate the world's mass media. They confidently predict by the 1990s, five to ten corporate giants will control most of the world's important newspapers, magazines, books, broadcast stations, movies, recordings, and video cassettes.

According to media scholar Ben Bagdikian, these lords of the global village have their own political and economic agenda. All resist economic changes that do not support their own financial interests. Together, they exert a homogenizing power over ideas, culture, and commerce that affect populations larger than any in history.

At this time, the five big media corporations that dominate the fight for the hundreds of millions of minds in the global village are: Time Warner Inc., the world's largest media corporation; the German-based Bertelsmann AG, owned by Reinhard Mohn; Rupert Murdoch's News Corporation Ltd. of Australia; Hatchette SA, of France, the world's largest producer of magazines; and U.S.-based Capital Cities/ABC Inc.

While monopolistic power may dominate many other industries, Bagdikian points out, "Media giants have two enormous advantages: They control the public image of national leaders who, as a result, fear and favor the media magnates' political agenda; and they control the information and

THIS MODERN WORLD by TOM TOMORROW

DISNEY'S RECENTLY ANNOUNCED INTENTION TO PURCHASE ABC HAS BY NOW UNDOUBTEDLY INSPIRED INNUMERABLE VARIATIONS ON THE SAME CARTOON...*

COMING UP NEXT-- AN EXCLUSIVE LOOK AT THE EXCITING NEW LINE OF POCAHONTAS ACTION FIGURES!

HERE'S LOVABLE BRIT HUME WITH OUR REPORT!

*INCLUDING THIS ONE, OF COURSE.

ABC NEWS

...BUT PAST THE EASY JOKES, THIS MERGER RAISES TROUBLING ISSUES... FOR INSTANCE, HOW WELL WILL THE PUBLIC INTEREST BE SERVED WHEN MOST SOURCES OF INFORMATION ARE CONTROLLED BY A HANDFUL OF CORPORATE CONGLOMERATES?

IT SAYS HERE THAT DISNEY REALLY DESERVES A LARGE TAX BREAK!

THAT WAS ON THE RADIO, TOO!

AND ON TV! IT MUST BE TRUE!

entertainment that help establish the social, political, and cultural attitudes of increasingly larger populations."

SOURCE: *The Nation*, 6/12/89, "Lords of the Global Village," by Ben Bagdikian.

UPDATE: With media merger mania in the U.S. running rampant, the only real question was who would end up as the world's largest media corporation. On July 31, 1995, Walt Disney answered that question when it announced it would buy Capital Cities/ABC Inc., thus making Disney the world's largest media corporation. However, less than two months later, on September 22, Time Warner and Turner Broadcasting merged, making it the world's largest media corporation. This dropped Germany's Bertelsmann down to third place—at least for the time being.

Please also see update of "Information Monopoly," #1, 1987.

2. Turning Africa Into the World's Garbage Can

1989 SYNOPSIS: Africa, already suffering from poverty, drought, famine, locusts, "contra" wars, and the AIDS epidemic, now appears destined to become the world's toxic waste dump. International sludge dealers have tried to dump U.S. and European waste onto at least 15 African countries, a trend exposed over the last couple of years by European environmentalists, but not widely covered by the U.S. press.

The need to find a dumping ground is increasingly imperative. Although the U.S. produces an estimated 87 percent of the world's toxic waste, West Germany exports the most. Switzerland lacks recycling or storage facilities.

France, a big waste recycler, had to stop taking in its neighbors' waste in 1988 because its recycling facilities were filled to capacity with domestic waste.

Until 1988, Europe's favorite solution to toxic waste was to incinerate it in the North Sea, until the sea died and 63 countries agreed to stop waste incineration in the North Sea as of 1994.

Africa, unfortunately, became a prime target. Geographically, most sub-Saharan countries have vast, sparsely populated territories that are not really controlled by any authority. There are also no serious controls of Africa's coastal waters. Populations are still largely illiterate and susceptible to persuasion. African countries lack the experts and facilities to determine the contents of shipments. Finally, the targeted countries are poor, in debt, and in need of funds Western countries are willing to pay to dump their waste.

The scandalous efforts to dump on Africa led to the 1989 Basel Convention, which recognized the "right of every country to refuse to accept toxic waste." The Organization for African Unity, concerned with having individual countries decide the issue, persuaded the African countries not to sign.

SOURCE: *In These Times*, 11/8/89, "Western Developmental Overdose Makes Africa Chemically Dependent," by Diana Johnston.

UPDATE: Please see update of "Dumping Toxics on the Third World," #8, 1987.

3. U.S. Supports "One of the Most Brutal Holocausts Since World War II"

1989 SYNOPSIS: Mozambique, a country on the Indian Ocean bordering South Africa, is one of the world's leading victims of terrorism. This nation of 14 million people is trying to resist brutal attack by the Mozambique National Resistance (RENAMO), a South African-armed and supported group. A U.S. State Department official called it "one of the most brutal holocausts against ordinary human beings since World War II."

The Mozambique government calls them "bandidos," but RENAMO, the 25,000-man army, says they are fighting to overthrow the predominantly black, socialist, one-party government in power. The atrocities are so horrible many cannot even be imagined. So far more than one million, mostly innocent men, women, and children have died as a result of this barbaric war. Many of the atrocities are committed against children. The numbers of girls raped is incredible; reports say girls as young as ten are being made sexual slaves for soldiers. There may be at least 100,000 children the RENAMO has trained and forced to kill. Children are kidnapped from their families and first trained to kill animals, then human beings. This process can begin at the age of eight. One out of every three Mozambique children will die before they reach the age of five.

Funding for RENAMO is believed to come from South African sources as well as conservative, right-wing groups in the United States and Europe. According to RENAMO watch groups, U.S. supporters of RENAMO include U.S. Representatives Dan Burton (R-Indiana) and Philip Crane (R-Illinois); Senators Bob Dole (R-Kansas), Bob Kasten (R-Wisconsin), and Jesse Helms (R-North Carolina); Jack Kemp, Secretary of Housing and Urban Development, and television evangelist Pat Robertson.

SOURCES: *UTNE Reader*, November/December 1989, "The Hidden War in Mozambique," by Kalamu Ya Salaam; *20/20*, 3/2/90, "Children of Terror," and "Against All Odds," by Janice Tomlin and Tom Jarriel; *RENAMO Watch*, February 1990, "RENAMO's U.S. Support."

UPDATE: The holocaust in Mozambique continued until 1990 when the ruling Frelimo government opened talks with RENAMO, which led to a cease fire in 1992. Ironically, RENAMO, which had once brutalized the country, turned to politics and millions of once-terrorized citizens started to support it. In the country's first election in 1994, brokered by the United Nations, Frelimo won a majority with about 55 percent of the votes, gaining 129 of the 250 seats in Parliament. However, RENAMO won 112 seats in Parliament with the remaining nine votes going to a coalition of small parties (*The Mining Journal*, 1/26/96).

Still struggling to overcome the ravages of war, Mozambique is one of the poorest nations in the world. *World Press Review* (January 1996), in an explosive article confirming the RENAMO use of children as warriors, noted that the average Mozambican earned about $80 in 1994.

According to an article in *The New York Times* (5/1/88), "RENAMO has the backing of several members of Congress, including Senator Jesse Helms and Representative Jack Kemp, who last September sent a letter to RENAMO's leader that closed with 'best wishes for continued success.'" Congressional support of the RENAMO was also later cited by *National Catholic Reporter* (12/10/93) which said Senator Bob Dole once referred to the RENAMO rebels as "freedom fighters."

4. Does the Bush Administration Really Want to Win the War on Drugs?

1989 SYNOPSIS: As the U.S. "War on Drugs" begins to look more and more like a losing battle, a number of stories tell of conflicting U.S. priorities and closed-door deals. One of the most extraordinary stories is about Richard Gregorie, who was one of the nation's most successful Mafia prosecutors when he was sent to Miami with orders to go after the top people in the cocaine business.

Gregorie did just that for eight years and became the top federal narcotics prosecutor in Miami. He became something of a local hero after making cases against big-time cocaine bosses and drug-corrupted officials from Miami to Medellin. But as Gregorie began penetrating the higher levels of the cocaine business, he began to target foreign officials of supposedly friendly nations, including General Manuel Noriega of Panama, while State Department officials were still courting the dictator.

Gregorie's elaborate undercover sting operations began to concern intelligence and State Department officials and he was soon told to stay away from certain sensitive areas. "I feel a lot like the soldiers in Vietnam felt. We are not being allowed to win this war," said Gregorie.

Gregorie's operations were subsequently stopped at the request of the State Department and he quit in protest in January 1989.

Meanwhile Gregorie's charges were validated by the findings of a Senate Foreign Relations Subcommittee on Narcotics, Terrorism, and International Operations, which concluded that foreign policy interests were permitted to sidetrack, disrupt, and undercut the war on drugs.

SOURCES: *NBC Nightly News*, 2/22/89; *San Francisco Chronicle*, 4/15/89, "Policy Reportedly Undercut Drug War," New York Times Service; Richard Gregorie, 10/10/89, telephone interview.

UPDATE: The nation's scandalous "war on drugs" has been cited often by Project Censored over the years. The #21 *Censored* story of 1989 reveals how government and media propagandized the war on drugs; the #5 story of 1990 reports the continued media blackout of drug war fraud; the #23 story of 1993 documents stories showing the highly touted DARE program was not effective; the #15 story of 1994 notes the DARE program cover-up continued. And on May 12, 1994, *USA Today* reported that despite $52 billion in federal anti-drug spending in the past five years, there was higher use and less fear of drugs.

Finally, on December 20, 1996, the *Washington Post* announced the latest bad news on the drug war front. A study by the National Institute on Drug Abuse revealed that illegal use of drugs, particularly marijuana, increased again in 1996. In something of an understatement, Health and Human Services Secretary Donna Shalala said, "Drug use among young people is at unacceptable levels."

Whistleblower Richard Gregorie is once again doing what he does best—going after drug dealers. He served as a Dade County prosecutor, and is now a senior prosecutor with the U.S. Attorney's Office in Miami.

5. Guatemalan Blood on U.S. Hands

1989 SYNOPSIS: The Bush Administration significantly strengthened ties with the Guatemalan military at the same time that human rights violations by the military rose sharply.

According to the 1989 review by Human Rights Watch, U.S. military involvement in Guatemala included: sales of rifles to the army; construction of a road by the U.S. Army; training of Guatemalan paratroopers by U.S. Green Berets; jungle survival training by U.S. Special Forces; and a series of training exercises by armed and uniformed National Guard units from Kentucky, Georgia, Iowa, Oklahoma, and Hawaii, in a Guatemalan province with considerable rebel activity.

Meanwhile the Guatemala Human Rights Commission/USA reported on the fate of a U.S. citizen that received little U.S. press coverage. On November 2, 1989, a U.S. citizen, Sister Diana Ortiz, 31, of the Ursuline order based in Maple Mount, Kentucky, was kidnapped, beaten, tortured, and sexually molested by three men, one of whom was a uniformed Guatemalan police officer.

The Human Rights Watch contended this should have triggered a suspension of U.S. training programs for the Guatemalan police, but the U.S. State Department didn't even register a protest, saying the case fell under Guatemalan jurisdiction. Compare this with the response by the Bush Administration to the *alleged sexual threat* to a U.S. lieutenant's wife by Panamanian armed forces that Bush used to partially justify the invasion of Panama by 26,000 U.S. troops.

SOURCES: *Guatemala Update,* February 1990, "U.S. Aid Said to Encourage Rights Violations," by Jana Schroeder; *Guatemala Human Rights Commission/USA,* 1/24/90, "U.S. Citizen Kidnapped and Tortured in Guatemala," by Joanne Heisel.

UPDATE: The report of "world-class" human rights atrocities in Guatemala was first cited in the #15 *Censored* story of 1988. But it wasn't until March and April of 1995 that the major media confirmed the full horrifying story. On March 11, 1995, seven years after the atrocities were revealed in the alternative press, wire services reported the Clinton Administration was suspending the last of its military aid to Guatemala. On April 13, 1995, *The New York Times* reported that a federal judge ordered an ex-Guatemalan general to pay $47.5 million to Sister Diana Ortiz and eight Guatemalans who were terrorized by the Guatemalan military. On July 26, 1995, *The Times* also reported an internal CIA investigation concluding that CIA officers covered up their clandestine Guatemalan activities. Finally, on June 29, 1996, the Associated Press reported that a presidential panel, the Intelligence Oversight Board, revealed evidence that several CIA agents in Guatemala had ordered, planned or taken part in human rights abuses in Guatemala, including assassination, since 1984.

It was not until 1997 that the full extent of U.S. interference in Guatemalan affairs was exposed. Newly declassified documents revealed that the CIA plotted to overthrow the Guatemalan government as early as the 1950s. It had compiled "hit lists" and started training Central American assassins to kill political and military Communist leaders (Associated Press, 5/24/97).

Guatemala's civil war, which began in 1960, was the longest and deadliest in Central America, having taken the lives of up to 200,000 unarmed civilians, primarily highland Indians, as reported in a well-documented article in *Foreign Policy* (6/22/96). In 1991, the Guatemalan army agreed to participate in peace negotiations to end the war. The United States, along with Mexico, Norway, Spain, Colombia, and Venezuela, known as the Group of Friends, offered to facilitate the peace process and support the United Nations as its moderator. *Foreign Policy* said Guatemala's new president, Alvaro Arzu, who took office in January 1996, vowed to advance the peace negotiations and to establish civilian control over the army. On November 11, 1996, the Guatemalan government and the guerrilla movement agreed to a formal cease-fire (Associated Press, 11/12/96). And on Sunday, December 29, 1996, guerrilla and government leaders signed the official accord ending the war and promising to address the poverty, repression, and discrimination that ignited the fighting 36 years earlier (Associated Press, 12/30/96).

Please also see update of "What's Happening in Central America," #5, 1982.

6. Radioactive Waste: As Close As Your Neighborhood Landfill

1989 SYNOPSIS: Radioactive waste may be joining old tires, banana peels, and other regular garbage at your local landfill. Radioactive waste may be sent to both solid waste and hazardous waste incinerators. Radioactive waste may be flushed down the drain to sewage treatment centers. And radioactive paper and metal may be recycled into consumer products.

All of this will happen if the Nuclear Regulatory Commission (NRC), the Environmental Protection Agency (EPA), and the nuclear industry implement their latest ingenious plan—deregulating low level radioactive waste to "Below Regulatory Concern," (BRC). BRC means that the formerly regulated radioactive waste will not require government regulation for radioactivity.

If the nuclear power industry application is approved by the NRC, as much as one third of the volume of what is currently considered "low-level" radioactive waste from U.S. nuclear power plants will become regular garbage. Unfortunately, once radioactive waste is deregulated, no records will be kept on the type of waste disposed of, the place of disposal, or the radioactivity contained in the waste.

Deregulating radioactive waste to "Below Regulatory Concern" could be the largest and most dangerous step in recent government history of "defining away" tough problems like radioactive waste and radiation risks.

SOURCE: *The Workbook*, April/June 1989, "NIMBY, Nukewaste In My Backyard?", by Diane D'Arrigo.

UPDATE: Despite the warning about the proposed "Below Regulatory Concern (BRC)" regulation cited above, the Nuclear Regulatory Commission's BRC policy was issued July 3, 1990. However, due to public protest, the NRC withdrew the policy on August 24, 1993. According to *Nuclear News* (December 1993), the NRC had hoped to keep the BRC prospect "alive through a consensus-building process, but most of the citizen organizations with which the consensus was to have been built wanted nothing to do with what they saw as a way to allow disposal of radioactive material with no special controls."

7. Oliver North & Co. Banned from Costa Rica

1989 SYNOPSIS: In July 1989, Oliver North and other major "contragate" figures were barred from Costa Rica. The order was issued by none other than Oscar Arias Sanchez, president of Costa Rica and winner of the 1987 Nobel Peace Prize. President Arias was acting on recommendations from a Costa Rican congressional commission investigating drug trafficking. The commission concluded that the contra re-supply network in Costa Rica, which North coordinated from the White House, doubled as a drug smuggling operation.

As a result of the commission's findings, North, former National Security Advisor John Poindexter, former U.S. Ambassador to Costa Rica Lewis Tambs, Major General Richard Secord, and former CIA station chief in Costa Rica Joseph Fernandez, are barred from ever setting foot in Costa Rica again.

The commission's probe of the contra network centered around the northern Costa Rican ranch of U.S. expatriate John Hull because of the quantity and frequency of drug shipments in the area.

The reaction of the U.S. press to this story was one of complete indifference. Despite a lengthy Associated Press wire report (7/22/89), mainstream media either ignored the story completely, or, like the *Washington Post* and the *Miami Herald*, relegated it to "News In Brief" sections. *The New York Times* and all three major television networks failed to mention the story at all.

SOURCE: *EXTRA!*, October/November 1989, "Censored News: Oliver North & Co. Banned from Costa Rica."

UPDATE: Being banned from Costa Rica did not seem to hinder Oliver North's quest for riches and fame. While he lost a hard-fought campaign for the U.S. Senate in Virginia to Democrat Charles S. Robb, he went on to become a radio talk-show host and a millionaire living on a sprawling, million-dollar 194-acre estate in the foothills of Virginia's Shenandoah Mountains.

U.S. News & World Report (6/6/94), in a scathing analysis of North's finances, reports North made $1.7 million from speaking fees and book contracts in 1992 and 1993 and that his total assets were estimated at $3 million. Chief among his assets is Guardian Technologies International, a maker of body armor, including bulletproof vests, in Sterling, Virginia (*The New York Times*, 4/24/96). North co-founded the company in 1989 with Joseph F. Fernandez, the former CIA station chief in Costa Rica who was indicted but not brought to trial for alleged crimes in the Iran-contra affair. In the *Times* report on North's efforts to take the company public in April 1996, North refused to be interviewed but Fernandez said, "We've worked very hard and very long to make this company what it is today. We want it to be equivalent to our own reputations, which are unblemished."

Shortly after going public on the NASDAQ Stock Market, Guardian shareholders got a "painful lesson in the risks of investing in small start-up companies," according to the *Washington Post* (8/19/96). Guardian stock sunk 69 percent from its high of $6.50 to $2 on August 16, 1996. By the end of 1996, *The New York Times* reported (12/28/96) the value of Guardian stock was down 90 percent.

Anyone wanting more information about Oliver North can check him out on his own home page at http://www.northamerican.com.

8. Biased and Censored News at CBS and *The Wall Street Journal*

1989 SYNOPSIS: *The Wall Street Journal*, one of the nation's most respected newspapers, censored one of its top reporters, Mary Williams Walsh, for exposing how one of the nation's most respected television news departments, *CBS News*, broadcast biased news coverage of the Afghanistan war.

The story by Walsh, originally slated to appear in *The Wall Street Journal*, was eventually published in the January 1990 cover article of *Columbia Journalism Review (CJR)*. It is a damning indictment of the role played by Kurt Lohbeck, CBS's Peshawar-based reporter, producer, and facilitator, in shaping the network's coverage of the Afghan war and, in turn, the nation's understanding of that war. Among Walsh's charges: Lohbeck, a partisan of the mujahideen, favored one guerrilla commander, Abdul Haq, and "served in effect as his publicist"; Lohbeck influenced other journalists' reporting of the war by feeding them disinformation; Lohbeck even tried to set up an arms deal between Abdul Haq and a New Jersey arms manufacturer for 10,000 machine pistols.

The article Walsh wrote for *CJR* was supposed to be the first of a three-part series which she spent five months researching for *The Wall Street Jour-*

nal in 1988. But it was not to be. In early fall of 1989, Walsh was based in Hong Kong as *The Journal's* principal correspondent in south and southeast Asia. Her coverage of the war in Afghanistan had attracted international attention and her editors at *The Journal* were planning to nominate her for the Pulitzer Prize.

Instead, by late fall, Walsh had resigned in fury and frustration from the *Journal*. The story she had been working on—the exposé of shamefully deceptive coverage of the Afghan war by CBS—had been killed by the *Journal*. "I was sold out," Walsh told Erwin Knoll, editor of *The Progressive*, in an interview.

In his cover story about the issue, Knoll wrote: "This is a story about faked and distorted coverage by *CBS News*, which boasts about its thorough and outstanding reporting on the Afghan War. It's a story about how *The Wall Street Journal*, presented with a thoroughly documented article about that fakery and distortion, decided not to publish it. And it's a story about how even a respected journal issued under academic auspices—*The Columbia Journalism Review*—was persuaded to tone down Walsh's exposé after accepting the story *The Wall Street Journal* had refused to print."

SOURCES: *Columbia Journalism Review*, January/February 1990, "Mission: Afghanistan," by Mary Williams Walsh; *Defense Media Review*, 3/31/90, "*Wall Street Journal* and CBS: Case of Professional Courtesy?", by Sean Naylor; *The Progressive*, May 1990, "Afghanistan: Holes in the Coverage of a Holy War," by Erwin Knoll.

UPDATE: In early 1990, the *Censored* story about CBS and Afghanistan was given mainstream media coverage including: *Newsday*, 1/17/90, "When News Organizations Stonewall"; *St. Petersburg Times*, 1/21/90, "When Propaganda Becomes News"; *Washington Post*, 4/17/90, "The Exposé They Declined To Publish"; and *The Washington Times*, 4/18/90, "Inside the Beltway: The Big Spike." *The New York Times* (2/4/90) noted how journalist Mary Williams Walsh was "suspended" from Peshawar's American Club "after reporting sardonically on the rebel boosterism she found" (among her colleagues). *The Times* further remarked that "when in the fall of 1989 word of her departure from the *Journal* reached the American Club, some of the freelancers involved called for drinks all around." It added that such attitudes did not encourage evenhanded reporting but instead led to selective reporting of the war itself: "When in November 1988 the rebels executed more than 70 government officers and men after they had surrendered at Torkham, the story was missed by many Peshawar-based American reporters." *The Times* also reported that there was little coverage in the U.S. media of massacres that occurred in areas taken by the rebels, even when Western human rights groups offered well-documented accounts of the events. (Covert U.S. aid to the rebels in Afghanistan was originally revealed in the #16 *Censored* story of 1984.)

After a stint at the *Los Angeles Times'* Toronto Bureau, Mary Williams Walsh became the *Times'* Berlin correspondent and has since covered major international stories with datelines from Berlin, Athens, Paris, Copenhagen, and Washington, D.C.

9. PCBs and Toxic Waste in Your Gasoline

1989 SYNOPSIS: Next time you pull into a gas station, you could be filling your tank with a deadly mixture of polychlorinated biphenyls (PCBs), toxic waste, solvents, and gasoline.

The General Accounting Office (GAO), Environmental Protection Agency (EPA), and the FBI are investigating sophisticated "waste laundering" schemes in which toxic wastes and solvents are mixed with gasoline, diesel, and industrial fuel. At least one of the schemes revealed connections to organized crime, including personal and business associations with members of La Cosa Nostra mafia families. The practice of mixing waste and fuel apparently started in the 1970s when oil costs began rising. It accelerated when toxic waste disposal costs increased and the number of legal disposal sites decreased. Proper disposal of PCBs can cost as much as $1,000 a drum in the U.S.

Law enforcement efforts have been hampered by the lack of cooperation among agencies to share information. The GAO told Congress that although the EPA had received information on a waste firm's suspected organized crime connections, it would not share the information with GAO officials. In May 1989, four congressmen introduced a bill to stiffen enforcement efforts, but the mass media have yet to cover this story. Representative Howard Wolpe (D-Michigan), one of the bill's sponsors warned, "Our own direct safety and public health may be jeopardized by this practice."

SOURCE: *Common Cause Magazine*, July/August 1989, "Toxic Fuel," by Andrew Porterfield.

UPDATE: The incredible story about mixing toxic waste in gasoline, diesel, and industrial fuel to avoid disposal costs was greeted with some skepticism. However, just over a year later, a Tacoma recycling firm was caught doing just that. Chris Gregoire, director of the Washington State Department of Ecology, charged that a Tacoma company sold fuel oil mixed with pesticides and other toxic chemicals. *The Seattle Times* (11/14/90) reported Gregoire's charge that Lilyblad Petroleum "allowed people to be unknowingly exposed to potentially hazardous conditions" by shipping contaminated fuel to steamship companies, a greenhouse, and a cement company. While Lilyblad is licensed as a solvent recycler, the Ecology Department charged it had engaged in "sham recycling" by improperly mixing waste materials.

10. Something Foul in the Chicken Industry and the USDA

1989 SYNOPSIS: The number of cases of salmonella rose to 2.5 million a year, leading to an estimated 500,000 hospitalizations and 9,000 deaths. This national epidemic was caused by a massive leap in consumer demand for the "healthier food" of chicken and by a massive failure of the U.S. Department of Agriculture (USDA) to adequately inspect processing plants.

While the chicken industry grew to $16 billion-a-year, the USDA cut its inspection staff, lowered health standards, and cracked down on employees who tried to inform the public about contaminated food. The relaxed inspection practices—known as the Streamlined Inspection System—are literally maiming workers and killing consumers. The rate of injury and illness for workers in poultry processing plants is twice that of textile or tobacco workers and even higher than miners.

The relaxed inspection practices have also led to an increase in contaminated chicken. Dr. Carl Telleen, a retired USDA veterinarian and safe food crusader, revealed how chicken "carcasses contaminated with feces, once routinely condemned or trimmed, are now simply rinsed with chlorinated water to remove the stains." According to Telleen, "thousands of dirty chickens are bathed together in a chill tank, creating a mixture known as 'fecal soup' that spreads contamination from bird to bird." Once the feces are mixed with water it creates what Telleen calls "instant sewage." Equally disturbing, consumers pay for the contaminated mixture every time they buy chicken since up to 15 percent of poultry weight consists of fecal soup.

SOURCES: *Southern Exposure*, Summer 1989, "Chicken Empires," by Bob Hall; "The Fox Guarding the Hen House," by Tom Devine.

UPDATE: Despite the thousands of deaths and hospitalizations from salmonella poisoning annually, and the E-coli epidemic of the early 1990s, it was not until July 6, 1996, that the federal government finally took action. President Clinton announced the biggest changes in the rules governing meat and poultry safety in 90 years. The U.S. Department of Agriculture safety plan, which involves scientific testing of meat, updates a 90-year-old system in which inspectors looked, touched, and smelled for bacteria-contaminated carcasses. *USA Today* (7/8/96) reported that "under the new system, called Hazard Analysis and Critical Control Points, companies in every step of meat and poultry production must identify the points in their production where contamination is most likely to occur and then create plans for preventing it or removing or killing the contaminants." Caroline Smith DeWaal, director of food safety for the Center for Science in the Public Interest, said the rules "put the lives and health of Americans before the fears and misgivings of the meat and poultry industry."

CHAPTER 15—1990

Truth is the First Casualty of War

While the Gulf War was the runaway best seller of 1990 in the mainstream media, the flawed news media coverage of the Gulf War was the top undercovered story, as reported in the alternative media. According to the Associated Press, the top ten news stories of the year were:

1. Iraqi invasion of Kuwait and multinational response
2. East and West Germany reunite
3. Political and economic reforms throw Soviet Union into turmoil
4. Savings and loan bailout grows larger
5. Relations warm between the U.S. and Soviet Union
6. White House/Congress budget struggle
7. U.S. economic slump: layoffs and foreclosures rise
8. Fledgling democracies in Eastern Europe in turmoil
9. Panamanian President Manuel Noriega surrenders
10. British Prime Minister Margaret Thatcher steps down.

THE TOP TEN CENSORED STORIES OF 1990

—And What Has Happened to Them Since

1. The Gulf War: Truth was the First Casualty

1990 SYNOPSIS: With the benefit of hindsight, we can safely say the mobilization of U.S. troops in Vietnam, Grenada, and Panama taught us a sobering lesson: When armed conflict is on the horizon, truth is the first casualty. The Gulf crisis indicates the press has still not learned its lesson.

Many journalists, carried away by the blare of the bugles in Saudi Arabia, fell into the unseemly role of Pentagon cheerleaders instead of being the honest, skeptical brokers of information they should have been.

As in Panama and Grenada, journalists and news executives took their cues from government officials. Surprisingly, Defense Department spokesman Pete Williams admitted, "the reporting has been largely a recitation of what administration people have said."

While the press was busy labeling Hussein as "the new Hitler," they were slow in uncovering the fact that just days before the invasion of Kuwait, the White House was lobbying Congress not to apply sanctions against Iraq. Further, the U.S. ambassador to Iraq, April Glaspie, was telling Hussein the U.S. had "no position" concerning Iraq's border dispute with Kuwait—which Hussein interpreted as tacit approval for his actions. Nor was there any coverage of the secret August 23 offer by Iraq to pull out of Kuwait and release all hostages (which President Bush rejected).

SOURCES: *Image Magazine*, 10/14/90, "The First Casualty," by Mark Hertsgaard; *Editor & Publisher*, 10/20/90, "Storytelling from the Persian Gulf," by Debra Gersh; *The Quill*, October 1990, "Imperial Thoughts," by Mike Moore; *The Spotlight*, 10/8/90, "Saddam Was Bush-Whacked On Invasion," by John McBrien.

UPDATE: Flawed media coverage of the Gulf War was subsequently discussed in a number of stories including: the #1 *Censored* story of 1991, which revealed how CBS and NBC spiked footage of the Iraq bombing carnage; the #6 story of 1991, which suggested that there was no evidence of the Iraqi threat to Saudi Arabia that President Bush used to rally the nation to war; the #14 *Censored* story of 1992, which revealed how the media lost the information war with the Pentagon; and the #14 *Censored* story of 1995, which highlighted the media's later shameful handling of the Gulf War Syndrome issue.

In early 1997 the final report of the Presidential Advisory Committee on Gulf War Veterans' Illnesses confirmed the Pentagon was slow in investigating whether chemical weapons could be causing health problems, saying there was no evidence of exposure to chemical weapons (*Washington Post*, 1/7/97).

It was not until January 21, 1997, that a federal agency, the Department of Veterans Affairs, acknowledged for the first time a direct link between toxic chemicals and Gulf War Syndrome (*The New York Times*, 1/22/97). Less than a month later, Bernard Rostker, the military's chief Gulf illness investigator, reported the number of U.S. troops that could have been exposed to chemical agents was greater than the 20,800 previously admitted by the Pentagon (*USA Today*, 2/12/97). In mid-June, 1997, the General Accounting Office released a report linking nerve gas and other chemical weapons to the health problems of the veterans (*The New York Times*, 6/15/97). Finally in late July 1997, the Department of Defense acknowledged that nearly 100,000 U.S. troops may have been exposed to Iraq nerve gas (*USA Today*, 7/24/97).

The media were equally slow in reporting the illness itself. Nor were the national media quick to report that geneticist Joshua Lederberg, head of the Pentagon panel that earlier dismissed links between biological weapons and the illnesses of Gulf War veterans, was also a director of American Type Culture Collection, the institute that had exported anthrax to Iraq (*Newsday*, 11/27/96).

As for April Glaspie, after some inconclusive congressional hearings—where she denied her statements to Saddam Hussein, she disappeared into obscurity as an ambassador-in-residence at a San Diego university. In 1993, she returned to active duty at the State Department's Bureau of African Affairs where she was criticized for provoking Somalia's warlord Mohammed Aideed's hostility. In January 1995, Glaspie took over operations of the United Nation's Relief and Works Agency for Palestinian refugees in the West Bank (*The Independent*, 3/13/95). By April 1995, Glaspie was reportedly in a turf battle with the U.N. special envoy responsible for distributing aid in Gaza (*The Washington Times*, 4/28/96).

2. The S&L Crisis: The Solution is Worse Than the Crime

1990 SYNOPSIS: An early estimate of the cost to taxpayers to bail out the savings and loan industry was $155 billion. In August of 1990, a *Wall Street*

Journal correspondent suggested a $1.4 trillion figure. But the most "acceptable" figure for the bailout appears to be $500 billion.

To put that $500 billion in perspective, it helps to realize that the entire cost of World War II, in current dollars and including service-connected veterans' benefits, was about $460 billion—or $40 billion less than the estimated S&L bailout. The cost of the Vietnam War, including benefits, was $172 billion; Korea was $70 billion; World War I was $63 billion; the Civil War was $7 billion. The combined 1988 profits of all the companies on the Fortune 500 list added up to just $115 billion. And the combined 1987 budgets of all 50 states didn't add up to $500 billion.

This "solution" was engineered by the Resolution Trust Corporation (RTC)—the government's misnamed S&L caretaker which is engaged in a massive giveaway that will make Teapot Dome look like a demitasse cup. Little known yesterday, the RTC is now the nation's largest operator of financial institutions, and, according to *The New York Times*, is "quickly becoming the biggest financial institution in the world, the largest single owner of real estate, the largest liquidation company, and the largest auction firm." The RTC solution includes a little known $500 million in outside legal fees and $37 million in administrative costs. The RTC was established without any meaningful public debate nor with any serious consideration of alternatives.

What is taking place with the RTC "solution" involves fraud, malfeasance, misfeasance, and nonfeasance of a scope never seen before. And no war, no defense program, no social program, no other scandal has ever cost what this will cost.

SOURCES: *The Progressive Review*, August 1990, "No-Fault Capitalism Meets Lemon Socialism," by Sam Smith; *The Wall Street Journal*, 8/9/90, "Viewpoint: Biggest Robbery in History—You're the Victim," by Michael Gartner.

UPDATE: On July 13, 1996, the General Accounting Office announced that the total cost for the S&L debacle was nearly half a trillion dollars—the most "acceptable" figure cited in the 1990 *Censored* story and more than the total cost of World War II. According to *The New York Times* report (7/13/96), the money went to clean up the financial mess caused by the failure of more than 700 savings institutions. Due to bonds issued, taxpayer accountability will continue through the year 2030. Incredibly, $500 billion dollars may not be the end of it. In July 1996, the Supreme Court ruled that the government could be liable for billions more in damages for arbitrarily changing accounting rules, hurting or forcing out of business dozens of institutions that had agreed to acquire failing savings and loan institutions.

3. The CIA Role in the Savings and Loan Crisis

1990 SYNOPSIS: It is now estimated that some 500 billion taxpayer dollars will be needed to bail out the savings and loan crisis. One very obvious question regarding this scandal is what happened to so much money? At least one investigative journalist, Pete Brewton, of *The Houston Post*, believes he has the answer. On February 4, 1990, Brewton wrote, "During an eight-month investigation into the role of fraud in the nation's savings and loan crisis, *The Post* has found evidence suggesting a possible link between the Central Intelligence Agency and organized crime in the failure of at least 22 thrifts, including 16 in Texas."

It was the first in a series of S&L articles by Brewton that found links between S&Ls, organized crime figures, and CIA operatives, including some involved in gun running, drug smuggling, money laundering, and covert aid to Nicaraguan contras. If S&L funds went to the contras or other covert operations, it would help explain where at least some of the money went.

Despite the blockbuster nature of Brewton's exposés, the major news media have not been quick to follow-up. As Robert Sherrill points out in his extraordinary analysis of the S&L crisis in an unusual single subject issue of *The Nation* (11/19/90), "Brewton's stories have not exactly stirred the national press to action."

The ominous silence on the part of the press led Steve Weinberg, former executive director of Investigative Reporters and Editors, to investigate the accuracy of Brewton's charges. Weinberg raises two key questions: If Brewton's information is wrong, what should other journalists be doing to set the record straight, and if he is right, why have most news organizations failed to assign their own reporters to the scandal?

SOURCES: *Houston Post*, "Savings and Loan" series starting 2/4/90, by Pete Brewton; *The Nation*, 11/19/90, "The Looting Decade," by Robert Sherrill"; *Columbia Journalism Review*, November/December 1990, "The Mob, The CIA, and the S&L Scandal," by Steve Weinberg.

UPDATE: Despite the sensational nature of the charges Brewton made, tying the CIA in with the S&L scandal, the major media failed to follow-up on the story. More than two years later, David Shaw, media critic for the *Los Angeles Times*, reported (10/26/92) that Brewton "wrote many of the best early stories about the S&L crisis." He noted that Jonathan Kwitney, a former *Wall Street Journal* reporter who had written extensively about the CIA and the Mafia, called Brewton's work "maybe the best job of reporting I had ever seen." Nonetheless, Shaw reported that Brewton and *The Houston Post* were very much alone in their coverage of the story. One reason for this was offered by Richard Smith, editor-in-chief of *Newsweek*, who said the national media often have "a kind of dismissive attitude" about stories broken outside the New York-Washington media axis. This is the same attitude that may have led the major news media to disparage the CIA contra-drug involvement, as cited in the update of the "U.S. and its Contra-drug Connection," #2, 1987.

Please also see update of the "S&L Crisis," #2, 1990.

4. NASA Space Shuttles Destroy the Ozone Shield

1990 SYNOPSIS: "Every time the space shuttle is launched, 250 tons of hydrochloric acid is released into the air. With each launch, .25 percent of the ozone is destroyed. So far, the space shuttle has destroyed 10 percent of the ozone."

Dr. Helen Caldicott, world renown physician and environmentalist, stuns audiences when she makes that statement in her talks across the country.

A brief article in a small-circulation environmental publication supports Dr. Caldicott's charges. Two Soviet rocket scientists warned that the solid fuel rocket boosters used on the space shuttle release 187 tons of ozone destroying chlorine molecules into the atmosphere with every launch. (Please also see update of "Ozone Crisis," #5, 1994.)

Valery Burdakov, co-designer of the Russian "Energiya" rocket engine, also noted that each shuttle launch produces seven tons of nitrogen (another ozone depleter), 387 tons of carbon dioxide (a major contributor to the "greenhouse effect"), and 177 tons of aluminum oxide (thought to be linked to Alzheimer's Disease) before reaching an altitude of 31 miles.

Burdakov also said the history of ozone depletion correlates closely with the increase of chlorine discharged by solid fuel rockets since 1981. According to Burdakov and his colleague, Vyacheslav Filin, a single shuttle launch can destroy as much as 10 million tons of ozone. Theoretically, this means that some 300 shuttle flights could completely destroy the Earth's protective ozone shield.

SOURCES: *Sonoma State University Star*, 5/8/90, "Doc Caldicott Prescribes Medicine," by Mindi Levine; *Earth Island Journal*, Fall 1990, "Soviets Say Shuttles Rip Ozone Layer," by Gar Smith; *San Francisco Chronicle*, 8/21/90, "Group Says Space Shuttle Damages Earth's Ozone," by David Sylvester.

UPDATE: While Dr. Helen Caldicott's charge about the space shuttle's destruction of the ozone was initially controversial, subsequent reports confirmed that a small percentage of chloro-fluorocarbons, the chemicals used in refrigerants and solvents, does come from the launch of solid-fuel rockets, including those on NASA's space shuttles (*Orlando Sentinel Tribune*, 5/1/92). Ironically, the NASA space shuttle itself is being used to measure and record the thinning of the ozone layer (*Orlando Sentinel Tribune*, 11/14/94).

5. Continued Media Blackout of Drug War Fraud

1990 SYNOPSIS: While the fire and brimstone of the government's drug war rhetoric continues to saturate the mainstream press, high-ranking drug war insiders continue to come forward in attempts to expose the "war" for what it really is: a battle for the hearts, minds, and tax dollars of the American public.

The latest insider to "go public" is Michael Levine, who retired from the U.S. Drug Enforcement Agency (DEA) after 25 years as a leading undercover agent for various law enforcement agencies. Over the course of his career, Levine personally accounted for at least 3,000 people serving a total of 15,000 years in jail, as well as several tons of various illegal substances seized. Upon his retirement, Levine published a critical exposé of the DEA in which he documents his journey from true believer to drug war heretic.

Levine documents numerous instances of CIA involvement in the drug trade, State Department intervention, and DEA cooperation with both parties. Levine's story closely parallels that of Richard Gregorie whose defection from the Attorney General's office was the fourth ranked *Censored* story of 1989.

According to Levine, "The only thing we know with certainty is that the drug war is not for real. The drug economy in the United States is as much as $200 billion a year, and it is being used to finance political operations, pay international debts—all sorts of things."

SOURCES: *EXTRA!*, July/August 1990, "Ex-DEA Agent Calls Drug War a Fraud," by Martin A. Lee; *The Humanist*, September/October 1990, "A Funny, Dirty Little Drug War," by Rick Szykowny.

UPDATE: Michael Levine continues to try to spread the word about the dangers and impact of drugs. In an interview with the *Chicago Sun-Times* (8/9/96), Levine charges that drugs are out of control in the United States. He and his wife, Laura Kavanau, wrote a novel, *Triangle of Death*, which one reviewer characterized as "a real story that can't be published as nonfiction because of secrecy laws and because many of the criminals involved are still protected by covert agencies like the CIA and French intelligence" (*Toronto Sun*, 9/1/96).

Please also see update of "War on Drugs," #4, 1989.

6. What Really Happened in Panama is a Different Story

1990 SYNOPSIS: According to a variety of non-mainstream but authoritative sources, the U.S. invasion of Panama on December 20, 1989, received inadequate and erroneous news coverage. It now appears that the legal implications of the invasion, the Bush-Noriega relationship, and the actual post-invasion conditions in Panama were all misrepresented to the American people. However, perhaps the most fraudulent news coverage dealt with the true numbers of civilian and combat fatalities.

Official accounts spoke of 202 dead Panamanian civilians, 314 dead Panamanian soldiers, and 23 dead Americans. The press was oddly silent two months after the invasion when a Southern Command official acknowledged to the *Los Angeles Times* that only 50 Panamanian soldiers died. Meanwhile, American soldiers reported that at least 60 to 70 Americans were killed, possibly more. The new findings indicate the U.S. lost more soldiers than Panama.

Physicians for Human Rights (PHR) challenged the government figure of 202 dead civilians and former U.S. Attorney General Ramsey Clark put the figure at 3,000, using the phrase "conspiracy of silence" to describe efforts to bury the true civilian death toll.

CBS's *60 Minutes*, in a September 1990 exposé, reported the existence of at least six yet-to-be-exhumed mass graves to conclude that Panamanian civilian deaths could run as high as 4,000. The findings of many watch groups, including the Central American Human Rights Commission, support the *60 Minutes* casualty report.

SOURCES: *Panama Delegation Report*, 3/1/90, by the Central American Human Rights Commission; *San Francisco Bay Guardian*, 9/26/90, "The

Hidden Body Count," by Jonathan Franklin; *CBS News, 60 Minutes*, 9/30/90, "Victims of Just Cause," by Mike Wallace; *Washington Post*, 6/30/90, "How Many Died in Panama?", letter from the Guatemalan Human Rights Commission, by Joanne Heisel; *The Nation*, 6/18/90, "The Press and the Panama Invasion," by Marc Cooper.

UPDATE: In 1992, a powerful award-winning documentary film titled, "The Panama Deception," produced by Barbara Trent, charged: "The U.S. government continues to insist that casualty figures from the 1989 invasion were low and the 'human costs' kept to a minimum...an official lie still endlessly repeated by the U.S. media." The film reported an estimated 20,000 Panamanians were left homeless by American bombing and shelling, 7,000 were detained by military authorities for vague reasons, and as many as 4,000 remained unaccounted for, most of them murdered and buried in mass graves under U.S. military supervision (*San Francisco Chronicle*, 9/11/92).

The National Censorship Board of Panama banned the release of the documentary in any form in Panama. With a few local exceptions, it was also denied broadcast rights on both commercial and public television stations in the United States. "The Panama Deception" received the Academy Award for Best Feature-Length Documentary from the Academy of Motion Pictures Arts and Sciences on March 29, 1993 (*The Humanist*, May 1993). While the official number of dead American soldiers is still reported at 23, there has been no updated figure concerning the number of dead Panamanian solders and civilians.

7. The Pentagon's Secret Billion Dollar Black Budget

1990 SYNOPSIS: Despite the extraordinary changes in international relationships and the end of the Cold War, the Pentagon has a secret stash called the "Black Budget" that costs taxpayers $100 million a day.

The "Black Budget" funds every program the President of the United States, the Secretary of Defense, and the Director of the Central Intelligence Agency want to keep hidden from view; in the past three years, $100 billion has disappeared into the Pentagon's secret cache.

While the money to run America's eleven intelligence agencies has always been hidden in the Pentagon's budget, something new transformed the "Black Budget" when Ronald Reagan took office. A White House obsessed with secrecy began to conceal the costs of many of its most expensive weapons, enshrouding them in the deep cover once reserved for espionage. The "Black Budget" quadrupled in size, reaching $36 billion a year.

The Pentagon keeps this money hidden by keeping two sets of books: one for the general public, one for the generals. Hundreds of "black programs" are concealed in the public budget it submits to Congress, camouflaged under false names, their costs deleted, their goals disguised. The Pentagon simply stamps a secret code on the price of a bomber, a missile, or a spy satellite, and open debate ceases. The Pentagon also pads seemingly unclassified programs with billions intended for "black projects." In short, the Pentagon budget, which is nationally debated, is a false document, an elaborate cover story—a lie not exposed by the press.

SOURCE: *Rolling Stone*, 9/6/90, "How the Pentagon Hides Its Secret Spending," by Tim Weiner.

UPDATE: On July 17, 1993, *The New York Times* reported that U.S. Senator Dennis DeConcini (D-Arizona), chair of the Senate intelligence committee, announced the "Black Budget" would now be subject to public debate on the floor of the Senate. Contributing to the new openness approach but with no thanks to the Senate was Steven Aftergood's *Secrecy & Government Bulletin* (11/4/94), which revealed top-secret, highly classified data about U.S. spy activities in 1994. Believe it or not, the Pentagon simply forgot to delete the secret numbers from subcommittee hearing transcripts before they were made public. For a critical analysis and historical review of "Black Budget" projects and the billions of dollars involved, please see "Black Holes: How Secret Military and Intelligence Appropriations Suck Up Your Tax Dollars," the cover story in the May 1996 issue of *The Humanist*, and "Special Projects Come Out of the Black," in the May 29, 1996, issue of *Jane's Defence Weekly*.

8. The Bill of Rights had a Close Call in 1990

1990 SYNOPSIS: An anti-crime bill was introduced in both the U.S. Senate and the House in 1990 which, had it been enacted and signed into law, would have essentially nullified the Bill of Rights. Fortunately, neither the Senate version, S.2245, introduced by Senator Phil Gramm (R-Texas), nor the House version, H.R.4079, introduced by Representative Newt Gingrich, (R-Georgia), the minority whip, passed either chamber.

The Gramm-Gingrich bills both start out stating that the U.S. criminal justice system is failing and both bills call for "A Declaration of National Drug and Crime Emergency." The legislation stated: "Guided by the principles that energized and sustained the mobilization of World War II, and in order to remove violent criminals from the streets and meet the extraordinary threat that is posed to the nation by the trafficking of illegal drugs, the Congress declares the existence of a National Drug and Crime Emergency beginning on the date of enactment of the act and ending on the date that is 5 years after the day of enactment of this act."

The bill prescribes mandatory incarceration, for at least five years, of "every person who is convicted in a federal court of a crime of violence against a person or a drug trafficking felony, other than simple possession." A crime of violence is defined as the "use, attempted use, or threatened use of physical force against the person or property of another."

The bills would also suspend protection from unreasonable search and seizure; excessive fines, bail, or punishment; and the right to be brought to trial. Both bills have provisions for utilizing tents and various other shelters, including unused military facilities, for the confinement of state and federal "violent criminals."

SOURCE: *The Spotlight,* 8/6/90, "Repressive Gingrich Bill: Dangerous Attack on Rights;" 10/15/90, "Danger to Bill of Rights," by Mike Blair.

UPDATE: The Gramm-Gingrich anti-crime bills of 1990 failed and the nation was not subjected to "A Declaration of National Drug and Crime Emergency" with its onerous provisions infringing on civil rights. On September 13, 1994, President Clinton signed what he called the "toughest, smartest" crime bill in the nation's history. Among other provisions, it banned several military-style semi-automatic weapons and promised to put 100,000 more police on city streets (*Cleveland Plain Dealer,* 9/14/94). The FBI's annual report on "Crime in the United States," released October 13, 1996, revealed that crime in the U.S. was down for the fourth straight year. Elected officials, including President Clinton, say the decline is due to the new anti-crime programs. Criminologists suggest crime rates are influenced by demographic forces and cite the gradual maturing of the baby boomer generation from the crime-prone age group to a more mellow middle age (*Dallas Morning News,* 10/13/96).

9. Where Was George During the Iran-contra Affair?

1990 SYNOPSIS: Despite the vast experience George Bush acquired while serving as U.S. ambassador to China, director of the CIA, and head of the Reagan Administration's task force on combatting terrorism, his assertion that he was "out of the loop" on the Iran-contra affair has yet to be challenged or explored by the mainstream media.

However, new material from Oliver North's diaries, which has yet to be widely examined or disseminated by the mainstream media, combines with previous evidence to offer a different picture of Bush's role. The new evidence was obtained through a Freedom of Information Act lawsuit filed by the National Security Archive and *Public Citizen.*

The diaries provide additional evidence that Bush played a major role in Iran-contra from the beginning, passing up repeated opportunities to cut the transactions short. While the secretaries of state and defense were both cut out of the arms-for-hostages deals after objecting to it, Bush attended almost every key meeting.

While Bush publicly stated, "It never became clear to me, the arms for hostages thing, until it was fully debriefed, investigated and debriefed by (the Senate Intelligence Committee on December 20, 1986)," White House logs show that Bush attended the first key Iran-contra meeting on August 6, 1985. It was at this meeting that National Security Advisor Robert McFarlane presented the first deal—a swap of 100 TOW anti-tank missiles in Iran in exchange for the release of four American hostages in Lebanon.

Additionally, the combination of the North diaries, the congressional committee's report, and White House logs place Bush at key meetings on January 6, 7, and 17; May 29; July 1 and 29; August 6; and October 3 of 1986.

SOURCE: *The Washington Post*, 7/10/90, "Outlook: Where George Was," by Tom Blanton, National Security Archive.

UPDATE: As it turned out, George *was* at those meetings and had lied about being "out of the loop." As *The Nation* reported (6/17/96), "When Vice President Bush mounted his presidential bid in 1988, he successfully hid behind his cover story that he was "out of the loop" on Iran-contra. That lie survived until the eve of the 1992 election, when Iran-contra special prosecutor Lawrence Walsh released documents that exposed Bush's far deeper role." The documents included a diary log by former defense Secretary Cap

Weinberger that revealed Bush was present at a January 7, 1986, top-level discussion about sending TOW anti-tank missiles to Iran as part of a deal to free five American hostages (*Bangor Daily News*, 6/22/96). On December 24, 1992, after losing the election to Bill Clinton, Bush pardoned six Iran-contra defendants. While Bush was never held accountable for his actions he was, incredibly, awarded $272,352 for legal expenses during the special prosecutor's investigation. The Ethics in Government Act allows reimbursement of lawyers' fees for people who are investigated but not indicted (*Los Angeles Times*, 6/10/95).

10. America's Banking Crisis: Coming to a Bank Near You

1990 SYNOPSIS: A new nationwide financial crisis is brewing and, thanks to the disinterest of the mainstream media, Americans will be just as surprised by it as they were by the massive failure of the savings and loan industry with its huge 500 billion-dollar price tag. The bill for a decade of federal deregulation, wild financial speculation in the private sector, and the Reagan Administration's immense military expenditures is about to come due.

"The looming crisis highlights the fragility of the debt-plagued financial system in the United States," writes John Miller, professor of economics at Wheaton College. The same economic conditions that led to the demise of the S&L industry have been eating away at commercial banks, and, according to Dan Brumbaugh, a Stanford economist and expert on the S&L debacle, the same kinds of accounting gimmicks that hid the S&L crisis are now being used to cover up the commercial banking crisis.

Because of the record number of bank failures this year, the Federal Deposit Insurance Corporation (FDIC), which insures the $2.7 trillion deposited in U.S. commercial banks, has lost money for the third year in a row. It now holds only 60 cents per $100 of insured deposits, the lowest level in its 57-year history. In 1988, the FDIC, for the first time in its history, paid out more than it took in. Bank failures soared from an average of ten per year in 1981 to more than 200 per year by the end of the decade. In the first half of 1990, 112 banks failed. More banks—almost 1,000—have failed in the last five years than in the previous 51 years of the FDIC fund combined.

SOURCE: *Dollars & Sense*, October 1990, "If You Liked the S&L Crisis...You'll Love the Banking Crisis," by John Miller.

UPDATE: The May/June 1991 issue of *Harvard Business Review* confirmed the impending banking crisis cited in the 1990 *Censored* story above and warned that if something wasn't done, it could lead to the most serious economic collapse since the Great Depression.

While a collapse of that magnitude did not materialize, according to *U.S. Banker* (August 1996), the banking industry suffered a record number of bank failures during the commercial real estate disaster that ended in 1992. That experience also resulted in restrictive new federal regulations. By 1996, fewer than half a dozen banks failed in the first half of the year, compared with the 112 that failed in the first half of 1990 (*The American Banker*, 8/20/96). Nonetheless, by mid-August 1996 some experts were beginning to wonder if banking is again on the verge of another loan loss debacle, this time on the consumer side. What alarms them is the increasing number of credit card delinquencies, mortgage loan delinquencies, and personal bankruptcies. And, as *U.S. Banker* warned, "If credit trends are this troublesome in a growing economy, what happens if a recession hits?"

CHAPTER 16—1991

Two Top TV Networks Censor Iraq Bomb Devastation

Again, while the Gulf War repeated as the top mainstream news story of the year, the top under-covered story of the year revealed how two major networks censored surprising video coverage of that war. According to the Associated Press, the top ten news stories of the year were:

1. U.S.-led war to liberate Kuwait from Iraqi occupation
2. Unsuccessful coup against Gorbachev who was later unseated
3. Nomination of Clarence Thomas to the Supreme Court
4. U.S. hostages in Middle East released
5. U.S. economy falters, consumer confidence plummets, unemployment rises
6. The Cold War ends
7. AIDS epidemic is a decade old
8. Mass-murderer Jeffrey Dahmer is arrested
9. Israelis and Arabs meet to discuss peace in the Middle East
10. Police beating of Rodney King.

THE TOP TEN CENSORED STORIES OF 1991

—And What Has Happened to Them Since

1. CBS and NBC Spiked Footage of Iraq Bombing Carnage

1991 SYNOPSIS: CBS and NBC refused to broadcast rare, uncensored footage taken deep inside Iraq at the height of the air war. The footage, initially commissioned by NBC with two producers whose earlier work had earned the network seven Emmy awards, substantially contradicted U.S. Administration claims that civilian damage from the American-led bombing campaign was light.

The exclusive videotape, shot by producers Jon Alpert and Maryanne Deleo, during a trip to Iraq in early February, portrayed heavy civilian carnage as a result of allied bombing.

"I thought it was substantial," said *NBC Nightly News* Executive Producer Steven Friedman, who initially approved the material for broadcast. After a meeting with Friedman, anchor Tom Brokaw, and Tom Capra, executive producer of the *Today Show*, producer Jon Alpert said, "Everybody felt the film was very good. They asked for three minutes, to be shown on the *Nightly News* and the *Today Show*, and we reached a financial agreement." But despite the enthusiasm shown by Friedman and Brokaw, who reportedly fought hard for its airing, NBC President Michael Gartner killed the footage.

The producers then took the video to CBS, where they got the go-ahead from *CBS Evening News* Executive Director Tom Bettag. "He told me, 'You'll appear on the show with Dan (Rather) tomorrow night.'" Alpert said. However, while Alpert was editing the piece for CBS, he got a call from the network; Bettag had been fired in the middle of the night and the piece had been killed.

Both networks stated publicly that spiking the story had nothing to do with the controversial nature of the material. But a series of interviews with network producers who requested anonymity charged there was intense pressure to put out a pro-war, pro-administration message.

SOURCE: *San Francisco Bay Guardian*, 3/20/91, "Sights Unseen," by Dennis Bernstein and Sasha Futran.

UPDATE: While the controversial documentary footage was never shown on the commercial networks, the *Los Angeles Times* reports (5/21/91) that excerpts of it were shown on "The '90s," an unconventional PBS series that shows the work of independent filmmakers seldom seen on mainstream TV. The *Times* noted the film was "reportedly personally rejected by Michael Gartner, president of the *NBC News* division." A subsequent story in *The Observer* (4/10/94) reported the censored images had "contradicted the official line that Allied 'surgical strikes' caused minimal civilian casualties."

Meanwhile, in a major article that appeared in *Foreign Policy* (3/22/93), John G. Heidenrich, a former military analyst with the Defense Intelligence Agency (DIA) and an analyst for the Department of Defense during the Gulf War, rejected the reports of high Iraqi casualties. While he noted the DIA's own report of 100,000 Iraqis killed, 300,000 wounded in action, and about 300,000 deserters, he pointed out the study had an error factor of 50 percent or higher. He suggested that a more realistic estimate would be a total death toll (from both air and ground offensive) of only 1,500 soldiers and less than 1,000 dead Iraqi civilians.

Please also see the following "Operation Censored War" story and update.

2. Operation Censored War

1991 SYNOPSIS: A secretive Bush Administration, aided and abetted by a press more interested in cheerleading than in journalism, persuaded the American people to support the Gulf War by media manipulation, censorship, and intimidation. Some of the events covered up by the military and/or the media included: the extent of casualties from "friendly fire"; use of Napalm bombs on Iraqi ground troops; inaccuracy of U.S. bombs dropped on Iraq and occupied Kuwait; the "fuel-air bomb" experiment; television networks' refusal to run available footage of the mass destruction from the "turkey shoot" on the road to Basra; the networks' refusal to broadcast uncensored footage of civilian casualties as cited in the #1 *Censored* story above; and U.S. battlefield casualties disguised as training accidents. In addition, reporters in the Gulf were routinely and openly censored and harassed by military public affairs officers.

SOURCES: *Editor & Publisher*, 7/13/91, "Military Obstacles Detailed"; *San Francisco Bay Guardian*, 3/6/91, "Inside the Desert Storm Mortuary," by

Jonathan Franklin; *The Progressive Review*, March 1991, "Collateral Damage, What We've Lost Already," by Sam Smith.

UPDATE: In a lengthy analysis, entitled "National Security and the Persian Gulf War on Television News: Ethics and the First Amendment Paradox," the December 1995 issue of the authoritative *Communications & the Law*, concluded, "The Pentagon held a strong rein on any and all substantive information about the war, disregarding the freedom of the press and the right to access guaranteed in the First Amendment." It noted that the failure to accurately portray the ravages of war was most likely a case of censorship. Indeed, news media censorship was so bad that Walter Cronkite, America's longtime esteemed television news anchor, charged that the Pentagon's censorship was "the real horror of the Persian Gulf war."

Ironically, given all the lives lost and all the lies, *Jane's Intelligence Review* reported in its November 1996 issue that "Saddam Hussein has rebuilt the devastated Iraqi army into a credible fighting force by reviving the military industries and smuggling in hardware components." Iraq was not prohibited from increasing the size or quality of its military under the terms of the Gulf War cease-fire.

It was not until mid-1997 that the American people learned the truth about the performance of Gulf War weapons that were so highly praised during the conflict. A newly declassified report by the General Accounting Office, released in late June, revealed that the Pentagon and weapons makers overstated the effectiveness of high-technology aircraft, bombs and other systems during the war. Representative John Dingell (D-Michigan) said the report documents "a pattern of overstated, misleading, inconsistent, or unverifiable claims on the performance of individual, particularly high-technology, weapons systems." He charged the military with withholding this information from the taxpayers (Associated Press, 6/29/97).

3. Voodoo Economics: The Untold Story

1991 SYNOPSIS: The nation is in serious financial trouble, but the public doesn't know why nor does it know who should be held accountable.

The deficit: By September 30, 1992, when the fiscal year ends, the federal government's total outstanding debt—which took some 200 years to reach $1 trillion in 1981—will total $4 trillion. Incredibly, as of October 1991, it appears the interest alone on the federal debt will be the nation's single largest expenditure this year—exceeding even the military budget.

Voodoo economics: A two-year investigative research effort by *Philadelphia Inquirer* reporters Donald L. Barlett and James B. Steele reveals that the rules by which the economy operates have been rigged, by design and default, to favor the privileged, the powerful, and the influential. The result is that the rich are richer than ever before; the middle class is being dismantled; life for the working class is deteriorating; and those at the bottom are trapped. The authors found the rules that govern America's economy have:

✔ Created a tax system that is firmly weighted against the middle class

✔ Enabled companies to cancel health-care and pension benefits for employees

✔ Granted subsidies to businesses that create low-wage jobs that in turn erode living standards

✔ Rewarded companies that transfer jobs abroad and eliminate jobs in this country

✔ Placed home ownership out of the reach for a growing number of Americans and made a college education impossible without incurring a hefty debt.

SOURCES: Knight-Ridder Newspapers, 11/2/91-11/8/91, "Caught in the Middle," by Donald L. Barlett and James B. Steele, of the *Philadelphia Inquirer*; *USA Today*, 10/1/91, "Interest to Take Largest Slice of Budget Pie," by Mark Memmott.

UPDATE: In 1995, the federal government paid out $332 billion in interest, more than it spent for defense and foreign aid combined, and nearly as much as in Social Security payments. On April 1, 1996, the Treasury Department reported the national debt reached $5 trillion (*Charleston Post and Courier*, 4/13/96).

Donald L. Barlett and James B. Steele, sources of the *Censored* story above, published a new book, *America: Who Really Pays the Taxes?*, in 1994. *Publishers Weekly* (2/21/94) said the book provides the facts, figures, names and anecdotes for readers who have ever had the sneaking suspicion they're being shafted. In its review of the book, *Time* (4/18/94) notes that two-thirds of the federal deficit could be wiped out overnight simply by restoring corporate taxes to their 1950s levels. *Time* warns that maybe "the dread class war is already over, and the suits have run away with the loot." In discussing the current economic situation, Daniel Hamermesh, an economist at the University of Texas at Austin, said, "This is worse than voodoo economics. This is doodoo economics."

4. The 250 Billion Dollar S&L Political Cover-up

1991 SYNOPSIS: As we know, the press failed to cover the S&L crisis during the critical 1988 election year; not a single question about the S&L problem was asked during the three national political debates between George Bush and Michael Dukakis in 1988; the media also failed to follow up on why the costs of the bailout kept escalating and did not explore whether politics had played a part in the 1988 executive actions on the bailout.

An investigative television documentary by the Center For Investigative Reporting and PBS-TV's *Frontline* provided some important answers. The potentially explosive documentary, titled "The Great American Bailout," was essentially ignored by the major media and received minimal exposure.

The documentary revealed that high administration officials had lied to prevent the public from knowing the full scope of the S&L crisis before the 1988 election. At a luncheon meeting in late summer of 1988, William Seidman, then head of the Federal Deposit Insurance Corporation, admitted to Federal Home Loan (FHL) Bank Board member Roger Martin that he and Danny Wall, chair of the FHL Bank Board, had been told by George Gould, Deputy Under-Secretary for Finance, to lie about the true size of the problem. Gould was working under Treasury Secretary Jim Baker and was the administration's political point man on the S&L crisis. Seidman later said he didn't remember any conversation like that.

Jim Barth, Danny Wall's chief economist at the Bank Board, was asked how much money could have been saved if the S&L problem had been addressed honestly and frankly before the 1988 election. Barth said $250 million.

George Bush was elected the 41st President of the United States on November 8, 1988.

SOURCES: Center for Investigative Reporting and PBS-TV *Frontline,* 10/22/91, "The Great American Bailout."

UPDATE: Please see update of "The S&L Crisis," #2, 1990, and update of "CIA Role in S&L Crisis," #3, 1990.

5. Operation Ill Wind—DOD's Untold Scandal

1991 SYNOPSIS: In late 1990, *Common Cause Magazine* published an explosive article examining the scandal-plagued history of the Northrop Corporation, one of the nation's major defense contractors. It documented how Northrop's former CEO, Thomas V. Jones, kept the company thriving despite scandals involving overseas payoffs, illegal Watergate contributions, and falsified tests on U.S. jet parts used in the Persian Gulf War.

As it turned out, Northrop was just another culprit unearthed by a massive investigation into possible fraud and bribery in securing defense contracts. In 1988, the Justice Department discovered that ex-Department of Defense workers were paid for the exclusive use of their knowledge. The story, involving McDonnell Douglas, a major aerospace corporation, was called "Operation Ill Wind" and it was expected to blow the lid off one of the nation's biggest scandals.

But it didn't. With just one exception, the search warrants and affidavits that contain transcripts of wiretapped conversations of employees at McDonnell Douglas were sealed by court order. Despite the best efforts of the *St. Louis Post-Dispatch* to obtain the potentially incriminating affidavits, including an appeal to the U.S. Supreme Court, the transcripts remain sealed.

SOURCES: *Common Cause Magazine*, November/December 1990, "The Devil and Mr. Jones," by John Hanrahan; *St. Louis Journalism Review*, March 1991, "The Documents Were Sealed and the Public Shut Out," by Philip Dunn.

UPDATE: By the time the dust settled, the Justice Department's investigation into Pentagon and military-contractor corruption known as Operation Ill Wind resulted in more than 50 convictions and corporate and personal fines. But, as *The New York Times* pointed out (9/13/92), "The impressive-sounding sum of $420 million in total Ill Wind penalties is less than half the cost of a single B-2 Stealth bomber."

6. No Evidence of Iraqi Threat to Saudi Arabia

1991 SYNOPSIS: On September 11, 1990, President George Bush rallied a surprised nation to support a war in the Persian Gulf with reports of a massive Iraqi army that had poured into Kuwait and moved south to threaten Saudi Arabia. At the time, the Department of Defense (DOD) estimated there were as many as 250,000 Iraqi troops and 1,500 tanks in Kuwait.

On January 6, 1991, Jean Heller, a journalist with the *St. Petersburg (FL) Times*, reported that satellite photos of Kuwait did not support Bush's claim of an imminent Iraqi invasion of Saudi Arabia. In fact, the photos showed no sign of a massive Iraqi troop buildup in Kuwait.

Journalist Heller told *In These Times*, which reprinted her article, "The troops that were said to be massing on the Saudi border and that constituted the possible threat to Saudi Arabia that justified the U.S. sending of troops do not show up in these photographs. And when the Department of Defense was asked to provide evidence that would contradict our satellite evidence, it refused to do it."

The pictures, taken by a Soviet satellite on September 11 and 13, 1990, were acquired by the *St. Petersburg Times* in December. *The Times* contacted two satellite image specialists to analyze the photos: Peter Zimmerman, a nuclear physicist who is now a professor of engineering at George Washington University in Washington, D.C.; and a former image specialist for the Defense Intelligence Agency who asked to remain anonymous.

The specialists saw extensive U.S. occupation at the Dhahran Airport in Saudi Arabia, but few Iraqi troops or weapons in Kuwait. They said the roads showed no evidence of a massive tank invasion, there were no tent cities or troop concentrations, and the main Kuwaiti air base appeared deserted.

While the *St. Petersburg Times* submitted the story to both the Associated Press and the Scripps-Howard News Service, neither wire service carried the story.

SOURCES: *St. Petersburg Times*, 1/6/91, reprinted in *In These Times*, 2/27/91, "Public Doesn't Get Picture with Gulf Satellite Photos," by Jean Heller.

UPDATE: A year after the Russian satellite photos were taken, Peter Zimmerman, a nuclear physicist and expert in satellite imagery, again reviewed the photos and confirmed the Iraqi army hadn't sent tanks sweeping across the Kuwaiti desert, nor had it established large base camps in Kuwait (*St. Petersburg Times*, 9/15/91). "The Soviet photos were, in retrospect, the first clue that U.S. intelligence overestimated Iraq's numbers, a fact the Defense Department has confirmed, at least in part," according to Zimmerman. When President Bush decided to go to war with Iraq, he used U.S. satellite photos that reportedly showed more than a quarter of a million Iraqi troops massed on the Saudi border ready to invade Saudi Arabia (*The London Guardian*, 12/16/95). Those photos are still not available to the press.

7. Freedom of Information Act is an Oxymoron

1991 SYNOPSIS: In theory at least, the 25-year-old Freedom of Information Act (FOIA) is supposed to counter the bureaucratic impulse for secrecy.

In reality, however, the executive branch and federal courts are exploiting the law's exemptions to circumvent the FOIA.

The erosion of FOIA over the past ten years coincides with a new and particularly hostile attitude towards the public's right to know that came in with the Reagan and Bush Administrations. "National security" was expansively redefined to cover virtually all aspects of international activity. A 1982 executive order told government officials to classify documents whenever in doubt. It even reclassified material already released under FOIA. The new strategy became: fight every possible case, even if the only defense against disclosure was a technicality.

FOIA is supposed to work this way: You make your request and the government has ten days to fill the request or explain why it won't do so. But in most agencies roadblocks are endemic. So are delays. The FDA often takes two years to fill requests; the State Department often takes a year. Last year the FBI calculated that its average response time was more than 300 days.

One problem is that the Office of Management and Budget keeps FOIA offices underfunded and understaffed. The Navy's central FOIA office has a staff of two and no fax machine. Another problem is that the D.C. Circuit Court of Appeals, which handles most FOIA cases, and the Supreme Court have moved aggressively to expand the government's power to withhold information.

SOURCE: *Common Cause*, July/August 1991, "The Fight To Know," by Peter Montgomery and Peter Overby.

UPDATE: In 1991, Senator Patrick Leahy, of Vermont, introduced the Electronic Freedom of Information Improvement Act (EFIIA) which was designed to bring the original Freedom of Information Act (FOIA) into the computer age. It died in a committee hearing in 1992. The Senate passed a modified version in 1994 but the House did nothing. Then, in 1996, Senator Leahy and Representative Randy Tate of Washington used the occasion of FOIA's 30th anniversary to re-introduce the EFIIA. It was approved by both houses and signed into law by President Clinton on October 2, 1996 (Associated Press, 10/3/96). The legislation, which was supported by 23 different organizations including major press organizations, requires that information available in the Federal Register or "available for public inspection and copying" under FOIA be available electronically and in the form requested (*Editor & Publisher*, 5/11/96).

8. Corporate America's Anti-Environmental Campaign

1991 SYNOPSIS: It would seem that in these times of heightened environmental consciousness, companies with questionable environmental records should be concerned with regulations. Instead, they are adopting an array of tactics and attack strategies aimed at disrupting environmental and citizen groups.

Some of the more recent anti-environmental innovations include multimillion-dollar SLAPP suits, the harassment and surveillance (including electronic) of activists, the infiltration of environmental groups by "agent provocateurs," and the creation of dummy ecology groups to ferret out whistleblowers. Another disturbing trend is the proliferation of groups such as "The Oregon Committee for Recycling," an industry front group whose real purpose was to lobby *against* a recycling initiative on the state ballot.

The new corporate mind-set may be best exemplified by a copy of a "Crisis Management Plan," commissioned by the Clorox Corporation, which was leaked to Greenpeace. The plan was prepared by Ketchum Communications, one of the nation's largest advertising and public relations firms.

Part of the Ketchum strategy was to suggest ways to discredit the findings of studies linking chlorine use to cancer, should the findings ever become public. The firm also recommends that Clorox "cast doubts on the methodology and findings" of potentially damaging scientific reports that haven't been written yet. Ketchum also recommends labeling Greenpeace as violent self-serving "eco-terrorists"; attempting to sue newspaper columnists who advocate the use of non-toxic bleaches and cleaners for the home; dispatching "independent" scientists on media tours; and recruiting "scientific ambassadors" to tout the Clorox cause and call for further study.

SOURCES: *E Magazine*, November/December 1991, "Stop the Greens," by Eve Pell; *Greenpeace News*, 5/10/91, "Clorox Company's Public Relations 'Crisis Management Plan.'"

UPDATE: The success of the corporate anti-environmental campaign was the subject of discussion by environmental lobbyists in Washington, D.C., in May 1994. One observer said the environmentalists "are trying to figure out what hit them" (*Greenwire*, 5/10/94). Among the reasons given for the environmental backlash included a hostile media that have turned on the environmental movement. Further, noting a potential ally in Congress, corporate America started funneling large sums of money to what some came to see as the most anti-environmental Congress in history. On September 11, 1996, the Sierra Club reported that 660 anti-environment PACs gave nearly $46 million between December 1993 and June 1996 to members of the 104th Congress (*Wisconsin State Journal*, 9/12/96). Among the PACs funneling the most money to politicians were the Realtors Political Action Committee, Philip Morris Co., Associated General Contractors, Mid-America Dairymen, and the Exxon Corp.

9. Inslaw Software Theft: Conspiracy at the Justice Department?

1991 SYNOPSIS: In a little publicized legal battle, the Inslaw Corp. charged that the U.S. Department of Justice (DOJ) robbed it of its computer software program, conspired to send the company into bankruptcy, then initiated a cover-up.

The Inslaw software in question, called Promis, was a potential goldmine. A case-management and criminal-tracking program, the software can also be used to track complex covert operations. For this reason, Promis had sales appeal to both law-enforcement agencies and the international intelligence community. In March 1982, Inslaw won a $10 million, three-year contract with the Justice Department. Then Justice reneged on the contract, withholding nearly $2 million. Consequently, Inslaw sought refuge in Chapter 11 bankruptcy and proceeded to sue Justice.

In September 1987, federal bankruptcy judge George Bason found the Justice Department used "trickery, fraud and deceit" to take Inslaw's property, and in February 1988, Bason awarded Inslaw $8 million. Not quite one month later, Judge Bason was denied re-appointment to the bench. (In the previous four years, only four of 136 federal bankruptcy judges had been denied re-appointment.) Incredibly, Bason was replaced by S. Martin Teel, one of the Justice Department attorneys who unsuccessfully argued the Inslaw case before him. Teel immediately appealed Bason's ruling, but in November 1989 a federal district court upheld the decision. Nevertheless, in the spring of 1991, the U.S. Court of Appeals set aside the ruling on the grounds that the bankruptcy court lacked jurisdiction.

According to Inslaw's attorney, former Attorney General Elliot Richardson, "Evidence to support the most serious accusations came from 30 people, including Justice Department sources." Additionally, the files of the Justice Department's chief litigating attorney on the case disappeared.

SOURCES: *In These Times*, 5/29/91, "Software Pirates," by Joel Bleifuss; *Random Lengths*, 10/3/91, "Software To Die For," by James Ridgeway.

UPDATE: On September 27, 1994, the Justice Department announced, "It could find no credible evidence that department officials conspired to steal computer software from the private firm of Inslaw Inc." The 187-page report also reaffirmed police findings that Daniel Casolaro, a freelance journalist investigating the Inslaw matter, committed suicide (*Reuter Business Report*, 9/28/94).

Not surprisingly, this was not the end of the Inslaw case. In May 1995, *Law Practice Management*, published a report from *Wired* magazine charging "senior intelligence and DOJ officials say that PROMIS (the Inslaw software) was appropriated as part of a covert intelligence operation—that it was installed on various computer systems with a secret 'backdoor' to let the U.S. government browse through the computers of foreign banks and intelligence services. Under that view, any thorough investigation into the Inslaw case would have jeopardized the operation, and any announcement that PROMIS was being protected as a matter of 'national security' would have tipped off those being watched." As *Law Practice Management* concluded, "Stay tuned."

Finally, the *Legal Times* (1/1/96) reported that Elliot Richardson, the attorney for Inslaw, had been cleared of libel charges resulting from an op-ed piece he had written about the Inslaw case that was published in *The New York Times* on October 21, 1991.

10. The Bush Family and Its Conflicts of Interest

1991 SYNOPSIS: Richard Nixon had his brother Donald; Jimmy Carter had his brother Billy; Ronald Reagan had his brother Neil. But no president in recent history has had the blatant familial conflicts of interest that George Bush has:

Prescott Bush, Brother. Munenobu Shoji, president of a Japanese real estate firm, reported that his firm and another, both run by a former Japanese crime boss, paid Prescott $200,000 for investment advice. Shoji said he was introduced to Prescott by the president of a firm with connections to an organized-crime syndicate.

George W. Bush, Son. When Harken Energy Corp. of Grand Prairie, Texas, signed an oil-production sharing agreement with Bahrain, a tiny island off the coast of Saudi Arabia, industry experts marveled over how a virtually unknown company, with no previous international drilling experience, could land such a potentially valuable concession. Perhaps the experts were not aware that George W. Bush, eldest son of the President, was on Harken's board of directors and a $50,000-a-year "consultant" to the company's chief executive officer.

Jeb Bush, Son. Jeb, a Miami real estate developer, knew Leonel Martinez, a Miami builder, as a generous contributor to Bush family causes. Others knew that Martinez imported more than 3 1/2 tons of cocaine and more than 75 tons of marijuana into the United States and was under investigation for more than four murders.

Neil Bush, Son. Neil was a director of Silverado Savings and Loan in Colorado, which was shut down by regulators in December 1988 and is expected to cost taxpayers about $1 billion. Regulators were told to delay closing Silverado until after election day in 1988.

SOURCES: *San Francisco Examiner*, 7/28/91, "Crime-linked Firms Hired Prescott Bush"; *Santa Rosa Press Democrat*, 7/19/91 and 8/6/91, "Neil Bush's New Boss" and "Son's S&L Not Closed"; *SPIN*, 12/3/91, "See No Evil," by Jefferson Morley; *The Texas Observer*, 7/12/91 and 8/6/91, "Oil in the Family" and "Global Entanglements," by David Armstrong.

UPDATE: Prescott Bush Jr., Brother. In May 1996, Prescott Bush Jr. was the guest of honor at the annual Connecticut Republicans Prescott Bush Awards Dinner named after his father (*Tampa Tribune*, 6/2/96). No mention of his reported ties to Japanese mobsters was found in any recent media reports.

George W. Bush, Son. On November 8, 1994, George W. Bush easily won the Texas governor's race defeating incumbent governor Ann Richards. Security and Exchange Commission documents revealing Bush had unloaded $840,000 in Harken Energy Corp. stock several weeks before it reported a $23-million loss apparently had no influence in the outcome of the gubernatorial race (*Los Angeles Times*, 10/28/94).

Jeb Bush, Son. On January 17, 1993, the *Washington Post* reported how Leonel Martinez, one of the most successful drug dealers in the United States, was transporting cocaine by the kilo and marijuana by the ton at the same time he was making generous contributions to political campaigns chaired by Jeb Bush. While it noted there was no evidence that Jeb, or his dad George, knew that Martinez was a drug trafficker when they accepted his contributions, the *Post* also noted there was no evidence the Bushes attempted to return his contributions when they learned that he had been arrested on drug charges. Martinez pleaded guilty in 1990, was sentenced to 12 1/2 years in prison, and is expected to get out around 1998.

Jeb Bush, who also had a partnership with Cuban-born Armando Codina, a successful real estate developer, narrowly lost the Florida gubernatorial race in 1994 to incumbent governor Lawton Chiles. The Summer 1996 issue of *Common Cause* noted Bush had exceeded voluntary spending limits in his losing campaign. Nonetheless, *Florida Trend* (June 1996) reports that Jeb Bush is expected to be the GOP's choice for another run at the Florida state house in 1998.

Neil Bush, Son. Neil's involvement in the Silverado S&L debacle, which cost taxpayers a billion dollars, was subsequently confirmed by a number of sources who said his explanation that he had no direct involvement was specious at best. Actually, he sat on Silverado's board of directors until the thrift was declared functionally insolvent (*Mother Jones*, March 1994).

For more detailed information on the Bush boys' escapades and the media's gentle treatment, please see *Mother Jones*, September/October 1992 cover story, "My Three Sons," and *Mother Jones*, March 1994 issue, "Whitewashing the Bush boys: Gentle Media Treatment of Neil, Jeb, and George W. Bush."

CHAPTER 17—1992

The Clinton-Bush Media Horse Race

As is customary during a presidential election year, the major media focused on the horse race between the two major candidates. At the same time, the alternative media focused on censored election issues. According to the Associated Press, the top ten news stories of the year were:

1. Bill Clinton wins election as president
2. Los Angeles riots after Rodney King jury acquits four policemen
3. Hurricane Andrew hits South Florida and Louisiana
4. U.S. troops sent to Somalia
5. Yugoslavia's civil war
6. U.S. economy in recession
7. Emergence of Former Soviet Republics
8. Supreme Court's abortion ruling
9. Two hostages released in Lebanon
10. Jeffrey Dahmer trial.

THE TOP TEN CENSORED STORIES OF 1992

—And What Has Happened to Them Since

1. The Great Media Sell-Out to Reaganism

1992 SYNOPSIS: During the 1980s, the big media owners had reason to celebrate—Reaganism ushered in the era of giant, monopolistic media empires. Take, for example, the three big networks—ABC, CBS, and NBC. Each was acquired by corporations that might have been deemed unqualified under earlier FCC standards. In return, big media dispensed relentlessly positive news about Reaganism and the great trickle-down dream. The FCC also relieved broadcasters of traditional public service requirements, made it almost impossible for citizens' groups to challenge station license renewals, and lifted limits on the number of stations a single corporation can acquire.

Newspapers enjoyed the Reagan era as well. In 98 percent of U.S. cities, the daily news business was already controlled by monopolies. However, the administration further sedated antitrust laws to permit the biggest newspaper chains to create local monopolies. In addition, the National Labor Relations Board, stacked with pro-management members, gave media giants permission to go on a ten-year union busting spree. And, like all big business, broadcasters and print publishers benefited from Reagan's shifting of corporate taxes onto the middle class and the poor.

Meanwhile, top editors were made part of the business-management team, responsible for keeping up advertising lineage as well as overseeing editorial content. Many Time Inc. editors received stock options, and, not surprisingly, many editors started to think more like stockholders than journalists. A new management practice called for the screening of new reporters to keep out journalists who might not readily comply with corporate wishes or who might join newspaper unions. Some major news companies, including Knight-Ridder, do such screening through mandatory, lengthy psychological questionnaires of potential news reporters. Others, including some papers in Gannett, the largest newspaper chain, order editors to be deliberately blunt in interviews so that applicants know the company wants only "team players" who won't rock the boat and aren't in favor of unions.

SOURCE: *Mother Jones*, May/June 1992, "Journalism of Joy," by Ben H. Bagdikian.

UPDATE: The threats to a free, aggressive press voiced by media critic Ben Bagdikian in the story above and his classic, *The Media Monopoly*, were fulfilled in the mid-1990s with the birth of giant, greedy, monopolistic media empires. As *The New York Times* (8/26/96) critic Edward Rothstein, commenting on the alliance between NBC and Microsoft, said, "This is yet another turn of the screw, as technology companies, conglomerates, and the entertainment industry spoon-feed the public ever more plentiful 'products' and prepackaged information." He lauded Bagdikian's prescience in predicting uniformity of news content.

On June 3, 1996, *The Nation* published an extraordinary chart/map delineating corporate ownership of mass media and invited media critics to comment on it. Following are some of the comments: James Fallows, then Washington editor of *The Atlantic Monthly* said, "The more basic concern is the conversion of the news business to just another corporate operation, where whoever is in charge must be as driven by the demands of the financial market as their counterparts in the banking and steel-making and fast-food industries; Peggy Charren, Founder, Action for Children's Television commented, "The media map depicts the dawn of a new world where three or five or ten CEOs could determine who says what to whom in America"; Herbert I. Schiller, educator and author said, "Gigantic entertainment-information complexes exercise a near-seamless and unified private corporate control over what we think, and think about"; Walter Cronkite, Dean of America's television news anchors said, "Nearly every important publishing and broadcasting company today is caught up in the plague of the nineties that has swept the business world—the stockholder demand to increase profits."

Please also see update of "Media Merger Mania," story #5, 1985.

2. Corporate Crime Dwarfs Street Crime and Violence

1992 SYNOPSIS: While the press continues to frighten the public with stories of street crime and violence, corporate violators run rampant and unwatched by the major media. Writer Russell Mokhiber, in his analysis of ten of the worst corporations of 1991 for the *Multinational Monitor*, charges that public corruption, environmental degradation, financial fraud, procurement fraud, and occupational homicide are on the rise.

The distortion of street crime versus corporate crime is promulgated by comments such as those of *Washington Post* columnist Richard Cohen, who wrote, "Young black males commit most of the crime in Washington,

D.C." As Mokhiber points out, Cohen doesn't acknowledge the criminal activities of Exxon, International Paper, United Technologies, Weyerhauser, Pillsbury, Ashland Oil, Texaco, Nabisco, and Ralston-Purina, all convicted of environmental crimes in recent years. "All of these convicted corporations operate in Washington, D.C. None of them are young black males," writes Mokhiber.

SOURCE: *Multinational Monitor*, December 1991, "Corporate Crime & Violence in Review," by Russell Mokhiber.

UPDATE: By the mid-90s, corporate America was finally forced to confront the truth in the old cliché—crime doesn't pay. *The Financial Review* (February 1996) reported a study revealing that convictions for major corporate crimes have a significant and lasting negative impact upon shareholder wealth. It also suggested that one way to deal with corporate crime is to punish executives guilty of fraud by structuring deferred compensation and retirement income plans so they could be reduced or forfeited. Given the cost and public perception of increasing corporate crime, U.S. companies started to spend hundreds of millions of dollars on ethics-training programs designed to keep employees honest (*Houston Chronicle*, 8/11/96). Consultants are also brought in to identify ethics-related business risks and to investigate accusations of wrongdoing—from the public, a whistleblower, or regulators.

Please also see "The Real Welfare Cheats: America's Corporations," #4, 1993.

3. Censored Election Year Issues

1992 SYNOPSIS: While the presidential candidates and the media were focusing on alleged infidelities, family values, and rap-music lyrics, other far more important issues were ignored or under-reported during the 1992 election. Here are just some of the stories that played second fiddle to Gennifer Flowers, Sister Souljah, and Murphy Brown:

George Bush and Iran-contra: Unanswered questions still lingering from the 1988 campaign remained unanswered and largely ignored by the mainstream media before election day.

Bush's Team 100: *Common Cause Magazine* documented how major campaign contributors to George Bush were given ambassadorships and federal advisory committee appointments and how federal regulatory issues that adversely affected members of "Team 100" were toned down.

Homelessness: Despite a critical status report by the National Conference of Mayors that showed 25 cities suffered a serious problem with homelessness, and reported an average 13 percent increase in requests for shelter, the presidential candidates barely mentioned it and the press did not pursue it.

Dan Quayle's Council on Competitiveness: Many questionable and unpublicized actions, often with an anti-environmental impact, stemmed from this committee, whose role and policies were never made clear by the media.

Unpublicized Result of the Iraq War: The death rate of Iraqi children rose dramatically by the tens of thousands in the months after the Gulf War, largely because of an outbreak of diarrhea caused by disabled water and sewage systems.

Where Was Bill?: Covert operations run from a clandestine airfield at Mena, Arkansas, while Bill Clinton was governor, included guns, drugs, and other activities related to the Iran-contra travesty.

SOURCES: *Common Cause Magazine*, April/May/June 1992, "George Bush's Ruling Class," by Jeffrey Denny, Vicki Kemper, Viveca Novak, Peter Overby, and Amy Young; *Washington Post*, 1/9/92, "A Profound Silence on Homelessness," by Mary McGrory; *The Progressive*, May 1992, "Deregulatory Creep: Dan Quayle Clears the Way for Industry," by Arthur E. Rowse; *San Francisco Examiner*, "This World," 10/11/92, "46,900 Unspectacular Deaths," by Mike Royko; *Unclassified*, February/March 1992, "The Mena, Arkansas, Story," by David MacMichael.

UPDATE: In the 1996 presidential election, the media once again tended to highlight alleged infidelities, candidate age differences, and the horse-race aspect of the campaign while ignoring other more important issues such as the increasing economic class division, environmental degradation, health care reform, corporate welfare, international trade treaties such as NAFTA and GATT, and the future of affirmative action.

Following is an update on some of the issues cited in the 1992 *Censored* story:

Homelessness: *American Demographics* (August 1996) reported that efforts to count the homeless have been all but impossible. "Some researchers estimate the number of homeless Americans at between 500,000 and 600,000," but the 1990 Census Bureau came up with less than half that number.

Quayle's Council on Competitiveness: While Quayle's controversial Council faded with the Bush Administration loss in 1992, the Republican Congress elected in 1994 resurrected it. In a little-noted attachment to the Small Business Regulatory Enforcement Fairness Act, passed in 1996, Congress "could put the brakes on new environmental labor, tax, and other regulations for all industry" (*National Law Journal*, 7/29/96). Representative David McIntosh (R-Indiana), former director of the Quayle Council, said this was a "revolutionary change" that "no one noticed" which would, in effect, "recreate" the role of Quayle's Council on Competitiveness.

Iraq War: Please see updates of Gulf War stories, #1 and #2, 1991.

Where was Bill?: The Mena, Arkansas, airfield/drug connection mystery continues to be perpetuated by the Republicans and denied by the Democrats. *Partners in Power*, written by Nixon biographer Roger Morris and published in 1996, reportedly "documents Clinton's knowledge, while governor of Arkansas, of drug and gun-running out of Mena" (*Washington Times*, 9/2/96). Conversely, on November 8, 1996, the CIA Inspector General told Congress there was no illegal CIA activity at Mena as alleged in the story above (*Washington Post*, 11/9/96).

4. United States: The World's Leading Merchant of Death

1992 SYNOPSIS: In the 1980s, global arms-spending rocketed to nearly $1 trillion annually—or about $2 million a minute. The two leading arms merchants were the United States and the former Soviet Union. Now the Soviet Union is gone, but its place has been taken by others with the U.S. leading the pack.

With the end of the Cold War, some Americans hoped U.S. arms production and sales would be reduced and arms plants converted to civilian factories. This has not happened; instead, the U.S. has kept its arms factories humming with exports.

Some facts from the Center for Defense Information include the following:

✔ The U.S. is the world's top weapons supplier.

✔ The U.S. has provided more than $128 billion in weaponry and military assistance to more than 125 of the world's 169 countries since 1982.

✔ The U.S. continues to provide arms to a number of nations with chronic records of human rights violations.

✔ In Latin America, El Salvador's bloody regime garners the largest share of U.S. military sales.

Meanwhile, there are reports of increasingly hostile world opinion against militarization, which the U.S. appears to be ignoring. Critics say the continued pathology of U.S. arms-spending, exacerbated by the decline in U.S. productivity in the '70s and '80s, can only further intensify the problems in America.

SOURCES: *World Press Review*, September 1992, "The World's Top Arms Merchant," by Frederick Clairmonte; *The Human Quest*, July/August 1992, "War 'Dividends'—Military Spending Out of Balance with Needy," by Tristram Coffin.

UPDATE: A well-documented analysis by the *British Medical Journal* (10/14/95) reported, "In 1986 the United States accounted for 13 percent of worldwide arms exports, but today its share of the weapons market is an astounding 70 percent. Furthermore, 66 percent of all United States arms exports are to developing nations, many with fragile autocracies that are easily destabilized." The *Journal* also noted that the risk of worldwide mass violence can be reduced if global arms sales are restricted. This is something the President can do unilaterally. The *New York Law Journal* (8/22/95) reported that the United States Arms Export Control Act of 1976 gives the President the power "to control the import and the export of...defense articles and defense services."

5. Iraqgate and the Quiet Death of the Watergate Law

1992 SYNOPSIS: Representative Henry B. Gonzales (D-Texas), chair of the House Bank Committee, launched an intensive investigation into the Iraqgate scandal in 1990. Since February 1991, he has been regularly addressing a mostly empty House and a loyal C-Span audience, about the role the Bush Administration played in building up Iraq prior to the Gulf War. His revelations were basically ignored by the press.

Gonzalez charged the Bush Administration: secretly sold nuclear, biological, chemical, and missile-related weapons materials to Iraq; blocked investigations into the use of the materials; suppressed warnings of the dangers of such sales; deliberately falsified documents on such sales submitted to Congress; interfered illegally to halt investigations into the criminal activities of the Banca Nazionale del Lavoro branch in Atlanta which was secretly diverting American agricultural loans to buy weapons for Iraq.

Finally, in September 1992, Senate Republicans quietly killed legislation that was necessary to renew the Watergate Law which had previously assured independent investigations of criminal acts by top officials. To their everlasting discredit, Senate Democrats sat silently by in order to avoid an effort to have the law apply to members of Congress as well as to executive branch officials.

SOURCES: *CovertAction Information Bulletin*, Fall 1992, "Bush Administration Uses CIA to Stonewall Iraqgate Investigation," by Jack Colhoun; *War & Peace Digest*, August 1992, "BNL-Iraqgate Scandal," by Kevin Sanders; *The Paper* of Sonoma County (CA), 10/22/92, "Is Bush a Felon?", by Stephen P. Pizzo; *The New York Times*," 10/20/92, "The Patsy Prosecutor," by William Safire.

UPDATE: With heavy Democratic support, on June 21, 1994, the 103rd Congress reinstated the independent counsel law. According to the *Washington Post* (6/22/94), "The legislation would continue the procedure under the old law of requiring an attorney general to conduct a preliminary investigation of credible allegations against 60 top officials, including the president, vice president, and Cabinet members." If "reasonable grounds" for further investigation are found, the attorney general could ask that an independent counsel be named. To their credit, Republicans criticized the bill for not including members of Congress in the list of automatically covered officials.

6. "We are Winning the War on Drugs" was a Lie

1992 SYNOPSIS: When President George Bush went before the nation on September 6, 1989, to give a special address about the seriousness of the drug problem in the United States, the media and the public responded with alarm.

By the end of that month, 64 percent of the public believed drugs posed a greater threat than nuclear war, environmental degradation, toxic waste, AIDS, poverty, or the national debt. *The New York Times* alone published 238 articles on drugs—more than seven articles a day—that month.

Fast-forward to 1992: The federal anti-drug budget mushroomed to more than $10 billion and President Bush proclaimed, "We are winning the war on drugs." The problem with this optimistic proclamation is that it was a lie.

The sobering fact is that Americans are in greater danger from drugs today than ever before. In fact, despite glowingingly positive rhetoric, drug deaths in the U.S. are skyrocketing at a much higher rate than drug arrests. Before the Reagan and Bush Administrations began their war on drugs, deaths from drug abuse and drug-related murders had declined from a peak of 8,500 per year in the early 1970s to 7,700 in 1982. Since 1982, the numbers have steadily climbed. Drug abuse deaths have risen by 50 percent and drug-related murders have tripled to more than 13,000 in 1990. This is the steepest increase and highest level in history.

SOURCES: *In These Times*, 5/20/92, "Drug Deaths Rise as the War Continues," by Mike Males; *EXTRA!*, September 1992, "Don't Forget the Hype: Media, Drugs and Public Opinion," by Micah Fink.

UPDATE: Please see update of "War on Drugs," #4, 1989.

7. Trashing Federal Regulations for Corporate Contributions

1992 SYNOPSIS: In his State of the Union address on January 28, 1992, President George Bush declared a 90-day "moratorium" on new federal regulations. Public Citizen and OMB Watch compiled a list of the affected regulations and what they might have accomplished:

1. Prevention of worker exposure to toxic chemicals. A 90-day delay could cost an estimated 289 workers' lives.

2. Cooperation of manufacturers and hospitals to report adverse effects associated with medical devices to the FDA. Such reports would keep the public up to date on hazards such as those associated with silicone breast implants.

3. Prevention of a replay of the S&L fiasco. A regulation pending at the FDIC would require banks, not the taxpayers, to pay for their own bailout.

4. Protection of farm workers from exposure to dangerous pesticides.

Polls show the general public opposes deregulation of business, especially when the purity of air, water, food, drugs, and other necessities is involved. Why then did the Bush Administration pursue deregulation so zealously? Consider these coincidences between contributions to the Bush/Quayle campaign/Republican National Committee and some federal decisions:

Developers contribute $2,277,490. Wetland protection acreage is reduced.

Food industry contributes $1,352,000. Nutrition guidelines are pulled back; nutrition labeling is delayed a year.

Oil and gas industry contributes $1,150,360. Stripper-well fees are reduced; rules on natural gas usage are relaxed; and limits on hazardous air are blocked.

Air polluters contribute $788,270. Emission standards are delayed.

Insurance industry contributes $450,000. Product-liability limits are pushed.

Airlines contribute $315,700. Limits on noisy engines are reduced.

The coincidental relationship between contributions and deregulation was not lost on George Bush. On April 29, he extended his original 90-day moratorium on new federal regulations for another 120 days.

SOURCES: *The Nation*, 3/23/92, "Bush's Regulatory Chill: Immoral, Illegal, and Deadly"; *The Progressive*, May 1992, "Deregulatory Creep: Dan Quayle Clears the Way for Industry," by Arthur E. Rowse.

UPDATE: During his acceptance speech as the presidential nominee at the Republican convention held in Houston in October 1992, President George Bush said, "I will extend for one year the freeze on paperwork and unnecessary federal regulations that I imposed last winter" (*Occupational Hazards*, October 1992). As we now know, Bush didn't have an opportunity to follow through with that promise. However, the newly Republican-controlled House of Representatives did and they passed a bill establishing a one-year moratorium on new federal regulations. With somewhat more foresight, the Senate, albeit also Republican-controlled, soundly rejected the attempt to impose a moratorium and the bill ended there.

8. Government Secrecy Makes a Mockery of Democracy

1992 SYNOPSIS: In 1991, some 6,500 U.S. government employees classified 7,107,017 documents, an average of more than 19,000 documents per day. Steven Aftergood, a senior research analyst at the Federation of American Scientists in Washington, D.C., says our information policy is in disarray, with widespread over-classification and an inefficient and costly information system. Further, the classified files are overflowing with records of policy decisions, historical and budget documents, and reams of environmental data that could not possibly compromise our national security:

✔ Secret Historical Documents: As of 1991, the oldest classified military document in the National Archives was dated April 15, 1917, and concerned U.S. troop movements in Europe during World War I.

✔ National Security Directives: These secret presidential directives withhold basic policy documents concerning space, telecommunications, counternarcotics, etc., from Congress as well as the public.

✔ The Black Budget: About 15 percent of the Defense Department's budget for weapons acquisition has been classified in recent years, keeping the cost of a program, its purpose, and even its existence, a secret from Congress. (See also #7 *Censored* story, 1990.)

✔ Secret Environmental Impact Data: The Department of Energy has withheld data on the health effects of its nuclear weapons production facilities.

✔ Intelligence Information: There are more than a dozen intelligence agencies within the government supported by a secret budget, including the National Reconnaissance Office which is so secretive its very name and existence are classified.

Concerned with an ever-increasing criticism of its secrecy, the CIA last year prepared a report on how the agency might achieve greater openness—and then classified the report.

SOURCE: *Issues in Science and Technology*, Summer 1992, "The Perils of Government Secrecy," by Steven Aftergood.

UPDATE: On October 14, 1995, Bill Clinton's presidential order to declassify millions of old national security documents took effect. While the government will be spending more than $2.7 billion this year to keep secrets, the order should cut costs significantly by reducing the volume of classified documents dramatically (*Chicago Tribune*, 6/25/96). Nonetheless, Steven Aftergood, the source of the *Censored* story above, said even a year after Clinton's announcement, compliance with the executive order appears to be incomplete. For example, he points out, the U.S. Army resists declassification by claiming it needs $500 million to properly handle the job. "And they aren't going to get half-a-billion dollars so they're just sitting on their hands" (The Springfield *State Journal-Register*, 7/14/96).

9. How Advertising Pressure Can Corrupt a Free Press

1992 SYNOPSIS: The free press in America isn't free at all—at least from the influence of advertisers on the content of the news. While people fear governmental control of the media, a far more subtle yet pervasive influence comes from advertiser pressure. "Dictating Content: How Advertising Pressure Can Corrupt a Free Press," a report by the Center for the Study of Commercialism, documents dozens of examples of advertiser censorship in the media.

One of the crudest forms of censorship is defined as "direct economic censorship," which occurs when an advertiser overtly dictates to the mass media what the public shall or shall not see or hear. Other forms of media bias include reporter self-censorship (when the specter of an advertiser's reaction dissuades a reporter from even suggesting a particular story); reporting fake news (advertiser-created reports or news segments presented as legitimate, unbiased news accounts); using stories as bait (stories that purposefully flatter current or potential advertisers); using puff pieces to increase ad revenues.

On March 11, 1992, The Center for the Study of Commercialism invited 200 media outlets to a press conference in Washington, D.C., to announce the results of its study. Not a single radio or television station or network sent a reporter. Only two newspapers, the *Washington Post* and the *Washington Times*, bothered to attend. The *Post* didn't run a story at all; the *Times* ran one but didn't name the advertisers cited in the study. The press conference, designed to show how advertisers suppress the news, made its point.

SOURCE: Center for the Study of Commercialism, March 1992, "Dictating Content: How Advertising Pressure Can Corrupt a Free Press," by Ronald K.L. Collins.

UPDATE: The continuing influence of advertisers on the media is reported by *The Cincinnati Enquirer* (5/20/96) which states, "Major advertisers are taking an increasingly growing stake in producing shows for TV and in creating much of the material funneled through the Internet computer network." It also cites a prediction made by *New Media Age* in the fall of 1995: "We are at the threshold of a world where the vast majority of content is delivered directly by advertisers." It also cited Ron Collins, author of the *Censored* story above, who warned, "The biggest concern about advertisers involvement is self-censorship by writers who don't want to offend a major sponsor. " *By Invitation Only: How the Media Limit Political Debate*, published by Common Courage Press in 1995, a well documented critique of the press, cites the corrupting influences of government sources, corporate owners, and advertising pressures (*The Progressive*, March 1995).

10. Pentagon's Post-Cold War Black Budget is Alive and Prospering

1992 SYNOPSIS: Today, and every day, close to $100 million flow through underground pipelines from the U.S. Treasury to the Pentagon to fuel the national-security machinery of the United States. The "Black Budget" is the secret treasury of the nation's military and intelligence agencies. It is appropriated and spent with only the scantiest public debate or media scrutiny.

Of the roughly $36 billion in the secret budget, about $5 billion goes to build and develop weapons programs, many of which remain so highly classified that only the two most senior members of the congressional armed services and appropriations committees know anything about them.

Why isn't there more publicity? After all, public pressure and congressional anger forced the lid off the now infamous B-2 bomber. But the realization that the Cold War has ended apparently has not yet penetrated the inner catacombs of the Pentagon.

The solution is not difficult. Congress could demand disclosure of data on the cost and character of secret programs but has only done so on a piecemeal basis; nor has Congress ever confronted the underlying fact that the secrecy system itself defies the Constitution, which requires the government to publish a complete and accurate account of all federal spending.

SOURCE: *Mother Jones*, March/April 1992, "The Pentagon's Secret Stash," by Tim Weiner.

UPDATE: Please see update of "Pentagon's Black Budget," #7, 1990.

CHAPTER 18—1993

A Major Flood vs. 12 Million Hungry Children

While the mainstream media focused on a major flood as its top ranked news story of 1993, they didn't notice that the United States had become one of the most dangerous places in the world for young people. According to the Associated Press, the top ten news stories of the year were:

1. The Great Flood of 1993 that devastated the Midwest
2. The Branch Davidian cult inferno in Waco, Texas
3. Bill Clinton's controversial inaugural year
4. Terrorist bombing of World Trade Center
5. The failed mission to Somalia
6. Mideast peace progress with PLO
7. North American Free Trade Association
8. National health care reform
9. Turmoil in Russia
10. Bosnian bloodshed.

THE TOP TEN CENSORED STORIES OF 1993

—And What Has Happened to Them Since

1. The United States is Killing Its Young

1993 SYNOPSIS: The United States has become one of the most dangerous places in the world for young people—and it is getting worse.

An alarming report issued in mid-September of 1993 by the United Nations Children's Fund should have been a lead item on the network evening news programs, but wasn't. In fact, according to the *Tyndall Report*, which monitors the evening network news programs, the UN report did not even make the top ten list of news subjects on the networks during the period from September 13 to October 1, 1993.

According to the United Nations Children's Fund: 1) Nine out of ten young people murdered in industrialized countries are slain in the United States; 2) The U.S. homicide rate for young people ages 15 to 24 is five times greater than that of Canada, its nearest competitor; 3) The U.S. poverty rate for children is more than double that of any other major industrialized nation; and 4) Since the 1970s, while other industrialized nations were bringing children out of poverty, only the United States and Britain slipped backward.

An earlier report by researchers at Tufts University revealed that nearly 12 million children are going hungry in the United States now.

Emphasizing the lack of compassion for young children in the United States, journalist Gayle Reaves, who reported on the findings by the Children's Fund, noted, "Unlike every other industrialized nation, the United States has not signed or ratified the Convention on the Rights of the Child, a set of principles adopted by the U.N. General Assembly in 1989."

SOURCES: *Dallas Morning News*, 9/25/93, "U.N. Says U.S. Dangerous for Children," by Gayle Reaves; *USA Today*, 6/16/93, "Report: 12 Million Kids Go Hungry in USA."

UPDATE: As frightening as this story was when Project Censored cited it in 1993, the plight of America's children has grown worse since then. On November 4, 1994, the *National Catholic Reporter* said, "The number of children abused each year in the United States—now three million—has tripled since 1980. The number of children murdered in the United States has doubled over the past ten years. In the United States, 110 babies die every day without reaching their first birthday. Only 18 percent of those eligible for Head Start are enrolled. One million American girls get pregnant each year—the highest rate in the industrialized world."

On September 22, 1995, *Daedalus* reported, "Each year ten thousand children in the United States die as a direct result of living in poverty. Violence towards children has escalated dramatically: three children a day die of child abuse. Over the last thirteen years we have lost 80,000 children to gun deaths, thousands more than we lost during the 25 years of the Vietnam conflict." The U.S. teenage suicide rate, fifth highest in the world, nearly doubled from 5.9 deaths per 100,000 in 1970 to 11.1 deaths per 100,000 in 1991 (*Maclean's*, 1/29/96). And, according to a UNICEF report also cited in *Maclean's* (9/2/96), 300,000 children in the United States are involved in prostitution. The situation may only get worse. The *New York Daily News* (2/25/96) reported the "projected growth of the 'at risk' 13-to-17 age group over the next ten years will mean that the nation will see a dramatic increase in crime."

On February 6, 1997, the Centers for Disease Control and Prevention released a new study that revealed American youngsters are 12 times more likely to die by gunfire and five times more likely to be murdered than their counterparts in 25 other industrialized nations (Associated Press, 2/8/97).

Despite all this, the United States is still the only industrialized nation in the world which has not signed the most important international instrument for protecting children—the United Nations Convention on the Rights of the Child, cited in the 1993 *Censored* story above. More than 180 other countries have already ratified the U.N. Convention which obligates governments to secure the well-being of their children (*The Christian Century*, 11/15/95).

2. Why Are We Really In Somalia?

1993 SYNOPSIS: Investigative authors Rory Cox, in *Propaganda Review*, and Jim Naureckas, in *EXTRA!*, wondered whether the decision to send U.S. troops to Somalia was based more on potential oil reserves there than on the tragic images of starving Somalis that dominated major media outlets in late 1992 and 1993.

The U.S./UN military involvement in Somalia began in mid-November 1992, but it wasn't until January 18, 1993, two days before George Bush left office, that a major media outlet, the *Los Angeles Times*, published an article that revealed America's oil connection with Somalia.

Times staff writer Mark Fineman started his Mogadishu-datelined article with, "Far beneath the surface of the tragic drama of Somalia, four major U.S. oil companies are quietly sitting on a prospective fortune in exclusive concessions to explore and exploit tens of millions of acres of the Somali countryside. That land, in the opinion of geologists and industry sources, could yield significant amounts of oil and natural gas if the U.S.-led military mission can restore peace to the impoverished East African nation."

According to Fineman, nearly two-thirds of Somalia was allocated to the American oil giants Conoco, Amoco, Chevron, and Phillips before Somalia's pro-U.S. President Mohamed Siad Barre was overthrown. The U.S. oil companies are "well positioned to pursue Somalia's most promising potential oil reserves the moment the nation is pacified."

Oil industry spokesmen, along with Bush/Clinton Administration spokespersons, deny these allegations as "absurd" and "nonsense." However, Thomas E. O'Connor, the principal petroleum engineer for the World Bank, who headed an in-depth three-year study of oil prospects off Somalia's northern coast, said, "There's no doubt there's oil there...It's got high (commercial) potential...once the Somalis get their act together."

SOURCES: *Los Angeles Times*, 1/18/93, "The Oil Factor In Somalia," by Mark Fineman; *Propaganda Review*, No. 10, 1993, "Somoilia?", by Rory Cox; *EXTRA!*, March 1993, "The Somalia Intervention: Tragedy Made Simple," by Jim Naureckas.

UPDATE: Somalia has been torn apart by clan fighting since 1991 when dictator Mohamed Siad Barre was overthrown. In mid-November 1992, the United States launched Operation Restore Hope with the avowed purpose to find and expel faction leader Mohamed Farah Aidid, in an effort to bring peace to the nation. Instead, in a media-sensationalized night invasion, U.S. Marines went ashore in Somalia on February 28, 1995, to protect final withdrawal of U.N. forces after the failed mission which cost $2 billion and the lives of 140 American and U.N. peacekeepers. Aidid died shortly after a gun battle in late July 1996 and two of his archrivals announced unilateral cease-fires (Associated Press, 8/3/96). The cease-fire lasted until September 16, when one of the faction leaders called an end to the agreement and fighting resumed (*Orange County Register*, 9/17/96). *Jane's Intelligence Review* (10/1/96) concluded: "Peace will not come to Somalia until a leadership

emerges that is perceivably working for all Somalis from whatever clan."
And so the oil companies bide their time until the "Somalis get their act
together," as one oil company spokesman said above.

3. The Sandia Report On Education: A Lesson In Censorship

1993 SYNOPSIS: One of the most thorough investigations into the quality
of public education did not produce the expected results and instead, ended
up being censored.

When state governors and President George Bush set national education goals after the 1989 education summit, the administration charged Sandia National Laboratories, a scientific research organization, with
investigating the state of public education.

In 1991, Sandia presented its first findings to the U.S. Department of
Education and the National Science Foundation. While the response from
these government agencies should have been one of some celebration,
instead it was one of silence—a silence compounded by the national media.
The results did not reveal a seriously deficient educational system in dire
need of profound changes such as a nationwide voucher program.
Nonetheless, the report was suppressed.

Instead, the Sandia Report revealed a steady or slightly improving trend
in public education on nearly every measure employed in the survey. Overall, the 85 percent high school completion rate in the U.S. ranks as one of
the highest in the world. The already low dropout rate is inflated by a growing immigrant school population. Falling SAT scores are not the result of
decreasing student performance but rather increasing participation from students in the lower percentiles. One quarter of young people will achieve a
bachelor's degree. Spending on education, often characterized as out of control, has risen by 30 percent—but this money has gone into special education programs, not the "regular" classroom. Areas of concern raised by
the report focused on the performance of minorities who were still lagging
behind whites.

The lack of coverage of the report, and the rancor with which the report
was met from government departments and, more importantly, from the
"Education President" George Bush, was astounding. Clearly the report contradicted the political philosophy of "deregulating" public education and
would have seriously weakened the school choice movement.

SOURCES: *Phi Delta Kappan*, May 1993, "Perspective on Education In America," by Robert M. Huelskamp; *The Education Digest*, September 1993, "The Second Coming of the Sandia Report," reprinted from *Phi Delta Kappan*.

UPDATE: The December 22, 1994, issue of *Mothering* provides a review of how the Sandia Report was covered up and a well-documented analysis of the report and its findings. It noted that after word of the report came out, "Sandia received nearly 1,000 requests for the report. School board members, teachers, and administrators spoke positively about it at meetings. Many were heartened by its fresh analyses of the facts and its sometimes surprising conclusions." *Mothering* concluded that almost all educators familiar with the study took the results as confirmation that the educational system is not as bad as had been thought.

4. The Real Welfare Cheats: America's Corporations

1993 SYNOPSIS: In his 1992 presidential campaign, Bill Clinton called for welfare reform, decried welfare cheats, and emphasized workfare. However, he failed to mention the largest recipients of taxpayer support—corporate welfare. A January/February 1993 issue of Ralph Nader's magazine, *Multinational Monitor*, contained articles documenting five major areas of government giveaways to corporations:

1. "Public Assets, Private Profits" by Chris Lewis. In 1980, the Government Patent Policy Act opened a floodgate of government research and development money to universities and private firms, then allowed these recipients to keep the patents and profits on products developed with public funds.

2. "Bankruptcy Bailouts" by Laurence H. Kallen. In 1986, the new bankruptcy code was established. Chapter 11 of this code, known as business reorganization under protection and supervision of a bankruptcy court, has allowed corporations, many of them solvent, to jettison debts. These "debts have included EPA-required toxic site clean-up costs, personal injury judgments, union contracts, and even retirement benefits.

3. "Gold-Plated Giveaways" by Jonathan Dushoff. Under the Mining Act of 1872, companies can mine valuable minerals and metals from federal lands without paying a cent in royalties and buy federal lands for as little as five dollars an acre.

4. "The Price of Power" by David Lapp. The 1992 Energy Policy Act guarantees our government will continue to subsidize the nuclear power

industry. These taxpayer dollars go to an industry with a dismal record on safety and efficiency.

5. "Last Stand" by Randal O'Toole. U.S. taxpayers own more than 192 million acres of forest land that are managed by the U.S. Forest Service and Department of Agriculture. Over the past 15 years, the Forest Service has lost between one and two billion dollars annually in undervalued timber sales to the logging industry.

SOURCE: *Multinational Monitor*, January/February 1993, "Public Assets, Private Profits: The U.S. Corporate Welfare Rolls," by Chris Lewis, Laurence H. Kallen, Jonathan Dushoff, David Lapp, and Randal O'Toole.

UPDATE: An investigative report by the *Boston Globe* (8/11/96) confirmed the charges of "corporate welfare" noted above and revealed the extent of this ongoing political outrage. It reported an estimated $150 billion, in the form of direct federal subsidies and tax breaks, is given American companies in what critics call "corporate welfare." It noted, "The $150 billion eclipses the annual budget deficit of $130 billion. It's more than the $145 billion paid out annually for the core programs of the social welfare state: Aid to Families with Dependent Children, student aid, housing, food and nutrition, and all direct public assistance, excluding Social Security and medical care."

Some of the examples of corporate welfare found by the *Boston Globe* include:

✔ The $200 million-a-year Market Promotion Program, which gives companies like Gallo and Ocean Spray enormous sums to market their products overseas.

✔ Federal programs costing millions of dollars that are designed to create jobs. Corporate recipients like AT&T, General Electric, Raytheon, Digital, and Lockheed Martin have instead laid off hundreds of thousands of workers.

✔ Government subsidies to the high-tech industry which resulted in tens of thousands of jobs going overseas.

✔ Poorly thought-out studies such as the Advanced Technology Program, a $90 million Massachusetts project to create jobs and stimulate the economy, which created a sum total of 150 jobs.

But now welfare as we know it is being privatized. According to a *USA Today* report (10/21/96), "Within a few years, welfare will be a multibillion-dollar industry, tightly regulated by government, but run in many states by high-tech giants such as Lockheed Martin IMS, Andersen Consulting,

EDS, Unisys, and IBM." The nation's $28-billion-a-year welfare adminis-
tration system could be the largest peacetime prize for corporate America.
Ironically, the same group that already is the largest welfare recipient of
taxpayer support may well become the administrator of welfare for the
nation's less fortunate. And tens of thousands of government employees who
now administer the welfare program may lose their jobs.

5. The Hidden Tragedy of Chernobyl Has Worldwide Implications

1993 SYNOPSIS: A devastating book on the far-reaching dimensions of the
1986 Chernobyl disaster, written by Vladimir Chernousenko, a Ukrainian
nuclear physicist involved in the emergency cleanup, has not received the
international media attention it deserves and probably will never be published in the Ukraine or Russia.

Chernousenko explodes many of the Chernobyl myths propagated by
Soviet authorities and eagerly accepted by the international nuclear establishment. He points out the accident was not the result of operator error
but was caused by major flaws of design present in 15 other Soviet reactors still in operation.

In contrast to the widely accepted belief that only 31 people died from
exposure to radiation in the effort to contain the emissions, Chernousenko
asserts that between 7,000 and 10,000 volunteers were killed.

The most serious charge made by Chernousenko was that the accident
released the lethal contents of 80 percent of the reactor core rather than
the three percent figure announced to the world. Using Chernousenko's figures, the radiation released was roughly equivalent to the explosion of 1,000
Hiroshima bombs.

While the fallout was concentrated mainly in the three Soviet
republics of Belarus, Ukraine, and Russia, the reluctance of the Soviet
authorities to recognize the true extent of the contamination of farmland
resulted in the shipment of contaminated food and grain to all the former
Soviet republics, thus spreading radiation illness.

SOURCE: *The Nation,* 3/15/93, "Chernobyl—The Hidden Tragedy," by Jay
M. Gould.

UPDATE: On the tenth anniversary of the Chernobyl disaster, *The Nation*
(4/29/96) devoted its cover story to an update of the issue. It said Cher-

nobyl's molten radioactive rubble continues to smolder and kill—and could explode again. It also noted that Chernobyl's lethal runoff now threatens the water supply of tens of millions of people; its airborne fallout caused a massive increase in childhood thyroid cancer rates; in Poland, Germany, Italy, and throughout the rest of Europe, massive quantities of farm produce were severely irradiated; and in the countryside around the reactor itself, local farmers and veterinarians reported a wave of animal deformities, sterility, and deaths. Nonetheless, the Soviets still admit to only 31 deaths among reactor operators and "liquidators." However, a staggering 800,000 or more of these workers were exposed at the site, and there has been no full follow-up on their health. The Ukrainian government says more than 8,000 have already died, with another 12,000 sick.

Ukrainian officials now predict at least 200,000 local deaths, and are reporting increases in bone tumors as well as cancers of the kidney, bladder, lung, and breast. Estimates of the worldwide death toll vary ranging up to 20,000 deaths.

Vladimir Chernousenko, the source of the 1993 *Censored* story, who spent seven months within a six-mile radius of the core, is now in his 50s and seriously ill. Chernousenko says "150 of my friends are dead; 12,000 people, total, have died; 300,000 are alive but very ill. For them this disaster is only now beginning."

The major media continue to downplay the impact of Chernobyl. *The Nation* also reported that a front-page story in the March 31, 1996, issue of *The New York Times*, attributed the brunt of Chernobyl's health impact to psychological rather than radioactive fallout and reported that "many suspect Chernobyl's effects will not be nearly as severe as once feared."

6. U.S. Army Quietly Resumes Biowarfare Testing After Ten-Year Hiatus

1993 SYNOPSIS: Although few people outside of Dugway, Utah, are aware of it, the U.S. Army has brought biological warfare testing back to a site it declared unsafe a decade earlier.

In 1983, residents of western Utah breathed a healthy sigh of relief when the Army discontinued testing biological warfare agents at its Dugway Proving Ground. The reason given was the Army's testing facility was getting old, and its safety—the ability to prevent potentially deadly diseases from escaping into the air outside the facility and thence to the rest of the world—could no longer be guaranteed. Now the deadly bugs are back.

Military scientists are testing a device called the Biological Integrated Detection System (BIDS), described as a defensive weapon, at the renovated Dugway facility. A Dugway representative said the tests, which include viruses and bacterium such as anthrax, botulism, and the plague, would initially be liquid, not aerosol, tests. Aerosol tests are the most hazardous form of testing; one tiny air leak could result in a catastrophic release of deadly diseases. It was precisely this hazard that led to the closing of the Dugway facility in 1983. The biowarfare lab has been renovated since then and Army experts claim their elaborate safety precautions will prevent such a leak.

Nonetheless, new safety concerns were raised in September 1993, when the Dugway Proving Ground was cited for 22 violations of state hazardous-waste regulations, ranging from inadequate record-keeping to improper dumping of poisonous chemicals.

Critics also point out it was the Army that denied for a year that it was responsible for the 1968 accidental release of nerve gas from Dugway that killed some 6,000 sheep in the area.

SOURCES: *Salt Lake Tribune*, 1/27/93, "Army Resumes Biological-Agent Tests at Dugway After 10-Year Cessation," 7/28/93, "Dugway to Test Disease-causing Agents at Remote Lab," both by Jim Woolf; 9/21/93, "Dugway Base Cited for 22 Waste Violations," by Laurie Sullivan; *High Country News*, 8/9/93, "Biowarfare is Back," by Jon Christensen; *High Desert Advocate*, 9/15/93, "Utah Biowarfare Oversight Group Wants to Do Its Work Behind Closed Doors."

UPDATE: Please see update of "Biological Weapons," #10, 1981.

7. The Ecological Disaster That Challenges The Exxon Valdez

1993 SYNOPSIS: "It's hard to believe, but the ecological disasters caused by the oil spills from the Exxon Valdez, in Prince William Sound, Alaska, in 1989, and the Braer, off Scotland's Shetland Island, in 1993, seem to pale when compared with the chronic environmental nightmare being wrought by selenium-contaminated drainwater flowing from irrigated lands in California and 13 other Western states," warns environmental writer Robert H. Boyle, president of the Hudson Riverkeeper Fund.

Ironically, selenium is not a new problem; poisoned water holes and sinks have existed for years in the West with the first recorded case of selenium poisoning reported in 1857 in Nebraska.

Now, however, man-made "lakes" and ponds saturated with selenium from agricultural run-off are threatening our drinking water and wildlife. Hardest hit is the Kesterson National Wildlife Refuge in California's San Joaquin Valley.

In 1983, Harry M. Ohlendorf, a wildlife research biologist, studying nesting birds at Kesterson, found a high incidence of dead adult birds, dead embryos, deformed embryos and deformed young coots, ducks, eared grebes, black-necked stilt, and killdeers. When he reported these findings to the U.S. Fish and Wildlife Service, he was told to delete those references in his report. In 1984, virtually no nesting birds were seen at Kesterson; instead, 16,000 adult birds died from selenium poisoning.

Boyle estimates that tens of thousands—some say hundreds of thousands—of birds have died or have been born dead or with grotesque deformities. The selenium crisis has now grown to extraordinary proportions in California, with the selenium runoff now threatening entire 500-mile-long Central Valley as well as the water supply for Los Angeles.

SOURCE: *Sports Illustrated*, 3/22/93, "The Killing Fields," by Robert H. Boyle.

UPDATE: Three years after the 1993 *Censored* story, San Joaquin Valley farmers and the government reached an agreement to clean up the selenium-poisoned Kesterson Reservoir (*The Fresno Bee*, 7/16/96). Under the settlement, farmers will pay $25.9 million for the clean-up and will help cover an additional $4.6 million for broader studies of drainage problems. On September 25, 1996, the *San Diego Union-Tribune* reported that the San Luis Drain, which was closed by the federal government in 1985 for causing the selenium problem, was opened again. However, this time, instead of carrying selenium-tainted irrigation runoff through duck marshes, the San Luis Drain will flow more directly to the San Joaquin River. Meanwhile, David Kennedy, executive director of California's Department of Water Resources, warned that the Salton Sea may become the site of a future selenium ecological disaster (*Riverside Press-Enterprise*, 12/13/96).

8. America's Deadly Doctors

1993 SYNOPSIS: The trust Americans put into their doctors may be sorely misplaced. According to estimates, five to ten percent of doctors—some 30,000 to 60,000—could be hazardous to your health. A study by the Public Citizen's Health Research Group concluded that medical negligence in hospitals alone injures or kills 150,000 to 300,000 Americans each year.

Experts cite two major reasons why some doctors are dangerous: They've become physically or mentally impaired, or they were poorly trained or incompetent to start with.

Charles Inlander, president of the People's Medical Society, said impairment is the number one reason doctors are dangerous. Impairment takes many forms including alcoholism (10 percent of all physicians) and drug addiction (three percent, which accounts for some 78,000 doctors nationwide). Another impairment is mental illness; a 1989 New Jersey report on incompetent physicians revealed that one percent, or about 6,000 doctors are mentally unbalanced. Senility is another problem with many doctors continuing to practice long after they reach retirement age. A final reason is ignorance—doctors who are otherwise mentally and physically healthy may fail to keep up with medical research.

The second major reason doctors can be deadly is simple incompetence and poor training. Students who could not qualify for admission to American medical schools often attend unaccredited schools in the Caribbean. Sometimes those who can't get a medical license simply practice without one or use a fraudulent degree. Some doctors lack the appropriate skills when they practice beyond their area of expertise. Finally, there are doctors who are driven by greed. One New Jersey doctor did so many needless surgeries he lost his malpractice insurance, yet he kept treating patients.

SOURCE: *Woman's Day*, 10/12/93, "Deadly Doctors," by Sue Browder.

UPDATE: On November 5, 1996, *USA Today* reported the results of a study conducted at RAND and the Harvard School of Public Health that revealed the full extent of medical negligence in the United States. The annual toll of medical harm includes: 1.3 million injuries, 180,000 deaths, and total costs of $50 billion.

But now, after years of medical incompetence and cover-up, the nation's medical system may finally be responding to increasing public skepticism about its infallibility. On October 13, 1996, two major medical groups announced new programs to figure out why mistakes like fatal overdoses or wrong amputations occur and what can be done to prevent them (*USA Today*, 10/14/96). The American Medical Association is launching the National Patient Safety Foundation to fund research into error prevention and to promote safety measures. The Joint Commission on Accreditation of Healthcare Organizations will establish an "accreditation watch" to be given healthcare organizations if it finds a significant error has occurred. The organization will have 30 days to produce a "root-cause analysis."

States are also watching a Massachusetts plan to publish a broad range of details on the state's 30,000 licensed physicians, profiling everything from scholarly achievements to scrapes with the law (*Modern Healthcare*, 8/5/96). Shortly after the program started, Massachusetts officials rushed to double the number of phone lines and operators taking calls from people checking up on physicians' disciplinary and malpractice records (*USA Today*, 11/11/96). Massachusetts was the first state to provide such a broad range of physician information. Florida passed similar legislation in May 1997 and it's being considered in eight other states: California, Connecticut, Illinois, Maine, Maryland, Rhode Island, Texas, and Vermont (*USA Today*, 5/14/97).

In late 1996, the American Association of Health Plans, the trade group for the nation's health maintenance organizations, sought to reduce patient concerns by issuing guidelines aimed at putting more information in the hands of consumers (*Washington Post*, 12/18/96).

In May 1997, the Association of State Medical Board Executive Directors launched an Internet site with information on doctors in Arizona, California, Massachusetts, North Carolina, and Texas. It can be reached at http://www.docboard.org (*USA Today*, 5/14/97).

9. There's A Lot Of Money To Be Made In Poverty

1993 SYNOPSIS: The Fall 1993 cover article of *Southern Exposure* magazine documents how huge national and international corporations, such as ITT, General Motors, and American Express, own and finance a growing "poverty industry" that targets low-income, blue-collar, and minority consumers for fraud, exploitation, and price gouging.

Money-making endeavors include: *Fringe banking*—pawn shops and check cashing outlets that serve low-income people, usually in urban ghettos, who don't fit into the picture at mainstream banks; *Second-mortgage companies*—making loans at 30 percent interest to pay off bills or make repairs; *Used-car dealers*—working in tandem with banks and finance companies to bilk people with "bad credit"; *Finance companies*—charging huge interest rates by acting as a lender of last resort for borrowers with limited incomes; *Rent-to-own stores*—which constitute a $3.7 billion-a-year business, charging customers about five times what they'd pay at traditional retailers; *Trade schools*—lending out federal loan money on the promise of giving usable skills to low-income students, then leaving them with no skills and a big debt; *Debt collectors*—the not-so-friendly people who badger, threaten, and coerce low-income borrowers to pay back funds regardless of the circumstances.

SOURCE: *Southern Exposure*, Fall 1993, "Poverty, Inc. Why the Poor Pay More—And Who Really Profits," by Mike Hudson, Eric Bates, Barry Yeoman, and Adam Feuerstein.

UPDATE: Profiteering from the poor apparently does not make for news in the U.S. As the authors of the *Censored* story above charged, "No one has called the 'poverty industry' what it is—a huge, multi-billion-dollar collection of companies fueled by Wall Street funding and propped up by a new veneer of corporate respectability."

Indeed, the prospect of profits to be made from the poor has encouraged some companies, after years of chasing after the haves, to start going after the have-nots, according to *Marketing News* (8/1/94): "Some marketers are learning that even those feeling the pinch have to buy the basics like everyone else."

The latest money-making endeavor to join those cited in the story above are the major banks which have instituted many new fees for banking. Steve Brobeck, executive director of the Consumer Federation of America, noting the new fee for transactions with a teller at banks like First National Bank of Chicago, Wells Fargo, and BankAmerica, said this particular fee "will clearly hurt those consumers, teenagers, the elderly, and low-income consumers who can least afford it" (*San Francisco Examiner*, 4/27/95).

10. Haiti: Drugs, Thugs, and the CIA

1993 SYNOPSIS: More than 4,000 civilians in Haiti have been killed since the 1991 bloody military coup that ousted duly-elected President Jean-Bertrand Aristide. But few Americans are aware of our secret involvement in Haitian politics.

Some of the high military officials involved in the coup have been on the CIA's payroll from "the mid-1980s at least until the 1991 coup." Further, the CIA "tried to intervene in Haiti's election with a covert action program that would have undercut the political strength" of Aristide. The aborted attempt to influence the 1988 election was authorized by then-President Ronald Reagan and the National Security Council. The program was blocked by the Senate Select Committee on Intelligence in a rare move.

Next, a confidential Drug Enforcement Agency (DEA) report revealed that Haiti is "a major transshipment point for cocaine traffickers" who are funneling drugs from Colombia and the Dominican Republic into the United States.

According to Patrick Elie, who was Aristide's anti-drug czar, Haitian police chief Lt. Col. Michel Francois is at the center of the drug trade. Francois' "attachés" reportedly have been responsible for a large number of murders and violence since the coup. Elie said he was constantly rebuffed by the CIA when he tried to alert it to the military's drug trafficking. Elie also reported how the CIA-created Haitian National Intelligence Service (NIS)—supposedly created to combat drugs—was actually involved with narcotics-trafficking, and "functioned as a political intimidation and assassination squad."

SOURCES: *The New York Times*, 11/1/93, "Key Haiti Leaders Said To Have Been In The CIA's Pay," by Tim Weiner; *Pacific News Service*, 10/20/93, "What's Behind Washington's Silence on Haiti Drug Connection?" and 11/2/93, "A Haitian Call to Arms," both by Dennis Bernstein; *San Francisco Bay Guardian*, 11/3/93, "The CIA's Haitian Connection," by Dennis Bernstein and Howard Levine; *Los Angeles Times*, 10/31/93, "CIA's Aid Plan Would Have Undercut Aristide in '87-'88," by Jim Mann.

UPDATE: On October 17, 1994, *Time* magazine revealed that Emmanuel "Toto" Constant, head of the FRAPH, a brutal gang of Haitian thugs known for murder, torture, and beatings, was on the payroll of both the CIA and the U.S. Defense Intelligence Agency. *The New York Times* reported (12/3/95) that Constant himself had confirmed he was a paid agent of the CIA. An American force of 20,000 threw out the Haitian military junta in September 1994 and paved the way for the return of Aristide in October. While the American force is long gone, U.N. peacekeepers, paid for by the United States, remain in Haiti (*Christian Science Monitor*, 9/4/96). Ironically, investigative reporter Allan Nairn revealed the "U.S. military intelligence and the CIA are still, to this day, continuing their secret work with the repressive paramilitary organization known as FRAPH" (*The Nation*, 1/8/96).

THIS MODERN WORLD by TOM TOMORROW

Panel 1:
THE SIMPSON TRIAL IS FINALLY OVER-- AND AMERICANS HAVE BEGUN TO DRAW CONCLUSIONS ABOUT ITS ULTIMATE MEANING...

ONE THING'S FOR SURE-- IT WAS THE *TRIAL OF THE CENTURY!*

{COUGH}--EXCLUDING THAT LITTLE UN-PLEASANTNESS AT *NUREMBERG*, OF COURSE?

WHERE?

Panel 2:
WE'VE LEARNED MUCH ABOUT OUR LEGAL SYS-TEM... SUCH AS THE ASTONISHING EXTREMES TO WHICH THE CONCEPT OF "REASONABLE DOUBT" CAN BE PUSHED BY A MULTI-MILLION DOLLAR DEFENSE TEAM...

LADIES AND GENTLEMEN OF THE JURY-- YOU MUST ADMIT THE *POSSIBILITY* THAT O.J. SIMPSON *COULD* HAVE BEEN *ABDUCTED BY ALIENS*--

--WHILE *ELVIS* COMMITTED THESE MURDERS!

TIP O' THE PEN (GUIN) TO THOM ZAJAC!

Panel 3:
IN HIS CLOSING STATEMENT, JOHNNIE COCHRAN SUMMARIZED THE DEFENSE'S ARGUMENT WITH A RHYMING COUPLET-- "IF IT DOESN'T FIT, YOU MUST ACQUIT"-- WHICH WAS ALMOST CERTAINLY THE RESULT OF *TEST MARKETING* AND *FOCUS GROUP* RESEARCH...

OKAY-- WHAT DO YOU THINK OF *THIS* ONE?

"IF THE GLOVE'S TOO TIGHT THEN THIS CASE *BITES!*"

Panel 4:
AT ANY RATE, THE TRIAL IS NOW *HISTORY*-- WHICH MEANS THAT THE FIRST WAVE OF O.J. NOSTALGIA SHOULD SWEEP THE COUNTRY ANY *DAY* NOW...

HEY FOLKS-- REMEMBER THE *BLOODY GLOVE?* THE *BARKING DOG?* THE *RACIST COP?* WELL, NOW YOU CAN *RE-LIVE* THOSE GOLDEN MEMORIES WITH *"THE BEST OF O.J."* -- NOT AVAILABLE IN ANY STORE!

FOR K-TEL PRO-DUCTIONS -- *I'M* STILL JOHNNIE COCHRAN IN A CAP!

THE BEST OF O.J.!

CHAPTER 19—1994

First Year of the O.J. Simpson Phenomenon

Nineteen-ninety-four was the first year of the O.J. Simpson media phenomenon, a media-hyped story that was to dominate the mainstream news agenda for three years. According to the Associated Press, the top ten news stories of the year were:

1. The murders of Nicole Brown and Ronald Goldman and the O.J. Simpson charge
2. The Republican Congressional victories in November
3. Baseball strike
4. Susan Smith drowns sons
5. Tonya Harding and the Nancy Kerrigan attack
6. Aristide's return to Haiti
7. Universal health insurance
8. The Northridge, California, earthquake
9. The tragedy in Rwanda
10. Palestinians in the Gaza Strip.

While the news media flooded America with O.J. Simpson sensationalism, a host of important domestic issues, led by critical health and environmental stories, dominated the list of overlooked news stories.

—And What Has Happened to Them Since

1. The Deadly Secrets of the Occupational Safety Agency

1994 SYNOPSIS: In the early 1980s, the National Institute for Occupational Safety and Health (NIOSH) completed 69 epidemiological studies that revealed that 240,450 American workers were exposed to hazardous materials at 258 worksites.

Many of the affected workers were unaware they were being exposed to hazardous substances (such as asbestos, silica, and uranium) that were determined in those studies to increase the risk of cancer and other serious diseases.

In 1983, NIOSH and the Health and Human Services Department's Centers for Disease Control and Prevention (CDC) concluded that NIOSH had a duty to inform workers of exposure "particularly when NIOSH is the exclusive holder of information and when there is clear evidence of a cause and effect relationship between exposure and health risk." Thus workers who learned they were at risk could undergo screening that could lead to earlier detection of cancer.

Despite the 1983 recommendations of its own scientific and ethical experts to notify exposed workers, the Reagan Administration refused to fund a $4 million pilot notification program and opposed legislation that would have required such notification.

As a result, by 1994, fewer than 30 percent of the workers covered by the studies have been notified. The Public Citizen's Health Research Group learned that NIOSH has individually notified only 71,180 of the original 240,450 workers, leaving 169,270 still in the dark about health risks from on-the-job exposure.

SOURCES: *Health Letter*, March 1994, "Unfinished Business: Occupational Safety Agency Keeps 170,000 Exposed Workers in the Dark About Risks Incurred on Job," by Peter Lurie, Sidney Wolfe, and Susan Goodwin.

UPDATE: Following publication of the original *Censored* story concerning the failure to inform workers of health hazards from the workplace, the Public Citizen's Health Research Group contacted (6/23/94) NIOSH for the latest status of notifications. Linda Rosenstock, director of NIOSH, responded (7/19/94) that worker notification had occurred or was in the process of being accomplished in 45 of the 61 studies where notification was indicated. However, NIOSH said notification was not recommended for 16 of the 61 studies (26 percent) for various reasons. Rosenstock also said NIOSH was committed to completing the notification process and that NIOSH planned to make notification an integral part of future epidemiological studies. Rosenstock added that NIOSH had not received increased funding for such notification but was doing its best to accomplish it within the limits of current funding (correspondence, Susan Goodwin, Public Citizen Health Research Group, 6/23/94, and Linda Rosenstock, Director, National Institute for Occupational Safety and Health, 7/19/96).

2. Powerful Group of Ultra-Conservatives Has Secret Plans for Your Future

1994 SYNOPSIS: In May 1981, under a tent in the backyard of political strategist Richard Viguerie's suburban Virginia home, 160 new-right political leaders celebrated their political fortunes and the election of President Ronald Reagan the previous November.

This elite group of administration officials, congressmen, industrialists, and conservative Christians—calling themselves the Council for National Policy (CNP)—launched a political federation to coordinate their own political agenda. One of their members, R.J. Rushdoony, a leader of the Christian Reconstruction movement, argues that right-thinking Christians should take "dominion" over the United States and do away with the "heresy" that is democracy.

After the public inauguration of the group, the CNP went underground. The group meets quarterly behind closed doors and is so secretive that its Washington office will neither confirm nor deny where, or even if, the group meets.

While the roster of the 500 CNP members is confidential, it is known to include former Interior Secretary James Watt, Phyllis Schlafly, Joseph Coors, Paul Weyrich (founding president of the Heritage Foundation), Jerry Falwell (Liberty Alliance), Oliver North, Senator John East (R-North Carolina), Senator Orrin Hatch (R-Utah), Senator Trent Lott (R-Mississippi), Senator Jesse Helms (R-North Carolina), Representative Bob Dornan (R-California), Iran-contra figure General John Singlaub, Richard Shoff (former leader of the KKK in Indiana), and former attorney general Edwin Meese, CNP president in 1994.

SOURCE: *In These Times*, 8/8/94, "Right-wing Confidential," by Joel Bleifuss.

UPDATE: Perhaps the most important meeting at the August 1996 Republican convention in San Diego, didn't take place in the Convention Hall but rather across the harbor on Coronado Island where the secretive Council for National Policy met. As the Memphis *Commercial Appeal* reported (8/11/96), "Observers say the Council, not the Moral majority or the Christian Coalition, is the driving force behind the growth of the religious right's influence in the Republican Party." Skip Porteous, director of the Institute for First Amendment Studies, charged, "They have the money, the machinery, the manpower, and the motivation to push their ideas as national policies, or to oppose such policies." The Council, whose membership is by invitation only, now meets secretly two or three times a year in undisclosed locations. Its members are sworn to secrecy and refuse to discuss any details of the meetings.

3. The Secret Pentagon Plan to Subsidize Defense Contractor Mergers

1994 SYNOPSIS: The Pentagon is secretly funneling taxpayer dollars to giant military contractors to help them grow even larger. This extraordinary Pentagon ploy to pay defense contractors billions of dollars to underwrite expenses connected with acquisitions and mergers was approved without any announcement in 1993.

According to Deputy Defense Secretary John Deutch, the unprecedented payment plan will save taxpayers money. However, David Cooper, of the General Accounting Office, said that while no specific savings could be seen, the new policy could involve "several billions of dollars" in payments to defense contractors.

Norman Augustine, chairman of Martin Marietta, a giant billion-dollar defense contractor, argued that the federal government would reap lower costs from defense mergers over the long term. Under the plan, Augustine's company would get $270 million from the Pentagon to cover expenses related to the purchase of a subsidiary from General Electric. Martin Marietta already quietly received a $60 million payment from the Pentagon to buy a General Dynamics subsidiary.

It was Martin Marietta's Augustine who originally persuaded Defense Secretary William Perry and Deutch to approve the money-for-merger plan. Both Perry and Deutch were on the Martin Marietta payroll before joining the Clinton Administration.

SOURCE: *Newsday*, 7/28/94, "Flak for Defense Merger," by Patrick J. Sloyan.

UPDATE: As information about the "money-for-merger" program spread, the program was also called "payoffs for layoffs" and Congress started to argue over the appropriateness of the program. By July 22, 1996, some 32 defense contractors were lined up to receive taxpayer funds under the program, with the newly merged Lockheed-Martin Corporation leading the way by asking for $1.6 billion (*Asbury Park Press*, 7/22/96). Despite the efforts of Representative Christopher H. Smith (R-New Jersey) and Senator Tom Harkin (D-Iowa), the House and Senate conference committee on the defense budget agreed to continue the controversial practice of paying the costs of mergers (*Wall Street Journal*, 9/25/96). President Clinton subsequently signed the defense bill that included billions of dollars more than he requested which had been added by the Republicans. Not surprisingly, following the re-election of Clinton and a Republican Congress, investment analysts started touting defense stocks as attractive buys.

4. Poisoning the Public with Toxic Incinerators

1994 SYNOPSIS: By the latter part of the 1980s, the U.S. Environmental Protection Agency (EPA) understood two very important facts that should have fundamentally altered the nation's waste disposal policy.

First, government officials knew incineration produced dioxin as a byproduct. Dioxin is one of the most potent, toxic, and carcinogenic chemicals known to science.

Second, EPA scientists knew dioxin accumulates through the food chain much like the banned pesticide DDT accumulates in the environment. Dioxin is a persistent substance that stores easily in the tissues of plants and animals.

Despite this information, incineration has rapidly grown throughout the country as the "profitable answer" for disposal of the nation's stockpile of toxic waste and garbage. In fact, incineration does not destroy the waste, it transforms it. Dioxin, lead, mercury, polychlorinated biphenyls (PCBs), and other air emissions from incinerator smokestacks are widely dispersed, and like acid rain, result in uncontrolled pollution of the surrounding water, soil, and farmland.

Examples cited by critics include the infamous WTI incinerator in East Liverpool, Ohio, and the LWD incinerator in Calvert City, Kentucky.

SOURCE: *Government Accountability Project*, September 1994, "Poisoning Ourselves: The Impact of Incineration on Food and Human Health, An Executive Summary," by Mick G. Harrison, Esq.

UPDATE: Despite earlier indications of high amounts of dioxin in ash samples and the protests of environmentalists, the LWD incinerator at Calvert City, Kentucky, is still in operation. The WTI incinerator in East Liverpool, Ohio, considered to be one of the largest hazardous waste incinerators in the country, also continues to operate despite ongoing protests. In 1995, the plant burned 53,000 tons of industrial waste (*Columbus Dispatch*, 11/3/96). For an insight into the environmental costs of waste disposal, including toxic incinerator emissions, please see "Mankind Must Conserve Sustainable Materials" in *USA Today Magazine*, July 1995. The authors, researchers with the Worldwatch Institute, charge, "In the U.S., where national policy officially favors waste reduction, reuse, and recycling over landfilling and incineration, actual practice has been the reverse. Local communities have spent billions of dollars to finance construction of disposal facilities, while cheaper, more environmentally sound waste management options have received little funding."

Please also see update of "Biological Weapons," #10, 1981.

5. EPA Retreats on Ozone Crisis

1994 SYNOPSIS: Since the United States banned chlorofluorocarbon (CFC) aerosols in the late 1970s, increasing evidence has revealed that both the destruction of the ozone layer and the resulting dangers to human health and the ecosystem are far more serious than scientists had first recognized.

The ozone hole over Antarctica has continued to grow every year since its discovery in 1985 and damage to the ozone layer over heavily populated areas of the Northern Hemisphere has also been increasing rapidly. Scientists recorded all-time low levels of ozone over the United States in 1993.

The ultraviolet rays that penetrate a weakened ozone layer have been linked to increased cataracts, skin cancer, genetic damage, and infectious diseases among humans. Meanwhile the Clinton Administration has been dragging its feet on protecting the atmospheric ozone layer. This approach will encourage other industrial countries to stall on their own CFC phase-outs and puts the administration in a weaker position to argue for an accelerated phase-out of CFCs in the developing countries where CFC production is soaring.

DuPont, the giant chemical firm which developed the first industrial CFC, had planned to halt CFC production at the end of 1994. Yet, in late 1993, the EPA asked DuPont to keep making CFCs until 1996. The EPA defended its decision as a "consumer protection" measure that will make it easier for car owners to recharge their old air conditioners which use CFCs as a cooling agent. However, ozone-safe, environmentally sound cooling technologies already are available.

SOURCE: *In These Times*, 1/24/94, "Full of Holes: Clinton's Retreat on the Ozone Crisis," by David Moberg.

UPDATE: In the fall of 1996, the ozone hole over Antarctica widened to a record 7.7 million square miles, nearly the combined area of the U.S. and Canada (*Chicago Tribune*, 11/3/96).

On August 18, 1995, *The Detroit News* confirmed that DuPont had voluntarily chosen to cease CFC production in 1994 but the EPA, reportedly with some White House involvement, persuaded them to wait another year. Nonetheless, as required by the Clean Air Act, the production of chlorofluorocarbons officially ended in the United States on New Year's Day 1996. The *Heating, Piping, Air Conditioning* trade journal noted (January 1996) the timing was quite appropriate since the 1995 Nobel Prize in chemistry went to three scientists who developed the ozone depletion theory in 1994. However, no sooner did the ban take place than CFCs became readily available on the black market. *The New York Times* reported (11/10/96) that CFC contraband was running second only to marijuana in U.S. Customs seizures at the Mexican border near San Ysidro, California.

Nonetheless, in 1996, for the first time, scientists detected a decline in the amounts of a wide range of atmospheric chemicals that damage the ozone layer. The decline was attributed to the 1987 Montreal Protocol, an agreement to slash CFC production and use, signed by the United States and 22 other nations (*San Francisco Examiner*, 5/31/96).

6. 1947 AEC Memo Reveals Why Human Radiation Experiments were Censored

1994 SYNOPSIS: As the secrecy ban is finally lifted, the unethical, immoral, and illegal Cold War radiation experiments on unsuspecting humans by the Department of Defense are exposed by a most remarkable document that has emerged virtually unnoticed.

Dated April 17, 1947, an Atomic Energy Commission (AEC) memorandum, stamped "SECRET" and addressed to the attention of a Dr. Fidler, at the AEC in Oak Ridge, Tennessee, reads in part as follows: *"Subject: MEDICAL EXPERIMENTS ON HUMANS*

"1. It is desired that no document be released which refers to experiments with humans and might have adverse effect on public opinion or result in legal suits. Documents covering such work should be classified 'secret.'"

The memorandum was issued over the name of O.G. Haywood, Jr., Colonel, Corps of Engineers. Apparently it was effective, for it was not until November 15, 1993, 46 years later, when *The Albuquerque Tribune* (circulation 35,000) broke the story which was then catapulted into the national headlines by the forthright admissions and initiatives of Secretary of Energy Hazel O'Leary. Author Eileen Welsome's three-part investigative series for the *Tribune* won her a Pulitzer Prize.

Ironically, as Geoffrey Sea, author and radiological health physicist, points out, documentation of the inhumane program was massive, solid, and publicly available, as early as 1986. But it was only after the disclosures by a small daily newspaper and Secretary O'Leary—with all the victims dead and most of the perpetrators retired—that the news media put it on the national agenda.

SOURCES: *Secrecy & Government Bulletin*, March 1994, "Protecting Government Against the Public," by Steven Aftergood; *Columbia Journalism Review*, March/April 1994, "The Radiation Story No One Would Touch," by Geoffrey Sea.

UPDATE: The Gannett News Service confirmed (12/14/94) the discovery of the AEC memo cited above and reported how AEC researchers decided in the 1940s and '50s not to publish anything relating to the radiation experiments. One AEC researcher in 1948 wrote, "It appears almost impossible to rewrite it in an acceptable manner, which would not jeopardize our public relations."

An incredible internal Veterans Administration memo, written on May 13, 1959, revealed the concerns about publicizing the nuclear medicine research: "It was felt unwise to publicize unduly the probable adverse effects of exposure to radioactive materials. The use of nuclear energy at this time was so sensitive that unfavorable reaction might have jeopardized future developments in that field."

In what probably is the first of many settlements, under a draft legal settlement, the families of 12 of the thousands involved in the experiments will receive a total of $4.8 million and an official apology (Associated Press, 10/24/96).

Please also see update of "Human Radiation," #8, 1986.

7. 60 Billion Pounds of Fish Wasted Annually

1994 SYNOPSIS: While the world's oceans are almost totally fished out and while millions of people starve, the world's fishing fleets waste about 60 billion pounds of fish and seafood every year—enough for 120 billion meals.

Since 1979, New England cod, haddock, and yellowtail flounder have declined 70 percent; South Atlantic grouper and snapper, 80 percent; Atlantic bluefin tuna, 90 percent. More than 200 separate salmon spawning runs have vanished from the Pacific Northwest. The United Nation's Food and Agriculture Organization reported in April 1994 that roughly 60 percent of the fish populations they monitor are fully exploited or depleted.

As large-scale fishing technologies have taken over the world's oceans, they have become less and less selective in their catch. Fish too small to be taken and species not legally fished are caught, and then thrown overboard to die. Often the catch is tossed overboard because it is too small or too large to be processed on the factory trawlers dragging large, bag-like nets that scoop up both wanted and unwanted species.

Ironically, the federal government's efforts to manage the catch—such as limiting the seasons for different species of fish—has instead led to incredible waste, unsafe fishing practices, and economic chaos for the industry.

SOURCE: *Mother Jones*, July/August 1994, "Special Report: A Farewell To Fish?", by Peter Steinhart, Hal Bernton, Brad Matsen, Ray Troll, and Deborah Cramer.

UPDATE: The Charleston *Post Courier*, in an extensive three-part historic overview of the fishing industry, published June 24, 1996, reported, "The

United Nations says 13 of the world's 17 fishing zones are depleted or in steep decline. Never in human history have the waters been fished so heavily or efficiently." From the South Carolina coast, to the seas off New England, to the Gulf of Mexico, and up the west coast to Alaska, there are simply too many boats hunting for too few fish. The incredible waste and economic chaos for the fishing industry, warned about in the *Censored* story above, have already come to pass.

8. The Return of Tuberculosis

1994 SYNOPSIS: Tuberculosis (TB), thought to be a disease of the past, has surged back with a vengeance and now kills more people than any other infectious or communicable disease in the world—despite the fact it is curable and the costs are not prohibitive.

Today, the reemergence of tuberculosis threatens more people than AIDS, cholera, dengue fever, and other infectious diseases combined. In 1993, TB killed 2.7 million people around the world; it infected another 8.1 million people; and an estimated one-third of the world's population, or 1.7 billion people, were infected but had not yet developed the disease. In the United States, the U.S. Centers for Disease Control and Prevention (CDC) reported 26,000 cases of TB in 1992, an increase of nearly 20 percent from 1985.

By the year 2000, the global incidence of TB alone is expected to increase to 10.2 million cases per year, an increase of 36 percent over 1990's 7.5 million cases. Overall, tuberculosis deaths are predicted to increase by one-sixth, to 3.5 million by the year 2000, killing a total of 30 million people in this decade alone.

SOURCE: *World Watch*, July/August 1994, "Why Don't We Stop Tuberculosis?", by Anne E. Platt.

UPDATE: *Maclean's* (9/9/96) cited a World Health Organization (WHO) study that reported tuberculosis is now an epidemic of unprecedented proportions—the single most deadly infectious disease in the world. In 1995, "TB killed almost three million people—more than in any year during a global epidemic at the turn of the century." According to the WHO report, one-third of the world's population now carries tuberculosis bacteria, and at current rates as many as 500 million people will become sick from it in the next 50 years. Even worse, according to an international study, headquartered at the Harvard University School of Public Health, research for TB, pneumonia, and diarrheal diseases combined amount to a minuscule 0.2 percent of total health research and development funding worldwide, but account for nearly 20 percent of the global disease burden (*Los Angeles Times*, 9/16/96).

9. The Pentagon's Mysterious HAARP Project

1994 SYNOPSIS: The Pentagon's mysterious HAARP project, now under construction at an isolated Air Force facility near Gakona, Alaska, marks the first step toward creating the world's most powerful "ionospheric heater." When completed, the project will transmit a beam of high-frequency energy into the ionosphere, 35 miles to 500 miles above the earth.

The High Frequency Active Auroral Research Project (HAARP), a joint effort of the Air Force and the Navy, is the latest in a series of little-known Department of Defense (DOD) "active ionospheric experiments."

Internal HAARP documents state, "From a DOD point of view, the most exciting and challenging" part of the experiment is "its potential to *control* ionospheric processes" for military objectives. Scientists envision using the system's powerful 2.8-10 megahertz (MHz) beam to burn "holes" in the ionosphere and "create an artificial lens" in the sky that could focus large bursts of electromagnetic energy "to higher altitudes...than is presently possible."

For a project whose backers hail it as a major scientific feat, HAARP has remained extremely low-profile—almost unknown to most Alaskans and the rest of the country. HAARP surfaced publicly in Alaska in the spring of 1993 when the Federal Aviation Administration (FAA) began advising commercial pilots on how to avoid the large amount of intentional (and some unintentional) electromagnetic radiation that HAARP would generate. Despite protests of FAA engineers and Alaska bush pilots, the final Environmental Impact Statement gave HAARP the green light.

Scientists, environmentalists, and native people are concerned that HAARP's electronic transmitters could harm people, endanger wildlife, and trigger unforeseen environmental impacts.

SOURCE: *Earth Island Journal*, Fall 1994, "Project HAARP: The Military's Plan to Alter the Ionosphere," by Clare Zickuhr and Gar Smith.

UPDATE: Despite critics and local public concern, testing of the HAARP prototype started in April 1995 (*Alaska Journal of Commerce*, 10/9/95). When completed, the HAARP project will consist of 360 72-foot antennas near Gakona, northeast of Anchorage. HAARP program director John Heckscher assures critics that "although HAARP is being managed by the Air Force and Navy, it is purely a scientific research facility that poses no threat to potential adversaries and has no value as a military target."

Nonetheless, the authoritative *Jane's Defence Weekly* reported (4/1/95) potential military applications for HAARP including its use for communicating with submerged submarines and for over-the-horizon surveillance purposes for the detection of cruise missiles and low observables. It added, "Bathing orbiting spacecraft or sub-orbital missiles with accelerated electrons produced by HAARP could damage electronic components, achieving a 'soft kill.'"

10. News Media Mask Spousal Violence in the "Language of Love"

1994 SYNOPSIS: A man guns down his former wife and her new boyfriend; reporters call it a "love triangle."

A man shoots and kills several co-workers, including a woman who refused to date him; the press reports a "tragedy of spurned love."

A man kidnaps his estranged wife, rapes her, accuses her of an imaginary affair, and chokes her to death; a reporter writes that he "made love to his wife," then strangled her when "overcome with jealous passion."

A New York City cop drags his ex-girlfriend out of police headquarters where she works, shoots her four times, killing her, then kills himself; the *New York Post* headlines it: "Tragedy of a Lovesick Cop."

Ann Jones, journalism professor and author of *Next Time, She'll be Dead: Battering and How to Stop It*, charges that the media are part of the problem by masking violence in the language of love. She says, "This slipshod reporting has real consequences in the lives of real men and women. It affirms a batterer's most common excuse for assault: 'I did it because I love you so much.'"

Noting that every 12 seconds in this country, some man batters his current or former wife or girlfriend, Jones says that battering is currently the leading cause of injury to American women, sending more than one million to doctors' offices or emergency rooms every year.

According to Jones, it also drives women into the streets with a reported 50 percent of homeless women and kids fleeing from male violence; and it figures in one quarter of all suicide attempts by women and one half of all suicide attempts by black women. According to the American Medical Association, it also injures fetuses in utero: 37 percent of all obstetric patients are battered during pregnancy.

SOURCE: *USA Today*, 3/10/94, "Crimes Against Women: Media Part of Problem for Masking Violence in the Language of Love," by Ann Jones.

UPDATE: Ann Jones, author of the *Censored* story above, told Project Censored that as long as we "view lethal assault as romantic, men literally get away with murder. And so does the criminal justice system that refuses to hold them to account." In the September 1996 issue of *The American Lawyer*, Lucy N. Friedman, executive director of Victim Services for New York City, said, "It is encouraging that some jurisdictions are finally beginning to prosecute domestic violence as a serious public crime." But, she pointed out, the new strategies—mandatory arrest, more aggressive prosecution (with or without the victim's cooperation), special courts, and police training—are still not always effective. Friedman concluded, "We need a serious, long-term commitment to make the criminal justice system responsive to the legitimate fears and needs of battered women. And a multifaceted, coordinated community effort to change society's beliefs and actions." And this effort should include the national news media.

CHAPTER 20—1995

The Unreported Problem with Telecommunications Deregulation

It took the deaths of 168 people in the tragic bombing in Oklahoma City for the mainstream media to discover the dangers of domestic terrorism. According to the Associated Press, the top ten news stories of the year were:

1. Terrorist bombing of the Alfred P. Murrah Federal Building in Oklahoma City
2. The Balkans conflict
3. The O.J. Simpson trial
4. The assassination of Yitzhak Rabin
5. The Kobe, Japan, earthquake
6. Republicans' Contract with America
7. Tokyo subway poison gas attack
8. Rescue of USAF Pilot Scott O'Grady
9. Fatal Chicago heatwave
10. Susan Smith life sentence.

And while the national news media spoke glowingly of the benefits of telecommunications deregulation in 1995, it failed to report its negative impact on the public's right to know.

THE TOP TEN CENSORED STORIES OF 1995

—And What Has Happened to Them Since

1. Telecommunications Deregulation: Closing Up America's "Marketplace of Ideas"

1995 SYNOPSIS: America's "marketplace of ideas," upon which our democracy rests, began shutting its doors in the summer of 1995. The harbinger of the bad news for the public was aptly titled the Telecommunications Deregulation Bill, which moved through both houses of Congress. As the name implies, the bill eliminates virtually all regulation of the United States communication industry.

As tends to be the case with most anti-consumer legislation, the bill stealthily moved under the guise of "encouraging competition"—but will, in reality, have the opposite effect of creating huge new concentrations of media power.

The most troubling aspect of the bill allows easing—and outright elimination—of current anti-trust regulations. In what *The New York Times* described as "a dazzling display of political influence," the nation's broadcast networks scored big in the House version of the bill by successfully getting the limits on ownership eased so that any individual company can control television stations serving up to 50 percent of the country. The Senate version of the bill provides for a more modest 35 percent coverage.

The legislation also dismantles current regulations limiting the number of radio stations that can be owned by a single company. Previously no one single company could own more than 40 stations.

It also would lift the current FCC ban on joint ownership of a broadcast radio or TV license in the same market—allowing a single company to have 100 percent control over the three primary sources of news in a community.

Most disturbing was the major media's almost total avoidance of the dangers of "monopoly ownership" in their coverage of the bill's progress in Congress.

SOURCE: Consumer Project on Technology, 7/14/95, "Federal Telecommunications Legislation: Impact on Media Concentration," *TAP-INFO*, an Internet Newsletter, by Ralph Nader, James Love, and Andrew Saindon.

UPDATE: After the Telecommunications Act of 1996 was passed by Congress and signed by President Clinton in February 1996, some representatives of the news media suddenly started to examine the implications of media monopolization. *The Baltimore Sun* (4/3/96) reported that while the legislation provides for more competition among the television, telephone, and computer industries, "It also opens the door to unprecedented consolidation." It quoted media critic Ben Bagdikian warning the media giants have gone a long way to achieve their goal "to control the origination of content and the national delivery system." Nicholas Johnson, professor of communications law at the University of Iowa, charged, "We used to have businesses, however awful and crooked and greedy, run by people who understood that business, whether making shoes or making newspapers. Now it seems everything is run by a bunch of 14-year-old financiers driven by the bottom line. When it happens in the media, it means democracy fails."

The trade journal *Telephony* (6/17/96) predicted the future of the telecommunications industry following deregulation by comparing it with what happened after the airline industry was deregulated in 1978. It predicted, "The telecommunications industry will pare itself from ten or more major players to about three or so; mergers will lead to cultural turmoil as well as union and employee unrest, especially in the local and interexchange mix; workers in the industry will be paid less, work harder, and have fewer unique benefits and perquisites; and prices will fall for end users in some cases, but customers in some parts of the country will be no better off when the telecommunications revolution is over than they are today."

The prediction by *Telephony* of a takeover by a few big players was quickly fulfilled. The four largest corporate mergers announced in 1996, an all-time record year for mergers, were all telecommunications companies. They were: 1. Bell Atlantic-Nynex, $21.34 billion; 2. British Telecommunications-MCI, $21.27 billion; 3. SBC Communications-Pacific Telesis, $16.52 billion; and 4. WorldCom-MFS Communications, $13.56 billion.

Not surprisingly, Neil Hickey, contributing editor to *Columbia Journalism Review*, in a year-later analysis of the Telecommunications Act (January/February 1997), charged, "The stage is set, more so than ever in U.S. media history, for corporate bosses to suppress unwelcome news and otherwise meddle in editorial decisions." In fact, less than a year after President Clinton signed the telecommunications bill, C-Span, the nation's window on Congress, reported it was being removed from millions of homes by conglomerates selling its cable location to the highest bidder (*The New York Times*, 2/6/97).

In February 1997, the World Trade Organization announced an international agreement to open up telecommunications markets, paving the way for worldwide phone service competition. To foster competition, the agreement eliminated telecommunications monopolies. Ironically, they were not the kind of monopolies we're concerned with in the United States, but "inefficient, state-run monopolies" in Third World countries.

2. The Budget Does Not Have to be Balanced on the Backs of the Poor

1995 SYNOPSIS: Congress could go a long way toward balancing the budget by 2002 without slashing Medicare, Medicaid, education, and social welfare. In fact, the Washington-based Center for the Study of Responsive Law identified 153 federal programs that benefit wealthy corporations and cost taxpayers $167.2 billion annually. For comparative purposes, federal support for food stamps, housing aid, and child nutrition costs $50 billion a year.

An analysis by *Public Citizen* reveals how Congress could balance the budget by cutting "aid to dependent corporations." The federal budget and tax codes are rife with huge subsidies to business—the sums involved make traditional "pork barrel" spending look like chicken feed.

The beneficiaries of corporate welfare escape the Congressional budget axe through a variety of tactics including direct and indirect subsidies, bailouts, below-market and guaranteed governmental loans, liability limitations, tax loopholes, favorable trade quotas, and gifts of governmental intellectual property for private use.

SOURCE: *Public Citizen*, July/August 1995, "Cut Corporate Welfare Not Medicare," by John Canham-Clyne.

UPDATE: The 1997 federal budget was not balanced on the backs of the poor; nor was it balanced by eliminating huge subsidies for corporate welfare. It just was not balanced. In late September 1996, White House and congressional negotiators agreed on a compromise spending bill to avoid the impasse that led to two government shutdowns over the budget in 1995. (Knight-Ridder News Service, 9/29/96). Finally, on July 31, 1997, Congress and the Clinton Administration celebrated a 1998 budget that reputedly would lead to a balanced federal budget in 2002. An analysis by Center on Budget and Policy Priorities concluded that the richest one percent of taxpayers will receive more than 32 percent of the tax cuts; the 20 percent in the median income category will get 5.9 percent; those in the lowest 40 percent will receive virtually nothing (Scripps-McClatchy News Service, 8/2/97).

Please also see update of "Corporate Welfare," #4, 1993.

3. Child Labor in the U.S. is Worse Today Than During the 1930s

1995 SYNOPSIS: Every day, children across America are working in environments detrimental to their social and educational development, their health, and even their lives.

In 1992, a National Institute of Occupational Safety and Health (NIOSH) report found that 670 youths aged 16 to 17 were killed on the job from 1980 to 1989. Seventy percent of these deaths and injuries involved violations of state labor laws and the Fair Labor Standards Act (FLSA), the federal law that prohibits youths under age 18 from working in hazardous occupations. A second NIOSH report found that more than 64,100 children went to the emergency room for work-related injuries in 1992.

These numbers are a conservative estimate since even the best figures underestimate the number of working children by 25 to 30 percent. As of yet, there is no comprehensive national data collection system that accurately tracks the number of working youths, nor their occupations, where they work, or how many of them are injured or killed on the job.

The patchwork of inefficient data collection systems fails to monitor the total number, much less the well-being, of youth in the workplace. Enforcement of the FLSA is lax. Cultural beliefs about the worth of work for children are strong. Also, various PACs lobby successfully to keep child labor laws from being strengthened, and, in many cases, to weaken existing laws.

"Child labor today is at a point where violations are greater than at any point during the 1930s," said Jeffrey Newman of the National Child Labor Coalition, an advocacy group founded in 1904.

SOURCE: *Southern Exposure*, Fall/Winter 1995, "Working in Harm's Way," by Ron Nixon.

UPDATE: In 1996, the National Institute for Occupational Safety and Health (NIOSH) issued its most comprehensive analysis of work-related injuries and illnesses associated with child labor (*Morbidity and Mortality Weekly Report*, 6/7/96). The analysis, based on 1993 data for workers under 18 years of age, reveals that "Substantial numbers of persons aged under 18 sustain work-related injuries and illnesses each year." In 1993, workers under 18 incurred an estimated 21,620 injuries and illnesses involving lost work days. They were employed most frequently by eating and drinking establishments, grocery stores, nursing and personal-care facilities, and department stores. Approximately 70 young people die from work-related injuries each year. However, NIOSH points out these figures are probably an underestimate because they exclude some categories, such as self-employed workers, farms with less than 11 employees, private households, and government employees.

4. The Privatization of the Internet

1995 SYNOPSIS: You may not have noticed, but the Internet, one of the hottest news stories of 1995, was essentially sold last year. The federal government has been gradually transferring the backbone of the U.S. portion of the global computer network to companies such as IBM and MCI as part of a larger plan to privatize cyberspace. But the crucial step was taken on April 30, 1994, when the National Science Foundation shut down its part of the Internet, which began in the 1970s as a Defense Department communications tool. That left the corporate giants in charge.

Remarkably, this sellout of cyberspace has attracted almost no protest or media attention, in contrast to every other development in cyberspace such as the Communications Decency Act and cyberporn. What hasn't been discussed is the public's right to free speech in cyberspace. What is obvious is that speech in cyberspace will not be free if we allow big business to control the Net.

There already are warning signs about efforts to limit on-line debate. In 1990, the Prodigy on-line service started something of a revolt among some of its members when it decided to raise rates for those sending large volumes of e-mail. When some subscribers protested, Prodigy not only read and censored their messages, but it summarily dismissed the dissenting members from the service.

THIS MODERN WORLD   by TOM TOMORROW

HEY KIDS! IT'S TIME FOR ANOTHER EDITION OF *THIS MODERN WORLD'S* INCREDIBLY HIP, IN-THE-KNOW GUIDE TO *WHAT'S HAPPENING* -- WITH YOUR HOSTS, *BETTY* AND *BIFF!*

WHAT IT *IS!*

YOU *GO,* GIRL!

THIS WEEK: THE *INTER-NET*... IT'S *HAPPENING!*

THERE ARE *ALL KINDS* OF MAGAZINE STORIES! AND MANY AUTHORS HAVE RECEIVED *ENOR-MOUS BOOK ADVANCES* TO DISCUSS *THEIR* ADVENTURES ON THIS *NEW FRONTIER!*

A CONVERSATION ABOUT STAR TREK

The True Story of an Author Who "Logged On" to America Online

Two ways cyberspace speech already is less free than speech in a traditional public forum: First, cyberspeech is expensive, both in terms of initial outlay for hardware and recurring on-line charges; second, speech on the Net is subject to the whim of private censors who are not accountable to the First Amendment.

SOURCE: *The Nation*, 7/3/95, "Keeping On-line Speech Free: Street Corners in Cyberspace," by Andrew L. Shapiro.

UPDATE: In a comprehensive, well-documented six-part series on communications, the *Monthly Review* (July 1996) analyzes the origin and privatization of the Internet. In "Privatization of Telecommunications," the *Review* notes how "until a few years ago, the Internet was largely funded by the National Science Foundation, NASA, other government agencies, and academic institutions that pay for access to the Internet...The Internet today is almost entirely funded by private enterprises such as MCI, AT&T, and Bolt, Baranck, and Newman (BBN), along with other 'network service providers.'" Now the government is essentially just another commercial customer.

The *Review* also suggests that the Internet is now being "transformed into an electronic shopping mall and sales catalog." It reports that "tracking the nature of the Internet use generally can be done by watching the 'domains' into which usage fits." By 1994, .com (commercial) had replaced .edu (education) as the most common domain name. Finally, a January 1996 survey by Network Wizards shows 9.4 million host computers connected to the Internet, of which .com was easily the single largest domain, larger than academic (.edu) and government (.gov) sources combined.

A major victory for free speech on the Internet was realized on June 26, 1997, when the U.S. Supreme Court declared the Communications Decency Act to be unconstitutional (*The New York Times*, 6/27/97).

5. U.S. Pushes Nuclear Pact But Spends Billions to Add Bang to Nukes

1995 SYNOPSIS: Even as the United States urged the rest of the world to indefinitely extend a treaty requiring signatories to work toward elimination of nuclear weapons, the U.S. Department of Energy planned a multibillion-dollar project to resume production of tritium—a radioactive gas used to enhance the explosive power of nuclear warheads.

Apparently unfazed by the hypocrisy of such an effort, the only decision not yet made as the year drew to a close was what kind of facility the Energy Department plans to build and where it plans to build it.

The choice is between a huge particle accelerator, using theoretically workable but untested technology, and a nuclear reactor, which would be the first reactor ordered in the U.S. since the 1979 Three Mile Island nuclear accident.

Either choice involves immense political, financial, environmental, and national security risks, yet the American public is little aware of the enormity of the decision to be made.

Many officials in the Clinton Administration are averse to nuclear power and do not want the federal government to sponsor construction of a reactor. But many career staff members in the Energy Department and the Pentagon have long supported the nuclear industry and favor the reactor method of producing the tritium wanted for the weapons program.

THIS MODERN WORLD   by TOM TOMORROW

The American public deserves to be made aware of the critical issues involved and a third option: not to produce the tritium to add more bang to America's nuclear warheads.

SOURCE: *Washington Post*, 5/1/95, "U.S. Seeks Arms Ingredient As It Pushes Nuclear Pact," and 5/28/95, "House Bill Would Order Nuclear Reactor As New Source of Tritium," both by Thomas W. Lippman.

UPDATE: Even as the United States continued to urge the rest of the world to eliminate their nuclear weapons, in September 1996, the U.S. Department of Energy (DOE) announced an experimental program, potentially worth three billion dollars, to use a linear accelerator to produce tritium—the radioactive gas used to enhance the explosive power of nuclear warheads. The *San Diego Union-Tribune* (9/10/96) reported the DOE named Burns and Roe Enterprises Inc. of Oradell, New Jersey, as prime contractor for the demonstration program. Given the hypocrisy of enhancing nuclear weapons power while calling for nuclear weapon disarmament, some groups, including the Physicians for Social Responsibility, have challenged the need to produce any tritium.

Please also see update of "U.S. Against the World," #4, 1992.

6. Radical Plan From Newt Gingrich's Think Tank to Gut FDA

1995 SYNOPSIS: The Food and Drug Administration (FDA), sometimes criticized in the past for being too cozy with corporations, is now under attack for exactly the opposite reason. A powerful bloc of critics in the drug indus-

ONE OF THE UGLIEST *HISTORICAL* EXAMPLES OF CORPORATE MALFEASANCE IS PERSONIFIED BY IN-DUSTRIAL ICON *HENRY FORD*...A VIRULENT ANTI-SEMITE AND LONG-TIME ADMIRER OF ADOLF HITLER, FORD ACTUALLY SUPPLIED VEHICLES TO THE NAZIS *DURING* WORLD WAR II (THROUGH A BRANCH OF HIS COMPANY IN VICHY ALGIERS)...

FORD IS ALSO SAID TO HAVE SENT HITLER 50,000 REICHMARKS EACH YEAR ON HIS *BIRTHDAY*...

"DEAR ADOLF--YOU'RE NOT GETTING OLDER--YOU'RE GETTING *BETTER*!"

THAT HENRY--ALWAYS SO *THOUGHTFUL*... Happy Birthday

IN SHORT, THE SANITIZED PUBLIC FACE OF CORPORATE AMERICA HAS OFTEN MASKED SOME PRETTY UNPLEAS-ANT TRUTHS...WHICH IS WHY REVELATIONS THAT TEX-ACO EXECUTIVES USED RACIAL SLURS IN PRIVATE LEAD *US* TO ASK ONE SIMPLE QUESTION: IS ANYONE ACTUALLY *SURPRISED* BY THIS..?

WHAT? TOP OIL EXECS WERE LESS THAN COMPLETELY EN-LIGHTENED, SOCIALLY CON-SCIOUS INDIVIDUALS?

GOSH--I ALSO HEAR THERE'S NO *TOOTH FAIRY*!

EXCUSE ME? AND WHO EXACTLY DO YOU THINK USED TO LEAVE THOSE QUARTERS UNDER MY PIL-LOW, MISTER SMARTY PANTS?

try has joined hands with the Republican Congress and together they are pushing to overhaul the FDA. These critics claim the FDA is too tough on drug companies, unnecessarily inhibits innovation, and delays approval of new drugs and medical devices.

Leading the charge in Congress is Speaker of the House Newt Gingrich, who labeled the FDA the "number-one job killer" in the country. Gingrich's Progress & Freedom Foundation has a radical plan to privatize much of the FDA's supervision of drugs and medical devices.

If enacted, the Progress & Freedom Foundation's plan will place responsibility for drug development, testing, and review in the hands of private firms hired by the drug companies themselves, while retaining a weakened FDA to rubber-stamp their recommendations. Additionally, the plan would limit the liability of drug companies that sell dangerous drugs to the public.

SOURCE: *Mother Jones*, September/October 1995, "Agency Under Attack," by Leslie Weiss.

UPDATE: *Bioworld Today*, an industry trade journal, warned its readers (6/19/96) that "industry advocates hoping for passage of FDA reform legislation this year might be advised to start praying for a miracle." Any such prayers went unanswered, at least for the time being. Despite the efforts of Senate Majority Leader Trent Lott and House Commerce Committee chairman Representative Tom Bliley, the 104th Congress failed to approve Newt Gingrich's Draconian plan for gutting the Food and Drug Administration.

7. Russia Injects Earth With Nuke Waste

1995 SYNOPSIS: For more than three decades, the Soviet Union secretly pumped billions of gallons of atomic waste directly into the Earth and, according to Russian scientists, the practice continues today.

The scientists said Moscow had injected about half of all the nuclear waste it ever produced into the ground at three widely dispersed sites, all thoroughly wet and all near major rivers. The three sites are at Dimitrovgrad near the Volga River, Tomsk near the Ob River, and Krasnoyarsk on the Yenisei River. The Volga flows into the Caspian Sea and the Ob and Yenisei flow into the Arctic Ocean.

The injections violate the accepted rules of nuclear waste disposal that require it to be isolated in impermeable containers for thousands of years.

The Russian scientists claim their practice is safe because the wastes have been injected under layers of shale and clay, which in theory cut them off from Earth's surface.

However, the wastes at one site already have leaked beyond the expected range and "spread a great distance," the Russians said. They did not say whether the distance was meters or kilometers or whether the poison had reached the surface.

The amount of radioactivity injected by the Russians is up to three billion curies. By comparison, the accident at the Chernobyl nuclear power plant released about 50 million curies of radiation and the accident at Three Mile Island discharged about 50 curies.

The Russians are now working with the U.S. Department of Energy to try to better predict how far and fast the radioactive waste is likely to spread.

SOURCE: *The New York Times*, 11/21/94, "Poison in the Earth: A Special Report; Nuclear Roulette for Russia: Burying Uncontained Waste," by William J. Broad.

UPDATE: On November 30, 1994, shortly after *The New York Times* story cited above appeared, the *Kansas City Star* reported that "American scientists recently were shocked to learn that Russians secretly have injected much of their atomic waste directly into the ground for years." They claimed "this cavalier, on-the-cheap method is not used by the U.S. nuclear industry" and noted that a "spokesman for the Nuclear Energy Institute in Washington said the industry would never pursue injecting atomic waste into the Earth."

What these scientists and others have conveniently forgotten is that the United States already has injected the Earth with nuclear waste in a process known as hydrofracture. The *Knoxville News-Sentinel* (11/22/94) reported that hydrofracture was a type of nuclear waste injection used at Oak Ridge National Laboratory for about two decades, beginning in the 1960s. It added that Oak Ridge stopped injecting the Earth in the early 1980s after problems developed during a rapid series of waste operations: "There was evidence of possible migration of some radioactive pollutants in the underground formation."

Ironically, Evgeniy Mikerin, a leader of Russia's nuclear weapons program, was promoting its deep-well injection of nuclear waste process to the U.S. as a solution to our waste problem, according to a *Knoxville News-Sentinel* (10/4/95) report. "This technology is so reliable that there is no force that can bring the waste back and cause exposure to radiation," Mikerin said. Nonetheless, the report noted Mikerin's proposals were not likely to be accepted in the U.S. given the concerns already raised about the migration of radioactive substances at Oak Ridge. Ominously, the article concluded, "Those concerns still linger."

8. Medical Fraud Costs the Nation $100 Billion Annually—Or More

1995 SYNOPSIS: The United States' $1 trillion annual health bill is 14 percent of the gross domestic product, making the medical industry the largest business in the land.

Of this sum, a staggering amount is stolen. According to the National Health Care Anti-Fraud Association, the yearly loss totals between $31-$53 billion; according to the authoritative General Accounting Office, the annual loss is $100 billion; according to other investigators, the amount is as high as $250 billion. In fact, an extensive *Mother Jones* investigation discovered that no one really knows how much money is stolen from the medical system every year—and, possibly even worse, no one has any way of finding out.

Although Medicare and Medicaid were created in 1965, no monitoring measures were established until 1978, giving the bad guys, according to Bill Whatley, Jr., president of the National Association of Medicaid Fraud Control Units, "a 13-year head start, and we never caught up. The people who put this program together didn't believe that the [health care providers] in the program would commit fraud, because medicine was such a high calling."

Unfortunately, such optimism was misplaced; it did not take health care providers long before they developed a series of medscam techniques including upcoding, unbundling, pharmacy fraud, psychiatric schemes, home health care overbilling, and "ghost" patients.

SOURCE: *Mother Jones*, March/April 1995, "Medscam," by L.J. Davis.

UPDATE: Despite the skyrocketing costs of medical care, medical fraud continues unabated. The *Philadelphia Business Journal* (4/19/96) reported that the General Accounting Office estimates medical billing fraud and abuse diverts around ten percent of the estimated $1 trillion in health-care payments made annually in the United States, or about $100 billion a year. The *Massachusetts Lawyers Weekly* (5/20/96) points out the annual cost of money lost to health care fraud, waste, and abuse would more than cover the cost of providing health care for all of the approximately 37 million presently uninsured Americans.

9. U.S. Chemical Industry Fights for Toxic Ozone-Killing Pesticide

1995 SYNOPSIS: Methyl bromide (MB) is a pesticide that is at least 50 times more destructive to the ozone layer, atom for atom, than chlorofluorocarbons (CFCs), yet America's chemical industry is fighting to prevent it from being banned.

In 1992, the United Nations estimated that bromine atoms released into the upper atmosphere are responsible for five-to-ten percent of global ozone depletion, a share that is expected to increase to 15 percent by the year 2000.

In 1994, the UN listed elimination of methyl bromide as the most significant remaining approach (after phase-out of CFCs and halons) to reducing ozone depletion. UN scientists conclude that eliminating MB emissions from agricultural, structural, and industrial activities by the year 2001 would achieve a 13 percent reduction in ozone-depleting chemicals reaching the atmosphere over the next 50 years.

MB also is extremely toxic and can cause acute and chronic health effects. Farmworkers, pesticide applicators, and people living or working where MB is used can suffer poisoning, neurological damage, and reproductive harm. The chemical is so toxic to humans and animals that the Environmental Protection Agency (EPA) classifies it as a Category 1 acute toxin, the most deadly group of substances.

For 60 years, MB has been used to kill pests in soils and buildings and on agricultural products. Worldwide, most MB is used for luxury and export crops, like tomatoes, strawberries, peppers, tobacco, and nursery crops. Soil fumigation to sterilize soil before planting crops is by far the largest use of MB in the U.S. In 1991, the U.S. accounted for nearly 40 percent of the pesticide's worldwide use.

Under the Clean Air Act, the EPA has mandated a halt to MB production in, and imports to, the U.S. in 2001—but manufacturers and agricultural users have mounted a formidable campaign to delay the ban. The Methyl Bromide Global Coalition—a group of eight international MB users and producers (including Ethyl Corp. and Great Lakes Chemical Corp., the major MB producers in the U.S.)—has launched a multimillion-dollar lobbying campaign to keep the product on the market.

SOURCE: *Earth Island Journal*, Summer 1995, "Campaign Against Methyl Bromide: Ozone-Killing Pesticide Opposed," by Anne Schonfield.

UPDATE: Despite heavy lobbying by the Methyl Bromide Working Group representing pesticide users and producers, the 104th Congress did not amend the Clean Air Act to postpone the 2001 ban on use of methyl bromide (*Chemical Week*, 10/16/96). Now the MB proponents are hoping President Clinton will support their agenda during his second term. Meanwhile, scientists and regulators from 14 nations met in Orlando, Florida, in early November 1996 to discuss efforts to find alternatives to the use of methyl bromide. Preliminary tests in Florida and California show that methyl iodide appears to work at least as well as methyl bromide in controlling some pests in the soil, yet it does not harm ozone (*Orlando Sentinel*, 11/5/96).

10. The Broken Promises of NAFTA

1995 SYNOPSIS: The promises of prosperity that the North American Free Trade Agreement (NAFTA) would bring the USA and Mexico were most loudly proclaimed by USA*NAFTA, a pro-NAFTA business coalition. The USA*NAFTA coalition promised the free trade pact would improve the environment, reduce illegal immigration by raising Mexican wages, deter international drug trafficking, and most importantly, create a net increase in high-paying U.S. jobs.

Now, some two years after the agreement became law, USA*NAFTA's own members are blatantly breaking the coalition's grand promises. Many of the firms have cut jobs, moved plants to Mexico, or continued to violate labor rights and environmental regulations in Mexico.

An analysis by the Institute for Policy Studies revealed how the original promises are being broken in Mexico. While the standard of living may have improved for the wealthy, there's been a 30 percent increase in the number of Mexicans emigrating to the U.S. The peso devaluation of December 1994 cut the value of their wages by as much as 40 percent (making them far less able to buy U.S. goods today than they were before NAFTA). Furthermore, interest rates on credit cards climbed above 100 percent and retail sales in Mexico's three largest cities dropped by nearly 25 percent.

The continuing economic crisis in Mexico is expected to cause the loss of two million jobs in 1995, and economic desperation is blamed for the 30 percent increase in arrests by U.S. border patrols between January and May 1995.

NAFTA's promises to U.S. workers also have been broken: The Department of Labor's NAFTA Transitional Adjustment Assistance program reported that 35,000 U.S. workers qualified for retraining between January 1, 1994, and July 10, 1995, because of jobs lost to NAFTA. A University of Maryland study estimates that more than 150,000 U.S. jobs were cut in 1994 as a result of increased consumer imports from Mexico. Since the peso devaluation, the U.S. trade surplus with Mexico has turned into a deficit expanding from $885 million in May 1994 to $6.9 billion a year later, wiping out any basis for claiming that NAFTA is a net job creator for U.S. workers.

Finally, an investigative piece by *Mother Jones* revealed that the environmental impact of NAFTA has been as severe as the economic impact. While government officials promised that NAFTA would reduce the level of pesticides coating Mexico's fields, the opposite has occurred.

SOURCES: *CovertAction Quarterly,* Fall 1995, "NAFTA's Corporate Con Artists," by Sarah Anderson and Kristyne Peter; *Mother Jones,* January/February 1995, "A Giant Spraying Sound," by Esther Schrader.

UPDATE: On January 2, 1996, the Washington-based Public Citizen organization and the Red Mexicana de Accion Frente al Libre Comercio of Mexico City released a critical report charging promises by backers of the two-year-old NAFTA deal that the border would be cleaned up under the agreement had been betrayed. The 100-page report, titled "NAFTA's Broken Promises: The Border Betrayed," provides extensive data on trends in the concentration of maquiladora industries in the border area, air and water pollution, hazardous waste, and birth defects attributable to environmental causes over the past two years. Joan Claybrook, president of Public Citizen, said, "Not only is NAFTA not meeting these promises, it has actually made conditions worse than before it took effect two years ago" (Inter Press Service, 1/2/96).

A U.S. government-funded study, reputedly the most comprehensive analysis yet of the 1994 NAFTA accord, reported by the Associated Press on December 19, 1996, said that NAFTA has not taken a substantial number of jobs from Americans, but neither has it generated the new jobs its proponents had promised. However, subsequent data from the Department of Labor released in May 1997 confirmed that job losses to Mexico are accelerating, especially among workers already at the bottom in pay and skills (*The New York Times*, 5/8/97). According to *The Times* report, since NAFTA took effect in 1994, job losses, mostly to Mexico but some to Canada, had grown by more than a third each year.

A later report, "The Failed Experiment: NAFTA at Three Years," released June 26, 1997, confirmed that NAFTA led to the elimination of two million jobs in Mexico (as predicted in the 1995 *Censored* story) and 400,000 in the United States. The report by the Economics Policy Institute and five other groups, including the Sierra Club and the Institute for Policy Studies, also revealed that the number of U.S. companies closing down and moving jobs to Mexico more than doubled, rising from just over five percent to 13 percent since NAFTA was enacted (*Boston Globe*, 6/27/97).

Finally, on July 11, 1997, the Clinton Administration released its own report on NAFTA admitting that the sweeping claims made by President Clinton when he was trying to rally support for the program in 1993 hadn't materialized. The report did not even address how many U.S. jobs might have been lost as companies moved manufacturing plants to Mexico (*The New York Times*, 7/11/97).

Meanwhile, two prominent foes of the trade pact, Representative Marcy Kaptur (D-Ohio) and Senator Byron Dorgan (D-North Dakota), submitted the NAFTA Accountability Act legislation to Congress with more than 100 co-sponsors. The bill would require the Clinton Administration to certify that NAFTA's goals have been achieved and, if not, would require that the U.S. renegotiate or withdraw from NAFTA (*Los Angeles Times*, 9/25/96).

Index

factory workers, 28
FAIR, *see* Fairness and Accuracy in Reporting.
Fair Labor Standards Act, 323
Fairness and Accuracy in Reporting (FAIR), 10,
    18, 22, 156-157, 171, 211-212, 323
Falklands, 123, 149
Falwell, Jerry, 307
famine, 21, 98-99, 113, 153, 162, 169, 233
FBI, *see* Federal Bureau of Investigations.
FCC, *see* Federal Communications Commission.
FDA, *see* Food and Drug Administration.
FDN, *see* Nicaraguan Democratic Force.
Federal Aviation Administration (FAA), 174,
    315
Federal Bureau of Investigation (FBI), 68-69,
    93, 155-156, 164, 186-189, 224, 229, 243,
    257, 269
Federal Communications Commission (FCC),
    175, 276, 320
Federal Emergency Management Agency
    (FEMA), 164-165
Federal Energy Assistance Program, 68
Federal Energy Regulatory Commission, 51
federal environmental standards, 55
Federal Financing Bank (FFB), 90
Federal Insecticide, Fungicide and Rodenticide
    Act, 99
federal land leases, 45
Federal News Service, 58, 197
Federal Power Commission (FPC), 45
Federal Trade Commission (FTC), 45, 89
Federal Triangle project, 90
Federation of American Scientists, 199, 284
FEMA, *see* Federal Emergency Management
    Agency.
Ferraro, Geraldine, 153
fertility, 70, 78, 195
Fertility Research Foundation, 70
fertilizer, 135-136, 143
FFB, *see* Federal Financing Bank.
Fiji, 58
Financial Times, 58, 64, 103, 109, 166
First Amendment, 12, 21-22, 81, 131, 155, 163,
    264, 308, 325, 351-352
First Interstate Bancorp, 109
FISA, *see* Foreign Intelligence Surveillance Act.
fishing industry, 313-314
fishing rights, 57
FMLN, 93
FOI, *see* Freedom of Information Act.
Food and Agriculture Organization, 226, 313
Food and Drug Administration (FDA), 19, 37,
    43-44, 69, 78, 97, 99-100, 102, 124, 222,
    269, 283, 327-328
Food, Drug, and Cosmetic law, 44
food industry, 284
food irradiation, 221-222
Food Lion supermarket chain, 15

food production, 64, 98, 135
food safety, 100, 245
Forbes, 75, 90
Ford, Gerald, 87
Foreign Intelligence Surveillance Act (FISA),
    126
Foreign Intelligence Surveillance Court, 125,
    187
Foreign Policy, 39, 130, 132, 238, 263
Foundation for Advancement in Science and
    Education, 38
foundries, 41-42
foundry workers, 42
Four Arrows, 129
Fourth Amendment, 126
FPC, *see* Federal Power Commission.
France, 29, 38-39, 94-95, 133, 140, 161, 205-
    206, 232, 234
Freedom of Information (FOI) Act, 131, 133,
    188, 204, 208, 215, 258, 268-269
Freeport-McMoRan, 87
free radicals, 222
free speech, 93, 131, 324-326
Fresno Bee, The, 230, 299
FTC, *see* Federal Trade Commission.
fungicides, 70
FYI Media Alert 1987, 208
G-7, 39, 94, 225
G-8, 39, 94, 225, 226, 331
Galileo, 215, 221
Gandhi, Indira, 153
Gannett, 72, 203, 276, 312
gas, 40, 45, 67, 89, 103, 111, 121, 133, 153,
    172, 192-193, 243, 249, 284, 292, 298,
    319, 326-327, *see also* natural gas.
gas companies, 45
gas industry, 45, 284
gasoline prices, 38-39
gas reserves, 45
Gates, Bill, 75
General Accounting Office, 40, 135, 213, 229,
    243, 249-250, 264, 308, 330
General Electric, 62, 175, 203, 205, 295, 308
General Motors, 89, 133, 177, 301
General Service Administration, 181
General Services Administration, 90
genetically altered humans, 36
genetic damage, 311
genetic engineering, 36-37, 150
genetic mutations, 78, 99
genocide, 86-87, 162, 172
GE-RCA merger, 175
Germany, 39, 58, 95, 133, 147, 161, 206, 213,
    233, 247, 297
Ghost Bank, 89-90
Gingrich, Newt, 101, 256-257, 327-328
Global 500, 108-109
global economy, 79

Goddard Institute for Space Studies, 174
Golden Age of Muckraking, 12-13
Government Decisions Without Democracy, 207-208
government information, 187-188, 207-208
Great Britain, 166, *see also* England; United Kingdom.
Great Depression, the, 260
Greece, 35, 67
Greeley, Horace, 11
Green Berets, 237
Greenpeace, 84, 97, 220, 270
Grenada, 101, 139, 248
Grossman, Karl, 198, 215, 221
Ground Wave Emergency Network (GWEN), 179-80
Group of Eight, *see* G-8.
Group of Friends, 238
Group of Seven, *see* G-7.
Guardian, 11, 67, 101, 145, 156, 159, 164, 166, 192, 194, 212, 218, 241, 254, 262-263, 268, 303
Guatemala, 28, 129-130, 140, 157, 160, 211-212, 231, 237-238
Gulf War, 119-121, 197, 219, 247-249, 261, 263-264, 267, 279-281
Gulf War Syndrome, 197, 249
Gulf War veterans, 120, 197, 249
Guyana, 61
GWEN, *see* Ground Wave Emergency Network.
HAARP, *see* High Frequency Active Auroral Research Project.
Haiti, 40, 161, 226, 302-303, 305
Hanford, 41, 65, 111
Harper's, 174
Harrowsmith, 95
Hatchette SA, 232
health and safety regulations, 54, 81
health care, 22, 89, 279, 289, 330-331
health care fraud, 331
health costs, 19, 54
health problems, 64, 182, 249
heart disease, 42, 72
heavy-metal poisoning, 42
Helms, Jesse, 193, 235, 307
herbicides, 37, 70, 136
Heritage Foundation, 165, 307
High Frequency Active Auroral Research Project (HAARP), 315
Hightower, Jim, 28
Hiroshima, 85, 132, 296
History of the Standard Oil Company, The, 13
Hitler, 160, 248
Holocaust, the, 28, 86, 235
Homelands, the, 114, 161-162
    See also Transkei.
homelessness, 180-182, 279
Homeless Task Force, 180-181

Honduras, 129, 140, 211-212
Hong Kong, 82, 242
House Energy and Commerce Subcommittee, 195
House Committee on Government Operations, 180
House Government Operations Committee, 119, 180
House of Representatives, 228, 284
Houston Chronicle, The, 105, 114, 177
HRC,*see* Human Rights Commission.
HUD, *see* Department of Housing and Urban Development.
human reproduction, 70, 83
human rights, 53-54, 79-81, 85, 140, 158, 160, 173, 191, 211, 214, 237-238, 243, 254-255, 280
Human Rights Commission (HRC), 214, 237-238, 254-255
Human Rights Commission of El Salvador (CDHES), 214
Human Rights Watch, 214, 237
Hussein, Saddam, 249, 264
hydrogen ions, 56
hypertension, 72, 182
IAEA, *see* International Atomic Energy Agency.
IBM, 296, 324
IBT, *see* Industrial Bio-Test.
ICBMs, 116, 141
i.d.a.f. News Notes, 147
IFPRI, *see* International Food Policy Research Institute
illegal aliens, 58-60
illegal workers, 59
immigration, 60, 332
Independent, The, 82, 87, 121, 161, 249, 282
India, 38, 66-67, 78, 103, 132-133
Indochina, 29, 54
Indonesia, 28, 85-87
Indonesian Communist Party, 28
Industrial Bio-Test (IBT), 124-125, 128
industrial waste, 171, 310
infant formula, 52-53
infant formula manufacturers, 52
infectious diseases, 121, 210, 311, 314
inflation, 108, 139, 153
information monopoly, 8, 201-202, 233
Inquiry, 36, 80, 86, 101, 116, 119, 128
Inslaw Software Theft, 271
Institute for Policy Studies, 92, 100, 332, 334
Institute for Southern Studies, The, 109-110
Institutional Investor, 109
insurance industry, 284
Intelligence Authorization Bill, 188
Intelligence Oversight Board, 238
Internal Revenue Service (IRS), 186
    audits, 186
International Atomic Energy Agency (IAEA), 149, 206

About the Author

Dr. Carl Jensen is a professor emeritus of Communication Studies at Sonoma State University and Former Director of Project Censored, an internationally recognized media research project. Founded by Jensen in 1976, Project Censored is America's longest-running research project which annually explores news media censorship.

Jensen has been involved with the media for more than 45 years as a daily newspaper reporter, weekly newspaper publisher, public relations practitioner, advertising executive, and educator. He spent 15 years with Batten, Barton, Durstine, and Osborn, the international advertising agency, where he was an award-winning copywriter, account supervisor, and vice president.

Specializing in mass communications, Jensen received his B.A., M.A., and Ph.D. degrees in Sociology from the University of California, Santa Barbara, in 1971, 1972, and 1977, respectively.

From 1973 to 1996, he taught media, sociology, and journalism courses at Sonoma State University where he founded Sonoma State University's B.A. degree in Communication Studies and the University's Journalism Certificate Program.

Jensen founded the Lincoln Steffens Journalism Award for Investigative Reporting in Northern California in 1981. He also participated in the development of the Bay Area Censored awards program by the Media Alliance in San Francisco in 1989 and in the development of Project Censored Canada in 1993.

He has written and lectured extensively about press censorship, the First Amendment, and the mass media. His 1996 Project Censored Yearbook received the first national Firecracker Award from the American Wholesale Book Sellers Association for the best alternative non-fiction book of the year. He also was consulting editor for *Ready Reference: Censorship*, a three-volume encyclopedia set covering major aspects of censorship issues in both American and world history, published by Salem Press, Pasadena, in 1997.

Jensen has been cited by the national Association for Education in Journalism and Mass Communication for his "innovative approach to constructive media criticism and for providing a new model for media criticism." The Giraffe Project honored Jensen "for sticking his neck out for the common good" and for being a "role model for a caring society." The Media Alliance presented Jensen with the Media Alliance Meritorious Achievement Award in the "Unimpeachable Source" category. The Society of Professional Journalists in Los Angeles awarded him its 1990 Freedom of Information Award.

In 1992, Jensen was named the outstanding university professor of journalism in California by the California Newspaper Publishers Association and was awarded the 1992 Hugh M. Hefner First Amendment Award in education from the Playboy Foundation for his achievement in defending the First Amendment. In 1996, Jensen received The James Madison Freedom of Information Award for Career Achievement from the Northern California Chapter of the Society of Professional Journalists; the University President's Award of Appreciation for "Dedicated Service to Sonoma State University"; and was cited for outstanding achievement by the Sonoma State University Academic Senate.

He has been a guest on many radio/television news and talk shows including a Bill Moyers PBS television documentary on Project Censored.

Jensen is married and has four children and three grandchildren. He, wife Sandra, and Danske, their great Great Dane, live in beautiful downtown Cotati, in Northern California.